THE
COAST GUARD

THE COAST GUARD

Tom Beard—Editor-in-Chief

José Hanson—Managing Editor

CWO-4 Paul C. Scotti, USCG (Ret)—Graphics Editor

FOUNDATION FOR COAST GUARD HISTORY
HUGH LAUTER LEVIN ASSOCIATES, INC.

Foundation for Coast Guard History

The Coast Guard is an amalgam of services and organizations that began in 1716 with the construction of the Boston Harbor lighthouse. In 1790, the Revenue Cutter Service was established. With the addition of the Life-Saving Service in 1915, the name Coast Guard emerged in a law, which established the Service as "a member of the armed forces at all times." Additions to its missions and tasks continue to this day.

Better known for its humanitarian role, the Coast Guard is also the nation's primary marine law-enforcer and regulator of maritime commerce. However, the Coast Guard's demonstrated preeminent degree of efficiency and effectiveness stems directly from its discipline as a military organization, which allows its leaders to seamlessly shift focus and assets—of this historically under-resourced Service—to meet our country's emerging urgent needs.

The Coast Guard has seldom assigned a priority to chronicling both mundane and heroic actions by its men and women during their performance of myriad daily tasks. Far too many deeds, many with unparalleled historical importance, have gone unrecorded; as a result, the legacy of a justifiably proud Service suffers. The Foundation for Coast Guard History, a 501(c)3 nonprofit organization, was formed on 4 August 1999—the Coast Guard's 209th birthday—to assist the Coast Guard History Program and promote a better appreciation on the part of the general public—as well as within the Service itself—of the breadth of its heritage and ever-growing importance to our nation. It is our hope that this book will be a significant addition to that end.

Coast Guard Seaman Blair Wells aloft at the mizzenmast aboard Coast Guard cutter barque Eagle. *(Mike Hvozda, U.S. Coast Guard)*

Vice Admiral Howard B. Thorsen, USCG (Ret)
Chair, Board of Regents
Foundation for Coast Guard History
Memoria Semper   Semper Paratus

Captain Fred Herzberg, Jr., USCG (Ret)
Executive Director

Foundation for Coast Guard History
Coast Guard Museum Northwest
1519 Alaska Way South
Seattle, Washington 98134
http://www.fcgh.org

Published by Hugh Lauter Levin Associates, Inc.
© 2004 Foundation for Coast Guard History
Design: Lori S. Malkin
Project Editor: James O. Muschett
ISBN 0-88363-116-4
Printed in China
Distributed by Publishers Group West

Contents

Foreword

Gentle reader, please do not expect to find here the impartial, unemotional, well-balanced essay that you might anticipate from the pen of an old reporter who has staked his reputation on those qualities of good journalism.

Frankly, I'm a Coast Guard junkie. I have seen them in war and peace and I've admired at first hand their dedication, their leadership, their esprit de corps, their skills, and, always, their courage. It is a love affair that goes back at least to World War II.

As a war correspondent I was privileged to observe them in action as they were among the first to go into combat after Pearl Harbor. Snatched from peacetime chores, they were thrown into convoy duty manning escort vessels in the desperate Battle of the Atlantic against packs of German submarines determined to blockade England.

Above: *Mr. Cronkite might have seen the anchored 270-foot Coast Guard Cutter* Tahoma *from his apartment window overlooking the East River, after the cutter rushes from New Bedford to take on-scene command of the maritime defense of New York Harbor following the September 11 attack. The cutter is coordinating the activities of a fleet of Coast Guard and law-enforcement craft, controlling all vessel movements in the harbor, to prevent any maritime attacks. (Tom Sperduto, U.S. Coast Guard)*

Pages 6–7: *(Mike Hvozda, U.S. Coast Guard)*

When I saw them next they again were displaying a new skill for the first time—getting troops ashore on an enemy-infested coast. It was the Allied landing in North Africa and again they performed with bravery and distinction. Naturally!

That was a rehearsal for their incredible performance in one of the greatest engagements in the history of warfare—the landings in Normandy. They manned many of the ships that plowed through the seemingly impenetrable barrage of German artillery to land troops on the shores of France.

Almost with the first landings, other Coast Guardsmen in comparatively small boats but with unbelievable courage and seamanship defied the enemy fire and the tangle of burning and sinking ships to rescue wounded and drowning soldiers. Many Coast Guardsmen made the final sacrifice as they fell among the wounded they sought to help.

The Coast Guard was at Korea and I saw them again in Vietnam where they fought a nasty war trying to keep clear the country's many waterways. In many places the rivers were mere streams with heavy undergrowth on the banks. Our patrol vessels frequently ran into ambushes with the enemy so close the gunfire almost seemed to be hand-to-hand combat. The valiant Coast Guardsmen again were to be counted among the conflict's heroes.

In peacetime the Coast Guard has been a part of my life. The Coast Guard Auxiliary, that splendid corps of volunteers who give so much of their time assisting the Coast Guard promoting boating safety, some years ago made me their honorary national commander and I proudly fly their ensign.

And I was honored to be included among the personnel aboard the first American naval vessel to visit a Russian port after World War II. The visit in 1989 was part of an effort to push along the slowly thawing relationship between Moscow and Washington. Our government chose to send what else but the nation's only official tall ship, the Coast Guard's glorious barque, *Eagle*—the perfect choice for such delicate diplomatic chores. Not only is *Eagle* incredibly handsome, but the ship's service within a civilian agency (then still the Transportation Department) created an aura of non-belligerency that helped mollify the discomfort of some hard noses among host governments.

There perhaps is nothing so beautiful as *Eagle* parading down a harbor, its crew at attention along the yardarms, those great sails billowing about them. Unfortunately the people of St. Petersburg (then still bearing its Communist name of Leningrad), were denied that gorgeous scene. A lack of wind and treacherous obstructions in the long passage down the channel forced us to power to *Eagle*'s berth.

There weren't any cheering crowds of Russians to greet us at the dock anyway. The authorities kept sightseers behind a chain-link fence a block from our berth, but across that porous iron curtain they waved and shouted greetings.

Eagle's tall masts dominating the waterfront skyline and its smiling crew of well-behaved cadets were gestures of friendship that surely must have melted by a few degrees the ice of the Cold War.

Another Coast Guard success!

As an avid sailor I have had more than one occasion to fall to my knees in thanksgiving for the presence of the Coast Guard.

During the recent decades—when the drug war was at its peak—those of us who sailed offshore and among the Caribbean islands were terrified by ruthless smugglers who boarded pleasure boats, not infrequently murdered their occupants, and stole the vessels to augment their fleets of dope runners. You might imagine our joy—we actually shouted with relief—when we saw the orange stripe on the bow of an approaching boat and knew the Coast Guard was at hand. And the letdown was pretty intense, too, when the Coast Guard boat had to depart the vicinity to continue its tireless and dangerous search for the ruthless brigands.

No, there is nothing so heartening to a sailor in trouble as seeing a boat or a plane adorned with that orange stripe come over the horizon. Some years ago I was overrun by a powerful northeaster, part of that same unpredicted weather system that inspired the book and movie, *The Perfect Storm*.

For several hours we battled hurricane-force winds, waves almost as tall as our masts, and blinding scud as thick as a heavy fog. By the time we skimmed past the rocks that guard the entrance to Atlantic City the wind had shredded two of our three sails, the main was about to go and the huge waves we were taking over the sides were cascading down into the cabin and threatening to drown our engine. We clawed into the entrance channel with a sadly wounded boat and an exhausted and frightened crew. And there steaming at flank speed out of the channel was a Coast Guard cutter. Our short-handed crew had been too busy to even call for help but I had a hunch that someone in one of the buildings ashore might have seen our plight and alerted the Coast Guard.

"Are you looking for us?" I radioed.

"You look like it," came back the cutter. "Somebody ashore said a boat of your description looked like it was foundering trying to get into the channel. Do you need assistance?"

"I don't think so," I answered with more bravado than I felt. "But I wouldn't mind if you escorted us into the harbor."

I wouldn't mind, indeed! If I could have walked on water I would have boarded the cutter and kissed each member of its crew regardless of gender.

The wind and sea that we had survived out beyond the breakwater were dangerous to any kind of vessel and yet that Coast Guard crew was going out in those perilous conditions to look for a boat about which it knew nothing except for an anonymous call from a concerned citizen. That sort of mission is the regular business of these Coast Guard people for whom heroism is simply routine.

And let me regale you with another example. My boat with a captain and guest crew of neophytes was dismasted in a somewhat lesser but still serious storm a couple of hundred miles off Martha's Vineyard en route home from Bermuda.

When they tried to start the engine they discovered one of the crew had failed to fill the tank as instructed. Without sails or power the boat and crew were adrift and taking a terrible beating.

Naturally they called the Coast Guard. Now the Coast Guard is understandably not too pleased with careless boat crews that don't fill their tanks, but pleased or displeased they respond when boaters are in genuine danger.

Within an hour our crew heard the thump-thump of a helicopter circling in the clouds above as its radar searched for the stricken vessel below. Contact was made and the chopper pilot skillfully held his machine steady against the gusting winds while his crew lowered containers of fuel to the boat.

Coast Guard helicopters and their crews have been lost on similar missions but that night the mission was just another colorless entry in the log book of a Coast Guard station. I doubt any of its members would acknowledge the notation actually told another story of heroism that to the Coast Guard is routine.

As I write this in the month of November 2002, I look out my New York apartment window. The view is of the United Nations buildings and their perch on the bank of the broad East River. The United Nations Security Council is debating the Iraq question. Heavily armed security forces are in the streets and atop neighboring buildings. And at anchor out there in the river is a Coast Guard cutter.

It has been there for days. I watch small boats tie up to it occasionally, I suppose delivering supplies or a change of crew. At night I see its porthole lights and imagine the crew staring at the radar and other instruments as, tedious as this lookout duty may be, they stand on guard, protecting the UN from waterborne terrorists.

I know they are living up to the Coast Guard motto, *Semper Paratus*—Always Ready. That single Coast Guard boat in its lonely vigil in the middle of the broad East River bolsters my confidence that as a nation we, indeed, are ready.

—WALTER CRONKITE

Roles and Missions

Admiral Paul A. Yost, USCG (Ret)
Eighteenth Commandant of the Coast Guard

The United States Coast Guard traces the roots of its roles and missions to the founding of this great republic under the Constitution. Perhaps the greatest challenge confronting the young nation was paying its debts from the Revolutionary War and creating a strong financial foundation on which to build a prosperous future. After all, the United States in 1789, the year the Constitution was adopted, was the great experiment in self-government. Simply put, revolutionary Americans declared they were no longer subjects of a king but citizens accountable to each other. As much as royalty fascinates us today, it appalled Americans in 1776. The most honorable title a person could hold was "citizen," and the Constitution prohibited government employees from accepting titles of nobility from foreign governments. American citizens became the "stakeholders" of their future and there were many in Europe who did not believe, nor wish, that these new Americans would succeed in their dreams.

And the beginning was rocky. From 1776 to 1781 the country was governed by revolutionary congresses that were usually only one step in front of a pursuing British Army. Between 1781 and 1789 the nation sputtered along under the Articles of Confederation, a fragile instrument of government that was too weak to fulfill the promises of the future. The great challenge of the mid-1780s was to create a stronger Union that provided political, economic, and social stability. The Constitution of 1789 was the fulfillment of that determination.

The first revenue cutters in the 1790s took up the American flag as a sign of their identity and authority to stop and board ships entering into United States waters. The small, nondescript cutters were then the might of the nation imposing import duty and thwarting smugglers. After 214 years the Coast Guard still works behind this banner, the national ensign, carrying out their roles and missions now with well-recognized cutters. (U.S. Coast Guard)

Pages 10–11: Time is a critical element in the battle against death. Sometimes Coast Guard helicopter rescue is the only chance for those in peril. (George F. Schoenberger, U.S. Coast Guard Art Collection)

Opposite: The Coast Guard is "a military service and a branch of the Armed Forces of the United States at all times." (Georgina Wells, U.S. Coast Guard Art Collection)

Revenue Cutter Service

Alexander Hamilton, as the nation's first Secretary of the Treasury, tackled the job of putting finances in order. The economic health of the United States then depended upon the taxes collected from imports and exports. Hamilton faced a Herculean task. Laws needed to be written to regulate commerce. Custom houses needed to be built to administer the laws. And, a maritime force had to be established to enforce these laws—a

Above: *Hopley Yeaton was the United States' first commissioned seagoing officer. Yeaton commanded the cutter* Scammel. *Earning thirty dollars a month, he, with his crew of nine, patrolled the Massachusetts and New Hampshire coasts. (Russel Joseph Buckingham, U.S. Coast Guard Art Collection)*

Right: *Hopley Yeaton's commission, signed 21 March 1791 by President George Washington and Thomas Jefferson, as Secretary of State. The original commission is on display at the U.S. Coast Guard Academy in New London, Connecticut. (U.S. Coast Guard)*

GEORGE WASHINGTON, President of the United States of America.

TO ALL WHO SHALL SEE THESE PRESENTS, *GREETING.*

KNOW YE, That reposing special Trust and Confidence in the Integrity, Diligence and good Conduct of *Hopley Yeaton of New Hampshire* . . . . I DO APPOINT him *Master* of a Cutter in the Service of the United States, for the Protection of the Revenue; and do authorize and empower him to execute and fulfil the Duties of that Office according to Law; AND TO HAVE AND TO HOLD the said office, with all the Rights and Emoluments thereunto legally appertaining, unto him the said *Hopley Yeaton* . . . during the Pleasure of the President of the United States for the Time being.

IN TESTIMONY whereof I have caused these Letters to be made Patent, and the Seal of the United States to be hereunto affixed. GIVEN under my Hand, at the City of Philadelphia, the *Twenty first* Day of *March* in the Year of our Lord one thousand seven hundred and ninety *one*, and of the Independence of the United States of America the *Fifteenth.*

G Washington

By the President

Th Jefferson

military organization consisting of a system of revenue cutters. Enforcement was particularly challenging since smuggling had grown to be a patriotic duty. And from this beginning in 1790, the character of today's Coast Guard began to be molded. This new force was modest in size and demeanor. There were ten small schooner- and cutter-rigged vessels not much larger than some modern-day pleasure craft. The work was hard, and the pay modest. Without exaggeration, these beginning Coast Guardsmen were forging the roles and missions of a maritime service to the nation that today's Coast Guard continues.

Law enforcement has been as great a challenge through our history and into modern times as it was for the first days under the Constitution. In 1833 President Andrew Jackson sent eight cutters to Charleston, South Carolina, where merchants refused to pay a new sugar tax. The president told the rebellious governor that, should one hair be harmed on the head

Coast Guard Flags

Tom Beard

The Coast Guard has a unique tradition as a United States military origination. It has two official flags, the Coast Guard ensign and Coast Guard standard.

Coast Guard Ensign

Nine years after the establishment of the Revenue Cutter Service, Congress provided that cutters and boats employed in revenue collection should display a distinguishing and unique ensign. Secretary of the Treasury Oliver Wolcott's order was for an ensign and pennant of "16 perpendicular stripes—the number of states in the Union when this ensign was officially adopted—alternate red and white, the union of the ensign to be the arms of the United States in a dark blue on a white field."

This ensign soon became familiar in American waters and served as the sign of authority for the Revenue Cutter Service. Outside American waters, the cutters displayed the national ensign. However, this same flag was later adopted to fly over customhouses, then continued in use into the early twentieth century. President William Howard Taft issued an Executive Order in 1910 changing the revenue cutter ensign by adding an emblem such that a "distinguishing flag now used by vessels of the Revenue Cutter Service be marked by the distinctive emblem of that service, in blue and white... over the center of the seventh vertical red stripe."

Cutters then began flying the United States flag as their naval ensign, and the revenue ensign, now shifted to the flag-signal yard, became the

service's distinctive flag. Five years later, when the service adopted the name "United States Coast Guard," the Revenue Cutter Service's ensign became the distinguishing flag on all Coast Guard cutters, continuing the then 116-year legacy.

The colors used in the Coast Guard ensign today, as in the Revenue Cutter Service, are all symbolic. The color red stands for youth and the sacrifice of blood for liberty's sake. The color blue represents justice and a covenant against oppression. The white symbolizes a desire for light and purity.

As intended in 1799, the ensign is displayed as a mark of authority for vessel boarding, examination, seizure, and for the purpose of enforcing the laws of the United States. The ensign is never carried as a parade or ceremony standard.

Coast Guard Standard

The Coast Guard standard's origins are obscure. A painting from 1840 shows the Revenue Cutter Alexander Hamilton flying a jack—hoisted on a jack staff at the bowsprit cap in port—similar to the present Coast Guard standard. A 1917 illustration shows the same white flag with a blue eagle surrounded by stars in a semicircle. The words, "United States Coast Guard—Semper Paratus" were added later. Its present version came after 1950. The star semicircle was changed to thirteen stars enclosed in a cluster above the eagle. The Coast Guard standard is displayed in military parades and ceremonies typically decorated with thirty-four battle streamers.

Top right: Coast Guard Standard with battle streamers. (Gary Todoroff)

The Coast Guard Ensign (*left, top*) is flown from every Coast Guard vessel. It came into being to identify the federal authority of the cutters. The Union Jack (*left*), or "Jack," flies at the jack staff when a cutter is at anchor or in port. This is the canton of the American flag. As late as the 1830s the Coast Guard flew the canton of the Coast Guard Ensign as its jack. (William C. Sturm, U.S. Coast Guard Art Collection)

of a cutter man, he would hang him from the nearest oak tree. Even at the turn of the twentieth century, Coast Guardsmen provided the only law that many Alaskans knew. Cutters sometimes served as jails and court houses. Between 1920 and 1933 prohibition was the law of the land. Hundreds of cutters and ships manned by thousands of Coast Guardsmen patrolled America's coasts during the "Rum War." And, it was truly a war: Coast Guardsmen were killed in shoot-outs with the smugglers. Beginning in the 1960s, Coast Guardsmen entered yet another law enforcement war, this time the "Drug War." That war persists today.

The early years of America were ones of frequent foreign conflict. France and most of Latin America would soon be casting off old political orders. Many of these revolutions were violent and threatened American commerce. Almost immediately, cutter crews had to be concerned with pirates and privateers. These plunderers even boldly sailed into protected waters such as the Chesapeake Bay. And then our young nation came to blows with revolutionary France in a quasi-war.

In 1799 the President of the United States ordered the nine-year-old Revenue Cutter Service to cooperate with the newly created United States Navy, beginning a bond between the two maritime services in time of conflict that continues today. Eight cutters were ordered to patrol America's southern coast and trade lanes in the Caribbean Sea. Of the twenty-two prizes captured by United States' vessels between 1798 and 1799, eighteen ships were taken by cutters. The cutter *Pickering*, alone, took ten prizes, one of which was a forty-four-gun privateer three times the strength of *Pickering*, manned by some 200 adventurers.

Coast Guardsmen have always been in the forefront of fighting America's wars. Cutters dueled with British privateers in American coastal waters during the War of 1812. Cutters worked with the Navy in the war with Mexico, supplying shallow draft ships for blockade and riverine duties. The cutter *Harriet Lane* put a shot across the bow of the steamer *Nashville* as it tried to enter Charleston Harbor without showing its colors in 1861—the first naval shot of the Civil War. The fast cutter *Miami* was stationed in Washington, D.C., during the Civil War should President Abraham Lincoln need to make a hasty exit. During the Spanish American War, the cutter *Hudson* rescued the damaged

Throughout seafaring history, dogs have been popular mascots with mariners aboard vessels. The Coast Guard still follows this tradition; however, in addition to crew companionship these devoted animals provide special K-9 talents for many tasks, from chasing birds off runways to uncovering illegal drugs. (U.S. Coast Guard)

The cutter Tampa pulls convoy duty between the Mediterranean Sea and the British Isles during World War I. (John D. Wisinski, U.S. Coast Guard Art Collection)

During the Confederate bombardment of Fort Sumter, the cutter Harriet Lane *spotted a ship without colors heading into Charleston harbor. Only after the cutter fired a shot across the steamer's bow did it promptly run up the Stars and Stripes and identify itself as* Nashville. *As a result,* Harriet Lane *is credited with firing the first shot from the deck of a ship during the Civil War. (Howard Koslow, U.S. Coast Guard Art Collection)*

naval torpedo-boat *Winslow* from the fire of enemy shore-batteries. In World War I, the loss of the Coast Guard cutter *Tampa* with all hands to an enemy submarine brought the percentage of Coast Guardsmen lost in the war to the highest of any American service. Eleven Coast Guardsmen from the cutter *Seneca* died trying to save the torpedoed British collier *Wellington* en route to Gibraltar during World War I. Yes, cutters were stationed at faraway Gibraltar during the "War to End All Wars," serving as anti-submarine escorts, a task at which they would excel during World War II.

The seven ship, 327-foot cutter class sank four German U-boats during the Second World War. Such achievements did not come without sacrifice: one, *Alexander Hamilton*, was lost to the enemy. Coast Guardsmen from *Escanaba* put on survival suits, tied ropes around their waists, and jumped into the freezing Arctic waters to rescue torpedoed sailors and soldiers from the *Dorchester*. *Escanaba*, too, would be torpedoed; 101 Coast Guardsmen died.

World War II port security needs saw the advent of what is now the Coast Guard Auxiliary. Americans from all walks of life volunteered to patrol port facilities and were known as the Coast Guard Temporary Reserve. Their wartime contribution was invaluable. Today, as the Coast Guard Auxiliary, they play major roles across all Coast Guard missions.

Saving Lives

Defending the nation and protecting its sources of revenue were not the only tasks of the early revenue cutters. Soon after being established, the cutters became involved in search and rescue. These were dangerous times for mariners. Wooden ships were kept watertight by pitch and tar; this virtually made them floating matchboxes only lacking a spark to

The Coast Guard Auxiliary is largely made up of boat-owning volunteers who lessen the Coast Guard's manpower burden by providing boating safety classes to hundreds of thousands of recreational boaters annually and by assisting the Coast Guard in performing its many missions. (U.S. Coast Guard)

change the ship into a blazing inferno. At the time, a small, wooden coastal trading ship that survived ten years had exceeded its life expectancy.

Cutters were outfitted with lifesaving equipment to aid those in distress. And rescuing those in danger soon became a routine occurrence. Compounding the dangers at sea were the vagaries of the wind that could unexpectedly drive a sailing ship aground. Merchant sailing-ships persisted in the American merchant trade until the close of World War I. Thus, these cutters from the beginning were not only at war with smugglers, privateers, and the nation's enemies, but battled nature as well.

The United States Coast Guard also traces its roles and missions to those brave individuals who saved lives on beaches. The first organized surf lifesavers were citizen volunteers outfitted at private expense. Though commendable and self-sacrificing, this effort was unable to keep up with the increasing number of shipwrecks caused by the expanding trade and

Before the era of motorized surfboats, it took sheer physical strength to force a rescue boat through the surf. The crew then rowed to the distressed vessel, pulled aboard survivors, and then rowed back through the surf. Each rescue was in itself a prodigious feat of human resolve. (Sherman Groenke, U.S. Coast Guard Art Collection)

The Pea Island Lifesaving Station near Cape Hatteras, North Carolina, had an all African-American crew. In October 1896 they made an extraordinary rescue of nine people, including a three-year-old, from a wrecked schooner by entering the waves two at a time bound together. A survivor was then tied to them and the group hauled ashore. This tactic was repeated for each person rescued. (Roy LaGrone, U.S. Coast Guard Art Collection)

Above: *Similar to service on the open ocean, Coast Guard vessels and aircraft work together to save a ship and its crew on an inland river. (U.S. Coast Guard)*

Above, right: *The Coast Guard is always ready to toss a lifeline. Every day, courageous Coast Guard men and women save an average of ten lives, assist 192 people in distress, and protect $2.8 million in property. (Rita Brue Stanziani, U.S. Coast Guard Art Collection)*

Above: *A fleet of 200, both helicopter and fixed-winged, aircraft are always ready to respond to environmental disasters, law enforcement, and military needs, as well as to traditional search and rescue missions. These distinctively painted aircraft can be spotted globally as they fulfill Coast Guard missions anywhere. (U.S. Coast Guard)*

Right: *Coast Guard rescue crews hone their skills at the Service's National Motor Lifeboat School, in Ilwaco, Washington. At the mouth of the Columbia River is one of the nation's most dangerous bars, depicted here being crossed by a training cutter. (David Stone, U.S. Coast Guard Art Collection)*

the flood of immigrants coming to America. Thirty-two million Europeans flooded to this "land of the free" between 1815 and 1914, many crammed into sailing ships. All too frequently a storm would drive ships bearing hopeful souls onto America's shoreline. Newspapers were filled with accounts of hundreds of immigrants perishing in the pounding surf as they neared their goal. In 1848, the United States government began paying for the equipment of the life-saving volunteers, and starting in 1871, the government gradually federalized these life-savers. These bold Americans—black and white—saved thousands of lives. One of the most famous life-saving stations was that of Pea Island, North Carolina. Its all-black crew set a standard for duty and bravery that earned them awards. The Life-Saving Service and the Revenue Cutter Service came together in 1915 to create the modern United States Coast Guard.

Life-saving remains a prime mission of the Coast Guard. Many old challenges are gone but new ones have arisen, met by the self-righting motor surf-boat and the helicopter as primary tools. The Coast Guard makes thousands of rescues a year. Some are spectacular—such as the

rescue of hundreds from the cruise ship *Prinsendam* almost 200 miles off the coast of Alaska in 1980 without loss of life. Others are more routine—a recreational boater who went too far or misjudged the weather.

Proficiency navigating shallow waters, gained through decades of coastal life-saving experiences, became a Coast Guard hallmark. Soon the Coast Guard was performing these skills throughout the world in the service of America. Coast Guardsmen manned landing craft during World War II amphibious assaults, including Guadalcanal, where Coast Guardsman Douglas Munro was awarded a Congressional Medal of Honor. Coast Guardsmen are buried in Normandy cemeteries having lost their lives on D-Day. In June 1944, sixty Coast Guard eighty-three-foot cutters patrolled off Normandy beaches rescuing hundreds of soldiers and sailors. Twenty-six, eighty-two-foot cutters served in the Vietnam War. Many of the Coast Guard's high-endurance cutters also saw action in Vietnam providing off-shore interdiction and in-shore gunfire support. The cutters' 5-inch/38 guns could reach far inland and were in constant demand.

Coast Guard patrol boats in the Vietnam War interdicted the enemy along the coast and in the rivers. (George Gray, U.S. Coast Guard Art Collection)

Coast Guardsmen took part in amphibious beach assaults in the European and Pacific Theaters during World War II. They transported men and supplies in ships and ran troops ashore in landing craft. (U.S. Coast Guard Art Collection)

Above: *Coast Guard buoy tender crews have the arduous and grimy chore of hauling out buoys, servicing them, and dropping them back on station. (U.S. Coast Guard)*

Above, right: *The lighthouse is one of many types of navigational aids a maritime nation uses for the safe transit of waterborne commerce. In 1939 the Coast Guard combined with the U.S. Lighthouse Service and took over responsibility for the nation's marine aids to navigation. (U.S. Coast Guard)*

Above: *A Coast Guardsman clings to a rocking buoy as he makes repairs to its light. (Dale Dumas, U.S. Coast Guard Art Collection)*

Opposite, top: *An icebreaker nudged into an iceberg, lying to while scientists conduct studies. The arctic waters and ice may hold secrets to affects brought on by global temperature changes. A helicopter deck and hangar on the stern provide the ship with two helicopters used searching for leads in the ice while making passage, hauling supplies, and moving scientists about on the ice. (U.S. Coast Guard)*

Opposite, bottom left: *These unique icebreaking cutters clear paths for supply ships through the Arctic and Antarctic. At home they keep shipping moving when winter ice covers lakes and rivers, bolstering the economic viability of the country for more months of the year. (Evelyn Peters, U.S. Coast Guard Art Collection)*

Lighthouse Service

Yet another place that the Coast Guard traces its roles and missions is the U.S. Lighthouse Service. If the Revenue Cutter Service and the Life Saving Service were the "pound of cure" for rescuing those in distress during the early days of the Republic, the Lighthouse Service was the "ounce of prevention." The ninth bill passed by the First Congress under the Constitution federalized the state-owned lighthouses in 1789. This attests to Congress' belief in the importance of providing reliable aids to navigation. The growth of America as a maritime nation was amazing. By 1829, the United States possessed the second largest merchant fleet in the world. The nation's fleet was 3.535 million gross tons. Only Great Britain led with a fleet of 3.565 million gross tons.

Lighthouses sprang up all along our coasts, including the inland sea—the Great Lakes. Thousands were built. They were the measure of man's technological achievement. But more important than the bricks and mortar were the blood and muscle that manned these outposts of civilization. These fearless keepers—many of them women—not only kept the lights burning even during the fiercest of storms, but boldly rushed forth to save those in distress. One need only to recount the exploits of two individuals, Ida Lewis and Marcus Hanna, to gain an appreciation of why the modern Coast Guard men and women are proud to trace the roots of their missions to such individuals. Ida Lewis became so famous she was featured on the cover of *Harper's Weekly Illustrated*. President Ulysses S. Grant even paid a visit to Lewis at her Lighthouse. And Marcus Hanna was awarded both a gold life-saving medal for a rescue in 1885 and a Congressional Medal of Honor for bravery while in the U.S. Army. He is the only individual in the history of this nation to have won America's two highest medals for heroism. And although lighthouses are now all automated, Coast Guard men and women still maintain some 40,000 aids to navigation in America's ports and waterways to mark safe passage.

Ice Breakers

Another role that has grown out of aids to navigation is ice breaking. Coast Guardsmen began this task at the end of the nineteenth century to help coastal communities which had been isolated during the winter by severe weather. Like so many of the Coast Guard's missions, what started out small has bloomed into a major responsibility. During World War II, thousands of combatant vessels, including landing craft and submarines, were built in the upper Mississippi River complex. It was the Coast Guard's ice breaking that permitted those vessels and craft to sail their way into combat long before they could have if they had not been freed from the ice during the winter months. During the 1970s, the Coast Guard

Above: *A scientist from a Coast Guard icebreaker taking ice-core samples in the Arctic Circle. Since the late 1970s, the icebreakers based in Seattle, Washington, have been traveling in the polar regions accomplishing scientific and logistical support, their primary mission. (U.S. Coast Guard)*

Above: *Since the tragic sinking of the passenger liner* Titanic *in 1912, the Coast Guard has been patrolling the iceberg-infested region of the North Atlantic, first by ships then later by aircraft. Iceberg sightings are plotted and reported to the maritime community. (U.S. Coast Guard)*

took the lead in polar ice breaking, a mission that it still performs today, with its three world-class icebreakers, *Polar Sea*, *Polar Star*, and *Michael Healy*. Coast Guard icebreakers were ordered by President Ford in 1975 to break the ice at Point Barrow to allow a commercial fleet of tugs and barges to commence the building of the North Slope oil pipeline. The president's order, based on a national security need, assured oil would flow at least a year earlier than would have been possible otherwise.

The Coast Guard's expertise in ice breaking and high seas search-and-rescue brought on the task of the International Ice Patrol. Shortly following the sinking of *Titanic*, the Coast Guard began patrolling, iceberg-infested North Atlantic waters. For many years this was done by sturdy cutters maintaining a dangerous, yet constant vigil. In the modern era, this vigil has been taken over by Coast Guard aircraft. And there have been no more *Titanics*. Not one ship has been lost to ice within the patrolled area since the International Ice Patrol began.

A part of merchant marine safety is the inspection program that oversees new ship construction and regularly examines ships in service. (Ron Wells, U.S. Coast Guard Art Collection)

Merchant marine safety is a major Coast Guard mission. Here the cutter Morris *prepares to inspect a passenger ship in 1861. No irregularities were found on the ship carrying Scottish and Irish immigrants to New York. Federal law allotted that sufficient lifeboat space must be available to accommodate shipboard passengers. (Gil Cohen, U.S. Coast Guard Art Collection)*

Marine Inspection

Marine inspection, like aids to navigation, is a preventative form of safety, and, like aids to navigation, it has been performed by Coast Guard men and women for many decades. The nineteenth century was truly the age of the technological revolution. Machinery multiplied man's productivity. As these new innovations were taken to sea, they helped reduce some old dangers, but at the same time introduced new ones. Steam engines

With the purchase of Alaska, the Coast Guard began patrolling through the cold and fog of Alaskan waters to bring law and order plus humanitarian aid to the new territory. Cutters with icebreaking capability, such as the cutter Bear, were at times the only ships able to reach isolated communities. (Edward Trosset, U.S. Coast Guard Art Collection)

were placed into ships and now merchantmen were less likely of being driven onto shoals by a sudden storm because the ship possessed a power source other than wind. But like all new inventions, frequently the limits of safety were exceeded by the new technology. Boilers would explode with catastrophic effect. In 1865, the boiler of *Sultana* exploded while bringing home Union soldiers from a Confederate prisoner of war camp. More lives were lost than in the sinking of *Titanic* decades later. New laws were passed establishing steamboat operating parameters to assure safety, and inspectors were needed to guarantee compliance. In 1942 this mission, including the Marine Inspection Service, was added to the Coast Guard's responsibilities. Today, Coast Guard inspectors review construction plans and crawl through the bowels of ships to guarantee compliance with the laws. In fact, Coast Guard naval architects must approve the detailed plans of every American-flagged ship before construction commences.

Environmental Protection

We think of environmental protection as a more recent concern of this republic, and yet Coast Guard men and women have been doing this for a very long time. In the first half of the nineteenth century, cutters patrolled the Florida coast to prevent the theft of live-oak trees, an important resource in the building of warships. In the late nineteenth century, cutters patrolled the islands off Alaska to prevent seal poaching.

The cutter Rush at Valdez, Alaska, in the late nineteenth century, as it and other cutters patrolled the islands throughout Alaska to prevent seal poaching in their role of environmental protection. The expression, "Come early to avoid the Rush," might have originated with the poachers of the era. (U.S. Coast Guard)

Above: *The uniqueness of the Coast Guard is that it is both a military force and a federal law enforcement agency with authority to board, search, and seize vessels in American waters. (U.S. Coast Guard)*

Above, right: *Fighting fires is a regular part of Coast Guard port operations. (Joan Theras Collins, U.S. Coast Guard Art Collection)*

A Coast Guard fisheries boarding team inspects a fishing vessel for safety and fisheries violations. A vessel cited for major violations might be taken into custody and escorted to a port for a complete inspection. Foreign fishing boats violating United States treaty waters can also be impounded. (U.S. Coast Guard)

Coast Guard inspectors must know the fishing laws. Here they are measuring net sizes and probing through the nets to determine if they meet legal standards for webbing sizes and escapements if required. (U.S. Coast Guard)

The expression "Come early to avoid the *Rush*" originated with the poachers of the era. *Rush* was the patrolling revenue-cutter.

During the summer of 1890, Captain "Hell Roaring" Mike Healy and his crew on the famous *Bear* sailed to Siberia, purchased reindeer, and transported the animals back to Alaska, where they became part of the sustenance for the Native Americans. At the beginning of the twentieth century, cutters were ordered to prevent the over-fishing of sponges in the Gulf of Mexico. More recently, in 1976 the U.S. Congress passed the Magnuson-Stevens Fishery Conservation and Management Act. This established a 200-nautical-mile Exclusive Economic Zone, a law that the Coast Guard has the primary responsibility to enforce.

No event illustrated the mission of environmental protection to the world better than the grounding of the oil tanker *Exxon Valdez* in March 1989 with the release of some 11 million gallons of North Slope crude oil. This spill did for the marine environmental protection mission what the loss of *Titanic* did for the marine safety mission seventy-seven years previously.

And Coast Guard history is filled with what to some might be considered interesting trivia, but these facts demonstrate the great flexibility of the Coast Guard. In 1906, Congress authorized the construction of *Seneca* as a "derelict destroyer" to patrol the seas and to use dynamite to blow up semi-submerged wooden ships; this was "preventative" life-saving. In the last annual report of the Revenue Cutter Service to Congress in 1912, the cutter *Algonquin* is credited with driving off a group of "piratical native wreckers." The Hamburg-American steamer *Prinz Joachem*, with a large party of American tourists, was stranded on Atwood Cay in the Bahama Islands. The vessel was surrounded by "insolent and aggressive" wreckers whose intent was to steal the cargo. When *Algonquin* arrived both vessel and cargo were saved.

In 1914, the U.S Lighthouse Service became responsible for maintaining the aids to navigation in the Panama Canal. During the 1930s Coast Guard officers were assigned to commercial whalers to enforce recently passed conservation laws. Such Coast Guard expertise was an outgrowth of law enforcement skills learned in the enforcement of prohibition. In 1946, a Coast Guard team traveled to China to help train the Chinese in the handling of patrol dogs; this Coast Guard know-how was

The Coast Guard cruises the seas protecting marine mammals. Crews also board foreign and domestic fishing vessels to prevent over-fishing within the 200-mile exclusive economic zone. (William J. Burgess, U.S. Coast Guard Art Collection)

A Coast Guard small-boat crew watches over a fleet of recreational salmon fishermen off the California coast. Patrols, whether within busy harbors for homeland security or watching the fishing fleets, are another way for Coast Guard crews to live up to their motto, Semper Paratus, always ready. (Gary Todoroff)

an outgrowth of the World War II beach patrols. Also following World War II, Coast Guardsmen went to Japan and the Philippines to help those nations create their own coast guards.

For nearly four decades beginning in the 1940s, cutters manned mid-ocean stations, regardless of seas and weather, to provide weather information and a potential rescue site for the growing, intercontinental air-passenger trade. On more than one occasion, a distressed airliner intentionally ditched near a cutter so that its passengers might be rescued. It was a Coast Guardsman who wrote the "how-to" emergency crash-landing manual based on knowledge gained in landing large sea planes in rescue missions at sea.

In 1957, three cutters successfully navigated the Northwest Passage across the top of the North American continent to study the feasibility of that route. While these missions are no longer being performed, they demonstrate the great flexibility that the Coast Guard has shown in the past. And lest we forget, each mission was hard and dangerous work for the Coast Guardsmen of yesterday.

The Coast Guard's unique status as a military service accountable to a civilian agency has allowed it to undertake sensitive international tasks. During the Cuban Boat Lift of 1980, cutters manned rescue stations close to Cuba to demonstrate America's peaceful resolve to aid those fleeing the Castro government. During the 1990s, the Coast Guard re-flagged Kuwaiti tankers to put them under the protection of the U.S. during the Gulf War. Coast Guard officers are assigned as attachés to a number of American embassies. A Coast Guard contingent is present on the annual UNITAS, U.S.-South American Allied Exercise, cruises that circumnavigate South America, offering maritime aid to our neighbors.

The Coast Guard has grown as its missions have grown. In 1988, the First Sea Lord of Great Britain noted to the Commandant, with some surprise, that the Coast Guard rivaled in size the Royal Navy. The Coast Guard would rank as the seventh largest navy in the world.

The Coast Guard has reaction teams around the country to respond immediately to contain and remove oil from maritime spills. (U.S. Coast Guard)

Oil-soaked birds receive a helping hand. (James E. Dyekman, U.S. Coast Guard Art Collection)

"Honors Duty" wall at the U.S. Coast Guard Academy. (U.S. Coast Guard)

By request of President John F. Kennedy, the Coast Guard established the Ceremonial Honor Guard. For the first time, soon after President Kennedy took office, the Coast Guard took their place on the parade field with the Joint Services Honor Guards. This unit performs in parades and exhibitions for public and military audiences nationwide as well as for solemn internments at Arlington National Cemetery. Major units also form small color guards from within their ranks, such as pictured here, for local formal ceremonies. (U.S. Coast Guard)

Coast Guard Values

We have written much about what Coast Guard men and women have done in the past and what they are doing today. Perhaps more important, it is necessary to say how they do these missions. Like its sister military services, the Coast Guard, through its history, has evolved core values. These values collectively are a pledge by Coast Guard men and women to each other, but also to those they serve, all Americans. These values are honor, respect, and devotion to duty.

Honor—integrity is the Coast Guard standard. Its men and women demonstrate uncompromising ethical conduct and moral behavior in all of their professional and organizational actions. They are loyal and accountable to the public trust. Respect—they value its diverse workforce, and treat each other and those they serve with fairness, dignity, respect, and compassion. They encourage individual opportunity and growth. They encourage creativity through empowerment. They work as a team. Devotion to Duty—they are professionals, military and civilian men and women, who seek responsibility, accept accountability, and are committed to the successful achievement of organizational goals. They exist to serve, and serve with pride. These are difficult promises to keep. But this great nation deserves no less, nor will Coast Guard men and women strive for less. At the U.S. Coast Guard Academy, the following inscription dominates the entrance to the Cadet barracks: "*He who lives here Reveres Honor, Honors Duty.*"

A New World Mission

The Coast Guard is at yet another crossroads. In late July 2002, the Commandant, Admiral Tom Collins, and five retired Commandants, Admirals Loy, Kramek, Kime, Yost, and Gracey, met in the Oval Office with President Bush. This meeting had no precedent, but more than that, the issue itself was historic. How could the service best be used to protect the homeland from terrorist incidents such as the attacks experienced on September 11? From that meeting came the commitment of the president to recommend to Congress the movement of the Coast Guard to the Department of Homeland Security. Such a movement will have a profound effect on the future Coast Guard. Missions such as military readiness, coastal sea control, and port security and defense will take on prioritized roles, while other missions make accommodations so as to provide the ships, people, and money for these priorities.

The president is committed to the Coast Guard's *Deepwater* initiative. This initiative is easily the most ambitious program the Coast Guard has ever undertaken to recapitalize its ships, boats, aircraft, and facilities. It is a program envisioned to spend a half-billion dollars a year in "FY '98 dollars" for the next twenty to twenty-five years to bring the fleet into the twenty-first century. The result will be a Coast Guard as different from today as today's is from the 1915 service. More effective, larger but less personnel-intensive, and with homeland security being an over-riding mission, the Coast Guard is destined to play an even greater role in our nation's future.

The first quarter of the twenty-first century will be the most exciting and challenging in the Coast Guard's more than 200-year history; challenges to keep our homeland safe and secure, challenges to acquire and operate billions of dollars of state-of-the-art assets, and challenges to balance our mission priorities in consonance with the needs of our nation. On that historic day in July 2002 in the Oval Office, the echo of the heroes of the air crash in Pennsylvania on 9/11 was pervasive. "Let's Roll." Coast Guard—"Let's Roll."

A vigilant Coast Guardsman from a port security unit walks his post in Al Jabayl, Saudi Arabia, during the Persian Gulf War. (W. D. Darrell, U.S. Coast Guard Art Collection)

The detonation of an anti-swimmer grenade results in a plume of water rising behind a twenty-five-foot transportable boat from Coast Guard Port Security Unit 309 in the Persian Gulf during the Iraqi War. (John Gaffney, U.S. Coast Guard)

The United States Coast Guard's roles and missions developed over more than 200 years—years devoted by individuals to the protection of the nation and its citizens. (George Skypeck, U.S. Coast Guard Art Collection)

History

1790-1915: That Others Might Live

John J. Galluzzo

W ho was the first true Coast Guardsman? Was it Joshua James, who for sixty years repeatedly threw himself into danger to save others? Or was it George Worthylake, the first man to live the lonely and unsung life of an appointed lighthouse keeper in the western hemisphere? Was it Alexander Hamilton, whose vision for the financial health of a young and hopeful nation led to the formation of a fleet of "cutters" to enforce anti-smuggling laws?

Today's Coast Guardsman is a composite of them all, embodying the bravery of James, the vigilance of Worthylake, and the foresight of Hamilton. Dedicating their lives to the safety of others and to the pursuit of the service's core values of Honor, Respect, and Devotion to Duty, America's Coast Guardsmen must be ready and able to react instantly to a call to action and be prepared for unexpected changes of circumstance that may turn standard operations into entirely different, life-threatening experiences. Such is the reasoning behind the adoption of the service's motto, *Semper Paratus*, or "Always Ready."

Revenue Cutter Service

The smoke had barely cleared from the battlefields of the American Revolution in 1790, when the seeds of today's United States Coast Guard were planted. The first generation of American citizens fought bravely for

In 1793 the French attempted to use American ports as a base for privateering against foreign vessels. Captain William Cooke, commanding officer of the revenue cutter Diligence, *intercepts privateers bringing ashore a trunk of gold taken from a Spanish prize ship. The gold was returned to the Spanish government. From its outset, the Coast Guard has enforced federal laws and assisted various law enforcement agencies. (John Thompson, U.S. Coast Guard Art Collection)*

Pages 30–31: The replacement lightship Nantucket, *here in a 1934 photograph, was anchored by 160 fathoms of chain over the grave of its predecessor. The crew did three-months duty aboard followed by one-month liberty ashore. Since the predecessor of this Nantucket Lightship was rammed and sunk by the liner* Olympic, *a weekly fire and lifeboat drill became a routine aboard lightships. (U.S. Coast Guard)*

Opposite: The Cadets of the Revenue Cutter Service, ship's company of 1906, on board the school of instruction practice cutter Chase. *Three cadets in this group later became Coast Guard commandants. (U.S. Coast Guard)*

33

CONFUSED IDENTITY

President Washington asked in 1790 for a "System of cutters" to chase smugglers and assist in revenue collection. The resultant government fleet carried confused titles for nearly a century. The most common name was ascribed by the Secretary of the Treasury, who in 1832 referred to it as the "Revenue Cutter Service." Earlier official documents cited it as "Revenue-Service," "Revenue-Marine," the "Revenue-Marine Service" and the "system of cutters."

The problem of a name was still not resolved in 1843 when the "Bureau of Marine" was created in the Treasury Department and staffed with Revenue Cutter Service personnel. Not until 1863 did the first specific reference to the service appear in any statutes. The published title then became, "United States Revenue Cutter Service."

Still the name did not stick. Adding more ambiguity, after over a century with a confused identity, 1894 Regulations for the "Revenue Cutter Service" was published by the "Bureau of Marine."

Prophetically, twenty-nine years before the service received its present name, Lieutenant Worth G. Ross wrote an article in Harper's Monthly *titled, ". . . Our Coast Guard." The service became known officially as the United States Coast Guard in 1915 after 125-years of name-calling.*

While this unique Service has one official name now, many people are mislead because today's name still suggests a sentry walking beaches and small boats working in harbors. Even today people frequently express surprise upon learning that Coast Guard men and women sail beyond forty miles from the nation's coast, let alone fight and serve overseas.

With its broad mission a mix of military duty, law enforcement, homeland protection, maritime protection, and life-saving, no single title can describe it all or guarantee it won't always be misunderstood. One name may be as good as another, but whatever it has been called, all its tasks have been carried out with courage and perseverance.

Nevertheless, for now, when in trouble, Call the Coast Guard!

Alexander Hamilton is the honored "father" of the Coast Guard. When he became the first Secretary of the Treasury, the new government was impoverished, and widespread smuggling of incoming goods thwarted the collection of tariff revenue. His solution was the creation of a revenue marine force equipped with swift cutters to catch smugglers and enforce customs laws. Congress authorized this seagoing arm on 4 August 1790. This date is celebrated as the birthday of the U.S. Coast Guard. (U.S. Coast Guard)

freedom, and now, with the eyes of the world upon them, they had to prove they could handle it. They lay down their muskets and swords and turned to the task of nation building.

Eight years of war left the new country with a $70,000,000 debt. Having made heroes of men and women who smuggled goods past British customs collectors for years, the founders of the new federal government now realized the necessity of proper taxation on imported goods. The Revenue Act of 1789 provided for a tariff to raise the money a nation needed to operate. Howard V. L. Bloomfield in *The Compact History of the United States Coast Guard* wrote that enforcement of the tariff would have to be strict, and undoubtedly would be unpopular, for the "Treasury Department was expected to make good taxpayers of Americans who disliked authority, who had become, through a century of practice, expert at dodging the King's taxes, and who had just fought a war to escape such burdens entirely."

The first Secretary of the Treasury, Alexander Hamilton, viewed the tariff as beneficial in several ways, including promoting American industrialism and the growth among the nation's merchant marine. Without a navy of its own, the country needed to find some way to protect and patrol the vast eastern seaboard. Hamilton's solution was to create the Treasury Department's own navy, and so on 4 August 1790 as Bloomfield noted, "ten armed revenue cutters, small, swift and manned by stout American sailormen unafraid of man or weather, became the nucleus of what later would be named the United States Coast Guard."

Worth G. Ross wrote in 1886 in *Harper's Monthly* that the "unpretending fleet of small, sharp-built, single-masted, (sic) light-draught sailing vessels" served multiple purposes. They had to be fast enough to chase down larger vessels on the open sea, yet nimble enough to maneuver through the harbors and up the rivers of the East Coast and the Gulf of Mexico. They bore names celebrating the states in which they were built, *Massachusetts*, *South Carolina*, *Virginia*, or denoting characteristics that would become synonymous with the American Coast Guard, *Vigilant*, *Active*, *Diligence*, or memorializing heroes of the young nation, *General Greene*, *Pickering*, *Scammel*. At about fifty feet, the boats of the original fleet measured just slightly longer than the principal search-and-rescue vessel introduced by the United States Coast Guard at the beginning of the twenty-first century, the forty-seven-foot motor lifeboat.

The short-term success of the young nation's endeavor could be measured by one indisputable fact: by 1796, the entire $70,000,000 debt to foreign creditors from the Revolution had been paid. The cutter fleet though, by hailing and boarding merchant vessels, would soon prove useful to the country for more than the collection of taxes. As early as 1797, the cutters had begun patrolling the nation's coastline to protect coastal cities and towns and American ships engaged in commerce.

Bloomfield further noted that on 2 March 1799, "Congress provided that the President, at his discretion, could place the Revenue-Marine under the orders of the Secretary of the Navy." Because the Navy Department had been formed only the year before and had no warships when hostilities broke out with France, the small cutters were the only vessels to defend the nation during the Quasi-War. Once new ships were commissioned, those of the Revenue Cutter Service served with distinction alongside those of the fledgling Navy, aiding in the capture of twenty French vessels and the freeing of five captured American ones. Thereafter, military service in times of war became a permanent mission of the Revenue Cutter Service and would remain so for its offspring, the Coast Guard.

In 1799 the Revenue Cutter Service added the task of quarantining ports during contagious-disease outbreaks. The belief that yellow fever, influenza, and other diseases were coming into the country from vessels trading in tropical regions led individual states to adopt health and quarantine measures. The enforcement of the embargo against slave smuggling came after 1808, and was later extended to the transport of illegal immigrants. The cutters also engaged pirates from the Caribbean who raided coastal trading, and actions against pirates by the cutters *Louisiana* and *Alabama* became legendary.

Maritime Safety

Maritime safety became a primary function of the service in 1832 when the Secretary of the Treasury directed several ships in the fleet to patrol the coastline in the winter to aid mariners in distress. That general order became law in 1837.

The great fiction writers of the late nineteenth century could not conjure better stories than the men of the Life-Saving Service provided to the public through their stoic refusal to let a single sailor perish without a fight on American shores. Men like Joshua James, Rasmus Midgett, and Fred Hatch threw themselves in harm's way repeatedly through the course of their lives to save others, weaving tales of heroism that today seem more like chivalric legend than fact. Yet, even with men like these watching over our shores, Mother Nature still found ways to rip life from the sea and toss it ashore. The lifesavers could give their all, but still not save every life. The battle continues today. (Frank Leslie's Illustrated Newspaper, 1878).

Just forty years after its founding, the service had maritime law enforcement and assistance-to-vessels-in-distress responsibilities added to its original customs role. Furthermore, the service imposed its authority over navigation laws, wrecking, plundering, piracy, slave trade, quarantine, and neutrality assurance. The cutter service enforced one of the first federal conservation statutes, the Timber Reserve Act, prohibiting export of Southern live-oak timber used in building warships. Cutter captains also acted as inspectors of lighthouses and buoys.

Following the Civil War, the cutters protected the country's newest territory, Alaska, and added to their tasks biological, geographical, and oceanographic research. They scouted new locations for lighthouses, custom houses, and other needed outposts for the federal government. Crews enforced hunting laws and prevented the illegal trade of firearms, ammunition, and alcohol in the new territory. Eventually their duties included destroying derelict ships impeding passage on sea-lanes and in ports.

Revenue Vessels

The ships of the Revenue Cutter Service changed with the service's ever-expanding list of missions. The small, lightly armed cutters built in the 1790s made way for heavier, fourteen-gun rated vessels for the Quasi-War with France in 1799. The new Navy kept some of these vessels after the war. By the 1830s, 100-ton cutters, up to twice the size of the earliest class, became common.

The invention of steam propulsion for ships led to experimentation, but early trials with steam-driven vessels nearly caused the service to be disbanded. It was a costly experiment, resulting in unsatisfactory and unreliable vessels and raising strong dissentions among officers. Steam propulsion did not return until the Civil War. Congress limited the service's spending to the point that in 1849, all the service's steam-driven cutters were deactivated. Not until 1857 would *Harriet Lane*, the service's first successful steam-driven cutter, be launched.

Below: *Cutter* Jefferson Davis *was a ninety-foot topsail schooner of some 150 tons. The cutter was sent to the West Coast in 1854 to defend settlers from Indian attacks. In 1859, the cutter was used as a show of force against British naval units in a territorial dispute. (Donald G. McGibbon, Jr., U.S. Coast Guard Art Collection)*

Below, right: *Cutter* Gallatin *in 1855 at Newport, Rhode Island, in the earliest known photograph of a revenue cutter. The seventy-three-foot topsail schooner, displacing 112 tons, was built at the New York Navy Yard in 1830. In 1832* Gallatin *accompanied the cutter* Andrew Jackson *and three others to Charleston, South Carolina, to enforce federal customs tariffs. (Newport Historical Society)*

The fleet expanded during the Civil War, but by the 1880s the service again found itself lurching under the weight of an outdated, underpowered fleet. A new wave of ship design and building took place at the end of the nineteenth century, bringing the fleet into compliance with the vessels of the U.S. Navy.

The steam vessel Miami *was one of the first propeller-driven cutters. The cutter supported the landing of Federal forces in the capture of Norfolk, Virginia, during the Civil War. Its boats carried infantry ashore during the May 1862 landings. Some of* Miami's *boats carried howitzers to protect the soldiers from attack. Originally built as a commercial vessel of expensive English oak, mahogany, and teak, it sported fine accommodations. (Charles Mazoujian, U.S. Coast Guard Art Collection)*

Cutter Fessenden, *an iron-hulled side-paddlewheel steamer, served on the Great Lakes. (Thomas Muchow, U.S. Coast Guard Art Collection)*

African-Americans in the Coast Guard

Vincent Patton, Ed.D.

In 1716 the first American lighthouse began operations near Boston, Massachusetts, but after only two years, its first keeper died in an accident on a trip out to it. Killed with him were his family and their black slave.

The accident was memorialized in a poem by thirteen-year-old Benjamin Franklin, and the recorded history of black involvement with what would one day become the U.S. Coast Guard began. Little else is known about the role of blacks in the early lighthouse service, but fragmentary evidence exists to show that if blacks were not lighthouse keepers, they at least assisted in the operation and maintenance of many lighthouses.

The ships Congress authorized in August 1790 were to be armed with "swivels" or small cannon mounted on a revolving base. Guns needed for outfitting one of the first revenue cutters built in Portsmouth, New Hampshire, had been ordered from a manufacturer in Philadelphia. A black woman, Maria Lee, was hired to head the wagon train taking the guns to Portsmouth. "Black Maria," as she was commonly known, was famous for her brawn, and was capable of dispatching more than her share of men in any rough and tumble, knock-down, drag-out brawl.

During the journey, when hijackers attacked the wagon train on the Philadelphia-New York road, "Black Maria" rose to the occasion by laying out six of the perpetrators herself, while the other male teamsters were driving off the rest. Thus by the grace of "Black Maria," Secretary Hamilton got his swivels, and Captain Hopley Yeaton took command of the revenue cutter Scammel with orders as the first holder of a seagoing commission in the service of the United States to "protect the revenue."

The practice of officers being permitted to utilize their slaves on board revenue cutters appears common as slaves were shipped in the capacity of stewards, cooks, and seamen. A Revenue Cutter Service regulation dated 1 November 1843 officially prohibited this practice, by providing "nor is any slave ever to be entered for the Service, or to form a complement of any vessel of the Revenue-Marine of the United States." Even before this date, however, some restrictions had been placed upon the use of blacks and slaves by the captain of the revenue cutters. Captain W. W. Polk, USRCS, commanding the revenue cutter Florida, penned the following comments to Secretary of Treasury Samuel D. Ingham on 22 June 1831:

"In the general instructions for the government of the Revenue Cutter Service of December last, by one paragraph is prohibited the employment of persons of colour, unless by the special permission of the Secretary of Treasury. I respectfully beg leave to offer a few remarks for consideration on the subject. The custom which prevails at the Port of Philadelphia (where I ship my crews) of having coloured persons for cooks & stewards, renders it very difficult to procure suitable white persons to fill those stations. In compliance with those instructions, I endeavored to ship white persons to fill those stations—being unable to procure a white cook—I rated one cook who had been shipped at Boy's wages. The steward, the officer assigned to that duty, shipped him for a white man. He is one of those persons whose complexion renders it doubtful (on cursory observation) to what race he belongs. He called himself a white man, and a native of Norfolk, born of French parents, but on becoming acquainted with him, I have no doubt

Alex Haley said, "You don't spend twenty years of your life in the service and not have a warm, nostalgic feeling left in you. It's a small service, the Coast Guard, and there is a lot of *esprit de corps*." This comment comes from a person who had to serve a military career as a mess cook and steward because of race, yet later achieved world-renowned acclaim as an author through his own striving. (U.S. Coast Guard)

he is a man of colour, and doubt whether he is a native. I beg leave here that I may be permitted to employ the boy as a servant on board. He is an expert sailor for his age and competent to the duty of a boy of the first class. I would further respectfully ask if the commanders of cutters are permitted to employ apprentices, and if so, how many."

Six days later Secretary Ingham replied, stating there "will be no objection to your retaining your servant Boy and shipping coloured persons as cooks and stewards." The following month, on 30 July 1831, Acting Secretary of the Treasury Asbery Dickens assured Captain Richard Derly, USRCS, commanding the revenue cutter Morris, that he had "permission of the department to employ free colored-persons as cook and steward of the MORRIS."

Since 1794 the U.S. Revenue Cutter Service had been carrying on an important mission—that of preventing the importation of slaves into the territorial limits of the United States. Although the law of 22 March 1794 that inhibited the slave trade between the United States and foreign countries did not specifically direct the revenue cutters to aid in its enforcement, they were nevertheless instructed to do so. Their efforts to suppress the traffic did not cease until the need for slaves had disappeared. For instance, the revenue cutters stationed at the

South Atlantic coast ports, operating under the authority of the acts of 2 March 1807 and 3 March 1819, captured numerous vessels, having on board "in the aggregate 487 negroes intended to be sold in bondage."

The following entry in the service's annual report for 1846 was typical: "Several captures of piratical vessels, which at the time infested the Florida Keys, were made by Captain Jackson and others, and, having full cargoes of slaves destined for Amelia Island, were carried into American waters and confined."

While the fratricidal bloodletting of the Civil War, coupled with the Emancipation Proclamation, drastically changed the status of African-Americans in the United States for all time, their position within the Revenue Cutter Service stayed pretty much the same—with only one startling exception: Captain Michael A. Healy.

In 1939, one the Coast Guard's most famous members, Alexander Palmer Haley, enlisted in the service. During his first ten years of duty, Haley was assigned as a steward, working in the officer's mess and wardroom, afloat and ashore. On the side he wrote articles for popular magazines, which earned him an opportunity to work "out of specialty" in the Third Coast Guard District's public affairs office in New York in 1950. It was during this period Haley's writing skills both on and off the job became well known. By constantly prodding his commanding officer, Haley was able to convince the Coast Guard to establish an enlisted specialty of journalist. He was then advanced to the rank of chief journalist, becoming the first in the Coast Guard to hold that position and specialty.

Haley retired from the Coast Guard in 1959, but he used the writing and research skills honed during his years in the service to write the best-selling book Autobiography of Malcolm X, to work as chief interviewer for Playboy magazine, and to author the Pulitzer Prize–winning novel Roots.

African-Americans were a vital part of the Coast Guard's contribution to the World War II effort. In 1942 Secretary of the Navy Knox announced blacks would be accepted in all ratings for which they qualified, rather than being restricted to the "Stewards Branch." This decision applied to the Coast Guard as well. During that same year the Coast Guard established an all-black station at Tina Beach on Hampton Bay, Long Island, New York. The station's principal mission was providing what is now called "homeland security." In addition to guarding against German submarines, the crews operated weather instruments and provided radio weather reports up and down the coast.

In June 1943 Lieutenant Carlton Skinner recommended to the Commandant of the Coast Guard, Vice Admiral Russell R. Waesche, that blacks be sent to sea as part of integrated crews rather than as all-black crews. This was considered a radical idea for the time. The Navy was experimenting with two all-black crews during this period, but previously established traditions of segregation were hard to break.

Waesche did not directly respond to Skinner's proposal. However, several months later Skinner received orders to report to Sea Cloud, a converted yacht being used for weather patrol. This duty required the ship maintain a designated position at sea for twenty–thirty days at a time and to make regular reports of the weather.

Skinner arrived for duty and just days before embarking on his first patrol, was met by twelve black crewmembers who had been assigned to his ship to

Master Chief Petty Officer of the Coast Guard Vincent W. Patton holds the Coast Guard's battle streamer commemorating the Revenue Cutter Service's heroic actions from 1790 to 1797. Patton, the eighth Master Chief Petty Officer of the Coast Guard, focused, during his tenure, primarily on quality of life issues, career development, work environment, and personnel matters for 36,000 active duty and Reserve enlisted personnel. In retirement, Patton holds titles of both Ed.D. and Reverend. (Pete Milnes, U.S. Coast Guard)

perform duties other than those of the traditional steward rating. Skinner's idea of an integrated crew had been accepted. During its various patrols, Sea Cloud had only one combat experience but was credited with assisting in the sinking of a German submarine. More importantly however, Sea Cloud proved blacks and whites could work together. As a result of this experiment and its test of all-black crews, the Navy issued a policy in 1944 that permitted up to 10 percent of the general ratings in non-combat ships to be black.

More significantly, Skinner's initiative and the success of Sea Cloud's integration of its crew was the first of its kind among all of the military services before President Truman signed Executive Order 9981 on 26 July 1948. Prior to the end of the war Skinner commanded yet another integrated ship, the destroyer escort Hoquim.

African-American women also played a role in the Coast Guard during World War II. In the fall of 1944 the Coast Guard recruited five black women as Reservists. Olivia Hooker became the first African-American woman to enlist, after repeated attempts were rejected because of her race. Undeterred, Hooker continued to attempt enlistment until the senior woman officer, Captain Dorothy Stratton, intervened on her behalf. Hooker enlisted as a yeoman second class and was assigned to assist in the mass separations from active duty of Coast Guardsmen during the reduction of forces toward the end of the war.

Since the close of World War II, roles, ranks, and responsibilities of African-Americans greatly increased. By the beginning of the twenty-first century, 12 percent of the Coast Guard's workforce was African-American. In 1998, for the first time in the service's history, African-Americans held two prominent senior ranks: Rear Admiral Errol S. Brown became the first African-American to attain flag-officer rank. An African-American myself, I was proud to serve as Master Chief Petty Officer of the Coast Guard, the service's most senior enlisted member. Today every rank and rating from seaman recruit to rear admiral includes an increasing number of African-American men and women.

Life Savers

Humanitarian motives behind the formation of the Humane Society of the Commonwealth of Massachusetts had manifested themselves elsewhere in the world before the first gathering of merchants, doctors, and philanthropists at the Bunch of Grapes Tavern in Boston, Massachusetts, on 5 January 1786. Similar organizations had come together in England and Holland a decade earlier, and the Chinese had been practicing lifeboat rescues since the formation of the Chinkiang Association for the Saving of Life in 1708. Although the Massachusetts Humane Society was originally founded with the medical objective of discovering methods for restoring the "apparently drowned," the scope of the organization quickly evolved to include shore-based lifesaving.

Its first actions were the development of three huts of refuge in 1787, one in Boston Harbor on Lovell's Island along the channel leading into the port, one on Nantasket Beach, and one at the base of Third Cliff in Scituate, just to the south. The huts, rudimentary at best, drew unfavorable comment from Henry David Thoreau. After coming across one on Cape Cod in 1847, he stated: "So we shivered round about, not being able to get into it, ever and anon looking through the knot-hole into that night without a star, until we concluded that it was not a humane house at all, but a sea-side box, now shut up." Yet where Thoreau saw failure in the humane experiment, others saw great potential and the first steps toward the realization of a noble dream.

The Humane Society brought their concept of saving mariners in distress one step further in 1807, twenty years after the placement of the first huts of refuge, when it located the first American shore-based lifeboat, built in Nantucket, in a cove at the South Shore town of Cohasset. This Cohasset lifeboat disappeared after 1813, however, and no record exists of any further activity until 1840.

Top: *Congress, in 1871, appropriated funds to build coastal lifeboat stations from which to launch surfboats to go to the rescue. Thus began the U.S. Life-Saving Service. This common layout, front view, and floor plan, for these small station buildings included one large room for the surfboat and minimum living-space for the surfmen. The bedroom measures only seven and a half feet by eight feet. (U.S. Coast Guard)*

Above: *Side views of a typical lifeboat station in the nineteenth century. (U.S. Coast Guard)*

After a particularly terrible winter that saw three successive hurricanes strike the Massachusetts coast in 1839, Humane Society President Benjamin Rich expressed a desire for the organization to reinvest in shore-based lifesaving with the construction of several new boats. Unfortunately, with empty coffers, the goal seemed impossible. Then in April 1840 the state legislature sent a communication to the surprised board of trustees. It stated, "That there be allowed and paid out of the Treasury of the Commonwealth, to the President and Trustees of the Massachusetts Humane Society, the sum of five thousand dollars, for the purpose of furnishing Life Boats to be stationed at the most exposed parts of the seacoast within this Commonwealth."

By January 1841, eleven boats had been constructed and placed along the coast. Within the year the state furnished more money, and the society built more boats. No longer would the people of Massachusetts simply wait ashore for storms to bring victims to them, alive or dead. From that moment on they would throw themselves to the storms and risk their lives to save others. Fishermen, lobstermen, Irish moss gatherers, merchantmen, yachtsmen, oystermen, whalers, and others answered the call to volunteer whenever the cry "Ship ashore!" rang out, their common motivation voiced by Joshua James' nephew Francis: "I'd like to think that if I was the one that was out there, someone would come for me."

The deeds of the lifesavers did not go unheralded or unrecorded. Men and women who performed daring rescues could earn gold, silver, or bronze medals, certificates, or in some cases, cash—a practice still carried on by the organization today.

By 1871, the Humane Society boasted seventy-six stations along the coast, the huts of refuge by that time having given way to lifeboat stations and mortar stations. That year, though, marked the end of the golden era of the organization's shore-based lifesaving practices. Although the Humane Society's lifeboat crews continued to save lives into the 1930s, from that day forward, the organization shared the spotlight with the men of the federal government's United States Life-Saving Service.

As with the Humane Society's first attempts at establishing a network of lifesaving structures, the federal government's initial approach could be classified as at least a start, if not a terribly good one. Congressman William Newell of New Jersey called for an appropriation of $10,000 in 1848 for lifesaving equipment to be placed along the New Jersey shoreline, and in August of that year, his proposal passed into law.

Unfortunately the appropriation did not provide either for maintenance and upkeep of the equipment or payment for personnel to use the "surfboats, rockets and carronades" in times of necessity. Captain Douglas Ottinger of the Revenue Cutter Service took charge of the establishment and outfitting of eight boathouses along the Jersey shore, but could do no more than hand the keys to local people he deemed trustworthy enough to watch over them.

The buildings and equipment had already started to deteriorate by the time of the Civil War. With a cessation of coastal trading between the North and the South, and the focus of the country shifting away from the

Boats at some stations were launched directly into the water from the boathouse by riding a carriage set on tracks. (U.S. Coast Guard)

shorelines to the great battlefields of the war, the need for a federal life-saving organization retreated to the background of American consciousness. Neglect caused the stations to fall into disrepair. Five years after the cessation of hostilities between the Union and the Confederacy, the nation once again focused on its dependence upon the sea. Still, in 1869 Congress defeated a plan for paid surfmen to replace the volunteer system.

Terrible winter storms beginning in 1870 and extending through the winter of 1871 convinced the country to make its own waterways safe for travel and trade. Concerned citizens called for action, and Congress responded in April 1871 with a $200,000 appropriation to create a better lifesaving system.

In conjunction with the humanitarian mission, those responsible for the new lifesaving system would also be charged with safeguarding the country's merchant fleet and the preservation of property. Much as Alexander Hamilton's Treasury accepted the mission in order to build a new nation after the American Revolution, Secretary of the Treasury George S. Boutwell's office viewed safeguarding the merchant fleet as a task of economic reconstruction after the Civil War.

Soon after his appointment in 1869, Boutwell created an interim bureau consisting of the Revenue Cutter Service, Steamboat Inspection, Marine Hospital, and Life-Saving Services. In an attempt to establish cohesive administrative practices within the various departments, Boutwell appointed the chief clerk of the Treasury, Sumner Increase Kimball, to reorganize the Revenue Cutter Service and Life-Saving Services. Kimball

Top, left: *U.S. Life-Saving Station, Chicago, Illinois, in 1889. (U.S. Coast Guard)*

Top, right: *The remoteness of a typical Life-Saving Station manifested itself in times of crises. Far removed from civilization, life-saving crews often opted to bury shipwreck victims, especially those men or women who were unidentified, on the beaches on which they washed ashore. Loved ones searching days, weeks, and in some cases months after a sailor's disappearance could ask for the remains of an unidentified victim to be disinterred, only to find that the bits of clothing hanging loosely from the rotting corpse did not match anything their brother, father, or uncle had ever worn. With 279 lifesaving stations around the United States, this scene played out all over the country. (Coast Guard Museum Northwest)*

took office on 1 February 1871 and for seven years he tirelessly worked at improving both organizations. He concluded that although the service was in poor condition, it might yet be shaped into an institution the citizenry could look upon with pride.

Armed with the 1870 and 1871 acts of Congress, Kimball, reported Evans, "assigned Revenue Cutter Service officers to supervise the reorganization in the field; they inspected the stations, repaired the existing plant, bought new equipment, drilled the crews, instituted beach patrols and lookouts, introduced a system of signaling to ships off shore, and helped draw up regulations for the whole establishment." Within ten years, 189 life-saving stations, arranged in districts, rimmed the country from Maine to Florida to the state of Washington, around the Great Lakes, and on the Ohio River.

In 1878, another reorganization of the Treasury Department established the United States Life-Saving Service as a bureau unto itself, with Kimball appointed as its first and only general superintendent. The results of Kimball's first decade in charge of the country's lifesaving system were impressive. "From 1871 to 1882," noted Evans, "death came to only one out of 306 persons wrecked on coasts patrolled by U.S. Life-Savers. In the same period, the station crews saved $18 million worth of property and rescued over 14,000 lives. Three thousand more, 'brought to the stations drenched, frozen, or starving, or nearly spent from the torture of the breakers,' were sheltered and given aid. And the total cost of the whole lifesaving program was no more than half a million annually."

The true heroes of the service, of course, walked the beaches and manned the oars of the lifeboats. In 1890, the average surfman could expect to be one of seven men assigned to a station under a keeper, with a seasonal man possibly brought on during the coldest months. He got June and July off, as the lifesaving "season"—before the rise of mass pleasure boating—was geared to the potential winter dangers to shipping. Together the crew manned the station's watch tower and patrolled the shoreline twenty-four hours a day for ten months of the year. The men mostly cooked their own meals, and, because of the isolation of many stations, had relatively little contact with other human beings.

Six mornings a week they drilled in their lifeboats and smaller surfboats, worked with the beach apparatus, and practiced resuscitation and with signal flags, so that when disaster struck, a keeper's orders could be carried out without hesitation. Should the need arise for a lifeboat launch, each man had an assigned station; should the beach cart be dragged to a ship in danger within the breakers, each man had an assigned task in unloading, arranging, and using the Lyle line-throwing gun, whip line, hawser, sand anchor, A-frame, and breeches buoy.

Above: It was often more practical to use beach apparatus instead of surfboats when vessels were stranded close to shore. The equipment was pulled to the wreck site on a beach cart where it was set up for rescue by breeches buoy or life car. (U.S. Coast Guard)

Opposite, center: Lifeboat stations were located principally in isolated locations. Boats were pulled along the beach to launching sites on carts pulled either by horse or manpower. Typically, a station had seven men assigned. They served constantly, twenty-four hours a day for ten months sharing station duties always looking for trouble at sea from a watchtower and by walking the beach. (U.S. Coast Guard)

Beach apparatus includes a Lyle gun—a small muzzle-loading cannon—and projectile with a line attached that is fired over to fall in the rigging of the wrecked ship. This light line is then used by ships' survivors to pull out a heavier line upon which rides the breeches buoy or life car. The line is coiled on long spindles attached to a backing board. This is then set into a box and the spindle board removed leaving a free-flowing pattern of line that can unwind at the speed of the bullet projectile to which it is attached. Note the box of line ready to run out and the spindle boards of line already woven ready to dump into the box. (U.S. Coast Guard)

Right: *A Lyle gun fires a nineteen-pound projectile during a breeches buoy drill. Note the line trailing from the projectile, which is heading for the rigging of a simulated ship. (U.S. Coast Guard)*

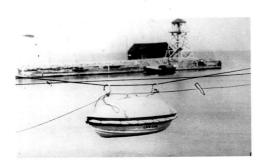

Above: *The alternative to the breeches buoy was the life car. It had room for eleven people, but the air supply for that many people reportedly was merely three minutes. Typically, a life car carried four to six people. (U.S. Coast Guard)*

Right: *In this beach-apparatus drill, a sand anchor (out of view) holds the set-up in place and one end of the line leading to the ship. The cross piece simulates a ship's mast where the other end is secured. A breeches buoy, seen here hanging from a block riding on the line, is hauled in and out through a pulley by surfmen, at left. (U.S. Coast Guard)*

Opposite, bottom: *During the Spanish-American War the cutter* Hudson, *a U.S. Navy gunboat, and torpedo boat* Winslow *were on reconnaissance near Cardenas, Cuba, when they came under attack by enemy batteries. When* Winslow *became disabled in shallow water, First Lieutenant Frank H. Newcomb maneuvered* Hudson *close to* Winslow, *while his crew continued to return enemy fire. The battle went on for a half hour before a towline could be made fast. A bursting shell killed an officer and three sailors on* Winslow, *but* Hudson *pulled the boat out of range, thus saving the rest of its crew. To acknowledge the heroism of Newcomb and his crew, Congress struck a special medal for all of the cutter's crew. (Dean Ellis, U.S. Coast Guard Art Collection)*

Individual heroes arose throughout the service. Surfman Frederick T. Hatch and eight other men at the Cleveland, Ohio, Life-Saving Station earned Gold Lifesaving Medals for rescuing twenty-nine men from three schooners during a two-day 1883 Lake Erie gale. Ten years later, Hatch earned a second gold medal for a rescue carried out while he served as

Above: *Spectators watch a real-life rescue of crewmembers being rescued by breeches buoy off a stranded ship. (U.S. Coast Guard)*

Right: *What a breeches buoy looks like with a "survivor." It is simply oversized canvas breeches with the legs cut short and the belt-line sewn inside a ring buoy. (U.S. Coast Guard)*

INTERIOR U.S. LIFE SAVING STATION. BANDON, OR.

a lighthouse keeper in Cleveland Harbor. Surfman William Drazel of the floating station on the Falls of the Ohio aided more than 6,000 people during his forty years in uniform with the Life-Saving Service and the Coast Guard, from 1880–1920 at Louisville, Kentucky.

Perhaps the most recognized American lifesaver, Joshua James was only eleven-years-old when he watched his mother perish before his eyes. Four years later the fifteen-year-old James snuck aboard a Massachusetts Humane Society pulling boat and joined in the rescue of

Joshua James

John J. Galluzzo

Disaster struck the United States Life-Saving Service on 17 March 1902, news of which sent shock-waves from station to station across the entire country. Responding to a distress signal from the stranded barge Wadena, *Keeper Marshall W. Eldredge of Massachusetts' Monomoy Life-Saving Station ordered the surfboat launched. The crew rowed south for Monomoy Point, the "elbow" of Cape Cod, battling heavy southeast winds and choppy seas. To the best of their estimation, though, due to the relatively stable condition of the barge resting on Shovelful Shoal, the rescue of the five stranded mariners aboard should not have been an especially dangerous one.*

When they reached the vessel, the lifesavers threw a heaving stick and line aboard, which the bargemen secured on deck. One by one they shinnied down a rope, each more frantic and excited than the one before him. After the fifth man dropped into the surfboat, Eldredge instructed his passengers to hunker down, keep quiet, and not move.

Just after the lifesavers pushed off from Wadena, a tremendous wave slammed the small boat, rousing the already terrified victims to an even higher state of fear. They reached up and grabbed at the surfmen, wrapping their arms around their necks and torsos, inhibiting their ability to row. Wave after wave continued to strike the surfboat until finally it overturned. The crew succeeded in righting the boat—twice—but eventually all but one of them gave way, lost to the powerful ocean's pull. Only surfman Seth Ellis, rescued by wrecker Elmer Mayo, survived to tell of the tragedy.

Two days after the loss of the Monomoy Station crew, Keeper Joshua James of the Point Allerton Life-Saving Station in Hull, Massachusetts, assembled his surfmen for an extra, unexpected drill in their new Beebe-McLellan self-righting, self-bailing surfboat. A

heavy northeast wind met them as they headed for Stony Beach across the road from the station.

With the seventy-five-year-old keeper at the steering oar, they practiced with the surfboat for a full hour. Just eleven months earlier, James had made Boston Globe headlines when he passed his annual physical with results better than any of the twenty- or thirty-year-olds under his command at the Point Allerton Station.

According to U.S.L.S.S. General Superintendent Sumner I. Kimball's 1909 biography of the keeper:

"The drill was very satisfactory, and the Captain expressed his great gratification both with the behavior of the boat in freeing itself of the torrents of water which boarded it, and with the skill of the men. At length he gave the orders for landing, and when the boat grounded upon the beach opposite the station he sprang out upon the wet sand and, glancing at the sea a moment, he remarked to his men, 'The tide is ebbing.' These were his last words, but little did he know how true they were for him, for as he uttered them, he fell dead upon the beach."

After sixty years of rescuing people from the dangers of the sea and with an unmatched record of having saved more than 1,000 sailors, lifelong storm warrior Joshua James passed into history as the most decorated lifesaver of the United States.

Above: Lifesaver Joshua James had an unmatched record of rescuing people from the dangers of the sea, according to accounts, by saving more than a thousand individuals. He began this phenomenal record at age fifteen when he joined the Massachusetts Humane Society and continued with the U.S. Life-Saving Service until his death at age seventy-five. (U.S. Coast Guard)

the crew of *Mohawk*. In 1876 the Humane Society appointed him keeper of their boats in the peninsular town of Hull, and in 1888 he led the rescues of twenty-nine men from six ships during a November snow storm. The following year the Life-Saving Service waived its age restriction to allow the sixty-two-year-old to become keeper of the new Point Allerton station. In November of 1898, at seventy-two, he led his combined USLSS and Humane Society team to rescue twenty men from four ships during the Portland Gale, which claimed more than 500 lives from Maine to New Jersey.

The most dramatic performance by a Life-Saving Service surfman, though, may have been that of Rasmus Midgett of the Gull Shoal, North Carolina, Station. Riding a horse on patrol from the station during a hurricane in August 1899, Midgett spied debris from a ship washing ashore, but could not see any vessel in danger. Continuing on for two more miles, he spotted the 643-ton barkentine *Priscilla* breaking up on the beach. Realizing the ten people on board stood no chance of survival if he went to the station for support—the sea had already wrested four to their deaths—Midgett quickly improvised a risky and dangerous plan. Timing the breaking waves, he ran in the shallows from the troughs out to the ship and yelled for those who could do so to jump

A lifeboat crew launches its boat to assist a grounded ship. The crew is wearing life vests made of cork. (U.S. Coast Guard)

49

Famed Apache leader Geronimo (seated center) in the uniform of an Army scout poses with members of U.S. Life-Saving Service in an 1898 exposition in Omaha, Nebraska. (U.S. Coast Guard)

Winter winds swirling sand amidst already dark skies at isolated rescue stations create an eerie setting such as "Old Salty" on the dunes near Cape May, New Jersey. (Lumen Martin Caseine Winter, U.S. Coast Guard Art Collection)

overboard. Seven times he ran to the ship, and each time a survivor leapt overboard. Keeping just ahead of the oncoming waves, he brought each person to shore. The final three survivors, though, could not help themselves. Again keeping in rhythm with the surf, he charged *Priscilla* an eighth time, and scaled the side of the ship by rope. Once aboard, he collapsed in exhaustion, regained his breath, and carried the next victim overboard and to the beach. Twice more he repeated this feat until he had single-handedly saved every person aboard. For his actions, Rasmus Midgett earned a Gold Lifesaving Medal.

PEA ISLAND — *VINCENT PATTON, ED.D.*

Records of the U.S. Life-Saving Service, commencing about 1875, showed the presence of African-Americans serving at a number of stations along the Maryland, Virginia, and North Carolina shores. Many were experienced fishermen and oystermen who lived nearby and were knowledgeable of the surf and sea. Upon clearance from the medical surgeon, these men were issued Articles of Engagements and became paid U.S. Lifesavers.

In 1880 Richard Etheridge, a "colored surfman," was designated keeper of the Pea Island Lifesaving Station on the outer banks of North Carolina, near where he was born and raised. His life outdoors along the coast enabled him to become an adept fisherman and surfman. While only fragmentary records of African-Americans in the U.S. Life-Saving Service exist from that time, Etheridge's promotion—on the recommendation of an inspecting officer—represents the first record of a black having been given such a responsible position.

Etheridge was assigned to the only all-black station crew in the Life-Saving Service. The rigorous drills Etheridge expected from his crew prepared the men to tackle any task they might face as lifesavers and soon earned them a reputation as a very efficient unit, one credited with saving many lives from wrecked or foundering ships.

Perhaps the most dramatic rescue for Etheridge's Pea Island crew occurred in October 1896. A schooner, E. S. Newman, left Providence, Rhode Island, for Norfolk, Virginia, and sailed into a "savage" hurricane, which stripped away its sails and pushed the stricken vessel down to the North Carolina coast. The captain, afraid of its being broken up by the huge waves, tried to beach the ship. E. S. Newman grounded offshore several miles below Pea Island Station. An alert surfman spotted the emergency flares and notified Etheridge.

High waves pounded the beach and shoreline, but Etheridge led his crew through the water-logged sand to the ship. When they reached E. S. Newman, they discovered their rescue equipment, which they had laboriously carried with them, could not be set up. Etheridge then tied ropes around two of his crewmen and they swam out to the ship and returned with the captain's daughter. Eight more times this arduous trek was made, alternating swimmers, until all E. S. Newman crew had been rescued. Not until 100 years later would the crew be formally recognized for this heroic feat: in 1996 the Coast Guard Commandant, Admiral Robert E. Kramek, awarded Gold Lifesaving Medals posthumously to the entire crew of Pea Island Station.

Although Etheridge died in 1900, Pea Island remained an all-black station into the 1950s. The station was deactivated in 1974.

Richard Etheridge (left) and his Pea Island life station crew in North Carolina. (U.S. Coast Guard)

Collectively, the stories of the deeds of the surfmen and keepers of the United States Life-Saving Service formed their own chapter in the mythos of America. Composite characters—part Joshua James, part Rasmus Midgett, part Frederick Hatch—graced the covers of magazines and newspapers from coast to coast under the generic name of "The American Life-Saver." Children's books allowed the young to fantasize about life as one of the country's storm warriors challenging the sea, all the while proudly living under the motto: "You have to go out, you don't have to come back."

Yet the reality of life at a station could hardly be called romantic. Low pay and a lack of upward mobility sent many men through the ranks of the lifesavers quickly as they left to find more financially rewarding work. The adrenaline rush of a rescue might come once every few years at some stations, while the drudgery of daily drills,

CAPTAIN MICHAEL A. HEALY — VINCENT PATTON, ED.D.

Captain Michael A. Healy was one of ten children born in Macon, Georgia, to an Irish immigrant and a mulatto slave girl. In his youth he constantly ran away from several schools. His brother felt sea life would discipline young Healy, so in 1855, at the age of fifteen, Healy was hired as a cabin boy aboard the clipper Jumna. *After traveling and learning the duties and responsibilities of sailors, Healy applied to, and was accepted by, the Revenue Cutter Service in March 1865.*

By June 1868 he had become a second lieutenant and was promoted to first lieutenant two years later. Healy became known as a brilliant seaman and was often considered the best sailor in the North. In 1884 **The New York Sun** *described Healy in a feature article: "Captain Mike Healy is a good deal more distinguished person in the waters of the far Northwest than any president of the United States or any potentate of Europe has yet become."*

Captain Mike Healy and his pet parrot rest easy on the main deck of the cutter *Bear*. Healy commanded *Bear* from 1886 to 1895 cruising Alaskan waters saving lives and enforcing federal laws. The foremost Arctic navigator of the period was a legend in his own time. (U.S. Coast Guard)

Healy's most remarkable period in service began in 1886 when he took command of the USRC **Bear**, *considered by many the greatest polar ship of its time. The ship's responsibilities included "seizing any vessel found sealing in the Bering Sea." By 1892 the revenue cutters* **Bear, Rush,** *and* **Corwin** *had made so many seizures, tension developed between the United States and the British merchants.*

Healy was also tasked with bringing medical and other aid to the natives of Alaska, making weather and ice reports, preparing navigation charts, rescuing vessels in distress, transporting special passengers and supplies, and fighting violators of federal laws. He served as deputy U.S. Marshal and was for many years the federal law in Alaska. He retired as the third ranking officer in the U.S. Revenue Cutter Service.

polishing, and patrolling came every day no matter what happened. When a ship did wreck, death remained a distinct possibility for both the rescued and the rescuers. From 1876, when the entire crew of the Little Island, North Carolina, Station died in a rescue attempt, until 1914, when Surfman Frank C. Bennett of Sleeping Bear Point, Michigan, succumbed to "disease contracted in line of duty," 330 surfmen and keepers died in action.

In 1915, the year the Life-Saving Service and the Revenue Cutter Service were joined as the United States Coast Guard, 279 stations protected America's shoreline. Each night, surfmen patrolled the beaches, islands, capes, points, ports, and inlets of the country, forming a thin line of hope for mariners in difficulty.

From 1871 to 1915, under the guidance of Sumner Kimball, the men of the United States Life-Saving Service saved more than 150,000 lives and warned tens of thousands more away from danger. So, in the words of J. H. Merryman in *The United States Life-Saving Service— 1880*: "In the thought of this deed let us close. A gallant soul whose name honors the rolls of the Life-Saving Service, once said: 'When I see a man clinging to a wreck, I see nothing else in the world, and I never think of family and friends until I have saved him.' It is certain that this is the spirit which pervades the men of the coast. All report, all records testify to it, and every winter their deeds sublimely respond to the divine declaration 'Greater love hath no man than this, that a man lay down his life for his friends.'"

Tucked away on a quiet seaside hill in Hull, Massachusetts, those very words are etched into the grave marker of Joshua James, a requiem to all of the men of the United States Life-Saving Service, men who risked their own lives, so that others might live.

The Coast Guard

The importance of the missions of the Revenue Cutter Service was never questioned, yet a recurrent discussion of the service's proper position in the federal government seemed never to go away. Several times during the nineteenth century, voices arose in support of moving the service under control of the Navy. The proposed federal restructuring that caused the service its greatest scare, though, came in 1911, 121 years into its existence. Acting under a directive to streamline the branches of the federal government and ensure that each organization in a given department adhered to the notion of "unifunctionalism," the governmental watchword of the day, Professor Frederick A. Cleveland of the newly appointed Commission on Economy and Efficiency told President William Howard Taft he believed the Revenue Cutter Service could simply be done away with.

With its myriad missions, many of which had never been assigned by Congress and others, that had long since become obsolete, such as stopping the flow of slaves into the United States, the service stood in direct opposition to the idea of this catchphrase. Other branches of the government, argued Cleveland, could take on the remainder of the service's mission. The commission also believed the Life-Saving Service should be merged with the Bureau of Lighthouses and moved into the Department of Commerce and Labor.

Institutional instability had been the norm for both the Life-Saving Service and the Revenue Cutter Service for the better parts of their existence. The Revenue Cutter Service had gone through name changes,

Crewmen stand tall with Bear surrounded by ice. For crewman Frank S. Sandel, the famous Bear was the only ship he really wanted to sail on. He went aboard shortly after the Revenue Cutter Service and the Life-Saving Service merged. Sandel recalled that the food aboard the ship was usually a fare of "salt horse," or beef, beans, and rice. Potatoes were a treat if they could be found, as was fresh fruit. There was no refrigeration and food had to be kept iced down. It was not uncommon to have the meat tied in the rigging during cold weather to keep it from spoiling. (U.S. Coast Guard Museum Northwest)

Above: Grant was a rare three-masted cutter. The square topsail schooner-rigged, iron-hulled Grant entered service in 1871 and served on both coasts, including in the Bering Sea. (U.S. Coast Guard)

Left: The cutter Gresham was launched on 12 September 1896, in Cleveland, Ohio. It was stationed in the Great Lakes until it came to the attention of Canada that this vessel was heavily armed and even carried bow-mounted torpedo tubes. A bilateral agreement established in 1817 limited the number of naval vessels and the armament permitted between Canada and the United States. This finding forced the cutter out of the Great Lakes during the Spanish-American War. However, there was a significant problem accomplishing this. Gresham was too long for the Welland Canal locks, so the ship was cut in half, with the two halves floated through the locks—aided by pontoons—and reassembled. By the time it was put back together the war was over. (U.S. Coast Guard)

continual expansion of purpose, and recurrent talk of annexation to the Navy. The Life-Saving Service grew out of a small appropriation in the 1840s. It fought battles for proper equipment and paid personnel. It suffered from poorly selected station keepers set in place by political patronage. From 1871 through 1878 the two services worked under the same masthead, with Sumner I. Kimball as superintendent of both operations.

Even after the organizations split in 1878, Revenue Cutter Service officers continued to act as inspectors of life-saving stations. Over the last quarter of the nineteenth century the men of both services demonstrated themselves as the true heroes of the American public, thrusting themselves into life-threatening situations in order to save the lives of strangers in peril.

The Cleveland Commission recommended that each of the three departments concerned—Treasury, Commerce and Labor, and Navy—be consulted before the bill went forward. Secretary Charles Nagel of Commerce and Labor agreed with the additions to his department, asking only that some of the revenue cutters be sent his way for life-saving purposes along the coast. Secretary George von L. Meyer of the Navy, however, did not want his service to take on the roles of the Revenue Cutter Service, arguing that their duties interfered with the Navy's training for war and were detrimental to fleet efficiency.

Secretary of the Treasury Franklin MacVeagh responded angrily, arguing that the idea of abolishing the Revenue Cutter Service "came out of a clear sky." He suggested instead that the Revenue Cutter Service and the Life-Saving Service be merged into one organization. Yet although MacVeagh and Captain Commandant Ellsworth Bertholf, hero of the Overland Expedition, argued that the removal of their service would lead to greater economic problems for the federal government rather than

"YOU HAVE TO GO OUT BUT YOU DON'T HAVE TO COME BACK." —
CAPTAIN GENE DAVIS, USCG (RET), DIRECTOR, COAST GUARD MUSEUM NORTHWEST

This old Coast Guard saying is traditionally attributed to a keeper of an Outer Banks, North Carolina, life-saving station back in the 1800s. During a horrific storm a vessel was seen to be in trouble off the beach. The surf was high and roaring. When a crewman questioned the sanity of trying to launch the station's boat into that surf, the keeper made his famous reply. You have but to read a section of the 1899 Regulations of the U.S. Lifesaving Service to understand the keeper's words:

Sec. 252. "In attempting a rescue the keeper will select either the boat, breeches buoy, or life car, as in his judgment is best suited to effectively cope with existing conditions. If the device first selected fails after such trial as satisfies him that no further attempt with it is feasible, he will resort to one of the others, and if that fails, then to the remaining one, and he will not desist from his efforts until by actual trial the impossibility of effecting rescue is demonstrated. The statement of the keeper that he did not try to use the boat because the sea or surf was too heavy will not be accepted unless attempts to launch it were actually made and failed, or unless the confirmation of the coast—as bluffs, precipitous banks, etc.—is such as to unquestionably preclude the use of a boat."

The slogan, "You have to go out but you don't have to come back" stuck as a motto through generations of Coast Guardsmen, as shown on this painting used as a cover for a small book portraying the story of the Coast Guard during World War II. (Coast Guard Museum Northwest)

---

saving it money, President Taft forwarded the commission report to Congress in April 1912, "recommending passage of the legislation necessary to put its various sections into effect."

Almost as if choreographed by fate and sent on stage for precisely timed dramatic effect, two stunning events occurred within the next ten days that returned both the cuttermen and the lifesavers to public awareness. In the early morning hours five days after the President sent the Cleveland Commission's report off to Congress with his wishes, the Merchant and Miners liner *Ontario*, on its way from Baltimore to Boston, caught fire near Montauk Point off Long Island.

Wireless calls from *Ontario* brought the revenue cutters *Mohawk* and *Acushnet* to the burning ship. Ashore, a surfman on patrol from the Ditch Plains Life-Saving Station saw the flames, and within moments the crew launched a lifeboat and soon after brought the passengers ashore. The lifesavers then returned to help the crew put out the flames, but when all was seen as hopeless, some in the ship's crew reached safety by breeches buoy; others managed to board the cutters. Not a single life was lost, thanks to cooperation from men of the two organizations.

Three days later, the White Star liner *Titanic*, on its maiden transatlantic voyage, struck an iceberg and 1,500 of the more than 2,200 passengers aboard lost their lives. Talk of disbanding of the Revenue Cutter Service lessened as that organization took on the challenge of the International Ice Patrol.

What once seemed a simple and straightforward solution to Taft and Cleveland—now stagnated in Congress—as the usefulness of the

From 1871 to 1915 Sumner Kimball guided the Life-Saving Service. Under his direction it became well organized and efficient. More than 150,000 lives were saved during his tenure. (U.S. Coast Guard)

There had been debate on disbanding the Revenue Cutter Service but that all but ended when in 1912 the passenger liner Titanic *hit an iceberg and sank with large loss of life. The Revenue Cutter* Service *was given the additional task of patrolling the iceberg lanes, as the cutter* Tampa *here, to warn ships of these floating dangers. Instead of being dissolved, the agency became stronger when in 1915 the Revenue Cutter Service and U.S. Life-Saving Service merged and was given the name Coast Guard. (John Wisinski, U.S. Coast Guard Art Collection)*

Revenue Cutter Service in its humanitarian mission and its potential for cooperation with the Life-Saving Service became apparent. Secretary MacVeagh's merger bill, as penned by Captain Commandant Bertholf of the Revenue Cutter Service and General Superintendent Kimball of the Life-Saving Service, drew strong bipartisan support after the change from a Republican to a Democratic White House and the election of Woodrow Wilson.

By March 1914 the bill had passed through the Senate, and urged on by the new president, made its way to the floor of the House of Representatives by the beginning of the following year. On 20 January 1915, the House voted 212 to 79 in favor of the Act to Create the United States Coast Guard. President Wilson signed the act into law eight days later.

That day, the 2,000 men of the Revenue Cutter Service and the 2,300 men of the Life-Saving Service came together under one banner, that of the United States Coast Guard. For the men of the latter organization, the merger signified movement from civilian to military life, as stated by Commandant Bertholf, "It is by means of military drills, training and discipline that the service is enabled to maintain that state of preparedness for the prompt performance of its most important civil duties." Therefore, he surmised, "the organization of the service must be and is by law military."

Overland Expedition

John J. Galluzzo

Beginning in the late 1870s, the Revenue Cutter Service established its reputation for search and rescue heroism through several long-distance missions to aid American merchant vessels in distress in the ice of Alaska. The Overland Expedition of 1897–1898 offered an even more dramatic demonstration of the tenacity and inventiveness of the Revenue Cuttermen when presented with a seemingly impossible mission of mercy. Rivaling Ernest Shackleton's amazing fight for life in Antarctica, the Overland Expedition differed in one major respect: while Shackleton and his men struggled to keep themselves alive, the men of the Revenue Cutter Service put their own lives at risk in an attempt to save others.

In 1897, as winter came, 273 men in a fleet of eight whalers were trapped by the early formation of ice near Point Barrow, Alaska, 300 miles north of the Arctic Circle. With supply ships only able to come barely within 1,000 miles of the ice-locked vessels, and the ice not expected to begin breaking up for at least ten months, the men faced almost certain starvation.

Some years earlier Captain "Hell-Roarin'" Mike Healy attempted to stave off starvation of Inuits, at a time when their traditional food sources were being exploited by non-native hunters. At the urging of Dr. Sheldon Jackson, a missionary appointed as an agent for education in the Alaska territory, Healy carried seventeen reindeer purchased in Siberia back to the Inuits aboard the cutter *Bear*. The reindeer could live on the same lichens that once supported great herds of caribou in Alaska, and, it was hoped, would provide a food source for the Inuits.

When President William McKinley handed the mission of saving the stranded whalers to the Revenue Cutter Service, its officers and men had to figure out the best

To the inhabitants of the remote and isolated Alaska Territory, the patrolling revenue cutters brought order and aid. Captain Mike Healy introduced domesticated reindeer as an alternative food source. In 1890 he loaded *Bear* with seventeen reindeer from a Siberian village and took them to Alaska. Fifty years after *Bear*'s first trip, the reindeer population had grown to more than one-half million. (Shannon Stirnweis, U.S. Coast Guard Art Collection)

way of effecting the rescue. Given their past successes in finding reindeer and transporting them to the Inuits, the solution seemed simple enough. The difficult part of the equation rested in locating more reindeer and transporting them across frozen lands.

With little time to ponder the problem, Captain Francis Tuttle and the crew of Bear left Port Townsend, Washington, in early December 1897. The plan was that Bear would sail as close to Point Barrow as possible and leave it to a volunteer party to disembark and herd as many reindeer as they could find overland to the stranded ships for use as food.

The relief party, consisting of First Lieutenant David H. Jarvis, Second Lieutenant Ellsworth P. Bertholf, Surgeon Samuel J. Call, and a Russian guide named Koltchoff, stepped ashore on Nelson Island near Cape Vancouver, Alaska, on 16 December. Between them and their destination lay 1,500 miles of snow, ice, and mountains. To avoid risking Bear becoming trapped in the ice, Tuttle sailed 400 miles south to the safety of a winter station at Unalaska. This left the relief party, Bloomfield noted, with "seven dogs, two sleds, 1,300 pounds of provisions, medicines for the whalers, an eight-by-ten wall tent, a small sheet-iron stove improvised on the Bear, woolen clothes, sleeping bags unfit for subzero cold, and seventy pounds of mail." Immediately they lost some provisions, when seawater ruined much of the bread and flour they carried.

Cutter Bear is one of the Coast Guard's most famous ships. For forty years it sailed off Alaska serving as lifesaver, doctor, federal court, mail carrier, newspaper, supply vessel, law enforcer, oceanographer, and weather data collector. The Coast Guard remembers this ship's distinguished service by handing down its name to subsequent cutters. (Hunter Wood, U.S. Coast Guard Art Collection)

A trader at an abandoned Catholic mission site on the island rounded up thirty-four more dogs, and four Eskimo drivers advised the cuttermen on sleds to use and gave them three lighter, shorter sleds. The rescue team set out two days after arriving. The temperature stood at about 32 degrees F., but as the party pressed ahead through the winter darkness, going along the coast where firewood could be found more easily, they would endure temperatures of 45 F. below zero.

Splitting up, Jarvis and Call pressed on to the north with two native guides, leaving Bertholf and Koltcholf to scout for replacement sled dogs. Two weeks out they made their first contact with the stranded whalers. George Tilton, third mate on the bark Belvedere, had volunteered to head to St. Michael's, more than 1,000 miles to the south, for help when it became clear that starvation was imminent among the crews. He told Jarvis the grim news, as related by Irving H. King in The Coast Guard Expands, 1865–1915, that "the steamers Belvedere, Orca, and Jesse H. Freeman were caught in the ice west of Point Barrow. The Orca had been crushed by the ice, and the Freeman had been abandoned. . . . The Rosario was in the ice west of Point Barrow, the steamers Fearless and Newport and the four-masted schooner Jeanie to the east of Barrow, and much farther east was the bark Wanderer. Worst of all, the Navarch was a wrecked derelict, and she was too east of Barrow." When Tilton heard Jarvis' plans, he decided he had better push on toward civilization to the south, as he had no faith that Jarvis and Call would reach the ships alive.

Pushing forward along the eastern shore on Norton Sound, Jarvis and Call hired a Lapp reindeer driver to help them continue toward their goal. On 14 January a raging snowstorm forced them to pull into a small village to find cover. Five days later they negotiated with a local herder for the purchase of 138 reindeer. Call drove the herd forward as Jarvis and the trader, whom they hired as a guide, swept the coast in search of more deer.

"It was a continuous jumble of dogs, sleds, men and ice—particularly ice," Jarvis later wrote, "and it would be hard to tell which suffered most, men or dogs. Once in helping the sled over a particularly bad place, I was

thrown 8 or 9 feet down a slide, landing on the back of my head with the sled on top of me. Though the mercury was -30 degrees, I was wet through with perspiration from the violence of the work."

At Cape Prince of Wales, the extreme western tip of the Seward Peninsula, Jarvis negotiated the purchase of 292 more reindeer from an American missionary, W. Thomas Lopp, who volunteered to drive them to Point Barrow himself. Continuing his push forward, Jarvis rendezvoused with Bertholf and Koltchoff on 12 February, finding them waiting with supplies they had gathered. Driving on to Point Hope, on the Chuchki Sea, Jarvis and Call met whaler Ned Arey, who reported three men at Point Barrow had already died and scurvy had invaded the little camp. Receiving a message from Lopp, Jarvis ordered Call on to Point Barrow with word that help was nearby.

Soon after, Jarvis sent word for Call to return, and the two of them drove a baggage train along the coast while Lopp moved the herd overland. On 6 March, Jarvis and Call left Point Hope to catch up with Lopp and the herd, and to complete the final 400-mile leg of the journey. On 29 March 1898, nearly three and a half months since waving good-bye to the crew of Bear, Jarvis and Call reached the stranded whalers at Point Barrow.

Jarvis took command of the situation immediately, ordering the men to rejoin their own ships and to leave the local native villages alone, as, noted Bloomfield, "hoodlumism had crept in; natives had been abused and some of their food stores had been looted." According to King, "The

Above, left: Officers from the cutter Bear: Second Lieutenant Ellsworth P. Bertholf (left), Surgeon Samuel J. Call (center), and expedition leader, First Lieutenant David H. Jarvis (right). (U.S. Coast Guard)

Above, center: Relief supplies from cutter Bear hauled by sleds to sailors ice-bound in Point Barrow, Alaska, in the Arctic Circle. (U.S. Coast Guard)

Above, right: Part of the more than two hundred trapped whalers saved from starvation when First Lieutenant David H. Jarvis led an overland expedition to bring a reindeer herd to feed the sailors. (U.S. Coast Guard)

slaughter of the reindeer began and each man was given 2½ pounds of fresh meat, the only antiscorbutic available. Jarvis noted that before long the general appearance of the men greatly improved. Later in the spring, signs of scurvy reappeared, and Jarvis increased the fresh meat allotment to 4 pounds per man per week." Only 382 of the 448 reindeer that started the trip survived. Call went to work on improving the health of the men and their living conditions. Noted Bloomfield, "Between all the whalemen and the natives, Dr. Call found he had a busy practice. From intestinal diseases to frostbite he treated 1,557 cases." One seaman suffered a heart attack and two others committed suicide.

On 14 June Bear began its trek north, reaching Point Barrow on 28 July. Newport, Fearless, and Jeanie had broken free of the ice, but Rosario and Orca had been crushed, Navarch left behind as a derelict, and Jessie H. Freeman was abandoned. Ninety-seven whalemen, the sailors of Orca, Freeman, Rosario, and Navarch, boarded the cutter and sailed for Seattle with their rescuers, Jarvis, Call, and Bertholf. When they reached that city on 13 September, the crew of Bear was surprised to hear that the United States had in the meantime fought and won a war with Spain.

On behalf of the nation, President William McKinley thanked Jarvis, Bertholf, and Call for their intrepidity, determination, and resourcefulness: "I commend this heroic deed to the grateful consideration of Congress and the American people. The year just closed [1898] has been fruitful of noble achievements in the field of war, and while I have commended to your consideration the names of heroes who have shed luster upon the American name in valorous contests and battles by land and sea, it is no less my pleasure to invite your attention to a victory of peace." Congress responded on 28 June 1902 by awarding each man a special gold medal for "heroic service rendered."

Course Changes

José Hanson

Birth at the Edge of a Storm

Toward the end of January 1915, on a clear summer day in the South Atlantic midway between Brazil and Africa, the German auxiliary cruiser *Prinz Eitel Friedrich* came upon the American merchantman *William P. Frye*. Some three months before, *Frye*, a four-masted barque, left Seattle with a cargo of wheat. The ship, bound for England, had rounded the Horn and was making its way north when the winds failed. Becalmed and helpless against the approaching engine-driven German warship, *Frye* had no choice, and the American skipper allowed his ship boarded and inspected.

World War I had begun six months earlier, but from the beginning the United States had declared itself neutral, and Germany had not yet announced the establishment of a war zone around the British Isles. Nonetheless, when the Germans found *Frye* carried wheat destined for the English enemy, the cargo was declared contraband and *Frye*'s crew was ordered to dump it overboard.

On the following morning, 28 January, the warship's captain decided the unloading was not going fast enough and ordered *Frye* sunk—the first ship of the United States to be lost in the Great War.

As *Frye* was settling to the bottom, thousands of miles away in Washington, D.C., President Woodrow Wilson put his name to an act rearranging the Treasury Department. This act, authorizing the merger of the Revenue Cutter Service and the U.S. Life Saving Service, was thought to be a logical and efficient consolidation of two organizations that had supported each other for fifty years. This new service was to be called the Coast Guard. It was born on the edge of a storm, and as the rush of international events would soon prove, the organization was destined to

Stern and side paddlewheel riverboats—reminiscent of the Mark Twain era—served the Coast Guard on western rivers into the mid-twentieth century with vessels such as Willow, a side paddlewheel river-tender. Willow was built by Dubuque Boat and Boiler Works for the U.S. Lighthouse Service for use on the Mississippi River in 1924. The Coast Guard maintained river navigation-aids with this vessel until 1945, when the paddle-wheeler was transferred to the Army Corps of Engineers. Two non-condensing steam engines powered by six "western river"-type, 225-psi oil-fired boilers gave a maximum speed of 7.5 knots; however, it cruised normally at a stately four knots—a fast walking pace. (U.S. Coast Guard)

Above: *Airplanes line the beach at the Naval Aeronautic Station, Pensacola, during World War I. Third Lieutenant Elmer Stone and Second Lieutenant Charles E. Sugden arrived here for flight training in April 1916. Stone became the Coast Guard's first and the Navy's thirty-eighth aviator in March 1917; Sugden followed as number two and forty-three. (U.S. Coast Guard)*

Opposite: *CGC Mohawk crewmember scans the horizon on the waters of the Windward Pass between Haiti and Cuba looking for Haitians attempting to sail to United States, often in overloaded or unseaworthy boats. (Robin Ressler, U.S. Coast Guard)*

SENECA — *TOM BEARD*

Revenue Service and Coast Guard Cutter Seneca *was built by Newport News Shipbuilding & Drydock Company in 1908 for $244,500 as a "derelict destroyer." Its task was to cruise the Atlantic seaboard locating and destroying abandoned wrecks still afloat as a menace to navigation. Wooden sailing ships, still in use, often failed to sink when breaking up or abandoned at sea.* Seneca *was to go on and create a nearly forty-year account with many different adventures beginning with International Ice Patrol in the North Atlantic. It followed ice patrols by fighting submarines in World War I then chasing and capturing rum runners in Prohibition. During all its voyages,* Seneca *saved lives from Greenland to Puerto Rico, from Gibraltar to the Gulf of Mexico. The 204-foot ship ended its active career as a training ship.*

Seneca *joined the International Ice Patrol in 1913 following the* Titanic *disaster in April 1912.* Seneca *and* Miami *were the first two Revenue Service cutters to perform this duty, patrolling out of Halifax, Nova Scotia.* Seneca, *on one patrol, rescued four survivors ten days adrift in a lifeboat in the North Atlantic from the British freighter* Columbian. *Ten* Columbian *crewmen died from starvation and exposure prior to their rescue.*

On 10 August 1914 Seneca, *operating with USS* Florida, *began patrols enforcing United States neutrality following the outbreak of war in Europe. The cutter then was assigned in 1917 to the Navy's Atlantic Patrol Fleet Squadron Four for war duty. A battery of four 3-inch guns was installed for the vessel's duty searching for enemy submarines in Cuban and Bahamian waters. Later that year* Seneca *crossed the Atlantic to serve with the Navy's Squadron Two in Gibraltar escorting convoys to Tangiers. It pursued and attacked several submarines and rescued crews from three British cargo ships torpedoed by German submarines.* Seneca *was at Gibraltar on 11 November 1918 when the Armistice ending World War I was signed.* Seneca's *wartime service included escorting thirty convoys consisting of 580 ships. Only four ships were lost under the Coast Guard cutter's protection, and from these, 139 survivors were rescued.* Seneca *responded to twenty-one submarine contacts, one which proved to be a bloated dead whale with four bullet holes, proving* Seneca's *gunnery crew accuracy. The cutter experienced four near misses from submarine-fired torpedoes, and was credited with one probable submarine sinking.*

Returning to the Treasury department from the Navy in 1919, Seneca *resumed the Coast Guard's International Ice Patrol. Also about this time,* Seneca *engaged in Prohibition patrols between ice patrols and in one episode of note in 1922, captured the schooner* Tomoka, *owned by the notorious rumrunner William F. McCoy ("Real McCoy").*

Seneca *was sold out of service in 1936 but later returned to Coast Guard service in 1941, was overhauled and used for a short period before being turned over to the state of Pennsylvania, where it remained in service training naval cadets as the training vessel* Keystone State *until 1948. This original Revenue Service vessel's adventurous life ended when sold for scrap in 1950.*

Revenue Cutter Seneca *among the bergs in 1914 during an International Ice Patrol. (U.S. Coast Guard)*

become something far greater, far wider ranging, than those who christened it ever could have expected.

All of these events taking place on its birthday would of course have their effects on the new Coast Guard, and an increasingly unstable international situation virtually guaranteed that sooner or later the new organization, designated a full-fledged military service and branch of the armed services, would be needed beyond the nation's coasts.

Indeed, the first mission well outside American waters had fallen almost unnoticed to the Revenue Cutter Service just two years before. In the spring of 1912 the magnificent British luxury-liner *Titanic* on its maiden voyage across the North Atlantic met destruction in a collision with an iceberg. Given the abundance of icebergs in those waters, one reasonable response to the danger would have been to route shipping farther south during the April-to-September iceberg season. This, however, would have increased both the cost and distance of trans-Atlantic passages. Commercial interests, both British and American, dismissed the idea as out of the question and raised a clamor for an Ice Patrol off the Grand Banks. It was a job the new Coast Guard would inherit.

In January 1912, The President's Commission on Economy and Efficiency had decided the Revenue Cutter Service could be eliminated. President Taft agreed. The catch, of course, was which government agency would be able to take over and do what the Revenue Cutter Service had been doing since 1790—duties considered essential to the survival of the nation. During wartime the Revenue Cutter Service had always gone under control of the Navy and each time after the war ended there was talk of leaving it there. This time however, the plan was to abolish the service altogether, and the Navy would take over its responsibilities. This might well have come to pass had it not been for the loss of *Titanic* and for the persistence of the Commandant of the Revenue Cutter Service, Captain Ellsworth Price Bertholf.

Ever since the idea of eliminating the service first arose, Bertholf had been fighting a fierce bureaucratic battle to deflect it. He provided the figures to show the move would save less money than believed, and at the same time he introduced measures to cut costs in his organization. He also pointed out that the Navy would have to be greatly expanded before it could handle the new missions, and this would cost a bundle.

As it turned out, Congress was slow to act; the Republican Taft administration went out; the Democratic Wilson administration came in, and the decision was postponed. Anyway, the service was now patrolling for icebergs—something the Navy had decided it could not do at the moment. And war was coming—a war more horrible than had ever been seen before. The Revenue Cutter Service was saved and became part of the new Coast Guard, with Bertholf at its head.

This first Commandant deserves more than passing mention, and not just for his fight to keep the service from being taken apart and scattered among other government agencies. A competent administrator who took his political baptism-under-fire fighting for survival of the service, Bertholf nonetheless was first and foremost a seafaring man. He entered the service as a cadet at nineteen and served through all grades. In 1897, at age thirty-one, he joined a relief party sent across the Alaskan wilderness in mid-winter to save the lives of the crews of eight whaling ships locked in the ice—a feat that moved Congress to award him a gold medal.

Besides courage, Bertholf was gifted with a good deal of foresight and the conviction to act on it. Expecting the United States would be drawn into the fighting eventually, over a year before that happened, Bertholf, together with Captain H. G. Bullard of the Navy, began outlining how the Coast Guard and the Navy could work as a team once war came. Knowing his cutters were not prepared for the long sea-keeping necessary for naval vessels, Bertholf planned for their use as radio-relay ships, for laying and sweeping mines, coastal patrols, and to escort merchant vessels. Life-Saving Service personnel would act as a coast-watch and also protect vulnerable shore-side installations. To better prepare the two military services to fight side by side, the Bertholf-Bullard plan called for the temporary exchange of personnel for training—a sensible enough idea, but one that was never acted upon.

Seneca's crew is rigging an oceanographic instrument while being tossed about in heavy seas. (U.S. Coast Guard)

Seneca crew with a ship's boat on a small ice floe in 1915 while on International Ice Patrol. The cutter was undertaking studies to determine the source of icebergs. Seneca would alternate cruises between springtime iceberg patrols in the North Atlantic and wintertime coastal patrols from Gay Head, Massachusetts, to the Delaware breakwater. (U.S. Coast Guard)

Officers and crew of Seneca in New York, January 1924. Commanding officer was Lieutenant Commander P. F. Roach. (M. V. Young, U.S. Coast Guard)

The Great Sea War

Captain Commandant Ellsworth P. Bertholf, born in New York City on 7 April 1866, entered the Revenue Cutter Service as a cadet in 1885 and was appointed a third lieutenant in June 1889. In 1897 Bertholf participated in the relief party making the overland trip in mid-winter to Point Barrow, Alaska, for which he received a gold medal for bringing relief to over 200 American whalers in danger of starving. Bertholf made another sledge trip in the winter of 1901 across northern Siberia to purchase a reindeer herd for the Inuits of northern Alaska. He was appointed Captain Commandant of the Revenue Cutter Service in June 1911 and reappointed to the same post in January 1915 when President Wilson joined the Revenue Cutter Service with the Life-Saving Service to form the Coast Guard. Bertholf died in New York City on 11 November 1921. (U.S. Coast Guard)

In April 1917, after German U-boats sank five American ships without warning in a single month, President Wilson asked Congress to declare war. "The world must be made safe for democracy," he warned. Within four days Congress complied, and within hours the Coast Guard received orders placing it under operational control of the Navy. The first action by the service was to seize enemy merchant ships in U.S. waters, and twenty-six German vessels found themselves impounded by the Coast Guard in New York and Baltimore harbors. Nothing could make up for the lives taken in the German attacks on American shipping, but within a few hours the Kaiser had lost a good number of ships just as completely as if they had been sunk—worse, they were now in the hands of the enemy and might be used against German forces.

War brought a whole new burden of duties, and yet the Coast Guard nonetheless had to continue most of its peacetime missions as well. International Ice Patrol was suspended, but not Bering Sea Patrol. This latter duty had fallen to the Revenue Cutter Service after the Civil War, and since that time Alaskans, as well as commercial fishermen, whalers, and sealers, had come to depend on the regular visits of the cutters for everything from law-enforcement and search-and-rescue to providing medical assistance and legal services. It was an important mission, one the northern territory could not do without even in wartime. Nor could many other domestic responsibilities be curtailed, for just as many sailors and their vessels could be counted on to seek help or rescue as in peacetime, and smugglers were not likely to be so patriotic as to reduce their activities to free up Coast Guardsmen for the front. To help meet manpower shortages, recruiting offices were opened, but the service would have been hard up for people indeed had not a draft been instituted a few months after the nation went to war.

In June, three months after America entered the fray, the Espionage Act removed jurisdiction for anchorages from the Army Corps of Engineers and gave it to the Treasury Department. Although the Coast Guard was now under the Navy, the secretary of the Treasury was able to appoint four Coast Guard officers as the first Captains of the Port. One of the foremost duties of the new position would be to thwart sabotage and assure the safety of vessels transporting the huge cargoes of wartime explosives.

If anyone questioned the importance of the utmost caution in handling modern munitions, these doubts were loudly—and with astonishing violence—shattered six months later in Halifax, Nova Scotia. A French ship, *Mont Blanc*, carrying 200 tons of explosives taken on in New York, collided with an outbound ship while entering the Halifax Narrows and caught fire. The ensuing explosion, estimated to be the largest man-made detonation before the nuclear age, flattened a large part of the city, killing over 1,900 people and injuring 9,000. Survivors said the force was so great that water under *Mont Blanc* was forced out leaving the bottom of the bay momentarily visible. The ship itself seemed to vanish; a piece of a cannon was found three miles away, and a thousand-pound chunk of an anchor landed two miles off in the opposite direction. Windows were broken in Truro fifty miles distant, and hundreds of miles away on Cape Breton Island the ground shook. Crew of the Coast Guard cutter *Morrill*, anchored a mile from *Mont Blanc*, felt their ship shoot upward as if being lifted out of the water and then dropped safely down again.

The new Captains of the Port were given no jurisdiction over the handling of explosives on land, however, and less than a year after the Halifax disaster, a blast shook a private munitions firm in Morgan, New Jersey. Coast Guardsmen responded, and as further explosions came one after another, they fought the fire and at the same time repaired mangled railroad tracks so a TNT-loaded train could be moved to safety. Two Coast Guardsmen lost their lives, but a much worse disaster was averted. In cases like this, although the Captains of the Port were able to limit the damage, they could do nothing to prevent it. During the next war the authority of the position would be expanded to include inspection of shore-side facilities.

Among the numerous innovations of World War I, probably none seemed more astonishing than the appearance of something called a submarine. Within months of the outbreak of hostilities it became apparent to both sides the shortest route to victory would be to strangle the other's economy. The British Royal Navy put up a blockade; the German Imperial Navy replied with U-boats. If mention of the Great War evokes images of mustard gas, muddy trenches, and cloth-and-wood biplanes, victory nonetheless was to be decided at sea.

As if to prove the horrendous potential of the submarine, during one day in September 1914, a single U-boat sank three British cruisers and took the lives of nearly 1,500 British sailors. Within a year the U-boats were sinking vessels faster than the formidable British shipyards could replace them. Sonar and depth charges were yet to be perfected, and the only known way to fight submarines was to catch them on the surface and either ram them or take them out with gunfire. Until they could find another solution to the U-boats, the Allies would have to be content with defensive measures, and the idea of the escorted convoy was born. This simple step would decide the war.

In the late summer of 1917, six Coast Guard cutters—*Algonquin*, *Manning*, *Ossipee*, *Seneca*, *Tampa*, and *Yamacraw*—set out for Gibraltar to join the Atlantic Fleet. As convoy escorts they would be putting themselves on the line in a naval war of extraordinary ruthlessness. Two years before, HMS *Baralong* sank a U-boat and executed all survivors. For their part, the Germans also were willing to kill survivors of sunk Allied vessels, including the torpedoed hospital ship *Llandovery Castle*, whose lifeboats were rammed and shelled.

The Coast Guardsmen endlessly scanning the sea for signs of a submarine had no reason to expect mercy; death was always near and came without warning. In September 1918, with a year of escort duty behind it, the cutter *Tampa* had just delivered a convoy to England and was last seen heading for port. That night an explosion was heard, and when *Tampa* did not appear on schedule, a search was undertaken. Only bits of debris and two bodies were ever found. The cutter had gone down

Coast Guardsmen row the ship's doctor to a convoy ship to aid a crewman needing medical attention. United States Public Health Service doctors are regularly assigned to Coast Guard vessels. (Anton Otto Fischer, U.S. Coast Guard)

Six Coast Guard cutters formed the second squadron of the Atlantic Fleet Patrol Force's Sixth Division escorting convoys between England and Gibraltar in World War I. In late September 1918, six weeks before the end of the war, Tampa just concluded its eighteenth convoy when it was torpedoed by a German submarine. All hands were lost—111 Coast Guard and four Navy crewmen. (John Wisinski, U.S. Coast Guard)

with all 115 hands—the greatest American naval combat loss of the war and a devastating blow to the small Coast Guard.

After the United States entered the conflict some 17,000 merchant vessels in 1,200 convoys were escorted through U-boat ambushes, and only one ship in a hundred was lost. As predicted, Germany's ruthless implementation of unrestricted submarine warfare had brought America into the fight. It had been a desperate gamble, one intended to end the war before the United States could effectively intervene. Had it not been for the success of escorted convoys, the German bet might very well have paid off.

For the Coast Guard, not all the excitement took place "over there." In August 1918, the Chicamacomico Lifeboat Station in North Carolina was shaken by an explosion. Looking out to sea, the Coast Guardsmen saw the British tanker *Mirlo* in flames some seven miles offshore. To this day it is still disputed whether the vessel struck a mine or was torpedoed by a U-boat. In any event, other explosions followed, ripping open *Mirlo*'s hull and spraying burning oil across the water.

A ship in distress could not have chosen a better spot for seeking help. John Allen Midgett commanded the Chicamacomico station. The Midgetts came from a long line of tough, daring seafarers and were said to be descended from the pirates and the survivors of shipwrecks who

had been making names for themselves on the Outer Banks since colonial times. Above all, it was a family that produced heroes. Two members already had been awarded the Coast Guard Gold Lifesaving Medal: John H. Midgett for helping rescue nine sailors in 1884 and Rasmus Midgett for single-handedly saving ten more fifteen years later. The heroism on that August day in 1918 when *Mirlo* blew up would bring the family five more of those medals.

Seeing *Mirlo* on fire, Midgett ordered a power surfboat launched, and with five men, four of whom were also named Midgett, he set out to find survivors. For the next six-and-a-half hours the Coast Guardsmen drove the surfboat back and forth through the blazing sea, badly blistering their hands and singeing hair and clothes, but managing to rescue forty-two sailors. The surfmen would each receive the Gold Lifesaving Medal.

Three months later the war was over, and the cutters could return home. At one time or another each had been attacked by U-boats, and *Tampa* had gone down only six weeks before the Armistice. Serving at sea during the Great War had proved to be dangerous duty, and relative to its size, the Coast Guard had suffered greater loses than either the Army or the Navy. The sacrifice was rewarded, however, and in the end it was the escorted convoys that turned the tide for the Allies.

This sixteen-year-old British merchant seaman and his sixty-five-year-old shipmate were fortunate to be plucked up out of the Atlantic Ocean by a Coast Guard cutter. The young sailor tells his rescuers that he was in the galley making a morning cup of tea when a torpedo exploded in his ship without warning. He missed getting into the last lifeboat and had to jump overboard, swimming until his rescue. (U.S. Coast Guard)

In August 1918 the British steamship Mirlo, bearing a cargo of gasoline and oil, exploded. The sea surrounding the wreckage was aflame when a surfboat from the Chicamacomico Station, North Carolina, was forced into this mass of flaming flotsam. Despite heavy seas, masses of wreckage, and intense heat, the crew—John A. Midgett, pictured here, Zion S. Midgett, Arthur V. Midgett, Leroy S. Midgett, Clarence E. Midgett, and Prochorus L. O'Neal—saved forty-two members of Mirlo's crew. (U.S. Coast Guard)

Coast Guard crewmen on a 75-footer, or "six-bitter," load bales containing whiskey bottles following a seizure from a rumrunner. Bales or cases normally held six bottles wrapped in gunny—hemp or jute—sacking. The large "mother" ships, typically New England or Canadian fishing schooners, lying offshore could supply the small delivery boats with from one to three thousand cases of liquor. (U.S. Coast Guard)

Opposite, bottom: A naval architect's drawings of the rumrunner Arthur Delmar, done in 1927 at the height of fast-motorboat development. These plans were drawn by the noted designer, Lee Hill Coolidge of Seattle. The cost for creating these boats was not a consideration, therefore the best talents in creating them were obtained. This "black boat" was equipped with two Capital conversions of the famous Liberty "V"-12 aircraft engine at 400 horsepower each. This rumrunner carried more than a thousand gallons of gasoline in tanks set along the centerline protected from gunfire on each side by the cargo of bailed contraband alcohol. Sheets of steel were sometimes bolted inside the pilot house to shield the crew from bullets. Living space on the fifty-six-foot boats was spartan, with only two berths for crewmembers. (Seattle Museum of History and Industry)

68

The Great Experiment

For the Coast Guard one war had ended, but the last of its cutters had barely returned from Europe before another kind of "war" began. Like the Great War itself, this next one, brought on by the Great Experiment, quickly got out of hand and grew to be much more difficult to control than anyone foresaw at the outset.

The era of prohibition of alcohol in the United States is often said to have begun with the Eighteenth Amendment, which took effect in January 1920, and made illegal the manufacture, sale, or transport of liquor within the country. In fact such laws were older than the nation itself, reaching back to the attempt in the colony of Georgia in 1733 to ban liquor. When the United States entered the First World War in 1917, the government had ordered all distilleries closed and prohibited the import of alcohol as part of the war effort. Temperance was thus linked to patriotism, and even before Prohibition became national law, thirty-three states were already legally "dry." Since the average American seemed to favor such legislation, there was little reason for anyone in the Coast Guard—or anywhere else for that matter—to believe enforcement would present any special problems.

While the Coast Guard was charged with stopping smuggling, no extra funding, personnel, or ships were forthcoming, nor were other duties curtailed to free up resources. The Bering Sea Patrol would continue, and of course so would search-and-rescue missions and ice patrol. In 1922 alone, the service numbering some 4,000 members would—along with its other duties—save nearly 3,000 lives. Yet with the coming "Rum War" just over the horizon, the Coast Guard was losing people faster than it could replace them. The enlistments of those who joined during the war ended shortly after the signing of the peace treaty, and the promise of a recruit's pay of 75 cents a day for an often dangerous job was not attracting many takers.

At the same time, the Coast Guard was fighting what was beginning to seem like a perennial battle for survival. With the end of hostilities, the Service was supposed to return to the Treasury Department, but the Navy was balking at letting it go. In this, the Navy had powerful support, and many in government felt it should have absorbed the Coast Guard's duties long ago. Commandant Bertholf fought tooth and nail—as he had before—to keep the Coast Guard independent, but his tenure as commandant would end in June 1919. The issue continued uncertain, and not until two months after Bertholf's retirement, did President Wilson finally sign an order sending the Coast Guard back to the Treasury Department.

There was, however, at least a little time to take an organizational breath before the full-blown Rum War kicked off. The smugglers themselves often started small and it took them time both to learn the smuggling game and to get organized. The greatest volume of smuggled alcohol came from Canada, for although most Canadian provinces went "dry" at the time of the American 18th amendment, the export of liquor from Canada was legal.

Any Canadian booze invoiced for the Caribbean or Mexico and diverted to the United States came to be called "short-circuit." And a lot of short-circuit alcohol began turning up in American cities. Frequently

a ship carrying liquor would leave a Canadian port bound for Cuba and return the next day for another cargo. Or if a consignment for Bermuda was taken on by a rowboat, no one asked any questions. As profits in smuggling soared, so did the volume—one smuggler who started out with just such a rowboat was said to be raking in $100,000 a week toward the end of his career.

At the height of Prohibition millions of gallon of spirits were entering the country every year, and it was all the Coast Guard could do to nab even a small percentage of it. Along the East Coast large ships waited on "Rum Row" just beyond the three-mile limit of American territorial waters

It looks like a good day for the rumrunners. This Coast Guard patrol boat is in no condition to make an intercept. Weather was an important factor in success for both sides. (U.S. Coast Guard)

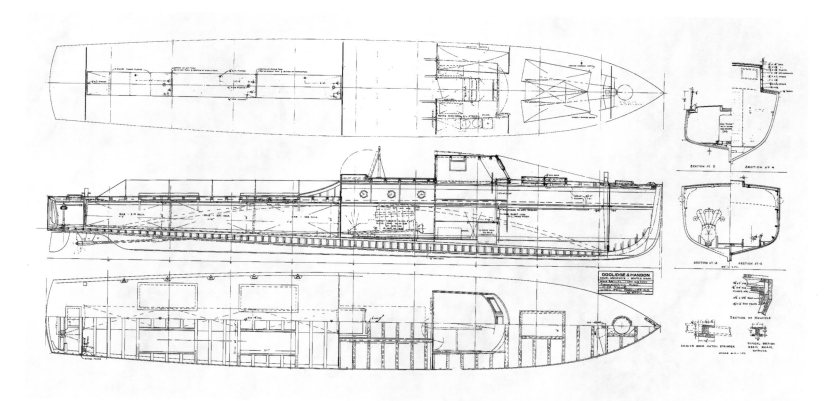

and unloaded liquor onto countless smaller boats that tried to evade Coast Guard patrols in order to supply the speakeasies of New York, Boston, and other large cities.

The service had no cutters that could match the speed of the small rum boats, nor was it easy to trap the larger ones in American waters. Nonetheless, enough vessels, large and small, were caught to make life increasingly difficult for the bootleggers. As time went on the Coast Guard of course got better at the game, but so did the smugglers.

The international boundary was pushed to twelve miles, and Rum Row simply relocated beyond that—an inconvenience to both sides, since it also increased the area the Coast Guard had to patrol. The Coast Guard asked for new cutters and got old Navy destroyers, which were fast but too clumsy for chasing smugglers and exorbitantly expensive to maintain besides. It also got various classes of hardy new patrol boats, some capable of speeds up to twenty-four knots, but the bootleggers upgraded too.

In 1916 the Coast Guard had been authorized to buy aircraft and build ten air stations—a good idea that went nowhere because no funding was approved. Finally, at the height of the Rum War nearly a decade later, the obvious usefulness of airplanes in spotting smugglers convinced Congress to give the service money for three Loening OL-5 amphibians and two Chance Vought UO4s. These were stationed on the East Coast and gave the service something of an edge on the smugglers.

Left: CG-237 *and cutter* Redwing *apprehended the seventy-eight-foot lumber schooner* Mary Langdon *of Rockland, Maine, in June 1925. The schooner was anchored and refused orders by boatswains mate Fish of CG-282 to move. The large deck-load of lumber was later removed by Coast Guard crews uncovering 2,000 cases of Scotch whisky in the hold. The vessel was seized and the six crewmen arrested. (U.S. Coast Guard)*

Above: *Two Coast Guard patrol boats picket a rumrunner operating outside enforcement boundaries. This crowding by Coast Guard vessels prevented smugglers from offloading contraband into smaller boats capable of running it ashore. (U.S. Coast Guard)*

Still, even if smuggling had been limited to the Rum Row off lower New England, the small, over-extended Coast Guard would have had its hands full. As it was, the number of rumrunners was too great, the country far too large, its coastline and waterways too long. Rumrunners were just as busy on the Great Lakes as on the oceans, and many neighborhoods of Chicago were said to have a bar on every corner. In Detroit, as much as 25 percent of the population was estimated to have some hand in smuggling. In the Northwest, Seattle became the hub of the illegal liquor trade, the liquor almost always arriving by ship from Canada and then being dispersed by truck throughout Washington and Oregon. Dozens of smuggling boats came and went along the foggy shores of northern California and countless beach shacks dotting the coast openly sold liquor.

Worse, the Coast Guard had to contend with more than boats on the waterways. Once boundary rivers like the St. Clair or the Detroit froze, booze-smuggling cars and trucks passed easily over them, and many locals came to believe Coast Guard ice-breaking operations were as much to prevent smuggling as to keep the channels open for shipping.

Smugglers used airplanes as well as boats. This smuggler was forced down near the Mexican border by a Coast Guard plane. Coast Guard aircraft were stationed along the Texas and New Mexico borders with Mexico. (U.S. Coast Guard)

During these years Congress greatly increased the Coast Guard's budget, and the service was able to grow in both personnel and ships, but as the first economic effects of the Depression came to be felt, the Coast Guard was required to reduce its size. At the height of the Rum War, over 9,000 men wore the uniform—twice the number as when the Great Experiment began. Yet even then the service was only half the size of the New York City Police Department. Still, tough times brought cutbacks, and a year before Prohibition ended, the service began closing bases and lifesaving stations and decommissioning cutters and patrol boats. Budget cuts led to the discharge of some 1,800 men and the reduction in rank of others. To some it appeared even more money could be saved by simply handing everything over to the Navy, and before long the Coast Guard would find itself yet again fighting for its life.

Coast Guard destroyers and patrol boats at State Pier in New London, Connecticut, about 1932. A year later the alcohol prohibition was rescinded, ending the fourteen-year Rum War. (U.S. Coast Guard)

The Gulf Stream Pirates

José Hanson

The situation in Florida highlights the tough spot the Coast Guard found itself in during the Rum Wars. Monster hurricanes twice swept the state in the 1920s, devastating Florida's economy even worse than its landscape. The first, in 1926, virtually obliterated Miami, the very heart of Florida's tourism-based wealth. To recover from financial disaster on top of natural ones, the state needed tourists, lots of them, and fast.

Prohibition, however, put a damper on the state's economic steam. Even before the hurricanes, tourists were showing a preference for rum-drenched holiday spots like Havana and Nassau, each just a hop across the sparkling water from Miami. In Florida then, booze came to be seen as the key to keeping vacationers and their dollars on American shores, and bootlegging became something of a civic duty. Since the Coast Guard interfered with rumrunning—and did so with increasing efficiency—the service was soon held by many to be almost as bad as a foreign occupying force.

Late on a Saturday afternoon in August 1927, a white thirty-foot boat left a Miami boatyard where its engine had just been rebuilt. The official owner, a man named Ross, had arranged to pay the yard-bill but was not present. Instead a group of men who had cared for the boat and apparently had some interest in it were there to see it off. On board were two ne'er-do-wells, Robert E. Weech and James Horace Alderman.

According to testimony given in federal court later, Alderman, an impoverished ex-con, was taking the boat for a "test drive," intending to buy it from Weech, who had bought it from Ross some days before—no one could remember exactly when. Weech had paid nothing and no papers were signed. With evening coming, Weech and Alderman stopped at a fuel dock, filled the boat's tanks and an auxiliary fifty-gallon drum mounted on the stern, and headed out to sea.

The next day, a bright Sunday morning, the seventy-five-foot patrol boat CG 249 also got underway, leaving Ft. Lauderdale under the command of Boatswain Sidney C. Sanderlin. The assignment—to ferry Secret Service Agent Robert K. Webster to Bimini some sixty miles away—promised to be a pleasure cruise, and passenger and crew alike were casually dressed in dungarees and t-shirts. None had reason to expect anything but a fine day on the water. In truth, they were sailing into a nightmare.

Just after dawn, a few hours before CG 249 headed out, Weech and Alderman met up with another boat a few miles off Bimini and took on forty-one burlap bags, each containing six quarts of scotch whisky. For the liquor Alderman paid around $4,000, a substantial sum in 1927, especially for a couple of guys down on their luck. They then headed west toward Florida and an unexpected rendezvous with CG 249.

No one will probably ever know what happened that day or why. Those present gave conflicting accounts, and their later writings disagreed not only with each other, but with their own sworn statements. Sean Rowe, a reporter for The New Times Broward-Palm Beach, investigated the case seventy years later, opening boxes in the National Archives to examine official documents that had not seen light for fifty years. Yet Rowe's careful detective work uncovered more questions than answers. Probably the court transcripts come closest to the truth, though these too are incomplete and inconclusive.

What is known is that in the Gulf Stream some thirty-five miles off Florida, the helmsman of CG 249 spotted something on the horizon about five miles away. Binoculars—still so novel in 1927 the jury had to be told what they were—showed the object to be a privately owned motor boat.

None of the surviving Coast Guardsmen was able to recall why the boat was pursued, but it was—and *finally brought to a halt by rifle shots across its bow. As the patrol boat came alongside, Sanderlin stuck a Colt .45 in his hip-pocket and jumped on the smaller boat. He immediately recognized Weech, said he knew him to be a bootlegger, and after a quick search found the liquor stowed below decks. While the Coast Guardsmen transferred the alcohol to CG 249, Sanderlin frisked the two rumrunners thoroughly, or half-heartedly, or not at all—here as elsewhere, testimony is contradictory—and told them to follow him.*

As the three were entering the CG 249's pilothouse, Alderman shot Sanderlin in the back and then shot Motor Machinist's Mate Victor Lamby, who was sitting close by. The skipper died instantly. Lamby fell through an open hatch and into the engine room, paralyzed, and would die a few days later.

None of the witnesses saw how Alderman got the gun. It was not the one in Sanderlin's pocket, because Alderman took that afterward. Two or three virtually identical weapons—again sworn testimony varies—were kept loaded on a shelf just inside the door, and Alderman said he grabbed one of these. Those who saw the pistol, however, were certain it was not military-issue, so perhaps it belonged to the Secret Service agent. The authorities were convinced it belonged to Alderman, and years later it was turned over to his widow.

In any event, although they were making an arrest, none of the other Coast Guardsmen or the Secret Service agent was armed. Alderman, helping himself to more pistols from the pilot house, herded the crew to the stern of the rum-runner, threatening to shoot them—or as the newspapers would have it, make them walk the plank. Seaman 1st class John Robinson, who a moment after the shootings had thrown a wrench at Alderman and dived into the water, now found sharks circling him and decided to climb back on board and join the others with their hands in the air.

Weech then broke CG 249's fuel lines, either to disable it so it could not give pursuit or more damningly, according to the survivors, to provide gasoline to burn up the patrol boat with the wounded Lamby still on board

and helpless. Although most, including Alderman, were smokers, the criminals seemed not to have any matches or really to look for any, and CG 249 was spared.

A few minutes later, while Weech was below decks struggling to coax his boat's engine into running, Webster dropped his hands and, as if on signal, he and the five Coast Guardsmen rushed Alderman. Alderman opened up with a pistol in each hand and went down fighting, shooting Webster dead and wounding Seaman 2nd class Jody Hollingsworth, who fell overboard.

The Coast Guardsmen quickly knocked Alderman senseless and disarmed him. As Weech came up out of the engine room, Seaman 1st class Hal Caudle stuck a pistol he'd taken from Alderman in Weech's back and pulled the trigger. Alderman had emptied it, however, and when the weapon failed to fire, Caudle shoved Weech overboard.

Alderman showed signs of coming to, and Motor Machinist's Mate 2nd class Frank Lehman knocked him unconscious again with a metal barnacle scraper and then helped bring Hollingsworth on deck. Shot up as he was, Hollingsworth took a .45 and stood guard over Weech and Alderman while the others checked Webster and Sanderlin for signs of life and brought the paralyzed Lamby up from the engine room. When the rest of the survivors returned, Hollingsworth admitted to not feeling well, went below on CG 249 where he cleaned up and changed clothes, and then returned to lay down across the sacks of whisky.

Above: The seventy-five-foot patrol boats like *CG249* became one of the Coast Guard's most effective weapons in the "Rum Wars." Their mission was to blockade coastal regions from encroaching smuggling boats. "Six-bitters," as they were called, upped the ante in the rum-running game, forcing smugglers to build ever faster, more specialized—and more expensive—boats.

Some two hours later Lieutenant Commander Beckwith Jordan, Section Base 6 commander, brought a Coast Guard rescue boat on to the gory scene. Two men were dead, a third was dying, and a fourth was badly wounded. Lehman and Coast Guardsmen from the rescue boat stayed with CG 249 while the rest of the survivors from the patrol boat, including the wounded Lamby and Hollingsworth, returned to the base with Jordan.

Lehman repaired the broken fuel lines and, with two criminals and two bodies on board, brought CG 249 home. In tow should have been the foremost article of evidence: Weech's boat with its cargo of whisky. Both boat and liquor had disappeared, however. Jordan testified Weech's boat was still tied to CG 249 when he left and he had no idea what happened to it. Lehman supposed the boat might have caught fire and sunk while being towed. If Alderman and Weech knew where their boat and liquor went they never said. There is no record of an investigation. Things like that happened during the Rum Wars.

Alderman, dubbed the "Gulf Stream Pirate," a modern-day Blackbeard, by the press because of the purported threat to make his captives walk the plank, testified he only grabbed a gun and began shooting when he realized Sanderlin intended to kill him.

Whether he really believed his life was in danger and the murders were in self-defense, many other Floridians did. The jury, however, did not. The trial lasted six days and Alderman was found guilty of murder on the high seas and sentenced to hang.

Weech turned state's evidence, testified against his partner, and was sentenced to one year in prison. The leniency of the punishment indicates full cooperation, and having proven to be talkative, Weech no doubt had a great deal to tell about rum-running in south Florida. He served his time and was free again before Alderman was executed. All records of Weech's interrogation were destroyed. The man himself vanished without a trace, perhaps just a jump ahead of the interested group who stood by to see him and Alderman off—carrying $4,000 in cash—that Saturday evening at the boatyard.

That an inveterate badman caught committing a felony could kill three law-enforcement officers, maim a fourth, and still enjoy any popular sympathy at all, gives an idea of the extreme emotional pitch of the Rum Wars and the increasingly widespread opposition to Prohibition. Although hardly imaginable now, so intense was the outrage and demand for Alderman's release it was thought prudent to shunt him to a lockup 400 miles away, and later to hold him on a Coast Guard ship offshore rather than in the local jail. The month of the trial, the Coast Guard reinforced its presence in Florida with extra seaplanes, ships, and 300 men.

In August 1929, a year and a half after his conviction, and after President Coolidge declined to overturn it, the Gulf Stream Pirate was taken to a seaplane hangar on Coast Guard Section Base 6 at Bahia Mar and executed. Passions had hardly cooled, and as Rowe reported, six carloads of armed guards were needed to escort Alderman through sympathetic crowds to his death. At the Coast Guard base, federal agents brandished tommy-guns to ward off hundreds of protesters.

The Rum Wars would drag on for four more years, generating more bitterness and frustration, and only in 1933, with the Twenty-first Amendment and the repeal of Prohibition, would the Coast Guard and the public it served begin to heal their wounds.

A photo taken shortly after the murders shows a Coast Guard 30-footer on the marine ways at Coast Guard Section Base 6 at Bahia Mar. The disappearance of the rum boat and its cargo has never been explained. *CG249* left this base on that fateful morning, and it was here Alderman was delivered two years later to be hanged. (U.S. Coast Guard)

Innovation and Change

For the other military services, it is their performance in time of war that is most exciting. For the Coast Guard—while there are plenty of gripping war stories—just as much drama and danger come when the nation is at peace. This was certainly the case between the First and Second World Wars.

During these years, Coast Guardsmen saved literally tens of thousands of lives, and some forty Gold Lifesaving Medals were awarded them. Without exception, accounts of these recognized acts of selflessness, bravery, skill, and endurance make exciting reading. Yet hundreds of other instances of heroism passed almost unnoticed, taken for granted in an occupation that deals almost daily with some form of catastrophe—storms, fires, floods, sinkings, groundings, collisions, and explosions on the water.

In 1919, the crew of *Marietta*, skippered by future Commandant Harry Hamlet, saved the lives of forty-seven men on board the floundering USS *James* as high seas in the Bay of Biscay repeatedly hurled the ships at one another. A few months later off Grand Marais, Michigan, Coast Guardsmen saved seventeen people from the steamer *H. E. Runnels* in high seas in a snowstorm. During the rescue, Coast Guardsmen were frequently swept into the icy waters, but no lives were lost. Five months after that, in violent seas off Massachusetts, two fishermen were pulled to safety as they clung to the mast of their sinking schooner. In heavy seas on an overcast night in 1923 in the Strait of Juan de Fuca, the cutter *Snohomish* rescued the crew from the burning steamship *Nika* in hurricane-force winds. Such rescues came with sobering regularity—one after another.

In 1933, Franklin D. Roosevelt, a former assistant secretary of the Navy and a man who always felt the proper place for the Coast Guard was in his department, now became president. Many believed the service would not survive long once the Navy got hold of it, and this time it certainly looked like the Coast Guard might be finished.

Commandant Frederick C. Billard, who had managed both the growth of the service during much of Prohibition, and then handled the subsequent reorganization and cuts, died suddenly after being appointed to a third term. The new commandant, Harry Hamlet, had been in charge less than a year before proposals to close the Coast Guard Academy and to transfer the entire service to the Navy began to surface. Hamlet, however, like the first commandant, Bertholf, proved he was equal to the occasion and made a strong case for keeping the service in the Treasury Department. Hamlet's position gained a good deal of congressional support, and in the end, the Coast Guard remained outside the Navy except in time of war. By all it accounts, it was another close call.

The International Ice Patrol had resumed after World War I, and soon scientific observers and oceanographers were assigned to the cutters. This led to the founding of the Coast Guard Oceanographic Unit and the service's enduring commitment to scientific exploration. In 1928, *Marion*, under the command of Lieutenant Commander Edward "Iceberg" Smith, conducted an oceanographic survey through the Davis Strait to

Frederick C. Billard, born in Washington, D.C., on 22 September 1873, was appointed a cadet and received his training, starting in 1894, on the practice ship USRC Chase. *He received his appointment as third lieutenant in April 1897. During the Spanish-American War Billard served on the cutter* Corwin *in the Navy's Pacific Fleet and later, 1906 to 1911, served as aide to Captain Worth J. Ross, Chief of the Revenue Cutter Service. Billard commanded USS* Aphrodite *operating in the European War Zone during World War I.* Aphrodite *was the first American war vessel to pass through the Kiel Canal after the signing of the Armistice. Billard succeeded William E. Reynolds as Commandant in January 1924. He managed the service's considerable growth, both in vessels and manpower, as a result of Prohibition. Billard saw reforms to the Academy curriculum and eventual construction and reestablishment of the institution at New London in 1932. Reportedly, he was personable and seemingly knew most of the Coast Guard officers—down to the junior levels. This attention engendered a deep sense of loyalty in all who served in his commands. Billard died in office on 17 May 1932 following the appointment to his third term as Commandant. "Frederic Chamberlayne Billard must rank with the greatest commandants of the Coast Guard." According to historian Robert E. Johnson, "He had guided his service through a very trying period, presiding over an unprecedented expansion and attempting to deal with the Herculean task of prohibition enforcement without neglecting his service's traditional responsibilities."*

Coast Guard aviation began to mature in mid-1930 with the joining of seaplanes and ships. The Grumman J2F carried aboard cutters then launched and recovered by taking off and landing in the ship's wake extended the ship's range for search and rescue. Seaplanes became the fundamental aircraft for Coast Guard operations. It would be over a quarter of a century before helicopters would take over the role of airplanes aboard cutters. (U.S. Coast Guard)

Russell R. Waesche was named commandant of the Coast Guard in 1936, when he was but a commander. His flag promotion leaped him over twenty captains and four other commanders. He went on to lead the Coast Guard for ten years, the longest period of any officer in that post. During his command Coast Guard missions expanded manyfold with the service involved in World War II. (U.S. Coast Guard)

Disko Bay in Greenland. The Coast Guard's new knowledge of those waters would pay off in a big way as the Second World War approached, but just as importantly, *Marion*'s mission would confirm a tradition of scientific research that would eventually take cutters around the world; it marks a commitment to discovery that continues today.

It was in these years too, that Coast Guard aviation became firmly established. Surfmen of the old U.S. Lifesaving Service had assisted the Wright brothers in 1903, and even before the First World War Coast Guardsmen were trained as pilots. But not until 1928 was an aviation section installed at Coast Guard headquarters. By the mid-1930s the service had forty-two aircraft, and when its new 327-foot ships were launched beginning in 1936, they were the first cutters able to handle airplanes. The planes would certainly prove their worth in thwarting smuggling and fisheries violations, but they also had another purpose: to protect the fledgling transoceanic commercial air service. It was the dawn of a new era.

Eight years earlier the first commercial air service had begun when a Fokker trimotor lifted off a dirt runway in Key West, Florida, and turned toward Havana, Cuba. Pan American Airlines, with two airplanes and two dozen employees, was launched "to provide mass air transportation for the average man." Within months airline passengers were flying between Florida and South America, and in 1935 the *China Clipper*, a Martin "flying boat," made a six-day trip between San Francisco and the Philippines—the first transpacific passenger flight.

In 1938, when Lieutenant Commander George Gelly proposed placing cutters far out to sea to provide storm warnings and navigation information for civilian aircraft, the success of airlines was anything but certain. Gelly—and the Coast Guard—showed uncanny foresight. Although the cutters' short-ranged seaplanes—with space aboard to carry one or two passengers—would not prove as successful in ocean rescues as hoped, and although Ocean Station duty would not blossom until after World War II, the service realized early on the need to support commercial airlines.

Much of the transformation of the Coast Guard from the old Revenue Cutter Service and Lifesaving Service into what it is today took place in the anything-but-dull years between the wars. In 1936 the service assumed responsibility for ice-breaking to keep shipping channels open—something it was already doing anyway. That same year it was legally empowered to board vessels on the high seas in order to enforce United States law—an astonishing confirmation of authority. It was that year, too, that the service was called upon to enforce international regulations on whaling worldwide. These new powers and obligations would have far-ranging implications.

In 1938 the Coast Guard assumed administration of the United States Maritime Service, including the training and licensing of mariners. Control of lighthouses passed to the Coast Guard in 1939, and along with it came responsibility to tend other aids to navigation like buoys and markers. In that same year, both the Coast Guard Reserve and the volunteer organization known today as the Coast Guard Auxiliary were created.

World War II

A German mine explodes as a Coast Guard LCI(L) transport nears a beach to unload troops. (U.S. Coast Guard)

By tradition, the claim to be first-to-fight goes to the Marine Corps, but as World War II began to unroll and the United States prepared for battle, it was the Coast Guard that would step in and deal America's first blow to the enemy.

In August 1941, with the United States still four months away from joining the war, Churchill and Roosevelt held a secret shipboard meeting in Placentia Bay, Newfoundland. Things did not look good: Japan had moved deeply into Southeast Asia and was holding what is now called Vietnam; Germany occupied France, Belgium, Holland, Denmark, and Norway, and was deep in Russia; in two years of war Britain had lost 2,000 ships to U-boats and vital supply lines were threatened. Without a dependable flow of foodstuffs, raw materials, machinery, and oil, Britain could not keep going much longer. Before they parted, the president and the prime minister agreed that when America entered the war—it was no longer "if"—control of the North Atlantic would be the key to victory. This war, like the one a quarter-century before, would be won or lost at sea.

Indeed, four months earlier, in order to reduce German opportunities in the crucial North Atlantic, Roosevelt had declared Greenland, which was under the jurisdiction of Denmark, and Iceland to be U.S. protectorates, and three Coast Guard cutters—*Bear*, *North Star*, and *Northland*—were assigned to Greenland's security. Commander "Iceberg" Smith, who had started charting those waters on board *Marion* a dozen summers earlier and knew them well, was given command of the new Greenland Patrol.

Ice above the keel is sometimes more of a problem than the ice below it. A Coast Guardsman on an ice-coated cutter carries a mallet as he decides where to begin his own icebreaking. (Mark Miller, U.S. Coast Guard)

Not a month after the meeting of the American and British leaders, and not far offshore from where it was held, a U-boat fired a torpedo at the U.S. Navy destroyer *Greer*. The torpedo passed harmlessly astern, but in his next "fireside chat" the president warned from now on American forces would shoot first—would shoot on sight—any threatening German ships or planes found "in the waters which we deem necessary for our defense." That same day elements of the Coast Guard passed to Navy jurisdiction. If it wasn't yet war, it certainly was no longer peace.

On the following day, Smith, on board *North Star*, got word a foreign fishing boat had landed men on Greenland. Smith sent *Northland*, captained by Commander Carl C. von Paulsen, to investigate, and soon *Northland* came upon the Norwegian sealer *Buskoe*. On board, the Coast Guard inspectors found an unusual amount of radio equipment, indicating the crew had more in mind than seal hunting, and under questioning, the Norwegians admitted to having landed a team to set up a radio station for Germany. Von Paulsen immediately declared *Buskoe* captured, left a Coast Guard prize crew on board, and set out to track down the radio station. After several hundred miles of hard going, *Northland* found the station. The cutter anchored some distance away and put ashore a landing party that was able to surprise those inside and capture their equipment and codes.

The only other German ship captured by the United States during World War II, *Externsteine*, would also be taken by Coast Guard icebreakers in Greenland, while in May 1942 the cutter *Icarus* would sink

a U-boat off North Carolina and pick up thirty-three survivors—the first official German prisoners of war captured by the United States. Altogether the Coast Guard had a hand in sinking thirteen U-boats as well as one, and probably two, Japanese submarines.

As in the previous war, much of the combat the Coast Guard saw during World War II was while escorting convoys across the Atlantic, and over 180,000 of its members were involved in this effort, mostly on Navy vessels. A quarter of a century of advances in antisubmarine warfare, however, had entirely changed the escort game since World War I. Sonar now allowed ships to track the U-boats when they submerged, and depth

When the Japanese attacked Pearl Harbor on 7 December 1941, the 327-foot cutter Taney *was tied up at Pier 6 in Honolulu Harbor.* Taney's *guns engaged enemy aircraft, concentrating its fire against the high altitude Kate bombers and Zero fighters.* Taney *followed this action, along with the six other cutters in its class, serving as convoy escort and in special operations throughout World War II. (Keith Ferris, U.S. Coast Guard Art Collection)*

The German vessel Externsteine, *supplying a covert radio-weather station in Greenland, surrenders after* Eastwind *fires three salvos from its deck guns. The ship was seized and its twenty crewmembers were taken prisoner. (U.S. Coast Guard)*

Above: *Captain James A. Hirschfield, commanding officer of* Campbell, *concentrates on a German U-boat wolf pack stalking his convoy. During a twelve-hour engagement, the cutter dropped depth-charges on a half dozen submarines, then rammed the German submarine U-606, sinking it. (U.S. Coast Guard)*

Right: *An explosion erupts the water's surface in* Spencer's *wake from depth charges dropped on a suspected German submarine. (U.S. Coast Guard)*

After destroyer escorts became available for convoy serviced and German submarine activity decreased in the Atlantic, Coast Guard 327-footers were pulled off escort duty and converted to amphibious command ships. From France to Okinawa and beyond, these cutters took part in fourteen invasions. (U.S. Coast Guard)

charges, often dropped in clusters, could be deadly effective. Even more devastating for the enemy, British experts had cracked the German codes and knew where to look for U-boats.

From the beginning, *Campbell*, the first cutter to join the escort fleet, demonstrated the exceptional suitability of the 327-foot cutters for such duty, proving itself superior in many ways to the destroyers. In a drama repeated during the war, a U-boat would be sighted, often after it fired a spread of torpedoes; a cutter would take after it, and the submarine might try to shake its pursuer by heading under the convoy. A white-knuckle chase would ensue, depth charges were dropped, and if they did not destroy the U-boat, they might drive it to surface so ships' guns could hammer it to pieces. Such actions frequently played out in the dark and in brutally bad weather—and often as not entailed dangerous search-and-rescue operations.

In the summer of 1943, having suffered extremely heavy U-boat losses, the Germans temporarily called back the wolf packs, and while escort duty would be dangerous until the end of the war, the worst was over. By this turning point in the battle for the North Atlantic, a handful

CGC Campbell *screening a convoy in the Atlantic against preying submarines. (Anton Otto Fischer, U.S. Coast Guard)*

Above: A Coast Guard landing craft runs Australian troops ashore at Balikpapan in Borneo. (U.S. Coast Guard)

Left: A German submarine attacked by Spencer *is photographed just before it sinks into its ocean grave. (U.S. Coast Guard)*

of Coast Guard cutters had sunk over half the submarines destroyed by American vessels.

War brought its losses too, for one of the 327s, *Alexander Hamilton*, was torpedoed and went down off Iceland. In the Caribbean a U-boat sunk *Acacia*, a 172-foot buoy tender. Two 125-footers, *Bedloe* and *Jackson*, trying to rescue a torpedoed cargo ship off North Carolina, were lost to a hurricane.

The service's war efforts were not limited to hunting down U-boats, however. Coast Guardsmen pitched in to get the troops ashore in the biggest landing ever, the D-Day assault on Normandy in June 1944, and saved 1,500 lives that day—in addition to the 1,000 men rescued during convoy duty over the course of the war. Thousands of service members also saw action in the Pacific, where they provided sorely needed boat-handling expertise for amphibious landings. Altogether, almost 2,000 Coast Guardsmen were killed in action during World War II.

Coast Guardsmen practice bringing troops ashore for amphibious invasions. During the war, the Coast Guard landed troops and supplies in both Pacific and European Theaters. (U.S. Coast Guard)

Douglas Munro at Guadalcanal

Robert M. Browning, Jr., Ph.D.

The Coast Guard's first major participation in the Pacific Theater was at Guadalcanal. So decisive was the success of its small-boat operators early in the war that they were later involved in every major World War II amphibious campaign. Coast Guard crews manned over 350 ships and hundreds more amphibious assault-craft. It was in these vessels the Coast Guard fulfilled one of its most dangerous but critical roles in the war. During one small engagement on Guadalcanal, Signalman First Class Douglas Albert Munro died while rescuing a group of Marines.

On 7 August 1942, the United States embarked on its first major amphibious assault of the war in the Pacific. Coast Guard personnel crewed eighteen of the twenty-two naval troop-ships attached to the campaign's task force. Furthermore, Coast Guardsmen from these crews were assigned as an integral part in the landings as operators of the landing craft. Many of the Coast Guard coxswains came from Life-Saving stations; their experience with small boats made them the most seasoned small-boat handlers in government service.

From the beginning of the battle, Munro drove the landing craft delivering Marines for the fierce fighting on Tulagi Island. About two weeks later he was sent twenty miles across the channel to Guadalcanal to land Marines there. Bloody battles ensued, and for six months both United States and Japanese troops poured onto Guadalcanal as each side attempted to gain control.

After the initial Guadalcanal landings, Munro and twenty-four other Coast Guard and Navy sailors were assigned ashore to Lunga Point Base commanded by Commander Dwight H. Dexter, USCG. Dexter was in charge of all small-boat operations for Guadalcanal. The base, on a Lever Brothers coconut plantation, consisting of a small house with a newly constructed coconut tree signal tower, served as the staging area for troop movements along the coast. A pool of landing craft from transports lay in the cove to expedite the transportation of supplies and men.

A month into the campaign a reinforced Marine garrison started a push beyond their defensive perimeter west across the Matanikau River. Each attempt to cross met tremendous resistance. On Sunday, 27 September, Marine Lieutenant Colonel Lewis B. "Chesty" Puller embarked three companies of his 7th Marines in landing craft to circle around by sea and land west of the river intending to drive out the Japanese and establish a new patrol base there.

The landing craft were dispatched from Lunga Base. Munro, two weeks short of his twenty-third birthday, took charge of ten LCP (landing craft personnel) and LCT (landing craft tanks) to transport Puller's Marines to a beach west of Point Cruz. The Marines landed under a five-inch gunfire support-barrage from the destroyer USS Monssen. Major Ortho L. Rodgers, commanding the landing party, assaulted the beach with two waves. The 500 unopposed Marines pushed inland quickly, reorganizing on a ridge about a quarter-mile from the beach. A Japanese aircraft bombing raid disrupted the Marines' gunfire support at their new position as Monssen maneuvered away from the bombers' threat. Then, with unexpected suddenness, the Marines were struck by an overwhelming Japanese force. Rodgers was killed and one company commander wounded.

No one anticipated a major withdrawal after the Marines landed, and only a single LCP had remained behind to take off the wounded. It was manned by Petty Officer Ray Evans, USCG, and Coxswain Samuel B. Roberts, USN. An encircling Japanese squad meanwhile set up near the beach behind the Marines. Without warning, a burst of machine-gun fire hit the LCP, severing the rudder cable and damaging the boat's controls. After jury-rigging the steering, Roberts was struck by enemy fire. Evans managed to jam the controls to full ahead, speeding back to Lunga Point Base where at full speed—and out of control—the boat ran onto the beach. Roberts died and was awarded the Navy Cross posthumously.

The trapped Marines, without means for communications, used undershirts to spell out the word "HELP" on the ridge. Marine Second Lieutenant Dale Leslie, piloting a Douglas SBD dive-bomber, spotted the message. Puller, receiving Leslie's communication and realizing his men were isolated and endangered, immediately directed surface and aerial covering fire for the retreating Marines desperately trying to reach the beach.

Munro, who had taken charge of the original landing, volunteered to lead the boats back to the beach. These boats were not heavily armed nor well protected: Munro's Higgins boat, carrying only two .30-caliber Lewis machine guns, was made of plywood.

From Point Cruz, the ridges abandoned by the Marines, and from positions east of the beach, the Japanese fired on the boat fleet led by Munro. The intense fire from three positions disrupted the landing, causing several casualties among the virtually defenseless boat crews. Despite this withering fire, Munro got the boats onto the beach in waves of two and three at a time and successfully picked up the Marines.

As escaping Marines reembarked, Japanese troops pressed toward the landing area, making the withdrawal

more dangerous. Japanese also kept up murderous fire from the retaken ridge. Munro, seeing the dangerous situation, maneuvered his boat between the enemy and those troops withdrawing in an attempt to protect the battalion's remnants. Munro and Petty Officer Raymond Evans provided covering fire. All Marines, including twenty-five wounded, managed to escape.

With all the Marines safely in the small craft, Munro and Evans steered their LCP away from the beach. Passing Point Cruz they noticed a grounded LCT full of Marines. Munro returned, directed another LCT to tow the stranded boat off, and provided protection. They succeeded, but before the three boats could get far from shore, Japanese rushed a machine gun to the beach and began firing. Evans shouted a warning to Munro. A single bullet hit Munro in the base of the skull. He died before reaching the operating base. For his extraordinary heroism, outstanding leadership, and gallantry, Munro posthumously received the Medal of Honor.

Left: Coast Guardsmen from the attack transport *Hunter Liggett* and Marines unload supplies at Guadalcanal. In the background is the Japanese ship *Kinugawa Maru,* stranded after a naval battle. (U.S. Coast Guard)

Above: When 500 Marines at Guadalcanal were attacked and trapped at water's edge, Signalman First Class Douglas A. Munro volunteered to lead landing-craft into the beach to pull them out. All the Marines got out, including the wounded; Munro died shortly after from wounds. He received, posthumously, the Congressional Medal of Honor. (Eric S. Gebhardt, U.S. Coast Guard)

The seventy-six Coast-Guard-manned LSTs in World War II took part in almost every amphibious operation involving Allied forces. (U.S. Coast Guard)

Wartime Duties

Just as important as the Coast Guard's front-line missions during the Second World War were its non-combat duties. As in the previous war, Captains of the Port played the major role in protecting America's water-front from sabotage and in assuring the safe and efficient movement of cargos—especially munitions—as well as in supervising merchant ship-ping and managing anchorages. Naturally, except for the International Ice Patrol, none of the Coast Guard's regular duties went away during the war. Lighthouses and aids to navigation still needed to be maintained, and during winter, channels still needed to be cleared through ice. Dangerous rescues were performed even more regularly than in peacetime, with countless lives saved.

In addition to these responsibilities, the Service also began perform-ing Beach Patrol. At night and when visibility was poor, Coast Guardsmen, either in pairs, with dogs, or sometimes even on horseback, patrolled long stretches of the nation's shoreline to prevent infiltration and sabotage. They also kept lookout for ships in need and were there to signal for help and to render aid. It could be lonely, rather thankless duty, often undertaken in isolated areas and frequently under cruelly harsh weather conditions.

Given the monumental scope of all these undertakings, it is not surprising the war's end found the Coast Guard much changed from what it had been at the beginning. As a military service, it relied on draftees to fill wartime shortages in personnel. Since the draft drew from the general male population within the age requirements, about 13 percent of the inductees were black. Although black Coast Guardsmen were still relatively few in number, by midway through the war they were being integrated into cutter crews, and the first black reserve officer graduated from the

Coast Guardsmen watched along the lonely coastlines of the nation by walking the iso-lated beaches or climbing over headlands, ever alert to enemies using these vulnerable approaches to the homeland. Some seamen rode horses while others walked the beaches, sometimes alone or accompanied by dogs. (U.S. Coast Guard)

OCS school located at the Academy in 1943. These were small first steps, but they marked the beginning of a trend leading to the end of segregation in the service.

In 1942 a Coast Guard women's reserve force was created. Initially the women who joined were limited to performing clerical duties and were recruited only in order to free up men needed elsewhere. The Army already had its WACS, the Navy its WAVES, and in keeping with the times, the new Coast Guardswomen were given the clever name SPARS (*Semper Paratus*, Always Ready)—hit upon by Lieutenant Commander Dorothy Stratton, head of the group. A well-known fashion designer created what, to the era at least, was said to be a snappy uniform in order to boost recruitment. Surely no one expected that in hardly more than a generation women would be serving alongside men on board Coast Guard high-endurance cutters.

Two technological innovations that would have far-ranging ramifications for the Service were introduced during the Second World War: loran, and the helicopter. Loran (LOng Range Aids to Navigation), using radio waves to determine the position of ships and aircraft, would be perhaps the most important breakthrough in navigation since the earth was discovered to be round and orbit around the sun. It would also be one of the most closely guarded secrets of the war, and the Coast Guard's Lieutenant Commander Lawrence Harding was instrumental in developing it. By 1943 loran stations were being established in both the Atlantic and Pacific theaters and soon became a major Coast Guard responsibility. As the first accurate, all-weather navigational system, loran's contribution to the winning of the war is immeasurable.

The helicopter has come to be almost as closely associated with the Coast Guard as the cutter. After witnessing a demonstration of one of these flying contraptions built by Sikorsky, an enthusiastic Lieutenant Commander Frank Erickson wrote Commandant Russell Waesche that helicopters would be just the ticket for the service, not only for lifesaving and law-enforcement, but also to protect convoys from submarines. The Navy wasn't interested in the odd machines, but the Army was getting thirteen, and Waesche was persuaded to attend a demonstration. Apparently the strange aircraft put on an impressive show, for the Coast Guard immediately ordered its first twenty-one helicopters from Vought-Sikorsky.

Knowing better than anyone else how slippery was the slope from the Treasury Department to the Navy and in the past how hard it had been to get back, before the war was half over, Waesche was staking out what the Coast Guard would do when peace came and what resources it would require. These would be the things the service was already doing and good at, and included providing loran and standing duty on the ocean stations. During the summer of 1944, the Navy and the Treasury Department came to an understanding on this plan, and when the war ended the service was able to return home with none of the bureaucratic infighting of earlier times. Waesche, the Coast Guard's longest-serving commandant—and one of its greatest—was already dying of stomach cancer, however, and would retire the last day of 1945, one day before the smooth return he had worked so hard to assure took place.

Marines on Guam salute the Coast Guardsmen who bore them to the Pacific Island beachheads in landing craft. Coast Guard crews operated many of the landing craft throughout both the European and Pacific assaults. The Marines recognized that the Coast Guardsmen stood exposed to sometimes withering gunfire while navigating the craft up onto the beaches and at the same time returning defensive machine-gun fire to protect Marines in the boats. (U.S. Coast Guard)

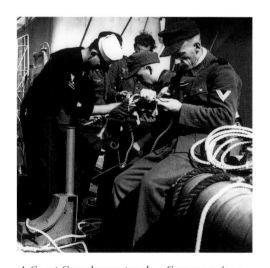

A Coast Guardsman teaches German prisoners of war nautical knot-tying while they are in transit aboard a Coast-Guard-crewed attack-transport en route to POW compounds in the United States. A small number of Coast Guardsmen thus kept hundreds of prisoners aboard ship occupied and less dangerous during the long and uncertain period in the prisoners' lives. (U.S. Coast Guard)

The Coast Guard at Normandy

Scott T. Price

Bullets slammed into the boat and the Coast Guard crew winced as the repeated thuds resonated through LCI(L)-85, a Landing Craft Infantry Large. Suddenly the hull jammed into the wooden stakes of a man-made forest of wooden piles driven into the sand to ward off Allied boats approaching the Normandy shore.

As the amphibian ground to a halt and its bow touched bottom, so did its luck. A mine exploded, ripping a gaping hole in the forward compartments. German defense-batteries pummeled the landing craft. Many soldiers on board were shredded by withering gunfire before they could get off the boat. Even those still unwounded could not disembark because the explosion had destroyed the vessel's opening ramp.

The crew backed the now burning vessel off the beach while at the same time fighting the fire. The boat began listing as water entered the hull through shell holes. Other landing craft came to its aid and removed the uninjured troops. The mortally wounded boat maneuvered back to the Coast-Guard-manned attack-transport USS Samuel Chase, where the dead and wounded were offloaded, and the crew abandoned ship.

Normandy waters slowly washed over the blood-stained decks as the stricken vessel, turning its stern skyward, settled beneath the waves. LCI(L)-85 was one of ninety-eight Coast-Guard-manned ships participating in the Normandy, D-Day invasion, Operation Neptune, 6 June 1944—a day that would prove to be the bloodiest in the Coast Guard's history.

Normandy Invasion

Coast Guardsmen took part primarily in attacks on Utah and Omaha beaches. The number of Coast-Guard-partially-crewed and Coast-Guard-manned Navy vessels at Normandy was larger than in any previous operation. Coast Guardsmen were aboard four attack transports and all of their landing craft plus ten Landing Ship Tanks, LST, twenty-four Landing Craft Infantry, LCI(L), and sixty USCG 83-footers.

Captain Edward H. Fritzsche commanded the assault group that landed 1st Division troops from Joseph T. Dickman on the easternmost Omaha beaches. The deputy assault commander was another experienced Coast Guard combatant, Captain Miles Imlay, a veteran of the Sicily and Salerno invasions, who doubled as the commander of the Coast-Guard-manned LCI(L) Flotilla 10.

Farther west from Omaha beaches was Utah. Navy Rear Admiral Don P. Moon commanded this assault from the Coast-Guard-manned attack transport USS Bayfield. The flagship was commanded by Captain Lyndon Spencer. The Coast Guard also participated in the British and Canadian landings. Four Coast Guard-manned Landing Ship Tanks, LST, transported British troops and equipment to the beach landings at Gold, Juno, and Sword. Coast Guard crews were also on the transport USS Charles Carroll.

Bayfield anchored in the transport area offshore at 2:30 a.m., 6 June. Over the ship's loudspeakers the troops heard the ominous words, "Now hear this. Stand by, all troops." Soon they were clambering down cargo nets into the pitching and heaving Landing Craft Mediums, LCM. With snorts and streams of smoke from diesel engines, landing craft were off toward French beaches. Joseph T. Dickman's boats were ordered away at 3:53 a.m. Landing craft loading proceeded satisfactorily despite the rough seas. Soon combat-troop-laden boats were off to Utah through mine-swept channels.

All was quiet on Samuel Chase when the order to "lower away" was given at 5:30 a.m. All that could be heard was the squeaking of the davits and the whispers of the soldiers as they loaded into the Landing Craft

Vehicles, Personnel, or LCVPs. The landing craft were lowered into the swells and headed toward France. Here too, as at Utah, they were well away from the coast and on the unsheltered waters of the Channel. All of Chase's boats got away without incident. Passing the battleships on their journey, men in the boats cringed as 14-inch guns nearby fired. Ernest Hemingway, in one of the LCVPs, described the huddled soldiers: "Under their steel helmets they looked like pikemen of the Middle Ages to whose aid in battle had suddenly come some strange and unbelievable monster."

Captain Imlay went to the beachhead with LCI(L)-87 to act as a traffic cop for landing vessels. He cajoled, threatened, and encouraged vessels in and out of Omaha all morning, ensuring they landed on the correct beaches at their appointed times.

Five-thousand yards seaward from the beach a group of Landing Craft Tanks, LCT, discharged their amphibious tanks, which were to "swim" through the water and land one minute before H-Hour. However, canvas sides erected to keep water out of these tanks collapsed under pounding seas. Most of those destined

to support the eastern landings foundered. The Coast Guard 83-footer, CG-3 rescued one tank's men, but most sinking "steel-coffins" took their crews with them. Only five out of thirty-two amphibious tanks made it ashore.

No Coast Guard vessels were lost off the British-assigned beaches on D-Day, but the same was not true at Omaha. This shoreline was ideal for defense. Bluffs above gave excellent fields of fire, and from the high ground the defenders could fire down into approaching landing craft. Vessels here were continually exposed to enemy gunfire while dodging obstacles, shuttling through the heavy seas between the landing areas and the transports. Both Coast-Guard-manned Navy trans-ports and their landing craft successfully disembarked troops, equipment, and ammunition on schedule. Never-theless, they did take losses. All Bayfield's landing craft returned; seven of Dickman's did not. Three swamped in the heavy surf; German artillery fire sunk four.

"You have no idea how miserable the Germans made that beach," a Coast Guard coxswain recounted. "From a half mile offshore we could see rows upon rows of jagged obstructions lining the beach. When our ramp went down and the soldiers started to charge ashore, the

Above: Soldiers embark from Coast-Guard-manned landing craft onto Normandy beaches. (U.S. Coast Guard)

Left: Injured soldiers cover the deck of an LCT as it returns from the Normandy beachhead. These Coast-Guard-manned Navy vessels continued their round trips between the off-lying ships and the beaches, hauling men and equipment into the battle and the wounded on the back trip. (U.S. Coast Guard)

[Germans] let loose with streams of hot lead which pinged all around us. Why they didn't kill everyone in our boat, I will never know."

Another Coast Guard LCVP skipper described his experience: "My eyes were glued to the boat coming in next to ours, and on the water in between, boiling with bullets from hidden shore emplacements, like a mud puddle in a hailstorm. It seemed impossible that we could make it in without being riddled."

LCI(L)-91 grounded to disembark its troops on the beach amid stakes topped with teller mines. As the tide came in, the landing craft moved up the beach. With 200 troops still to unload, it struck a mine, killing several men. The landing craft backed off and moved a hundred yards away, which allowed troops to get ashore. A violent explosion forward started a fire that first consumed the well deck, then raged out of control, and the vessel was abandoned. LCI(L)-91 burned all morning. Seven of its Coast Guard crew perished, eleven were wounded.

The crew of LCI(L)-92, with 192 troops aboard, approached the beach shortly after LCI(L)-91 and saw it burst into flames. So LCI(L)-92's coxswain beached his boat in the lee of the burning landing craft in the hope that smoke from its fire would help cover their landing. But German shells still struck. An explosion ripped through the forward compartments setting them afire. While disembarking troops, the crew fighting the flames was being cut down by German machine-gun fire. Shells continued to hit it and the fire spread. Eleven crewmen were wounded. All day the pyres created by these two

Coast-Guard-manned LCI(L)s served as landmarks for the incoming craft—as well as for German artillery spotters.

Down the beach, LCI(L)-93 delivered its first load of troops and emerged unscathed, but on the second trip it grounded on a sand bar off the beach and took ten direct hits. Within a few minutes of the first wave, four Coast-Guard-manned LCI(L)s were casualties.

Samuel Chase launched fifteen assault waves, and before noon all the 1st Division's troops were disembarked. LCTs then maneuvered alongside and soon all of their equipment was on the way to the beaches. The LCVPs and LCMs returned with wounded, who were cared for by the Samuel Chase's Public Health Service doctors. Some of the ship's small boats became rescue vessels.

Such incidents were common along the shores of Normandy on D-Day. It was a successful morning for this Coast-Guard-manned ship, but the day was not without loss: six LCVPs did not return. One impaled itself on an obstacle before it made it to the beach. Four swamped in the heavy surf, and one sank after taking a direct hit from a German 88, which killed one Coast Guardsman outright.

Matchbox Fleet

A few weeks prior to D-Day, President Roosevelt suggested that Operation Neptune have a rescue flotilla. The Navy had none available, so CNO Admiral Ernest King sought Coast Guard resources. The service was operating 83-foot patrol boats, referred to as the "matchbox fleet," on anti-submarine duty along the United States' East Coast. The sixty gasoline-powered wooden vessels quickly assembled in New York Harbor where they were hastily loaded aboard freighters and shipped to England. Once off-loaded, crews worked frantically removing

Left: Looking down on the dead and wounded aboard the Coast Guard *LCI(L) 85* damaged by a mine and struck some two-dozen times by German shells. The crew offloaded most of the soldiers before being forced away from the beach. The stricken vessel returned to the offshore attack transports in time to get the wounded and crew off before it sank. (U.S. Coast Guard)

Opposite: Barrage balloons float overhead protecting the ships from low-flying enemy aircraft while a continuous parade of trucks loaded with troops and supplies move inland supporting the invasion of Europe following D-Day. (U.S. Coast Guard)

anti-submarine equipment to provide room on deck for rescued soldiers pulled from the water. The final cutter completed its conversion just sixty hours before the invasion. Renamed Rescue Flotilla One for the invasion, its boats were numbered CG-1 through CG-60.

The newly assigned fleet of patrol-boats experienced a hectic and dangerous morning. The 83-footer CG-1 joined with the Omaha assault force escorting a group of LCVPs to the beach. While still offshore a lookout spotted men in the water from a sunken British craft. Ensign Bernard B. Wood maneuvered his vessel while crewmen jumped overboard tying lines to those too cold to clamber aboard unaided. Only a few minutes after H-Hour they pulled forty-seven British soldiers and sailors from the water. Three hours later CG-1 sailors recovered nineteen survivors from the burning LCI(L)-91.

The rescue flotilla saved more than 400 men on D-Day and by the time the unit was decommissioned it had pulled 1,438 from Channel waters. As at the shores of North Africa, Sicily, the Italian mainland, and throughout the Pacific, the Coast Guard was instrumental to the invasion's success.

Port Director

The Allies had no ports following the invasion on the Normandy beachhead for delivering supplies and reinforcements, so the British, with the assistance of Coast Guard officers, devised a series of temporary artificial harbors. Captain Imlay was assigned as the port director for Omaha area debarkation port, which soon was handling as much cargo as most of the world's larger ports.

Coast-Guard-manned landing craft shuttled reinforcements and supplies to France and returned to England with the wounded and with prisoners. LST-261 made fifty-three crossings following D-Day. Once the Normandy invasion was completed, many Coast Guard vessels and Coast-Guard-manned Navy ships went on to participate in other invasions.

The Coast Guard lost more vessels on D-Day than at any time in its history—testimony to the ferocity of the German defenders and the bravery of the Coast Guardsmen who carried the Allied infantry to the enemy's doorstep.

Above: *Navy and Coast Guard crewmembers discuss plans aboard a Coast Guard cutter off Cuba with the Navy ship in the background, during* Operation Able Vigil. *This operation began in August 1994 when the number of Cubans escaping across the Florida Strait in anything that could float jumped to 2,607 in a single week. The previous record was 1,173 people for the entire month of June. (Don Wagner, U.S. Coast Guard)*

Above, right: *CGC* Alex Haley—*named for the famed author of* Roots *and former Coast Guardsman—diverted from fisheries patrol in the Bering Sea takes the freighter* Alam Selaras *in tow after the ship's engine failed. The law enforcement role can instantly revert to one of the fundamental tasks of the Coast Guard, aiding victims at sea. (Tony Cortes, U.S. Coast Guard)*

Above: *Weapons and equipment taken from captured crewmen following a shootout between the cutter* Point Glover *and a Viet Cong junk. (U.S. Coast Guard)*

The Cold War Years

The Coast Guard shouldered the expanded burdens of maintaining loran stations in far corners of the world, as well as handling the ocean weather station program, which the Navy was only too happy to relinquish. Fortunately this latter mission proved to require fewer stations than expected. For a time, too, it looked as if Coast Guard aviation would be taken over by the Navy, but in the end the service was able to keep its pilots and aircraft. By 1950, some 23,000 people wore the Coast Guard uniform.

The Korean War, since it was not officially a war, came and went without the Coast Guard being placed under the Navy, although Coast Guardsmen were assigned to Navy destroyer escorts. In this conflict too, the Coast Guard loran stations proved invaluable, and one was set up in Pusan, South Korea. Again, maintaining the security of American ports took the highest priority. A few years earlier an accidental explosion on a foreign-flagged ship killed 500 and wounded thousands in a Texas harbor, demonstrating how vulnerable the nation's ports could be. Also, as a foretaste of similar concerns that would resurface half a century later after terrorists attacks on the United States, experts worried an enemy, in this case the Soviet Union, might try to slip nuclear weapons into the country. These, it was feared, could be detonated at a time of the enemy's choosing and bring the nation to its knees. The Coast Guard, of course, became the foremost line of defense against such a ploy.

Early in the Cold War the DEW line, the Distant Early Warning string of radar stations, was established across northern Canada, and the Coast Guard was soon sending icebreakers over the top of North America to determine the feasibility of supporting the stations by sea. During these voyages, the cutters also were able to gather invaluable oceanographic data. This was the time of the International Geophysical Year from 1957 to 1958, a massive global exploration effort involving scientists from around the world. A dozen Arctic and sixty Antarctic research stations were constructed by the United States and eleven other nations. Coast Guard icebreakers were called on to help establish and supply these outposts, a mission still going on today under *Operation Deep Freeze.*

In 1958, AMVER, the Automated Merchant Vessel Reporting System, came into being. Taking advantage of the technology newly available, a system was set up allowing merchant ships to regularly report their positions to the Coast Guard. The service tracked this data and when a ship found itself in trouble at sea, the Coast Guard could contact any vessels nearby and they could go to render aid. For most of the public it would remain one of the service's least known programs, and yet it was one of the most successful, with ever-growing numbers of merchant ships from many nations volunteering to participate.

By the 1960s, higher-flying, long-range jet planes had reduced the need for mid-ocean weather information, and the Ocean Stations would be phased out within a decade. While this freed the cutters from one task, another was growing to replace it: Russian and Japanese trawlers and whalers had begun plying the North Atlantic and Bering Sea in increasing numbers. Fisheries conservation duty, still an important mission of the service today, was soon involving more cutters and aircraft.

As the Cold War intensified, two seemingly minor Communist insurrections on opposite sides of the globe were gathering steam, and the service would soon feel the heat from both. The first of these, in Cuba in 1959, brought Fidel Castro to power. The ensuing flight of refugees, often in floating death-traps, rapidly entangled the service in huge lifesaving, humanitarian, and immigration operations still unfolding today. The second, in French Indochina, or Vietnam, would engage the Coast Guard in eight years of intense patrol, rescue, and security operations unlike any it had known before.

Above: *CGC* Seneca's *small boat approaches a listing Haitian freighter hauling 463 passengers bound for the United States. (U.S. Coast Guard)*

Above: *A gunner's mate tosses spent .50-caliber machine-gun rounds over the side. Along with intercepting the enemy moving along waterways, the crews were called upon by ground units for alongshore gunfire support. On one such occasion in 1968,* Point Caution *struck an enemy encampment with mortar and machine-gun fire. Reconnaissance units later counted eighty-four dead enemy troops. (U.S. Coast Guard)*

Opposite, bottom: *Haitian small boats overburdened with refugees attempting to sail to the United States.* Legare *rescues 301 migrants attempting to navigate the sometimes-perilous waters between Haiti and the coast of Florida. (U.S. Coast Guard)*

Clockwise from top left:
The deep draft cutters of Squadron Three patrol Vietnam's offshore waters. These ships frequently used their guns effectively on enemy land targets. (U.S. Coast Guard)

A Navy Swift boat and Coast Guard cutter Point Banks *prowling one of the many South Vietnam's inland waterways used by the Viet Cong to move weapons and supplies. (Noel Daggett, U.S. Coast Guard)*

A fiery donut hovers in front of the muzzle of a five-inch deck gun after sending a heavy shell against enemy forces just inland from the coast of Vietnam. (U.S. Coast Guard)

Coast Guardsmen in Vietnam not forgetting their humanitarian missions continued to involve themselves in aiding civilians where they could. Commissaryman Second Class John J. Sullivan cleans, applies ointment, and bandages a child's infected foot. (U.S. Coast Guard)

Along with the war itself, the number of cutters committed to the war escalated. In the summer of 1965 eight Coast Guard cutters arrived at Danang. There were seventeen in 1966, then an additional nine that same year, then five more in 1967. Altogether fifty-six cutters would find themselves in the "Brown Water War." Besides coast and river patrol, the Service also placed and maintained the aids to navigation necessary for bringing modern warfare to the region. In addition, Coast Guardsmen established loran stations both in Vietnam and neighboring Thailand. They provided port security for the massive shipments of arms and equipment pouring into the country, rescued downed pilots, and provided naval gunfire support for ground troops. They literally took fire from all sides, and some of the deadliest came by mistake from other Americans.

In hopes that South Vietnam, if properly equipped and trained, could hold back the Communists on its own, the United States set out to untangle itself from the war. Accordingly, in 1969, the Coast Guard took over the training of Vietnamese Navy crews for the patrols, and began transferring the first cutters to the South Vietnamese Government. More cutters were turned over the next year, and a final three in 1972. The next year, in May 1973, the last Coast Guardsman left Vietnam. South Vietnam continued fighting for two more years, holding out until April 1975.

Attack on Point Welcome

Paul C. Scotti, *Condensed by author from* Coast Guard Action in Vietnam *(Hellgate Press, 2000)*

"Captain! Captain! Captain! We're being illuminated!" yelled Gunner's Mate Third Class Mark D. McKenney bursting open the door to the cabin. Twenty-five-year-old Lieutenant (jg) David C. Brostrom threw off his blanket and jumped up from his bunk just as the 20mm projectiles from the attacking plane struck.

Chief Boatswain's Mate Richard H. Patterson climbing the ladder to the bridge to relieve the watch was thrown to the deck and momentarily blacked out. Inside the small bridge, executive officer, Lieutenant (jg) Ross Bell, hit the "General Quarters" alarm before he fell. Lying on the deck his vision began to cloud over, he saw that some of his toes were gone but felt no pain. A chunk of flesh was missing from his broken right arm and he bled in numerous places where metal fragments had raked him.

The alarm's urgent blare cruelly yanked the crew from their dreams. Piling out on deck they saw the cutter's stern afire. Patterson took charge and organized a fire fighting party as British freelance photographer Timothy J. Page stood in the doorway to the cabin recording the events with his camera. On the bridge, broken glass and shrapnel crunching under his feet, Brostrom stepped around Bell. He seized the radio microphone and called the operations center in Da Nang and told them he was being illuminated and attacked by planes. Da Nang acknowledged and began the difficult process of finding out who was doing it. Point Caution *on patrol to the south overheard the call and told Brostrom it was on its way to help.*

This was 11 August 1966, after 3:15 a.m., and Point Welcome, an eighty-two-foot Coast Guard patrol boat with thirteen men on board, was loitering without running lights three-quarters of a mile off the Demilitarized Zone, DMZ, and three-quarters of a mile below the 17th parallel, the demarcation line between North Vietnam and South Vietnam. This was nothing unusual.

These patrols had been going on for more than a year as Coast Guardsmen sought to intercept enemy movements.

The crew, having extinguished the fire caused from ignited gasoline cans used to fuel the cutter's small boat, stood amid the litter of firefighting equipment taking a breather. The residual gasoline had been washed overboard leaving behind paint blisters speckling the burned deck and transom. At this time, Brostrom ran out to the starboard side of the narrow platform behind the bridge and took up either a Very pistol or Aldis lamp for signaling. Before he could send an emergency recognition signal the aircraft cannons clattered behind Brostrom, and the lethal rounds nearly cut him in half. Almost opposite to Brostrom on the deck below, Engineman Second Class Jerry Phillips took mortal wounds in the abdomen. Fireman Houston J. Davidson coming back from the bow was starboard of the deckhouse when shrapnel mangled his hands into bloody uselessness. Tim Page, who had expected a relaxing photographic assignment lazing in the sunshine and swimming in the

Point Welcome mistakenly came under strafing attacks by a U.S. Air Force B-57 Canberra followed by bombings by F-4 Phantoms. The initial attack, with 20mm cannons, killed the commanding officer and severely wounded the executive officer. When *Point Welcome* returned to service its cartoon mascot, Wile E. Coyote, painted on the bridge, sported a Purple Heart Medal and Band-Aids. (William H. Wolf)

sea, spiced with a few fishing-junk boardings, was felled with multiple shrapnel wounds and lost his camera overboard. Up forward, in the paint locker, just below the open hatch, McKenney was stretching for foam when his exposed back was riddled with shell fragments. A hunk of metal lodged in his thigh and cuts in his forehead made paths of blood on his face. Down too, with wounds, went the South Vietnamese liaison officer.

After the plane roared past, Patterson ran up to the bridge. Giving little mind to his dead skipper and wounded executive officer he slammed the throttles ahead to get the idling boat from being a sitting target to a moving one. He shouted orders to get the wounded below and to stay off the main deck. He instructed Boatswain's Mate First Class Billy R. Russell to check on him after each pass and if he was hit Russell was to assume command.

The U.S. Air Force B-57 Canberra made another raking pass, this time from bow to stern. Reacting out of instinct bred by military comradeship, nineteen-year-old Seaman David E. O'Conner, threw himself over the mortally wounded Phillips, who lay crumpled where he had fallen.

Its ordnance expended, the Canberra's job was done; but the "enemy" was still afloat. Consequently, the C-130 airborne control aircraft running the attack continued circling above dropping flares while trying to find aircraft to finish the job.

Patterson searched for signal flares but found none. The radios were useless as the antennas were destroyed by the B-57. He dared not turn on his running lights fearing it would just make them an easier target to hit. So he opted to make a zigzag dash to a friendly base down the coast. His skillful boat handling was further challenged because the rudders would not respond to the helm and he had to use the two engine-throttles to make turns.

The lull had ended. Patterson leaned out the window and heard the deep roar of more jets. The C-130 had vectored in two F-4 Phantom fighters, one carried two cluster bombs, the other two 500-pound bombs.

Patterson felt the engines losing power. Realizing without power they were doomed, he ordered abandon ship. In the water the crew painfully swam for shore

when unbelievably they began taking machine-gun fire from two points. O'Connor swam back to the cutter intending to give his shipmates machine-gun covering fire. As he neared the boat, a spotlight captured him.

It was Point Caution. *Nearer to shore, the others in the water heard a cry of "They're Americans." Immediately after, the crews of the South Vietnamese Coastal Force junks with their U.S. Navy advisors began pulling them out of the water.*

The small arms fire had come from the South Vietnamese junks, as well as a probable Viet Cong position on shore. Point Welcome *lost power when the air supply to the engines choked. Repairs were made to the blowers and the cutter made it back to Da Nang on its own.*

The friendly fire incident lasted an hour. Basically, it happened because one hand did not know what the other hand was doing. Although the Coast Guard and Navy had been operating off the DMZ for more than a year, the Air Force had recently begun an operation in, and above, the DMZ, and was unaware of the regular naval activity. When the pilots were briefed that night they were emphatically told that there were no friendly maritime operations in progress. The tragedy was the result of poor information sharing, pilot zealousness, failure to follow recognition procedures, and just plain bad luck.

Chief Boatswain's Mate Richard H. Patterson relaxes on the bridge of *Point Welcome* on patrol off the coast of South Vietnam. Just hours later the cutter came under attack by U.S. Air Force aircraft. With the cutter's commanding officer dead and the executive officer severely wounded, Patterson took command. After losing rudder control from cannon-fire damage, he jockeyed the cutter's twin-engine throttles, successfully dodging repeated bombings until the attack ceased. His actions under fire saved the vessel and surviving crew, for which Patterson received the Bronze Star. (William H. Wolf)

New Times and
New Twists to Old Missions

In 1949, a commission had proposed moving the Coast Guard from the Department of Treasury to the Department of Commerce, and when this came up again some years later, the commandant, Admiral Alfred Richmond, managed to defeat it. In 1966, however, while the Coast Guard was waging its Brown Water War, President Lyndon Johnson was making plans for a new cabinet-level organization, the Department of Transportation. To many, including Commandant Willard Smith and Secretary of the Treasury Henry Fowler, there was no doubt Johnson intended to place the Coast Guard within the new department. When objections arose, the president assured them, in effect, that he could do as he pleased. And he did. In April of 1967, the Coast Guard was formally transferred to the newly created Department of Transportation.

As the war in Vietnam wound down, the Coast Guard suddenly confronted organized smuggling on a scale not seen since Prohibition, and the service was called on to fight an escalating Drug War against criminals as ruthless as any bootleggers. Thirty years later that war is still being waged.

Humanitarian missions, too, continued to test Coast Guard resourcefulness. After the initial flood of refugees from Cuba in the early years of the Castro regime, the problem waned for a time. Then suddenly, in April 1980, the Cuban Government authorized the departure from the port of Mariel of any citizens who wanted to leave. Several hundred small American boats, many of them by no means seaworthy, made the trip from Florida to shuttle the Cuban exiles to the United States.

Surprised by Castro's sudden announcement and the ensuing flotilla of small craft, the Coast Guard was nonetheless able to organize the largest peacetime operation in its history. Reservists were called up, and through speedy action by the service, some 125,000 Cuban immigrants arrived safely in the United States with the loss of only twenty-seven lives. Given the overloading of boats, their unsuitability for the passage, and

Above, left: Women's uniforms present more than just a military look. Attractive styling in clothing is an effective device in recruiting. (Clifford H. Schule, U.S. Coast Guard)

Above, center: Coast Guard and Navy uniforms have been alike for decades with differences only in devices and insignia. To distinguish the Coast Guard from the Navy and emphasize it as a separate organization, new Coast Guard uniforms came into being in the 1970s. (U.S. Coast Guard)

Above, right: As they have throughout the service's long history, today's Coast Guard members "suit up" every morning to take up the challenges on land, sea, and in the air. There are many variations on the workday uniform. However, most common for the mariner is the ubiquitous lifejacket. (Ferdinand Petrie, U.S. Coast Guard)

Two petty officers from Coast Guard Law Enforcement Detachment 406 in Miami, Jeff Turverey (left) and Edgar Figueroa, offload cocaine seized aboard a fishing vessel near Panama. Eight suspects and 3,700 pounds of cocaine from this seizure were transferred to federal law enforcement officials in Florida. (Scott Carr, U.S. Coast Guard)

95

Above: *Coast Guard Seaman Jennifer Mays holds a Haitian child. This youngster is one of 301 rescued Haitian migrants intercepted at sea and rescued by the cutter* Legare *on their attempt to sail to the United States. (U.S. Coast Guard)*

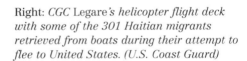

Right: *CGC* Legare's *helicopter flight deck with some of the 301 Haitian migrants retrieved from boats during their attempt to flee to United States. (U.S. Coast Guard)*

Above: *Coast Guard crews aboard the buoy tender* Walnut *and NOAA vessel* Townsend Cromwell *recover more than 57,500 pounds of abandoned fishing nets and human discarded debris from Lisianski Island and Pearl and Hermes Reefs in the Hawaiian Islands chain. The non-biodegradable plastic poses a constant killer for fish, marine mammals, and birds. (Jacquelyn Zettles, U.S. Coast Guard)*

the often-rough seas of the Florida Strait, the whole operation might be viewed as something of a miracle.

Over the following years the Coast Guard saved thousands more lives in numerous refugee boatlifts from Haiti and Cuba. In 1995, the cutter *Dauntless* rescued 578 migrants from an appallingly overloaded freighter—a record for the largest number taken off a single ship.

By the 1990s, a new, satellite-enabled technology, GPS, Global Positioning System, rendered many lighthouses obsolete. These were decommissioned, transferred to other agencies, or sold. Prior to this, automation took over the jobs of the lighthouse keepers, finally leaving only a single lighthouse, symbolically that of Boston Harbor, to be manned by the service. An era spanning nearly three centuries had ended.

The twentieth century might be looked back on as an age of the gigantic. Certainly this is so on the world's oceans, where behemoth oil tankers and driftnets nearly 100 miles long made their appearance. Preventing, or at least limiting, the environmental damage caused by the first and protecting marine life from the wanton destruction wrought by the second, remain high priorities of the service. These missions regularly demand the Coast Guard act on a worldwide scale in ways never imagined when it was created, and the service has assisted in international efforts to contain oil spills in such far-flung places as the Straits of Malacca at the equator and the Straits of Magellan near the Antarctic.

The absence of declared wars has never kept the Coast Guard away from military missions. Following the Iraqi invasion of Kuwait in 1990, Coast Guard Law Enforcement Detachments, LEDETs—boarding

teams—arrived in the Persian Gulf embarked on Navy ships to enforce United Nations sanctions. *Operations Desert Shield* and *Desert Storm* required 550 Coast Guard Reservists in three Port Security Units activated, and another 950 Reservists mobilized for vessel inspection and for supervising the loading of hazardous military cargoes. LEDETs also

Petty officer Damon Kizzar, Seaman Adam Walton, and Seaman Luke Pullen recover an abandon driftnet from the Gulf of Mexico. The overwhelming smell of rotten fish causes the crew to feel ill as they tug at the indiscriminant killer. A driftnet traps fish and marine mammals near the surface until the burden of dead carcasses drags it to the bottom where the animals decay. The buoyed net, free from the weight of rotted flesh, eventually rises to the surface beginning once more the cycle of death. Only by removing the net from the water can this pernicious cycle be stopped. (Keith Alholm, U.S. Coast Guard)

Left: *A crew from CGC* Jarvis, *in the ship's small boat, disentangles a sperm whale from abandoned fishing gear in the mid-North Pacific Ocean. The ship came upon the entrapped whale while searching for vessels fishing with illegal driftnets. (U.S. Coast Guard)*

helped in securing Iraqi oil platforms and the capture of twenty-three prisoners. And thirteen years later the Coast Guard would return to the region for *Operation Iraqi Freedom* in 2003.

Years of hard use—and *Semper Paratus*, being always ready—have taken their toll on Coast Guard equipment, and its "deepwater" assets; many of its cutters, patrol boats, and aircraft are reaching the end of their useful service lives. The answer, of course, is to replace as much of the worn-out equipment as possible, which led to the *Integrated Deepwater System Program*, often simply called *Deepwater*, which began in the 1990s and is the largest acquisition in the Coast Guard's history. When completed over the coming years, *Deepwater* promises to leave the service well equipped to handle future missions.

In the aftermath of the September 2001 terrorist attacks against the United States, President George W. Bush signed into legislation a new cabinet-level agency, the Department of Homeland Security. On 1 March 2003, Transportation Secretary Norman Mineta transferred leadership of the Coast Guard to Secretary Tom Ridge's Department of Homeland Security.

As the nation's oldest maritime agency, the Coast Guard traces its ancestral roots back to five federal agencies: the Revenue Cutter Service, the Lighthouse Service, the Steamboat Inspection Service, the Bureau of Navigation, and the Lifesaving Service. During numerous wars it has served under the Navy, and in peace operated within three departments: Treasury, Transportation, and now Homeland Security. Given the service's multitude of missions and responsibilities, who's to say but that this last organization may suit the Coast Guard best.

Or maybe the agency doesn't really matter. It's not the department the Coast Guard finds itself in that counts, but the people—the men and women serving on active-duty, the reservists, Auxiliarists, and the civilian workforce—who for over 200 years have made the service what it is today.

Opposite: Reservist, Petty Officer Bryce Douglas, just returned from overseas duty, shows his emotions as he holds his infant son. (Louis Hebert, U.S. Coast Guard)

Above: National security operations, a longtime Coast Guard role, expand following the Coast Guard moving into the Department of Homeland Security. Monuments in Washington, D.C., are under the watchful eyes of Fireman Janna Mason (left) and Petty Officer Jay Douglas, members of the Coast Guard's boat force located in the U.S. capital, during a security patrol along the Potomac River. (Telfair H. Brown, U.S. Coast Guard)

Left: This guidon is from Marine Safety and Security Team 91101, Seattle. Established in 2002, Marine Safety and Security Teams were modeled after the Coast Guard's Port Security Units and Law Enforcement Detachments. These units, with their boats specially designed for their service, protect military embarkations areas, enforce port security zones, defend waterside facilities in strategic ports, stop illegal activities such as narcotic trafficking and illegal migrant importation, and provide general shoreside protection. (Telfair H. Brown, U.S. Coast Guard)

Backup: Auxiliary, Reserve, & SPARs

John A. Tilley, Ph.D.

The Coast Guard differs from the other armed services in that it regularly calls upon part-time reservists and civilian volunteers to help carry out its missions. Born just before the Second World War, the Coast Guard Auxiliary and the Coast Guard Reserve today are integral components of the Coast Guard's "Total Force."

Volunteerism has a long tradition in the Coast Guard. When the federal government got into the business of maritime lifesaving in 1848, Captain Douglas Ottinger, U.S. Revenue Cutter Service, supervised the construction of a series of wooden sheds along the New Jersey coast. Each of these structures was outfitted with a surfboat, a mortar (for shooting lines to wrecked ships), stocks of ropes and flares, and a water-tight metal "life car" that could be loaded with survivors and hauled along a line from the wreck to the beach. The government paid for all this apparatus, but made no provision for employing people to use it. At each site Captain Ottinger handed some trustworthy-looking local a key to the shed and a set of printed instructions for using the gear. The federal government then officially forgot the matter.

Two years later this casual, if economical, system got a chance to prove itself in dramatic fashion when the British immigrant ship *Ayrshire* piled onto the New Jersey shore in a blizzard. Sailors and fishermen from nearby communities broke out the local lifesaving station's mortar and life car and rescued all but one of the 203 people on board. Those seamen who hauled *Ayrshire* survivors to safety in the middle of that stormy night in 1850 were, in a sense, the ancestors of the modern Coast Guard Auxiliary.

During the 1930s pleasure boating emerged as an American sport. Companies like Chris-Craft and Dodge were manufacturing motorboats

Coast Guard Auxiliary and Reserve craft at a marina near Wilmington, North Carolina, in World War II. Hundreds of motor boaters and yachtsmen responded to the Coast Guard's call for the loan of small craft that could be used for patrol duty. An Auxiliary boat, designated "CGA," was still operated by its owner, who donated his and its services to the Coast Guard for several hours each week. A boat labeled "CGR" had been lent to the Coast Guard for some agreed-upon period. (East Carolina University)

Opposite: A Coast Guard Auxiliarist helps to right a capsized catamaran. Volunteer Auxiliarists using their own boats frequently assist active duty Coast Guardsmen with search and rescue missions filling in at locations where regular active units may be scarce. An example is inland lakes and reservoirs, where typically there are no Coast Guard units. (U.S. Coast Guard)

The Coast Guard Reserve Act, passed in June 1939, created a civilian force to assist active duty Coast Guardsmen. The reserves were also to promote public awareness in sound boatmanship and water safety measures. Membership was limited to United States citizens who owned boats. (U.S. Coast Guard Auxiliary)

In its original form, the Reserve lasted less than two years. With war looming, Congress restructured the Coast Guard Reserve by splitting it into two forces. The civilian reserve became the Coast Guard Auxiliary and the Coast Guard Reserve became a military manpower source, similar to the reserves of the other armed forces. These boats underway in Florida in 1942 were part of the newly named Auxiliary. (U.S. Coast Guard Auxiliary)

The idea of a civilian reserve organization quickly caught the public's favor. By June of 1940—a year after its inception—the Coast Guard Reserve had enrolled 2,600 men and 2,300 boats. The yacht Spindrift, shown here in 1940, was typical of the boats acquired. (U.S. Coast Guard Auxiliary)

the upper middle class, at least, could buy in considerable numbers. By the end of the decade, despite the pressures of the Great Depression, over 300,000 motorboats and 4,000 sailing yachts with auxiliary power were registered in the United States.

Presiding over this congenial armada, at least in theory, was the Coast Guard, whose mission included enforcement of federal laws and safety standards relating to recreational watercraft. Limited finances, however, undermined the Coast Guard's ability to carry out that mandate as budget cuts reduced the service's manpower to about 10,000 officers and enlisted men. Few of those personnel were stationed on inland waterways, where the majority of pleasure boats operated, and most of the Coast Guard's energy was siphoned off by its other duties.

The Army and Navy had reserve forces—sizeable organizations of veterans and other trained personnel who were paid modest salaries to stay in training and make themselves available in an emergency. The idea of creating a similar Coast Guard reserve had surfaced occasionally, but the federal government had never acted on it. In the summer of 1934 a Hollywood scriptwriter and amateur sailor named Malcolm Stuart Boylan was elected commodore of the Pacific Writers' Yacht Club. When that organization laid plans to make a cruise from its home in Los Angeles to Catalina Island, Boylan asked a Coast Guard acquaintance, Lieutenant Commander C. W. Thomas of CGC Hermes, to inspect the club's boats before their departure. Another of Hermes's officers, Lieutenant F. C. Pollard, made the trip to Catalina on board Boylan's yacht, and the two men had a long discussion about the relationship between the Coast Guard and the boating community. Following their talk, Boylan sent Pollard a letter outlining a basic concept for a Coast Guard reserve:

> *My dear Lieutenant:*
> *I have been dwelling on our recent conversations concerning the Coast Guard and your most informative explanation of its origin, traditions, and function. Out of this, the thought has come to me that the Coast Guard alone of all the armed services has no organized reserve. . . . A Coast Guard Reserve would be an excellent thing to perpetuate its traditions, preserve its entity, and, more particularly, to place at the disposal of CG officers, auxiliary flotillas of small craft for the frequent emergencies incident to your . . . duties.*

A copy of Boylan's letter made its way to Washington and to the desk of Commander Russell R. Waesche, an aide to the Commandant of the Coast Guard. Waesche saw merit in the idea, but it languished for some five years. In 1936 when Waesche was appointed Commandant the creation of a Coast Guard reserve became one of his favorite projects. With the backing of the Secretary of the Treasury, the Secretary of the Navy, and several influential Congressmen, Waesche finally was able to gain Congressional approval.

The Coast Guard Reserve Act of 1939, passed in June of that year, created a unique institution and gave the new Reserve the broadly defined purposes of promoting safety on the water, boatmanship, knowledge of

German submarines sinking ships along America's East Coast drove the desperate U.S. Navy to commandeer "the maximum practical number of civilian craft in any way capable of going to sea in good weather for a period of at least forty-eight hours." These were manned by the Coast Guard Reserve "and operated along the 50-fathom curve of the Atlantic and Gulf Coasts." Brightly painted yachts with once-fancy names, went to sea in Navy-gray paint with numbers and "CGR" painted on their bows, and depth charges stowed inelegantly on their decks. Not one of the 2,000 CGR craft ever sank a submarine. (U.S.Coast Guard)

laws and regulations, and assistance of the Coast Guard. Membership was to be limited to United States citizens who owned boats.

While the Army and Navy Reserves were conceived as readily available sources of trained manpower in the event of war—many Army and Navy Reservists were World War I veterans—the new Coast Guard Reserve was to be a civilian organization. Members were not to hold military ranks, wear uniforms, receive military training, or "be vested with or exercise any right, privilege, power, or duty vested in or imposed upon the personnel of the Coast Guard." Reservists were invited to place their boats at the disposal of the Coast Guard "in the conduct of duties incident to the saving of life and property and in the patrol of marine parades and regattas"—with the understanding that each boat would be commanded by a regular Coast Guard officer or petty officer.

Nor were Coast Guard Reservists to be considered government employees. Apart from a provision that "appropriations for the Coast Guard shall be available for the payment of actual necessary expenses of operation of any such motorboat or yacht when so utilized" (i.e., the Coast Guard would pay for the gas), it was expected that the Reserve would cost the government no money whatsoever.

The idea of a civilian reserve organization was new, and no one could have been blamed for being skeptical about it. Initial membership benefits consisted of the right to buy a Coast Guard Reserve ensign (a blue rectangular flag bearing the Coast Guard emblem in white, with "United States Coast Guard Reserve" in the ring around the shield) and a lapel pin. The response in both the Coast Guard and the civilian boating community was, however, remarkably enthusiastic. By June of 1940 Commander Merlin O'Neill, the first chief director, had enrolled 2,600 men and 2,300 boats in the Coast Guard Reserve. With the support of Admiral Waesche, Coast Guard bases began offering training courses for reservists. Those who passed the courses were appointed to three reserve grades: Senior Navigator, Navigator, and Engineer.

A Coast Guard Auxiliary uniform cap device. Auxiliary insignia devices are in silver, where similar devices used on active duty Coast Guard uniforms are gold. (George Datz, U.S. Coast Guard Auxiliary)

Coast Guard Reservists in a signal class at New Brunswick, New Jersey, in 1941. Active duty Coast Guard members welcomed the addition of Reservists and Auxiliarists helping keep up with the staggering demands for personnel during the war. (U.S. Coast Guard Auxiliary)

In its original form the Reserve lasted less than two years. By early 1941 the Coast Guard was preparing for war, and events in Europe warned of the demands for manpower and boats the service could expect when the United States entered the Second World War. In February 1941 Congress passed a law restructuring the Coast Guard Reserve. Henceforth the Coast Guard was to operate two reserve forces. The existing civilian reserve organization was renamed the U.S. Coast Guard Auxiliary. A new U.S. Coast Guard Reserve was to be a source of wartime military manpower, like the reserves of the other armed services.

The officers running the Coast Guard appreciated the staggering demands that war would put on it and the value of the new reserve system in helping them meet those demands. By the summer of 1941 the district commanders were sending Coast Guard headquarters lists of Auxiliarists-owned boats that would make good patrol craft, and requisitioning Lewis machine guns, Thompson submachine guns, rifles, and pistols for them.

In November 1941, President Roosevelt ordered the transfer of the Coast Guard from the Treasury Department to the Navy Department. Five weeks later, Waesche got his chance to find out whether the system he had designed would work.

First Lady Eleanor Roosevelt (seated) transported by a Coast Guard Auxiliary boat during a 1943 visit to Seattle, Washington. The Auxiliary, a civilian volunteer adjunct to the Coast Guard, began in 1939 under the name Coast Guard Reserve. In 1941, Congress restructured the Reserve. The civilian component became the Coast Guard Auxiliary and the military segment became the Coast Guard Reserve. (East Carolina University)

Reservists and Auxiliarists Go to War

During the Second World War the Coast Guard underwent the most dramatic expansion in its history. The coming of war changed Admiral Waesche from the head of a small military service most Americans ignored most of the time into a key player in the war effort. Waesche understood from the beginning that the Coast Guard was going to have to preside over a range of activities far wider than any peacetime duties. One response was to expand the roles of the Coast Guard Reserve and the Coast Guard Auxiliary. In the first few weeks of the war no one in Washington or elsewhere was quite sure what the wartime function of the Auxiliary should be. Within a year after Pearl Harbor, however, the Auxiliary had become a major, if frequently unrecognized, supporter of the Coast Guard's military effort.

The Coast Guard, like the Army and Navy, used its Reserve for a massive expansion of personnel. Waesche and his staff created a complex but flexible administrative system that let the service put all available personnel, including thousands of people who otherwise would not have been eligible for military service, to constructive use.

More than 92 percent of the 214,000 men and women who wore Coast Guard uniforms during the war were "Active Duty Regular Reservists." They served full-time, were paid for their services, had to meet normal military physical standards, and could be assigned to stations anywhere the Coast Guard deemed appropriate. Coast Guard Regular Reservists served in all theaters of the war.

Individuals who could not pass the physical examination to get into the Coast Guard might become volunteers called Temporary Reservists, TR. Applicants without regard to age and reasonably healthy could be a TR serving their country. An art class student designs a poster for a recruiting campaign to enroll TRs for waterfront duty. (Coast Guard Museum Northwest)

Auxiliary craft manned by civilian volunteers early in World War II patrolling U.S. waters came in such a variety that the force was tagged with names like "Putt-Putt Fleet" and "Corsair Fleet." The Walt Disney Corporation designed this unofficial logo for this coastal picket force. (Courtesy Walt Disney Enterprises, Inc.)

Those who were unable to meet the physical requirements of the "Regular Reserve" were invited to become "Temporary Members of the Reserve." A "Coast Guard TR" was a volunteer who served in some designated geographic area, usually near his home or workplace, and less than full-time. TRs ages ranged in age between seventeen and seventy, meeting physical requirements that were not very stringent. In the Boston District, for instance, anyone who could climb the four flights of stairs to the TR recruiting office was deemed eligible.

During the Second World War, the Auxiliary served as the Coast Guard's general-purpose wartime assistant. Members were invited to enroll in the Reserve as TRs and bring their boats with them. The distinction between Temporary Reservist and Auxiliarists frequently was blurry, particularly after May 1942, when Auxiliarists were authorized to wear uniforms. In some districts the Auxiliary, as a 1943 directive put it, functioned as "a civilian organization which is engaged in the training of its members to qualify them for active duty whenever needed with the CG, as temporary members of the CG Reserve." In others, the jobs performed by Auxiliarists and Reservists were virtually indistinguishable. No one seemed to mind.

Early in 1942 five German U-boats arrived off the east coast of the United States, inaugurating the heartbreaking season known as "Bloody Winter." The Navy and the Coast Guard, woefully short of escort vessels with the necessary anti-submarine weaponry, could do little to keep the U-boats from running amok in the shipping lanes.

In desperation the Navy ordered the acquisition of "the maximum practical number of civilian craft in any way capable of going to sea in good weather for a period of at least 48 hours . . . to be manned by the Coast Guard as an expansion of the Coast Guard Reserve . . . and operated along the fifty-fathom curve of the Atlantic and Gulf Coasts." Motorboats and sailing yachts, with numbers preceded by "CGR" painted on their bows and depth charges stowed awkwardly on their decks, began appearing on patrol stations all along the coasts. Many were donated by temporary members of the Reserve, or bought outright by the Coast Guard. Others were owned and manned by Auxiliarists. Known variously as "the Putt-Putt Navy," "the Splinter Fleet," and "the Corsair Fleet," they made up much of the American response to the U-boat threat in coastal waters during the early months of the war. As newly constructed warships took over the load, the Coast Guard abandoned the concept. None of the 2,000 CGR craft ever sank a submarine, but they rescued several hundred survivors of torpedoed merchant ships and may have driven some U-boats away from tempting cruising grounds.

Perhaps the Auxiliary's most important contribution to the war effort came in the form of the Volunteer Port Security Force. An executive order of February 1942 directed the Secretary of the Navy to take the necessary steps to prevent "sabotage and subversive activities" on the nation's waterfronts. The task of protecting the hundreds of warehouses, piers, and other facilities that kept the American shipping industry in business fell to the Coast Guard, which in turn delegated it to the Reserve and the Auxiliary.

Early in World War II German submarines operated off the east coast of the United States with little fear of detection. This spurred the acquisition of civilian craft as an interim means of defense. In March 1942, a German submarine only sixteen miles off North Carolina torpedoed this loaded tanker. (U.S. Coast Guard)

A Coast Guard Temporary Reservist (TR) boat returns from patrol. A Coast Guard TR was a volunteer who served usually near his home or workplace and less than full time. (U.S. Coast Guard Auxiliary)

Opposite: *This sleek schooner, armed with depth charges and manned by Coast Guard Reservists, searched the North Atlantic for German submarines. Other similar yachts operated along all United States' coasts. (U.S. Coast Guard)*

CGR 52, formerly named Poodle Pup, *serving as a harbor patrol boat in World War II. It carried Coast Guard personnel out to board and inspect incoming merchant vessels. (U.S. Coast Guard)*

A luxurious seventy-three-foot cabin cruiser becomes a rakish Coast Guard Reserve patrol boat. Famous film stars of the period donated their yachts to the service. (U.S. Coast Guard)

With the constant threat from German submarines prowling the American coast, civilian craft manned by Reservists, Auxiliarists, and Temporary Reservists put to sea sometimes in grueling weather conditions for anti-submarine patrols. Although there is no record of these eclectic vessels sinking a U-boat, their crews did rescue hundreds of survivors from torpedoed ships and their presence likely drove away some submarines. (U.S. Coast Guard Auxiliary)

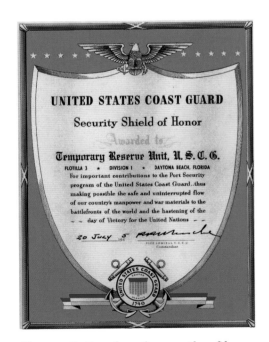

The contributions from the more than fifty thousand temporary reserve members were indispensable. Their presence relieved thousands of Coast Guardsmen for duty overseas. At the end of World War II, these individuals were awarded the Victory Medal. Temporary Reserve Units were given the Temporary Reserve Certificate. (U.S. Coast Guard Auxiliary)

In each port city a Coast Guard officer with the title Captain of the Port was placed in charge of a Port Security Force, consisting of TRs, Auxiliarists, and other civilians recruited for the purpose. The precise organizational structure varied from city to city. The Coast Guard set up a Reserve Training School in Philadelphia to train TRs in such subjects as anti-espionage methods, fire prevention, customs inspections, and small arms handling. Eventually some 20,000 Reservists and Auxiliarists participated in port security patrols. About 2,000 women enrolled as "TR SPARs," attending to the mountainous paperwork that dispatched ships, cargoes, and troops overseas.

As the war progressed and the Coast Guard's resources were stretched thinner, Auxiliarists and TRs were called upon to fill gaps left by active duty Coast Guardsmen. Auxiliarists' boats patrolled the waterfronts and inlets looking for saboteurs, enemy agents, and fires. Temporary Reservists, recruited from the Auxiliary, patrolled beaches on horseback. Other Auxiliarists manned lookout and lifesaving stations near their homes, freeing regular Coast Guardsmen for sea duty. When a flood struck St. Louis in the spring of 1943, Coast Guard Auxiliarists and Reservists evacuated 7,000 people and thousands of animals.

The Auxiliary and the Reserve attracted their share of celebrity members. Actor Humphrey Bogart took his yacht on several patrols out of Los Angeles, and Arthur Fiedler, conductor of the Boston Pops Orchestra, put in his twelve hours per week on patrol duty in Boston Harbor.

By 1945 the Coast Guard Auxiliary boasted a membership of 67,533, and 53,214 men and women (most of them Auxiliarists) were serving as temporary members of the Reserve. At the end of the war the Temporary Reserve program was abandoned, and all Coast Guard TRs were "honorably disenrolled." Many remained Auxiliarists for years afterward. Wartime service had earned them no veterans' benefits and precious little other public recognition. In 1946 the TRs were awarded the Victory Medal. Auxiliarists who had not joined the Reserve had to be satisfied with thanks from Waesche: *"The Auxiliary during the war years was indispensable. Many thousands of you served faithfully and loyally as Auxiliarists and as temporary members of the CG Reserve, performing hundreds of tasks and relieving thousands of Coast Guardsmen for duty outside the continental limits. The Coast Guard is deeply appreciative of this service."*

"The Best Clerical Assistance"

When World War II began, the concept of employing women in the armed forces was not new, but neither the military profession nor the government had shown much enthusiasm for it. American society in the early twentieth century saw four spheres of the professional world as proper domains for respectable women: the hospital, the office, the classroom, and the telephone exchange.

During the First World War the United States had undertaken an unprecedented expansion of its armed forces, simultaneously producing a manpower shortage and a stupefying mass of military paperwork. The Department of the Navy, which had been operating an auxiliary Nurse Corps since 1908, concluded with some reluctance that war had created a legitimate role for the woman in uniform. "Enroll women in the Naval Reserve as yeomen," proclaimed Secretary of the Navy Josephus Daniels, "and we will have the best clerical assistance the country can provide."

In March 1917 the Navy Department authorized the enlistment of women in the Naval Reserve, with the rating "Yeomen (F)" and the popular label "Yeomanettes." The Navy's policy was extended to the Coast Guard. Personnel records from World War I contain virtually no references to the Coast Guard Yeomanettes. A handful of them were employed at the diminutive Coast Guard headquarters building in Washington. Nineteen-year-old twin sisters Genevieve and Lucille Baker, who transferred from the Naval Coastal Defense Reserve, seem to have been the first uniformed women in the Coast Guard.

Top and above: *Young women off to war in a new role and uncertainties in a new kind of service, as evident in these official photographs taken in the early 1940s. (U.S. Coast Guard)*

ENLIST WITH
COAST GUARD

SPARS

APPLY NEAREST COAST GUARD OFFICE

SERVE WITH WOMEN'S RESERVE · U.S. COAST GUARD

SPARS

APPLY NEAREST OFFICE OF NAVAL OFFICER PROCUREMENT

ENLIST IN THE COAST GUARD SPARS

RELEASE A MAN TO FIGHT AT SEA

Apply to your nearest
NAVY RECRUITING STATION OR OFFICE OF NAVAL OFFICER PROCUREMEN

With the war's end the Coast Guard Yeomanettes, along with their Navy and Marine Corps counterparts (the Army refused to enlist women, except in its Nursing Corps), were mustered out of the service. Secretary Daniels bade them farewell: "As we embrace you in uniform today, we will embrace you without uniform tomorrow." Between the world wars the only women in the American armed forces were members of the Army and Navy Nursing Corps.

During the Second World War more than 16,000,000 men joined the American armed forces, and the country's industrial and agricultural production was expected to increase in their absence. The Joint Chiefs of Staff, noting the examples provided early in the war by Great Britain and the Soviet Union, realized even before Pearl Harbor that women would have to play a major role in the U.S. war effort.

In November 1942, President Roosevelt signed Public Law 772 of the 77th Congress, 2nd Session, creating the Women's Reserve of the Coast Guard. The purpose of the act was "to expedite the war effort by providing for releasing officers and men for duty at sea and their replacement by women in the shore establishment of the Coast Guard and for other purposes."

The Women's Reserve was modeled on the one the Navy created a few months earlier. Two restrictions placed on the use of Navy women were carried over to the Coast Guard: Women were not to serve outside the continental United States, and no woman, officer or enlisted, was empowered to issue orders to any male Coast Guardsman.

The armed forces, never having confronted the prospect of organizing a large contingent of young women, sought help from the academic world. Lieutenant Dorothy C. Stratton, USN, former Professor of Psychology and Dean of Women at Purdue University, agreed to transfer to the Coast Guard, and, with the rank of lieutenant commander, became Director of the Coast Guard Women's Reserve.

An informal proposal to call the Coast Guard women WORCOGS was mercifully abandoned. It was Commander Stratton who suggested that the Women's Reserve be known by the acronym SPARs, based on the Coast Guard motto: "*Semper Paratus*, Always Ready." By early 1943 the WAAC and WAVE recruiting posters on post office walls and phone poles were joined by placards urging women to "Make a Date With Uncle Sam," "Release a Man to Fight At Sea," and "Enlist in the Coast Guard SPARs."

Initially the Coast Guard estimated it would need 8,000 enlisted women and 400 women officers, with a recruiting target of 500 enlisted and twenty-five officers per month. Applicants were to be between twenty and thirty-six years-old—the maximum age for officers was fifty—and have no children under the age of eighteen. Enlisted women were required to have completed two years of high school and officers at least two years of college. Married women could enlist provided their husbands were not in the Coast Guard. Unmarried women had to agree not to marry until after finishing their period of training. After training, a SPAR could marry a civilian or a serviceman not in the Coast Guard. A SPAR who became pregnant was expected to "submit her resignation promptly."

CAPTAIN DOROTHY STRATTON

Captain Dorothy C. Stratton, USCG (Ret), was born in the nineteenth century and remained an active and inspirational leader in the twenty-first. She was a pioneer for women in the Coast Guard, leading the way for women in all the military services.

Stratton, a preacher's daughter, was born in 1899. After obtaining a Ph.D. from Columbia University she went on to become Dean of Women and a professor of psychology at Purdue University. At Purdue, where male students outnumbered females by a ratio of seven-to-one, she began a program to encourage women's studies.

"I tried from the beginning to establish a more positive atmosphere," Stratton recalled. Hoping to move women away from traditional roles by making science more appealing to them, she devised a women's curriculum. The enrollment of women at the university more than doubled.

Believing the military opened a new avenue for women, in June 1942, on a leave of absence from Purdue, Stratton joined the Army and served on a selection board for the first group of WAC officers. Later that summer Stratton joined the Navy's Women Appointed Volunteer Emergency Service (WAVES) and following graduation from the first WAVE class at U.S. Naval

Training Station at Smith College, received a commission in the Navy. Her first assignment was at the Naval Training Station, Madison, Wisconsin. Almost immediately she changed direction once more. In November the law establishing the Coast Guard Women's Reserve was signed by the president. Stratton was summoned to Washington, D.C., to begin as director, and first woman officer, in the newly created Coast Guard's women's corps.

Following her Coast Guard service in 1946, Stratton was awarded the Legion of Merit by Commandant Admiral Joseph F. Farley, who described her as "a brilliant organizer and administrator" with "a keen understanding of the abilities of women and the tasks suited to their performance." In accepting the award, Stratton pointed out that "the Coast Guard utilized the highest percentage of women of any of the services. This is adequate testimony to the adaptability of the Coast Guard, and to the ability of the women who entered its service."

Following her war duties Stratton became the director of personnel for the International Monetary Fund and national executive director of the Girl Scouts of America. When asked why she left her university position, she replied, "I was willing to do whatever I could to serve my country."

Following the attack on the World Trade Center in 2001, the alert and sprightly 102-year-old Stratton reportedly once more offered her services to the Coast Guard.

Captain Dorothy Stratton, director of the Coast Guard's SPARs, enjoys a light moment with other Coast Guard women. She originated the name SPAR, an acronym of the service's motto: *Semper Paratus*—Always Ready. (U.S. Coast Guard)

The first 153 enlisted SPARs and fifteen SPAR officers were former WAVES who, under an arrangement worked out by the Navy Department, agreed to be discharged from the Navy and join the Coast Guard. Several were promptly assigned as recruiters and dispatched throughout the country with the mission of convincing the populace that the Coast Guard offered a proper career for young women.

Recruiters were told not to sit in their offices and wait for women to walk in, but to "go out in the field to talk to prospects and their families." At least one recruiting office took that advice literally, sending its staff on treks through the cotton fields of the South to seek potential SPARs. Recruiters climbed to the stages of movie theaters between double features to remind women of their patriotic duty. "Mobile units" traveled the country in jeeps with "Don't Be a Spare—Be a SPAR" painted on the spare tires. A song-and-dance show called "Tars and Spars" played in the cities of the East Coast.

Opposite, top to bottom: *Recruiting posters for the SPAR purveyed the wholesome, businesslike, but distinctly feminine image that the armed forces wanted the public to see in a woman in uniform. (U.S. Coast Guard)*

111

The corner drug store opposite the Coast Guard training station at Palm Beach, Florida, was frequented for socializing and enjoying ice cream. (U.S. Coast Guard)

Military training for the first women recruits followed a similar plan used for men at the time. They, too, had to learn the fundamentals of marching. However, posed images such as this always show perfection in any task they are performing. (U.S. Coast Guard)

Opposite: *Reveille at the SPAR training station in Palm Beach, Florida. (U.S. Coast Guard)*

Recruiters confronted some serious obstacles, for military women were experiencing an image problem. In 1943 a bizarre nationwide rumor gave rise to public speculation about the nature of the American woman in uniform. One version had it that the female recruiting effort was a front for a government-sponsored prostitution ring, the function of which was to satisfy the ravenous sexual appetites of soldiers and sailors. Each uniformed woman supposedly was receiving a monthly issue of prophylactics to help her accomplish her mission. The story probably originated as a fantasy in a male barracks, but soon newspaper editors and clergymen were warning decent parents not to sell their daughters into slavery.

The Coast Guard constructed a much different image of the real SPAR: an attractive, wholesome, high-spirited young woman with impeccable grooming habits, perfect teeth, and no ambitions beyond serving her country, "freeing a man for sea duty," and getting married, preferably after the war. The SPARs adopted a slightly modified version of the WAVE uniform, which had been designed by Mainbocher of New York, a women's fashion firm. Newspapers and magazines were bombarded with glossy prints of SPARs smiling as they marched in formation, smiling at depth charges, smiling over steaming cook pots, smiling at assorted vehicles, and smiling at male Coast Guardsmen. One managed to look as though she was smiling while blowing a bugle. There is almost no such thing as a casual photograph of a World War II SPAR.

To train the new recruits, the Coast Guard again relied on assistance from academe. The first enlisted SPARs were former WAVES who had received their basic training at Oklahoma A&M University in Stillwater. When civilian women began joining the SPARs they were sent to Iowa

SPARs learning to be radio operators in typing and code class at radio school in Atlantic City, New Jersey. (Courtesy of Lois Bouton)

Right: No task was shunned by SPARs, not even loading aerial ordnance. (U.S. Coast Guard)

Above: SPARs attending cooks and bakers school refine their food preparation skills to learn how to make huge meals to feed the complements of Coast Guard units. (U.S. Coast Guard)

Right: SPARs were not shy about wearing a little grease makeup on the job, as an official caption might say in the period. However, like most official photographs of the early years of women in the service, their novelty was emphasized with a little dramatic license. (U.S. Coast Guard)

State Teachers College, in Cedar Falls. A joint training center for WAVES and SPARs was established at Hunter College in New York City.

In the middle of 1943 the Coast Guard set up its own indoctrination facility in what had been the Biltmore Hotel in Palm Beach, Florida. The slogan "Train under the Florida sun" was added to the recruiters' arsenal, and during the next eighteen months more than 7,000 SPARs received basic training at Palm Beach. The original four-week course was eventually expanded to six weeks.

After graduation the new SPARs were ordered to various specialized schools throughout the country, where they received the same training as their male counterparts. Late in the war, as the SPAR recruiting effort met its targets and the number of new recruits slowed, the Palm Beach facility shut down and newly enlisted women were trained alongside enlisted men at the Coast Guard training facility in Manhattan Beach, New York.

Coast Guard enlisted men were assigned specialties when they enlisted, but the service's initial policy was to give all enlisted SPARs the

rating of seaman second class, the same as men graduating from boot camp. It was assumed a woman could not bring any useful civilian skills other than typing or working a telephone switchboard into the military. Then a former policewoman demonstrated in boot camp that she knew how to shoot, and a former professional photographer suggested she could qualify as a photographer's mate. War introduced a flexibility that no American armed service ever demonstrated in peacetime. The policy changed, and by the end of the war, SPARs held forty-three different rates ranging from boatswain's mate to yeoman.

The first 200 SPAR officers were trained at a Navy facility on the campus of Smith College, a women's school in Northampton, Massachusetts. The Coast Guard realized, however, that it needed an indoctrination facility for its own female officers. In June 1943 the U.S. Coast Guard Academy at New London, Connecticut, opened its doors to women for the first time when a class of fifty SPAR officer candidates reported for indoctrination. SPAR officers, like male reserve officers, went through a streamlined program crammed into six weeks (later lengthened to eight) that bore little resemblance to the Academy's peacetime academic curriculum. But in using its service academy to train women the Coast Guard was taking a step that none of the other armed services emulated. More than 700 of the 955 SPAR officers commissioned during the war received their training at New London.

Air control operators give a pre-flight briefing to a pilot, one of many new roles for women in uniform. (U.S. Coast Guard)

Above: *While the wartime SPAR was destined to operate little more than a typewriter, some women trained with weapons. However, women were never considered for combat duty. (U.S. Coast Guard)*

Above: *SPARs learning parachute fundamentals taking part in a risky practice. (U.S. Coast Guard)*

Left: *Officers check out their sidearms before making a courier run carrying classified documents according to original press releases. (U.S. Coast Guard)*

115

SPARs were assigned only stateside until late in World War II, when some were finally deployed to Alaska and Hawaii. Ordinary transportation was by ship during that period, not aircraft as was later common. (U.S. Coast Guard)

Women typically were assigned duties that relieved men for combat. Most assignments involved clerical tasks, but women also filled some specialized jobs such as medical technicians from the tradition at the time that women were natural nurses. (U.S. Coast Guard)

Opposite, bottom: A traditional role for women in the 1930s and 1940s, along with the expected jobs of secretary or nurse, was telephone operator. The service had need for a great number of women in this task as well. (U.S. Coast Guard)

"I Don't Suppose You Could Take a Letter"

The largest single employer of SPARs was Coast Guard Headquarters, located in the former (and, rumor had it, condemned) Southern Railway Building at 1300 E Street in Washington. As the war went on, most of the clerical work in the eight-story structure came to be done by SPARs and female civilian employees.

Wartime Washington was hard pressed to find room for all the military women and civilian "government girls" who were crowding into the city. They were jammed into every building the government could locate that could accommodate a few bunks. SPAR Betty Splaine recalled how fortunate she felt when she and three other SPARs, after being shuttled from an insect-infested rooming house to the Plaza Hotel, were billeted in a dean's office at American University: "It had wall-to-wall carpeting, so we got individual solid maple beds rather than iron bunk beds." Eventually the SPARs were moved into a row of temporary barracks, named after Coast Guard cutters, on Independence Avenue.

Admiral Waesche was an early convert to the cause of the SPARs. Stratton asserted afterward "the thing that made the SPARs successful was the support of the Commandant." Not every male Coast Guardsman showed the same inclination. When Splaine reported for duty at Headquarters, the officer in charge of her office gave her a look of utter disgust and assigned her to a desk behind his, so he would not have to look at a woman in uniform. He refused to assign her any duties, and virtually ignored her until one day when his civilian secretary called in sick. The officer turned to the SPAR and said, "I don't suppose you could take a letter." She in fact could take shorthand faster than he could dictate, and soon was doing most of the clerical work in the office.

Late in 1942 the Coast Guard began setting up a new electronic navigation system called loran. The highly classified loran was futuristic in its sophistication; its existence was made public only after the war. Reports from the British Royal Air Force, whose WAAF radar operators had helped win the Battle of Britain, probably were instrumental in convincing the Coast Guard that a loran station would be an appropriate billet for SPARs. In the summer of 1943 Lieutenant (jg) Victoria Hamerschlag took command of the Chatham, Massachusetts, loran monitor station, which consisted of a 30-by-50-foot, one-story building and a 125-foot tower on a beach at Cape Cod. The eleven SPARs under Hamerschlag's command had responsibility for ascertaining and maintaining the accuracy of transmissions from several other loran stations on the east coast. The duty involved monitoring and recording those transmissions every two minutes, twenty-four hours a day. The SPARs were told "don't even think loran," and never to give anyone in or out of the service any hint of what was happening inside the mysterious building.

The policy of denying women authority over men inevitably created practical problems, particularly when female officers were assigned to stations that had male Coast Guardsmen on staff. The Coast Guard eventually got around the difficulty by means of an opinion from the Navy Judge Advocate General's office dated November 1943. The JAG concluded that the prohibition applied "only to authority which pertains to command," and that "the authority of [a] subordinate officer as a representative of the officer in command has full legal effect in the execution of his regulations, instructions and policies. The fact that the subordinate is a member of the Women's Reserve does not alter the effect." In other words, a SPAR could give orders to a male Coast Guardsman so long as her commanding officer was a man.

On 27 September 1944, Congress revised the law prohibiting WAVES and SPARs from serving outside the continental United States. Henceforth, SPARs with good records who requested such duty could be stationed in American overseas territories. The war in Europe was over by this time, but about 200 SPARs were sent to Alaska and 200 more to Hawaii before VJ Day.

In October 1944 the Secretary of the Navy ordered the WAVES and SPARs to begin accepting African-American recruits. The first black SPAR was Yeoman Second Class Olivia J. Hooker. By then the SPARs' initial recruiting goals almost had been achieved, and the service had stopped accepting civilian women for officer training. A few African-American enlisted women did go through OCS and were commissioned as ensigns before the end of the war. The personnel records are silent regarding the total number of black SPARs who enlisted in the three months before the recruiting effort began to shut down.

Publicity on the new face of women in the military went out with the same care as a movie star's promotional photographs. (U.S. Coast Guard)

SPARS did take on active roles outside the traditionally portrayed office duty. Women did assist with the ground details around aircraft such as refueling and cleaning. (U.S. Coast Guard)

The SPARs had enlisted for "duration plus six" — the length of the war plus six months. SPAR recruiting virtually ended in December 1944. Shortly after the surrender of Japan the women's reserve branches of all the services were disbanded, and the SPARs officially ceased to exist, although the label was still being applied informally to female Coast Guardsmen in the 1960s. During the next few years the federal government seems largely to have forgotten about the SPARs; many of the records of the Women's Reserve were destroyed. But the SPARs never forgot the years they had spent in uniform. Dorothy Gleason, who enlisted in 1943 and had just been commissioned an ensign when she was demobilized, recalled the pride she and her fellow SPARs felt at having played "an active part at a crucial time in our country's history. . . . We were the pathfinders; we ended up doing many things because we showed we could."

Above: *Following World War II, when most women returned to civilian life and no more were recruited, SPARS virtually disbanded. Uniformed women in the ranks were rarely seen for the next twenty years. However, with the equal rights movement, women came back to the service beginning in 1974. That year, mixed gender basic training began when the first group of women ever enlisted as "Regulars" reported to basic training at Cape May, New Jersey. The Coast Guard was the first military service academy to admit women. This happened in 1976. Finally, women came into the ranks as equals to their male counterparts. All roles were opened from this time forward to women in the Coast Guard. (U.S. Coast Guard)*

Left: *Having just heard the announcement that the Japanese surrendered, SPARs and TARs at district headquarters display their feelings. (U.S. Coast Guard)*

The Reserves

In June 1950, the United States found itself engaged in a "police action" in Korea. The military activity in the Far East produced a surge in the American merchant marine and a correspondingly heightened concern about port security. The Commandant, Admiral O'Neill, requested $4 million to activate the Coast Guard Reserve. Congress appropriated $1 million.

About 500 former Coast Guard officers and 4,500 enlisted men were called back to active duty in the Reserve and assigned to the major port cities, with the duty of guarding shipments of military supplies against Communist saboteurs. Those units established during the Korean conflict became the nucleus of the Coast Guard Reserve as it exists today. When the Korean "police action" ended most members remained active

Opposite: *The SPAR, the Women's Reserve of the Coast Guard, was inactivated in 1947 but reactivated in 1950. Legislation in 1973 finally ended the Woman's Reserve. Women for the first time were integrated on an equal bases with men into the Coast Guard. Today it is common to see women serving in all positions that once were considered males-only tasks. (Norma Johansen Struck, U.S. Coast Guard Art Collection)*

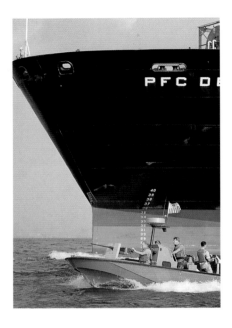

Top, left: *Coast Guard Reservists receive combat training at the U.S. Marine Corps' training site in Quantico, Virginia, for their job in port security. Among them are the Port Security units, which normally deploy overseas during war or conflict to protect American shipping interests. However the reserve port-security units were instantly activated following the September 11 attack to protect major ports and sensitive target areas within the continental United States. (U.S. Coast Guard)*

Top, center: *A United States Coast Guard port security "raider" boat crewed by Reservists escorts ships carrying American war materials into Jubayl, Saudi Arabia. The Coast Guard meets vessels at the sea buoy and shadows them safely into the harbor. (U.S. Coast Guard)*

Top, right: *Port Security Reservist Mike Jajner catches up on his letter writing between patrols. Boat crews patrol two hours, then are on standby for two hours, repeating this schedule around the clock. (U.S. Coast Guard)*

Right: *Filling sandbags may not be fun work, but it is necessary for these Coast Guard Reservists during the Persian Gulf War to fortify their outpost. (U.S. Coast Guard)*

Above: *Reservist Bob Miller checks engines on a Saudi Frontier Forces patrol boat. About once a week the Saudis would bring a boat over to the Coast Guard pier to have things fixed. The man in the blue coveralls is an Egyptian working for the Saudi Coast Guard. (U.S. Coast Guard)*

in the Reserves, attending regular drill weekend sessions and two-week summer training programs.

If the 1970s were years of only modest growth for the Auxiliary they were even rougher for the regular Coast Guard and the Reserve. The Nixon administration, as part of its effort to shrink the federal budget, proposed that the Coast Guard Reserve be phased out of existence. A Congressional debate in 1971 concluded that the Reserve should be retained, but with the proviso that the Coast Guard define a specific peacetime mission for it. In the following year Congress gave the Coast Guard authority to issue "involuntary recalls" of Reservists for peacetime disasters. Individual Coast Guard units also were invited to call on Reservists whenever extra hands were needed, and in those days of steadily shrinking Coast Guard resources, it frequently did. An "Augmentation Training Program" was established as a means of training Reservists for specific jobs. During the fiscal year 1973 Reservists performed nearly 2,000,000 hours of augmentation training.

Reserves Today

Captain John Dwyer, USCGR

The use of the Reserves in units separate from Regular forces increased in the 1980s. One notable use was in overseas expeditionary-warfare units. Another was maritime defense-zone operations. Regular Coast Guard forces relied on the Reserve's resources extensively for both these tasks. However, Reservists working side by side during their drill periods with active duty members continued. Reservists acquired skills working and training in company with their Regular forces counterparts while on their active duty periods by handling domestic contingencies, such as hurricane and flood responses.

Reserve port security units, beginning in the 1990s, were employed during the First Gulf War's Operations Desert Shield and Desert Storm. A Coast Guard Reserve port-security boat became the first Allied vessel to reenter the liberated Kuwait City's seaport.

By the mid 1990s, however, while the overseas and regional harbor defense missions continued successfully with Coast Guard Reserve support, the program assigning Reservists to work alongside their active duty counterpart had reached a crossroads. In 1995, determining that the active duty's use of Reservists in augmentation roles was inconsistent and often ineffectively applied, the Coast Guard dissolved the separate non-expeditionary warfare Reserve units, integrating them into the active duty units. This resulted in the Reserve being reduced to only 8,000 members from a previous high of over 16,000 during the Vietnam War. Training and use of Reservists generally improved as a result. Even so, the Reserve was still not considered by active duty planners a critical part of the Coast Guard organization. On September 11 that view changed dramatically.

Almost immediately after the attacks, the Coast Guard activated over a third of its Reserve force by recalling 2,623 Reservists—activating them within one month. The Reserve forces recalled to active duty boosted the Coast Guard's active duty strength to 37,671, with Reserve personnel then comprising 7 percent of the active Coast Guard. By October 2002 the number of recalled Reservists on active duty shrank to 698; however, Congress authorized the overall size of the Reserve to expand once more—to 9,000 in fiscal year 2003, and 10,000 in 2004.

This increase proved appropriate, as the reduction in mobilized Reservists was short lived. In 2003 the war in Iraq drove the Reserve recall to the highest level since World War II, with 4,412 Reservists once more mobilized to active duty by April 2003. This represented 56 percent of the total Reserve strength of 7,836 then available, by far the highest percentage of mobilized Reservists of any of the military services. By September 2003 the numbers of recalled Reservists were again reduced, to approximately 240 retained to meet critical requirements in manpower for both homeland security and military operations abroad. However, the continued potential for further terrorist attacks continues to underscore the importance of the Coast Guard Reserve.

Top: A Coast Guard Reservist pulls his guard stint during the Persian Gulf War. (U.S. Coast Guard)

Below: An important port security task overseas is boarding and inspecting boats. Boarding parties in war zones must be ever alert to actions hostile to their presence. (U.S. Coast Guard)

A senior Auxiliarist follows a SAR case in an operations center. A civilian volunteer serving in the Auxiliary can bring many years of experience to aid active duty members solving complex search and rescue problems. They might offer dozens of years of "local knowledge" and familiarity, from navigating on nearby waters to being an encyclopedia of local lore and having specific knowledge of many boats and vessels. (U.S. Coast Guard Auxiliary)

An Auxiliarist examines a compass on a sailboat as part of a courtesy vessel safety check. Boaters who complete boating safety courses and pass these inspections are generally rewarded with lower premiums on their vessels by insurance companies. (U.S. Coast Guard)

The Auxiliary

At the end of World War II Congress reduced the Coast Guard's strength to about 18,000, or about half the number that the Commandant estimated would be necessary to carry out all the service's peacetime missions. The Coast Guard Reserve virtually ceased to exist. Only the Auxiliary was left to plug the voids. During the last months of the war Auxiliarists in various districts held meetings to define how that organization should work.

The war had changed the character of the Auxiliary. It had been conceived as a boaters' organization; during the war the Coast Guard had used it as a means of recruiting and training temporary members of the Reserve. Virtually anybody who wanted to be a Temporary Reservist and could commit the time was welcomed. Many TRs did not own boats and, understandably, took little interest in the old Coast Guard Reserve's peacetime activities.

One subject of argument was the institution's name. The 1939 law had called it simply the U.S. Coast Guard Reserve. That title, however, had been usurped by the military "regular" reserve that had been created in 1941. When the Coast Guard got funding to retain a small military reserve after the war, the civilian institution was left with the label "Coast Guard Auxiliary." That development generated some grumbling; as the minutes of one postwar planning meeting put it, "the present name is too closely allied with women's organizations which are adjunct to military or church groups." But nobody came up with a better one.

On 19 March 1946, the District Commodores and Directors of the Auxiliary convened a three-day conference at Coast Guard Headquarters in Washington. This meeting of Auxiliarists and regular Coast Guard officers produced a blueprint for a streamlined Auxiliary that would function as a civilian arm of the peacetime Coast Guard. Each Auxiliarist would be required to own at least a 25 percent interest in a boat, airplane, or amateur radio station, or "by reason of . . . special training or experience" be "deemed by the Commandant to be qualified for membership in the Auxiliary." Inactive members would be encouraged to disenroll. As a 9th District Coast Guard publication put it, "a smaller number of strong flotillas is better than many weak ones. Get rid of the deadwood. Let's have a well-knit organization of active members—no matter how small. If we are strong and healthy, we will grow." By mid-1947 Auxiliary membership had shrunk to 24,273.

For all outward appearances, Auxiliary logos, badges, and uniforms appear the same as Coast Guard uniforms; however, where gold is used on badges and stripes for the Coast Guard, silver is used on Auxiliarist uniforms and badges. (Paul Mayer, U.S. Coast Guard Auxiliary)

The uniforms of the postwar Coast Guard Auxiliary were similar to those of regular Coast Guard officers, with distinctive Auxiliary buttons and insignia in silver, rather than the gold of the regular Coast Guard. A sleeve badge similar to that of Coast Guard enlisted personnel, minus the eagle, indicated each member's grade and specialty.

The postwar Coast Guard had a congressional mandate to cut its personnel from a wartime high of more than 175,000 to 18,000—before all its military duties were completed. As late as 1947, for example, regular Coast Guardsmen were still staffing several big Army transport vessels that were bringing troops home from Europe and the Far East. The Coast Guard came to rely on the Auxiliary to fill in the gaps. Postwar austerity threatened to close several Coast Guard stations on the Great Lakes; Auxiliarists operated them until the Coast Guard could find the necessary work force. When another series of floods struck the Mississippi Valley in 1947, 9th District Auxiliarists used their boats to evacuate victims and carry supplies.

Airplanes had joined the Auxiliary informally during the Second World War. The first official mention of a Coast Guard Auxiliary pilot dates from 1943. Public Law 451, passed by the Congress in September 1945, added owners of aircraft and radio stations to the list of those eligible for membership in the Auxiliary. Auxiliary aviators were particularly welcome in the late 1940s. The Coast Guard, fully aware of the value of aircraft in its search and rescue missions, had lost most of its regular aviation component to postwar cutbacks.

In the late 1940s, two of what would come to be known as the "four cornerstones" of the modern Auxiliary were established: vessel examination and education. Courtesy Marine Examination, CME, program quickly became one of the Auxiliary's most important assignments. The Coast Guard published a booklet of safety standards and regulations, and gave the Auxiliary the authority to train its own members as inspectors. The recreational boating community accepted the concept with enthusiasm. In May 1947, the Auxiliary issued more than 1,000 CME decals in the Miami area alone.

The Public Education program got under way in January 1948, when Auxiliarists offered a series of free courses at the annual Motorboat

After World War II, the Auxiliary was reaffirmed as a civilian arm of the peacetime Coast Guard. Each Auxiliarist was required to own at least a 25 percent interest in a boat, airplane, amateur radio station, or have some special training or experience. Here, an Auxiliarist pilot undergoes water-survival testing as part of his pilot requalification. (Richard Adomatis, U.S. Coast Guard)

An Auxiliarist in the Boston Lighthouse lens room making weather observation to be called into the Coast Guard operations center on the mainland. (U.S. Coast Guard Auxiliary)

A Coast Guard Auxiliarist conducts free courtesy vessel inspections at the invitation of boat owners. Auxiliarists examine vessels to determine if their safety features meet regulations and seek defects that might lead to unsafe conditions. Auxiliarists frequently offer owners advice and recommendations leading to safe and enjoyable boating experiences. (U.S. Coast Guard Auxiliary)

Auxiliary members, as boat owners, keep up with changes in waterborne craft. The very popular personal watercraft, used as an Auxiliary vessel, is becoming a common sight on safety patrols. Along with being nimble and able to cruise into shallow water, these powerful jet-skis are also capable of towing larger vessels. (Roger Wetherall, U.S. Coast Guard)

Show in New York City's Grand Central Palace. The boating public responded enthusiastically. The organization's tenth anniversary, 23 June 1949, was declared Coast Guard Auxiliary Day in New York.

The 1950s

By the early 1950s the Auxiliary was offering an eight-lesson course in "Outboard Safety." During the next few years, one-lesson and three-lesson basic courses were added. Individual flotillas experimented with their own education programs. In Falmouth, Massachusetts, for instance, the Auxiliary helped organize a Young Sailors' Organization for teenagers. By the mid-1950s more than 30,000 men and women had taken part in Auxiliary education programs. A strong boost came from the insurance industry. Several major insurance firms lowered the premiums they charged for boats that passed CMEs and owners who passed the courses.

In 1958, largely due to lobbying efforts by the Coast Guard Auxiliary, Congress passed Public Law 85-455. The President of the United States was thereby authorized "to proclaim annually the week including July 4th as National Safe Boating Week." The event was later moved to the second week of June. It is marked each year by a stepped-up campaign to encourage boat owners to get their CMEs, along with boating safety displays at regattas, boat shows, and shopping malls. Movie and television stars, along with other national celebrities, have helped publicize National Safe Boating Week over the years.

The third of the Auxiliary's "four cornerstones" is operations. Since its inception the Auxiliary has assisted the Coast Guard in several of its non-military functions, including search and rescue, safety, regatta, and harbor patrols and checking aids to navigation.

Fellowship is the Coast Guard Auxiliary's fourth cornerstone. The organization's leadership has always understood that it can only thrive if membership is a source of pride, satisfaction, and fun. Meetings on the flotilla, district, division, and national levels give Auxiliarists the opportunity to participate in the decision-making process, exchange ideas, and share their good will, not only with each other but with

AUXILIARISTS TO THE RESCUE

The Auxiliary is about people who care. Frank Mauro demonstrated this devotion. A rental boat with eleven people on board motored through a Ft. Lauderdale waterway. The tide was ebbing, and unexpectedly, a strong current captured the boat and carried it toward a moored barge. To the horror of diners watching from the patio of a nearby restaurant, the relentless tidal stream forced the boat beneath the barge's hull. Those on Coast Guard utility boat 41351 watched also. The boat's crew reacted and reached the scene as the boaters, now in the water, were being dragged under the barge. Despite the powerful current, Frank Mauro, an Auxiliarist on the utility boat, jumped into the water and reached a struggling nine-year-old girl about to be sucked under the barge. However, in the act of saving her, three panicked adults grabbed him to avoid being pulled under. Demonstrating extraordinary strength under the weight of four frightened people against a powerful current and a shifting barge threatening to crush him, Mauro still was able to make way against the current and wedge the group between the barge and a wooden piling. Seeing yet a fifth victim, Mauro tried to reach him too, but because the other four still held tightly to him, he was not fast enough, and the man went under. Mauro helped those clinging to him reach an inflatable raft launched by the utility boat's crew. Mauro then pushed away from the piling just as the barge shifted and ground against it. He narrowly missed being crushed. The rental boat disappeared beneath the barge and resurfaced at the far end, upside down with its engine still running. Mauro saved four lives; those assisting him saved five more. Two lost their lives. For this heroism the Coast Guard awarded Mauro the Gold Lifesaving Medal. (U.S. Coast Guard)

members of the public. Since 1964 the culminating event of each year has been the fall National Meeting, which features an address by the Commandant of the Coast Guard.

Just when the first woman joined the Auxiliary is unclear. At least a few women were members in the 7th District by late 1941, and by 1945 Coast Guard regulations for female Auxiliarists' uniforms were in print. The reception accorded female Auxiliarists by their male counterparts apparently varied from place to place. When four women joined Flotilla 61 in Sacramento, California, in 1957, the minutes of the next flotilla meeting hailed their arrival, "Welcome aboard, girls! It's time we glamorized a bit." In other cases, perhaps because they felt unwelcome in the existing flotillas, women formed their own. In the late 1940s at least one, Flotilla 525 in Boston, consisted entirely of women; it had no boats or aircraft and its operations apparently consisted of performing clerical work for its division. By the end of the 1950s all-female flotillas were operating in Detroit, Louisville, Memphis, Mobile, and Manasquan, New Jersey.

The 1950s saw the creation of the Coast Guard Bronze Plaque of Merit. Known informally as the "A" Award, it is presented by order of the Commandant of the Coast Guard to Auxiliarists who save lives at the risk of their own. A few years later the Coast Guard established the Certificate of Merit, or "B" Award, presented at the Commandant's discretion for "exceptional meritorious services in furtherance of the organization and its purposes."

Public education classes given by Auxiliary members in communities throughout the nation are frequently the first formal, and sometimes only, introduction to regulations, navigation, and seamanship for new boat owners. Skillfully tying a simple knot might mean the difference between a safe boating experience and disaster for the newcomer. (U.S. Coast Guard Auxiliary)

A Coast Guard Auxiliary airplane sits on the apron at Coast Guard Air Station, Houston, Texas. Airplanes came to the Auxiliary informally during World War II but since 1945 have been a recognized part of the organization and an invaluable asset for search-and-rescue missions. (James Dillard, U.S. Coast Guard)

Opposite: What once was an unused, dingy blue and yellow Alaska railroad caboose is now an attractive, modern Coast Guard Auxiliary Station in Whittier, Alaska, near Prince William Sound. The interior was gutted and restored with new lumber and carpeting. It was outfitted with radio communications, chart tables, computers, and the accouterments associated with operations and administration. The restoration was done by Auxiliarists and community volunteers. (Noreen Folkerts, U.S. Coast Guard Auxiliary)

Flares are an important signaling means when you are in trouble on the water. Auxiliarists check that they are available and in good condition. (Telfair H. Brown, U.S. Coast Guard).

The 1960s

By the early 1960s the number of registered yachts and motorboats in the United States had surpassed 5,000,000, and membership in the Coast Guard Auxiliary had reached 22,000. The task of administering the organization had outgrown the capacity of the National Board. In 1968 the staff at the national level was reorganized. The elected national commodore and vice commodore were authorized to appoint a staff of forty additional officers, who would preside over four departments: Comptroller, Public Relations, Operations, and Education. Each department was divided into divisions, which were in turn subdivided into branches—a scheme system similar to that of the Coast Guard. In 1969 the position of national rear commodore was added.

More recent organizational changes have elaborated on the system that was worked out in the 1960s. There are now three national rear commodores, representing the Eastern, Central, and Western Areas. The number and titles of departments have fluctuated over the years. In 1996 the number stood at nine: Public Affairs, Finance, Education, Information Services, Legal Affairs, Member Resources, Operations, Training, and Vessel Examination.

The first national-level Auxiliary journal was a newsletter called *Under the Blue Ensign*, which began publication in 1959. Since a national boating magazine was already using that title for its column of Auxiliary news, the name of the journal was changed in 1960 to *U.S. Coast Guard Auxiliary National Publication*—a masthead that, though descriptively accurate, had little to recommend it aesthetically. Later that year a contest was held to find a better name. The winner was *The Navigator*, which has been the title of the Auxiliary's magazine since 1961.

One of the Auxiliary's functions since its early days had been to provide the Coast Guard with reports on errors in official nautical charts. In 1962 that function was formalized when the Coast Guard and the Auxiliary signed an agreement with the National Oceanic Service. NOS was to provide copies of its charts to members of the Auxiliary, who were to identify and report any discrepancies. The sheer number of Auxiliarists constantly checking the accuracy of their charts became a significant asset to both NOS and the Coast Guard.

Since the Second World War the Coast Guard has been barely large enough to perform the missions assigned to it. On many occasions the Auxiliary has stepped into the breach. In the early 1960s, for example, it became clear that there were not enough Coast Guard radio stations in California. Auxiliarists of Flotilla 47 put their own radio sets to work, and eventually set up a permanent radio tower on the roof of a restaurant in Santa Cruz. It has since been responsible for handling hundreds of distress calls.

During the Vietnam conflict several Coast Guard cutters were taken off their normal stations and sent to Southeast Asia. Auxiliarists put their boats to work on patrol duty, and the 11th District set up a "Vietnam Cutters Fund" to buy books, magazines, and other recreational materials for the Coast Guardsmen who had taken their ships to war. The war in

Southeast Asia also saw the biggest call-up of Reservists since the Second World War. Membership in the Reserve peaked in 1965 at 18,378.

In December 1967, the retired British ocean liner *Queen Mary* ended its final voyage at Long Beach, California, where the great ship was to become a permanent tourist attraction. Hundreds of pleasure boats formed an unofficial welcoming committee; the *Queen Mary*'s captain commented, "There were more craft than at Dunkirk." Eighty-seven Coast Guard Auxiliary boats kept the channel into Long Beach Harbor clear.

In 1967 the Coast Guard took the Auxiliary with it from the Department of the Treasury to the Department of Transportation. The DOT's budgets were not generous to the Coast Guard. Headquarters had to accept that a greater role for the Auxiliary was not only desirable but necessary. At the end of 1967 the Coast Guard Auxiliary had 23,721 active members. During that year, 23,538 people took the eight-lesson Public Information Course; more than 145,000 took the one-lesson and three-lesson courses. The Auxiliary conducted 908 regatta patrols, 7,177 safety patrols, and 7,234 missions of assistance to boats or people in distress. Auxiliarists were responsible for saving 128 lives that year. Those statistics attracted the attention of the National Safety Council, which presented the Auxiliary with the National Safety Service Award for 1968.

Page 128, bottom: *A fun means to reach children about water safety is through Coastie, a robotic boat forty-four inches long, thirty inches wide, and forty-five inches tall. It has a working searchlight, rotating beacon, siren, and air horn. Coastie is remotely operated at a distance by an Auxiliarist wearing earphones so he or she can hear what is being said to the tug. Coastie will "sail" up close to kids, roll its eyes, flutter its eyelids, and begin talking. This startles the kids at first, but before long there is a happy two-way conversation in progress. Coastie will also playfully squirt water at them. (Courtesy of Elizabeth Scotti)*

Pages 128–129: *Auxiliarists and active duty Coast Guard members practice ice rescues on one of the Great Lakes. Similar joint training takes place throughout the country so Auxiliary members learn how to work in cooperation with active duty Coast Guard members on cases where their assistance is needed. (U.S. Coast Guard)*

The 1970s

Four years later Congress passed the Federal Safe Boating Act of 1971, which expanded the Coast Guard's role in supervising boating on inland waterways. The act also provided that the Auxiliary be placed at the service of individual state governments when they asked for its assistance.

Early in 1973 budget cuts forced the closing of seven Coast Guard stations on the Great Lakes. At the request of the affected communities, Congress ordered the stations to be reopened and operated by the Auxiliary. The local division captains took responsibility for manning them and ensuring that Auxiliarists' boats were always available to assist distressed vessels. The Auxiliary later took over seven more stations on the Mississippi and Ohio rivers.

Auxiliarists Lillian Phillips and Mary Roeder, of Tacoma, Washington, originated a water-safety education program called "Water 'n' Kids" in 1973. The Auxiliary adopted the course nationally, and since then more

Above: *Auxiliarist Jim Snyder standing a radio watch at an Auxiliary station. In addition to boats, Auxiliarists supply airplanes, radios, and other rescue support equipment. (U.S. Coast Guard Auxiliary)*

Above, right: *Who are these guys? They are Auxiliarists Bill Gardner and Dean Nimax training in firefighting gear aboard a cutter as part of the Coast Guard augmentation program. (Jeff Lowe, U.S. Coast Guard Auxiliary)*

Mickey Mouse at Disneyland does his part to encourage boating safety by undergoing a courtesy safety examination of his boat. (U.S. Coast Guard)

than a million children have taken it. Phillips and Roeder received Certificates of Administrative Merit from the Commandant for their efforts.

Any publicized event near the water attracts a swarm of enthusiastic but sometimes careless boaters. Auxiliarists performed maritime crowd control service at each Apollo moon shot and Space Shuttle launch and for OPSAIL '76, the parade of sail training vessels through New York Harbor on the nation's bicentennial. In June 1976 the Teton Dam in Idaho burst, flooding a considerable area and washing toxic chemicals out of a warehouse into the reservoir below the dam. Coast Guard Auxiliarists warned boaters to evacuate and helped build a levee that saved the city of Idaho Falls.

By the end of the decade Auxiliarists felt more a part of a truly national organization. In 1979 Auxiliary membership surpassed 46,000, a figure that exceeded the numerical strength of the Coast Guard by about 25 percent.

The 1980s

The new decade opened with two serious accidents in Tampa Bay, Florida. In January 1980, the Coast Guard tender *Blackthorn* sank after a collision with the tanker *Capricorn*, with the loss of twenty-three Coast Guardsmen. A few months later, the freighter *Summit Venture* rammed the Sunshine Skyway Bridge, knocking some 1,200 feet of roadway into the water and killing thirty-five people. In both cases the Auxiliary helped with search and rescue operations.

In the spring of 1980 the government of Cuba unexpectedly announced it would permit a massive emigration through the port of Mariel. For three weeks a steady stream of boats, 200 to 300 a day on the average, flowed from Cuba to Florida. The Coast Guard mobilized all its resources in the area, and Auxiliarists operated radios, performed search and rescue operations along the Florida coast, and stood watch in the Coast Guardsmen's absence.

In 1984, in an effort to set standards for training and efficiency in the Auxiliary, Coast Guard Headquarters initiated the Boat Crew Qualification

Program. In order to participate in operations on the water, each Auxiliarist would have to pass a rigorous series of courses supervised by specially trained Auxiliarists certified as Qualified Examiners. The reaction to the new program was mixed. Many Auxiliarists welcomed the opportunity to get the new training; others were unable or unwilling to commit the time. Another development that sapped enthusiasm was a toughening of Coast Guard policy regarding assists to vessels in trouble. One of the Auxiliary's most common activities had been towing boats that ran out of gas or had mechanical problems. Pressure from commercial towing firms led the Coast Guard to emphasize that Auxiliarists were authorized to pass towlines to other boats only in genuine emergencies.

The combination of rising standards and declining opportunities to be of service probably contributed to the fall in Auxiliary membership during the mid-1980s. In 1987 membership stood at 39,144, a decline of nearly 20 percent since 1976. Those figures attracted the attention of Congress, which ordered the Secretary of Transportation to prepare a detailed report on the subject.

The subsequent Coast Guard study, chaired by Captain William P. Hewel, deputy chief of the Office of Boating, Public, and Consumer Affairs, surmised the decline in membership was a natural, temporary consequence of the boat crew and non-emergency assistance policies. It further noted that for whatever reason, the size of the Coast Guard Auxiliary was not large enough to meet Coast Guard requirements. In order to keep up with the demands of the recreational boating community, Auxiliary membership needed to expand at about 3 percent a year.

The 1980s saw a number of massive public events on the water, each attended by throngs of small craft. Auxiliarists helped bring order to these events, and assisted the Coast Guard patrol at two "tall ship parades," *OPSAIL '80* in Boston and *OPSAIL '82* in Philadelphia, the Olympic Games

The Coast Guard Auxiliary is indispensable to the Coast Guard. During Operation Sail 2000, *more than ninety Auxiliary boats patrolled in New York Harbor as the Coast Guard training barque* Eagle *led the parade of Tall Ships. (Telfair H. Brown, U.S. Coast Guard)*

This Auxiliarist looks surreal in a protective garment donned for winter operations. The Auxiliary of today assists the Coast Guard in performing all of its missions. This means undergoing rigorous training in order to be able to work alongside their regular Coast Guard counterparts. (U.S. Coast Guard Auxiliary)

131

Auxiliarist Trish Connolly of Flotilla 12-1 at Fort Totten, New York, on a break as she waits to join the safety patrol in New York Harbor for the Statue of Liberty centennial celebration in 1986. (Fred J. Connolly)

Treacherous Alaskan waters provide interesting challenges for Auxiliarists. The Valdez Arm becomes an ice maze in early spring for this Auxiliary boat en route to a military exercise. (Noreen Folkerts, U.S. Coast Guard Auxiliary)

at Los Angeles in 1984, the America's Cup races of 1983 and 1988, and the Pan American Games of 1987. For the centennial of the Statue of Liberty on The Fourth of July 1986, more than 30,000 watercraft packed New York Harbor. Some 100 Coast Guard vessels and 380 Auxiliary boats provided safety patrols in the largest peacetime operation in Coast Guard history.

The 1990s and beyond

To fill a workforce shortage during the 1990–1991 Gulf War, Auxiliarists took over various duties at stateside Coast Guard stations. The years 1992 and 1993 saw Coast Guard ingenuity and dedication tested by weather and international politics. Coast Guardsmen, Reservists, and Auxiliarists evacuated hundreds of people from the path of Hurricane Andrew and from the scenes of devastating floods in the Midwest. In 1994 a military coup in Haiti released another surge of emigrants heading for Florida. In order to control this human tide and assist the many who set out ill-prepared and inadequately equipped for survival at sea, the Coast Guard, the Reserve, and the Auxiliary launched their largest search and rescue operation since the Second World War. In 1996 President Clinton signed the Coast Guard Auxiliary Act of 1996. That legislation made official a policy that had been in place for several years, declaring: "The purpose of the Auxiliary is to assist the Coast Guard, as authorized by the Commandant, in performing any Coast Guard function, power, duty, role, mission, or operation authorized by law." The Coast Guard was now authorized to use all its assets, including the Reserve and Auxiliary to carry out its missions.

Throughout its history the Coast Guard has been called upon repeatedly to "do more with less." Always the smallest of the armed services, it has watched its missions multiply faster than its resources have expanded. It has responded to that challenge by relying increasingly on the Coast Guard Reserve and the Coast Guard Auxiliary. It seems safe to say that both organizations will continue to be vital members of Team Coast Guard.

Auxiliary boat 256611 was the first Coast Guard-owned vessel purchased for use by the Auxiliary. The twenty-five-foot SAFE, Secure-All-around-Flotation Equipped, boat is operated solely by volunteers for search and rescue missions on Alaskan waters. The rigid foam collar around the boat provides additional flotation, making the boat virtually unsinkable and serves as a fender. (Noreen Folkerts, U.S. Coast Guard Auxiliary)

As a tanker leaves the Trans-Alaska Pipeline Terminal at Valdez, Alaska, Auxiliarist Mike Folkerts provides an extra set of eyes and ears for security. (Noreen Folkerts, U.S. Coast Guard Auxiliary)

Beacons

Ralph E. Eshelman, Ph.D.

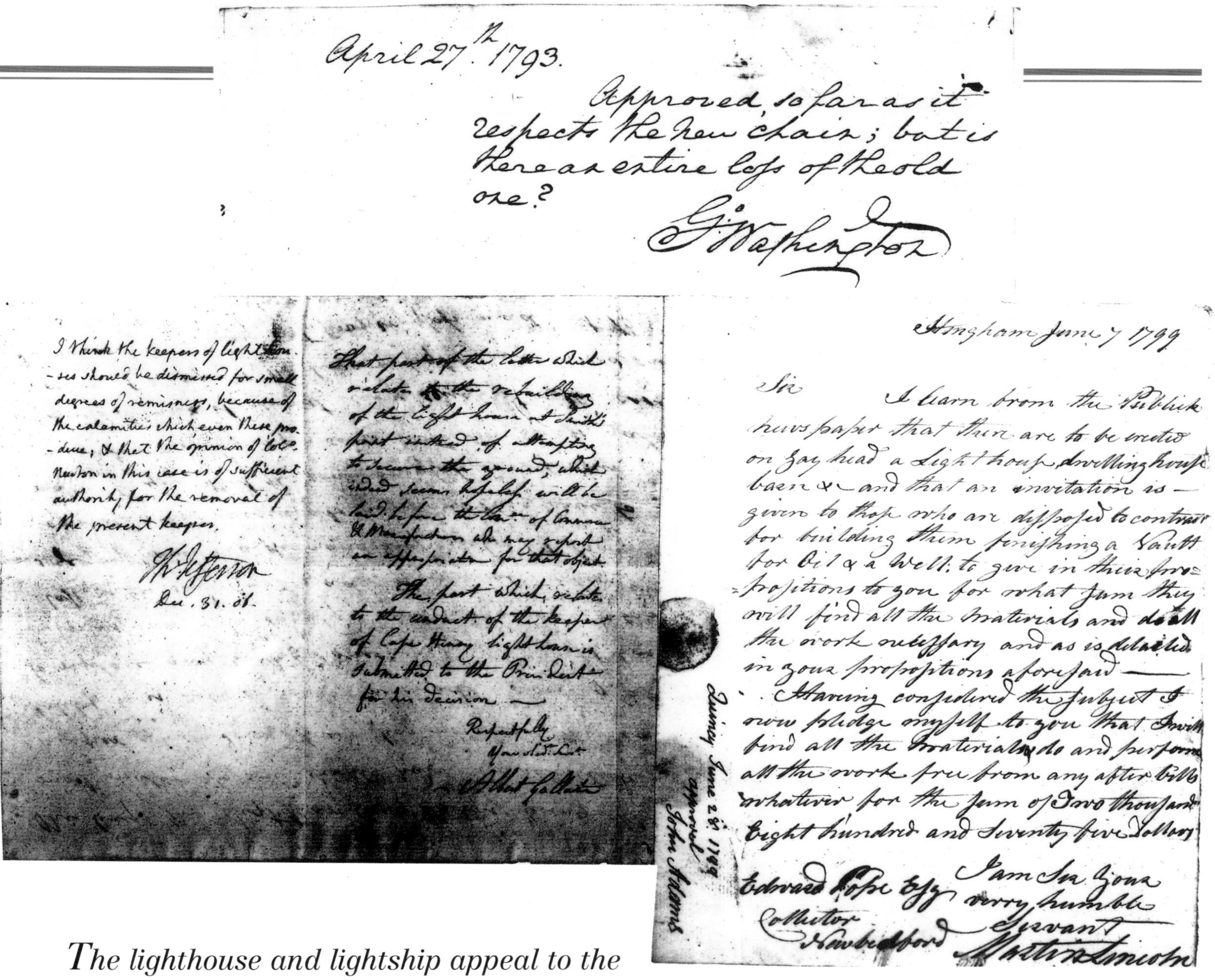

April 27th 1793.

Approved, so far as it respects the new chair; but is there an entire loss of the old one?

Go: Washington

I think the keepers of lighthouses should be dismissed for small degrees of remissness, because of the calamities which even these produce; & that the opinion of Col. Newton in this case is of sufficient authority for the removal of the present keeper.

Th: Jefferson
Dec. 31. 01.

That part of the letter which relates to the rebuilding of the light house at Smith's point instead of attempting to secure the ground, which would seem hopeless will be laid before the Com.ee of Commerce & Manufactures who may report an appropriation for that object.

The part which relates to the conduct of the keeper of Cape Henry light house is submitted to the President for his decision —

Respectfully
Your obt. Servt.
Albert Gallatin

Hingham June 7 1799

Sir I learn from the Publick newspaper that there are to be erected on Gay head a Light house dwelling house barn &c and that an invitation is given to those who are disposed to contract for building them finishing a Vault for Oil & a Well to give in their propositions to you for what sum they will find all the materials and do all the work necessary and as is detailed in your propositions aforesaid — Having considered the subject I now pledge myself to you that I will find all the materials do and perform all the work free from any after bills whatever for the sum of Two thousand Eight hundred and Seventy five Dollars

I am Sir your very humble Servant
Martin Lincoln

Edward Pope Esq
Collector
New Bedford

Quincy June 28. 1799
Approved
John Adams

Three handwritten letters pertaining to decisions regarding lighthouse business bear the signatures of George Washington, Thomas Jefferson, and John Adams. Washington appears to approve the purchase of new chairs but questions the status of the old. Jefferson supports the dismissal of the keeper of Cape Henry lighthouse. Martin Lincoln offers to build a lighthouse dwelling on Gay Head for $2,875. John Adams approves it. (U.S. Coast Guard)

The lighthouse and lightship appeal to the interest and better instinct of man because they are symbolic of never-ceasing watchfulness, of steadfast endurance in every exposure, and of widespread helpfulness. The building and the keeping of the lights is a picturesque and humanitarian work of the nation.

—George R. Putnam,
Commissioner of the Lighthouse Board, 1910–1935

The traditions of the lighthouse keeper, often lonely, sometimes heroic, but always faithful, are legendary. "The light must be kept going" was their unofficial motto, and there is arguably no better symbol of the humanitarian work of the U.S. Coast Guard.

Lighthouses have been a part of our nation since its inception. In 1789, after adopting the Constitution and the Bill of Rights, the First Congress of the United States in the passage of its ninth law, created the Lighthouse Establishment to take over the operation of the twelve colonial lighthouses, as well as to oversee the construction and operation of new lighthouses.

Opposite: *Lighthouses for many observers conjure feelings of romance, security, and beautiful settings. (U.S. Coast Guard)*

Given such early recognition of their importance, it is not surprising that the largest number and the most diverse lighthouses in the world are found in the United States. Lighthouses are located in thirty-one states, as well at St. Croix and Navassa Island, while fifteen are in Puerto Rico. By official count, the Coast Guard maintains 481 of these and even operates one at Guantánamo Bay, Cuba. The National Park Service's 1994 *Inventory of Historic Light Stations* lists 611 existing historic light stations encompassing 631 existing historic light towers— some stations such as Cape Henry, Virginia, have more than one light tower. Another 190 sites are listed as ruins. This list does not include more recent non-historic lighthouses such as Sullivan's Island, South Carolina, and Oak Island, North Carolina, or the offshore Texas-tower-type lighthouses built in the 1960s. All told, an estimated 1,000-plus lighthouses have been built in the United States and its territorial waters.

Killock Shoal Lighthouse is a light now only seen in pictures. This cottage over the water marks the north end of Chincoteague Channel next to Chincoteague Island, Virginia. It was completed in 1886 and appeared like this until 1939 when the building was removed and an automated light put in its place on the remaining skeletal supports. Later, when the channel changed course the light was no longer needed. (U.S. Coast Guard)

Bottom, left: *Lightships were eventually replaced by large navigational buoys and manned Texas Towers such as* Ambrose *at the entrance to New York Harbor. The Texas Towers, too, faded into the navigational past.* Ambrose *went into operation in 1967; in 1988 all personnel were removed and it was automated. After an oil tanker rammed it in 1996, damaging it beyond repair, it was demolished and replaced with a small light tower platform. (U.S. Coast Guard)*

Bottom, right: *The original Cape Henry Lighthouse tower was completed in 1792. However, now only the second, black and white, tower, built in 1881, shines for mariners at the south entrance to Chesapeake Bay. (Ralph E. Eshelman)*

136

Left: *Point Arena lighthouse towers above seaside cliffs in a classic scene. (Gary Todoroff)*

Above: *Lighthouses, like Table Bluff Lighthouse, might also sit at the harbor's entrance and low to the water where it is only seen a few miles distance—just enough for a vessel to make port. (Gary Todoroff)*

The word "lighthouse" brings an image of a tall, tapering tower perched high on a rocky prominence, its lantern warning mariners away from treacherous shoals. Yet many lighthouses were also built to guide mariners into ports and harbors, not away from reefs and dangerous

Above: *Located on the northern tip of Long Beach Island, Barnegat Lighthouse's sweeping beam once assisted mariners bound to and from New York Harbor along the New Jersey coast. Modern, electronic navigational aids render the light, like many others, no longer necessary. (U.S. Coast Guard)*

Left: *Sturgeon Bay Canal Light, built in 1899 off Lake Michigan, is an example of a steel skeletal tower with lantern. The light is on the Coast Guard small boat station at the east end of Sturgeon Bay Ship Canal. (U.S. Coast Guard)*

137

Top, left: *The first lighthouse on North America's Pacific Coast is considered to have been lighted in Sitka, Alaska. The governor, Aleksandr Baranov, placed a beacon light consisting of a wick in four copper cans containing seal or whale oil, placed in front of a large reflector in the cupola of his residence known as Baranov's Castle. The light continued in operation after the United States purchased Alaska in 1867. (Alaska State Library)*

Above: *Tortugas Harbor Lighthouse constructed in 1876 sits on the parapet of famous Fort Jefferson, Dry Tortugas Islands, offshore near Key West, Florida. (Ralph E. Eshelman)*

Above, right: *Yet sometimes they fall victim to the seas over which they watch, as does Smith Island lighthouse battered by the westerly storms screaming down the Strait of Juan de Fuca. (Coast Guard Museum Northwest)*

Right: *Split Rock Lighthouse sits on a bluff on Lake Superior's Minnesota north shore. The light, 168 feet above the lake's surface, is visible for twenty-two miles. From the lake the cliff appears split, hence the name Split Rock. (Paul C. Scotti)*

Far right: *Small, modern light-fixtures replaced the classic Fresnel lenses at nearly all lighthouses following the automation of lights beginning in the early 1970s. This plastic light-fixture is merely attached to the railing of the narrow walkway, once used by the keeper to clean the glass, outside the tower's original lantern room. (Gary Todoroff)*

rocks. Lighthouses have also been erected in a variety of shapes including conical, triangular, square, hexagonal, octagonal, with tapering sides, or vertically straight. While some do stand on wave-swept heights, many can be found at the edges of rivers, canals, and lakes. Others have been erected on fortifications or even incorporated into church steeples. Lighthouses are also inland: the Liston Rear Range Lighthouse serving the Delaware River is located three miles from the river shore.

Of course lighthouses can be located on any body of water where ships are present, and Michigan, with its Lakes Michigan and Huron, has more lighthouses than any other state. Surely most people still imagine lighthouses as did the Bureau of Lighthouses in 1915 as "lights where resident keepers were employed," yet today, by this definition, very few lighthouses in the United States would be classified as such: all but one are now automated and thus require no onsite keepers.

A lighthouse was not only a building that housed the light but often also had separate buildings for the keepers, as well as radio and

fog-signal buildings, workshops, cisterns, and storage sheds, garages, and, especially at island locations, tramways and boat houses. Such complexes are called "light stations."

Lighthouses also come in many sizes, ranging from towers only tens of feet tall to towers over 165 feet high. Height depends on location and requirements. Primary lighthouses are the tallest and contain the most powerful lights to be the first aid to navigation seen when approaching land. Harbor, river, and channel lighthouses are shorter and outfitted with less powerful lights because they do not need to be seen across long distances of water. Such lighthouses are referred to as "secondary lights" or "minor lights." Generally, coastal lighthouses on the low, flat south-eastern coast of the United States tend to be tall towers to elevate the light high enough to be seen from twenty or more miles at sea. Light-houses on the rugged West Coast, however, often do not need to be as tall, since the high cliffs themselves provide enough elevation. Ironically, the fog so characteristic of the West Coast caused one light station to be

The 1880 Jeffrey's Hook Lighthouse, better known as the "Little Red Lighthouse," was relocated in 1921 to the east bank of the Hudson River, just north of New York City. With the completion of the George Washington Bridge in 1932, the little lighthouse, now dwarfed by the large bridge, was no longer needed to aid navigation and was closed by the Coast Guard. The lighthouse fell into disrepair and was put up for auction in 1951. Ten-year-old Matthew Goldin, son of Harrison J. Goldin, comptroller of New York City, read about this lighthouse in Hildegard Hoyt Swift's The Little Red Lighthouse and the Great Gray Bridge, *and was saddened to see the lighthouse in such poor condition. In 1982 Goldin and the parks commissioner, Gordon J. Davis, announced the city would restore the lighthouse. The Little Red Lighthouse, now administered by the New York City Parks and Recreation department, stands proud under the great gray bridge. (Ralph E. Eshelman)*

Far left: *Along the southern Georgia coast sits St. Simon's Island Lighthouse, originally built in the early 1800s. Confederate forces dynamited the lighthouse in 1862, denying its use to Union ships. A tall barn on a nearby cotton plantation filled in as a navigational reference in postwar years until 1872 when the current lighthouse was built. The 104-foot-tall tower is made of "tabby," a mixture of lime, sand, oyster shells, and water. (Paul C. Scotti)*

Left: *Flowers on one side, the Pacific Ocean on the other make a "wish you were here" setting at Point Montara Lighthouse, a sentinel for the southern approaches to San Francisco's Golden Gate. A rash of shipwrecks first resulted in a fog signal being installed at this location in 1872. The lighthouse came in 1900. This thirty-foot tower built in 1928 replaced the original. (Ralph E. Eshelman)*

139

Above: *The ninety-seven-foot tall Minot's Ledge Lighthouse, located just off Cohasset, Massachusetts, is rooted to a granite ledge upon foundation stones weighing two tons each. The present tower, built of granite blocks in 1860, is referred to as the "lovers light" because of its one-four-three rhythmic flashes emulating the words "I Love You."* (U.S. Coast Guard)

Right: *Lighthouses have a multitude of appearances. Regardless of their shape they have strong artistic appeal such as Thomas Point Shoal Lighthouse in Chesapeake Bay. The rock piles are for structural protection to break up ice floes in the winter.* (William L. Trotter, U.S. Coast Guard Art Collection)

Lighthouses have a timeless appeal. From 1896 until 1939, Coquille River Lighthouse in Bandon, Oregon, guided mariners across the dangerous river bar. Even though it has not functioned as an aid to navigation for decades it is one of the most photographed lighthouses along the Oregon coast. (Paul C. Scotti)

built low in order to get the light below the foggy ceiling, but still high enough to be visible at sea.

The First Congress placed responsibility for aids to navigation within the Treasury Department, where Alexander Hamilton personally administered them. This high-level attention given to lighthouses by the newly created nation was tied directly to its need for commerce and the desire to become a maritime world power. Lighthouses not only encouraged trade with foreign nations, but symbolically proclaimed the United States was worthy of due recognition. In keeping with these aims, the first public works project in the United States was to build a lighthouse, the Cape Henry Lighthouse at the mouth of Chesapeake Bay, which was lighted in 1792. President George Washington personally signed the construction contracts and also the appointment letter for its first keeper.

Following the California Gold Rush half a century later, the U.S. government raised the first lighthouse on the West Coast. The Treasury Department had awarded a contract to a Baltimore, Maryland, firm to build sixteen lighthouses. Their company ship, appropriately named *Oriole*, departed Baltimore with men and supplies, sailing around Cape Horn to San Francisco, and by 1854 the company had completed the lighthouse at Alcatraz Island. The next year, at nearby Farallon Island another light was finished, although the construction crew was initially prevented from landing by egg harvesters, then making a good profit selling seabird eggs in San Francisco. These entrepreneurs feared a

lighthouse would scare away the seabirds and destroy their livelihood, and it wasn't until a Coast Survey ship, with armed sailors, subdued the egg gatherers that construction could begin.

Politics, needs, costs, location, and available technology all influenced lighthouse design, and construction often required a good deal of ingenuity. One of the most difficult to build was at Minot's Ledge, one mile off Cohasset, Massachusetts, near the entrance to Boston in the open Atlantic Ocean. Joseph G. Totten, borrowing ideas from the famous English Channel Eddystone Lighthouse, designed what was to be the first wave-swept lighthouse in the United States. Exposed to the full force of the sea, the 114-foot-tall masonry tower took five years to build. Each granite block was individually shaped so that every stone was locked together by the blocks around it—similar to a three-dimensional jigsaw puzzle. To further strengthen the structure, wooden rods were driven from one course to another through holes drilled in the blocks. When wet, the wood expanded and held the structure together even more firmly.

Initially men could only work on the foundation during extreme low tide on calm days. A rowboat was stationed off the rock to pick up any men who might get washed away by unexpected waves. Henry David Thoreau described the completed structure in 1871: "The lighthouse rises out of the sea like a beautiful stone cannon, mouth upward, belching only friendly fires."

Another wave-swept lighthouse was St. George Reef, built on tiny (300-feet in diameter) Northwest Seal Rock, off the Pacific Coast of California. Construction could be carried out only on every fifth day due to intermittent pounding seas. The St. George Reef Lighthouse, its foundation and

The palm tree appears stunted beneath the 160-foot tower of Cape Canaveral Lighthouse on Florida's Atlantic Coast. Tall towers are common in the low-lying coastal plains of the East and Gulf coasts of United States. Different paint schemes helped identify the individual lighthouses for daytime use by the offshore navigator. A distinctive light-flash combination identified a lighthouse by night. (U.S. Coast Guard)

The classic image of a lighthouse is one of a stoic sentinel perched high atop a jutting cliff, along a barren wave-beaten rocky coast. The building at right is the light keeper's dwelling. Heceta Head Lighthouse, twelve miles north of Florence, Oregon, is a model of that portrait. (Paul C. Scotti)

141

tower faced with cut granite blocks, the smallest weighing 17 tons, took ten years to complete and was finally lit in 1892.

As a result of a shipwreck off San Francisco in 1901 and the loss of 100 lives, Congress appropriated funds for a new lighthouse to be built on the wave-washed Mile Rocks. Called one of America's greatest engineering accomplishments, this station required workers to jump from small, bouncing boats onto slippery seaweed-and-barnacle-encrusted rock.

While the lighthouse was tantalizingly close to San Francisco, it was difficult to recruit men for this dangerous work. The four-man crew lived in cramped quarters, confined and isolated by the perilous landing that required a small boat to maneuver in up to fifteen-foot swells so that a keeper could scale a rope ladder hung under the lighthouse boom, while the oppressive sound of the fog signal seldom allowed any serenity around the station. Mile Rocks Lighthouse was automated in 1966 and the upper three floors of the tower were replaced by a helicopter platform, eliminating forever the dangerous and dreaded rope ladder.

In the time when coal was the primary fuel for heating light stations and for the fog signal's boilers, coal deliveries often required hours of backbreaking work, although when a station was outfitted with a dock or derrick the chore was not as difficult. Each fall during the 1920s, coal for Lovell's Island Range Lights, Boston Harbor, was delivered by the tender *Shrub*. The 60- to 100-pound coal bags were offloaded from the tender to a small lighter that landed them on the beach where they were stacked in huge piles. The crew carried the bags on their shoulders several hundred yards to the coal bins, often singing as they worked. Light stations located on high cliffs used cable cars to haul coal and other supplies. In the 1880s at Southeast Farallon Lighthouse off San Francisco, a mule was used to pull the cable car. At other stations a tramway, powered by a gasoline, and later, by electric winch, was used to convey coal and supplies. Regardless, the filling of the coal bins at a light station was an arduous and dirty job employing the men of both the tender and the station.

The Statue of Liberty served as a lighthouse in New York Harbor from 1886 to 1902. The first reported use of electricity in a lighthouse was by its first keeper, A. E. Littlefield, who maintained the electric-arc light beaming from the torch. (U.S. Coast Guard)

Opposite: *Construction on the St. George Reef Lighthouse began in 1882. America's most expensive lighthouse took builder George Ballantyne ten years to construct on treacherous rocks—six miles offshore from Crescent City in Northern California—before the first light beacon emitted from its ninety-foot tower in 1892. Abandoned since the 1970s, it is being restored by a chapter of the Lighthouse Preservation Society. This light was replaced by a large navigational buoy in the 1970s. (Gary Todoroff)*

Aids to Navigation

Ralph E. Eshelman, Ph.D.

Aids to navigation include buoys, daymarkers, lights, fog signals, ranges, lightships, radio beacons, and electronic navigation systems such as loran. While natural and man-made landmarks such as hills and smokestacks serve as land reference points, it is the aids to navigation, or floating or fixed markers that assist navigators safely through the water. The Coast Guard is responsible for aids to navigation in the waters of the United States and its territories. The service maintains more than 96,000 aids to navigation, which requires a workforce of more than 4,000 people, and consumes more than 20 percent of the Coast Guard budget. Imagine the difficulties and dangers of gathering in a 20-ton ice-covered buoy in wave-tossed, wind-swept waters, or when overgrowth conceals a day-mark and a crew must wade into snake-infested swamps to clear it. There are thousands of such jobs that Coast Guardsmen from Maine to Guam do every day to keep our nation's aid to navigation system working.

A new chapter in aiding navigation began during World War II when a long-range, all weather, electronic navigation system called loran was introduced. The system proved that accurate triangulation positioning was possible as far as 800 miles from transmitting stations in daytime and from 1,400 miles away at night. In 1942 a chain of stations was established along the North American Atlantic Coast from Bermuda to Greenland to guide convoys and planes crossing the Atlantic.

The following year a similar chain was established along the Bering Sea and Aleutian Islands. As the Pacific campaign got under way, mobile truck stations were used until permanent stations could be constructed. When the Marianas Islands were taken, a new loran chain was established to direct B-29s on the 1,500-mile flight to Tokyo. Much of the success of the bombing of Japan was made possible by these loran stations. Another loran chain assisted in the retaking of the Philippine Islands. By the end of the war there were seventy-five loran stations, thirty-one established in the Pacific theater alone, which extended over a third of the earth's surface—all built and operated by Coast Guardsmen.

Many loran stations were in isolated locations where food and stores were supplied only twice a year. A radio electrician spending the first winter at a loran station in Greenland, wrote in May 1943:

A Coast Guard HH-3F Pelican hoists heavy parts of a navigational day mark into place for the crew of Barnegat Inlet Coast Guard Station to finish its assembly. (William J. Triviline, U.S. Coast Guard)

Servicing an aid can mean clinging to a swaying framework tower with one hand while doing delicate repairs with the other. Lighted aids have the same problem as lamps in the home; they burn out. (U.S. Coast Guard)

Petty Officer Scott Galvin, of Coast Guard Station Burlington, Vermont, eases down a "skeleton" tower guiding a lantern Petty Officer Kevin Erwin is lowering with a rope from above. (Mike Hvozda, U.S. Coast Guard)

A Coast Guardsman pounds a day board into place. Day marks on pilings are generally used to mark channel boundaries in rivers and along shallow waterways and intercoastal routes. (Tom Gillespie, U.S. Coast Guard)

"Food proposition is really getting disastrous. Coffee has been out for months, got enough cocoa for a week, potatoes (dehydrated) are running out, powdered milk is getting low. Vienna sausage, balogna (sic), ground pork sausage is our regular diet. Sunday—ham. Cocoa for breakfast and dinner, tea for supper. Been like this for some time now. Think rationing wold (sic) be easier on us. Fresh meat has been out since the second week in March. Last vessel to come in here was Comanche *on 26 February. Last mail, drooped (sic) by plane 31 March. Great Life, isn't it."*

Radio electrician Everett B. Kopp, stationed at Iceland, wrote in February 1943, "When the weather is bad, waves climb up the cliff and spray the operations hut. With the two small stoves it is impossible to keep the hut dry."

The Aleutian Islands endure some of the world's worst weather, and their jagged coastlines, swept by violent tides, currents, and monumental surf, made landing of supplies for loran stations here "by the grace of God." A Christmas-package airdrop delivery made near one loran station was not recovered until April due to extreme weather conditions and a five-man team died in the attempt. By the time the packages were found, foxes had destroyed many of them.

Stations in the western Aleutians were built at the same time Japanese forces were being driven out. In the

South Pacific stations were sometimes attacked by Japanese planes. Stations were well guarded with sentries and dogs and armed with machine guns and grenades to ward off Japanese commandos intent on capturing the secret loran equipment. Surveying parties at future loran stations on Iwo Jima and Okinawa carried out their work under fire. At the Okinawa station, there were several uncomfortable experiences with the poisonous snakes abundant in that area. Along one particular path between the power and equipment huts, many Habu snakes were killed daily, and the area came to be known as "Habu Gulch." There was an enemy air raid almost daily and many dogfights were fought in the sky directly over the station.

The Iwo Jima loran station received the following report from the 73rd Wing, 21st Bomber Command: "Our navigators have been using your signals to great advantage. On several occasions we have managed to bring a plane back with LORAN when all other means have failed. There is no doubt that you have saved us several planes and many men. Your service will be appreciated more when the rain squall season covers this area as it is the only means of navigation."

Above: The remote Molokini Island light in the Hawaiian Islands is serviced by a crew delivered by a Coast Guard HH-65A Dolphin. For many remote lights, helicopters are the only quick way for crews to service ailing lights. (S. Epperson, U.S. Coast Guard)

Below: Coast Guard members operating the loran station at Attu are the only people on the remote island at the end of the Aleutian chain. For serving a year at a remote loran site without family, personnel get an extra month's leave and new assignment preference. (U.S. Coast Guard)

Wickies

The first lighthouse keeper in what is now the United States was George Lakeworthy, keeper of Boston Island Lighthouse, built in 1716. In 1718, while returning from Boston his boat capsized and he drowned, making Lakeworthy not only the first American lighthouse keeper, but the first to die in service. Benjamin Franklin, then only thirteen, was so moved by the accident he wrote a poem called "A Lighthouse Tragedy." The oldest lighthouse keeper on record was Anthony Christy, keeper of the Christiana Lighthouse, Delaware, who like Lakeworthy died on duty—but in this case apparently of natural causes—in 1862 at the age of 105.

The often monotonous, tedious, and isolated work of the lighthouse keeper was unlike most civil servant jobs in that it normally required the keeper to be at the site twenty-four-hours a day, 365 days a year. At some larger stations, assistant keepers enabled the responsibilities to be handled in shift work. Typically the assistant keeper was in charge of the first, or night shift, which ran from sunset to sunrise. Before the light came on, the Fresnel lens was cleaned and polished, the oil lamp cleaned and filled, and the wick trimmed or replaced. During this work the keeper wore a linen apron to prevent scratching the expensive glass lens. A properly trimmed wick kept the light burning brightly and minimized sooting: thus the lighthouse keeper's nickname "wickie."

Left: A light keeper's life, first and foremost, is one of exacting routine and absolute isolation. (U.S. Coast Guard)

Top: A Coast Guardsman inside a Fresnel lens replacing a light bulb. The unique lens, which somewhat resembles a rotating glass beehive, magnifies a diminutive light, focuses it, and beams it far to sea. The distance the light can be seen is based on the combined height of the tower and height of the navigator's eye reaching above the earth's curvature. (Coast Guard Museum Northwest, M.D. Williams)

Above: Baltimore Lighthouse was constructed in 1908 on a pneumatic caisson foundation. This photograph shows temporary buildings on piles surrounding the lighthouse used to store equipment and serve as living quarters for the workmen. These structures were removed upon the lighthouse's completion. (U.S. Coast Guard)

Fog-signal striking machines and lens-rotating machines were once powered by hanging weights, their workings similar to those of a grandfather clock. Every two to four hours the weights needed to be pulled up as high as permitted inside the tower. Finally, after sunrise, the light was extinguished and a curtain drawn around the lantern room to protect the lens from sunlight.

The head keeper handled the second, or day, shift. In the lantern and watch room the copper and brass lamp and lens fixtures, as well as utensils such as dust pans and oil measures, were cleaned and polished.

Above: *Scotch Cap Lighthouse keepers Oscar Lindberg and Barney Lokken pose with a Christmas tree given to them by a passing steamer in 1927. The gift is most welcome as no trees grow on Unimak Island in the Aleutians. In 1946, disaster struck this lighthouse when a seismic sea-wave destroyed it, killing the five Coast Guardsmen at the light station. (Coast Guard Museum Northwest)*

148

Daily polishing was also required of the parabolic reflectors, metal dishes that reflected light from behind the lamp. Another time-consuming job was cleaning the glass on the Fresnel lens and storm panes, which surrounded the lantern. The floor of the lantern room was swept and cleaned, as were the tower stairs and landings. When visibility was poor due to fog, snow, or heavy rain, the weights of the fog-signal striking machine and lens-rotating mechanism would need to be hoisted every few hours throughout the day as well. Other work such as scraping and painting of the tower and other buildings were routine maintenance, and handled by station keepers as time allowed.

At smaller stations with only one keeper, down-time was permitted only when weather and circumstances allowed, and leave was approved only when a relief keeper could be brought in. Daily entries in the station log assured the lighthouse was always manned.

The greatest drudgery was the daily cleaning and maintenance of the light apparatus. To avoid the problems of rust in the wet, often salty environment, brass was the preferred metal for lens frames and lamps, but brass required constant polishing. One keeper at Point Reyes Lighthouse in California wrote the following in the station log:

Oh, what is the bane of a lightkeeper's life
That causes him worry and struggles and strife,
That makes him use cuss words and beat up his wife,
It's brasswork.
I dig, scrub and polish, and work with a might,
And just when I get it all shining and bright,
In comes the fog like a thief in the night.
Goodbye brasswork.

There was plenty of other labor, however. Where fog was common, the task of winding the fog-bell weights was a continual and exhausting chore. James McCullough, keeper at Burnt Island Light Station, at the entrance to Boothbay Harbor, Maine, gave his son and daughter, ages eight and ten, the responsibility of winding the 2,200-pound weights. The

Opposite, top: *The first-order Fresnel lens atop the tower on Destruction Island off Washington's coast is viewed only from a distance by mariners except for the close-up encounters by a few lighthouse keepers—in its lofty space until 1995. After spending 104 years in the lantern room, the original lens installed in 1891 is now viewable up close. The lens created from nearly a thousand prisms set in a brass frame is almost eight feet tall and six feet in diameter. Its base once floated in a trough of mercury creating a near frictionless bearing for the three-ton structure to turn with little resistance. This book's graphics editor, Paul Scotti, is standing next to the lens now relocated to Westport Maritime Museum, Westport, Washington; a quarter century ago, the editor-in-chief climbed up inside this working lens as it rotated atop the lighthouse tower on Destruction Island. Entry is through the round ports shown along the lower edge. This is how light keepers entered the lens to tend the later-added electric lights and at one time to add fuel to the oil lantern and trim the wicks. (Elizabeth Scotti)*

Above: *A light keeper performs maintenance to keep the lantern rotating. (Coast Guard Museum Northwest)*

Opposite, bottom: *Destruction Island Lighthouse sits atop a thirty-acre island of steep bluffs located in the Pacific Ocean three miles off the Washington coast. Once having a "First-order" Fresnel lens, the tower now is automated with a modern light source. The original lens installed in 1891 is viewable at the Westport Maritime Museum. (U.S. Coast Guard)*

Left: *When the original Cape Hatteras Lighthouse showed growing cracks in its sandstone structure, the tower shown in the photograph was built to replace it in 1870, 1,500 feet from the water's edge. In the years since, this clearance continued to shrink and it would be only a matter of time until the ocean once more reached and destroyed the second Cape Hatteras Lighthouse. To save it, Cape Hatteras Lighthouse was moved intact, further inland in 1999 from this location to a safer spot, 1,600 feet from the Atlantic Ocean (Telfair Brown, U.S. Coast Guard)*

Located two miles northwest of Port Townsend, Washington, Point Wilson Lighthouse was activated in 1879. The first keeper was paid eight hundred dollars a year. (U.S. Coast Guard)

Portland Head Lighthouse in Maine was first established in 1791. (National Lighthouse Museum, E. Ross Holland Collection)

Dungeness Lighthouse sits at the tip of Dungeness Spit near Sequim, Washington, in the strait of Juan de Fuca. It is reached only at low tide by traveling seven miles along a narrow rock- and log-strewn beach. Established in 1857, it was the first American lighthouse in Puget Sound. Now fully automated, a group of local volunteers takes turns spending short stays living in the former keeper's quarters doing yard and building maintenance and visiting with the hikers making the trek to see this lighthouse. Note the modern, small light-fixture attached to the railing outside the original lantern room replacing the original Fresnel lens. (Joel Magisos)

children took their responsibility seriously and had to tend to it every two hours because their limited strength would not allow them to meet their task if the weights dropped too far. In 1869 the keeper at Petit Manan lighthouse reported the clockwork weights pulled lose from their fastener and fell with "such tremendous force that they snapped away eighteen steps of the cast-iron circular staircase."

Over the years the duties of the lighthouse keeper became more formalized and books of instruction were issued to ensure proper operation. Prior to this, some keepers were rather nonchalant in their duties. Sometimes they hired others to operate the light for them or had slaves assume the duties, with the keeper only occasionally visiting the lighthouse. Some keepers held extra jobs and left the lighthouse work to their wives and children; others had drinking problems that rendered them undependable, while a few simply walked away. Lighthouse work was not easy; it took a certain kind of dedication and conscientiousness as well as a tolerance for isolation.

Politics could play a role in lighthouse keeper appointments. Some keepers were appointed based on political favors rather than qualifications, and when the political winds changed, so did the lighthouse keeper. The Civil Service Reform Acts of 1871 and 1883 and President Cleveland's executive order of May 1896, which classified keepers' positions as civil service jobs, discouraged the former practice.

To ensure keepers were properly maintaining their stations, lighthouse inspectors typically made quarterly inspections, though at some isolated stations such as in Alaska, inspections were only once a year. In 1912, to promote efficiency and friendly rivalry among the lighthouse keepers, a system of stars and pennants was established. Keepers commended for efficiency at each quarterly inspection were entitled to wear the inspector's star for the next year, and those who received the inspector's star three successive years were entitled to wear the Commissioner's star.

A legendary West Coast inspector was Captain Harry Rhodes. Rhodes, notorious for his trivial demands and stingy ways, wore white gloves to discover dust or dirt anywhere in a lighthouse. He closely examined all brass for fingerprints and checked the station's logbook for

Above: *West Quoddy Head Lighthouse is a single tower built in 1858 and is located at the easternmost point of the continental United States. (Ralph E. Eshelman)*

Left: *"The light must be kept going," is the unofficial motto of the legendary light keepers. Fewer lighthouses are needed today because modern navigational aids define a surer and safer passage for seafarers. The deactivated light structures are being preserved thanks to the public's will and individual personal efforts. Through these restored maritime structures, the beacon that guided millions will always be shining in memories. In this manner, citizens are carrying on the light keepers' motto. (U.S. Coast Guard)*

The original Barnegat Lighthouse, New Jersey, dropped into the ocean after encroaching seas eroded the sand from its base. Military engineer Lieutenant George G. Meade designed and constructed the present lighthouse in the 1850s. Meade, a Civil War general, achieved fame for defeating General Robert E. Lee and his Confederate Army at the Battle of Gettysburg. A bust and plaque at the lighthouse recognizes his engineering contribution to the safe passage of seafarers. (Ralph E. Eshelman)

completeness. Extremely penny-pinching, he insisted brooms be used until worn down to stubble and no paintbrush be discarded so long as a few bristles remained. Although unpopular among the keepers, Rhodes gained a reputation as a frugal government manager.

Philmore Wass, who as the son of a keeper at Libby Islands Lighthouse, Maine, recalls the arrival of another such inspector aboard the tender *Hibiscus*:

> *This was always a moment of high drama. Father resplendent in his uniform, brass buttons shining, stepping forward to meet this godlike giant, Inspector Luther. Every eye of the audience was riveted upon them as they shook hands, turned, and marched through the boathouse and up the grassy path toward the houses. The urge to follow was too great to resist, so, keeping a safe distance, we all fell in behind, mothers with babes in arms, all the children, and, often, the horse, cow, and dogs. It was quite a parade.*

Keepers assigned land stations often kept gardens to supplement their provisions. One keeper stationed out in the Chesapeake Bay brought enough soil to plant a mini-garden in tubs kept on the walkway. The wife of another keeper maintained a flower planter outside the kitchen window, the only flowers she would see for months at a time. Adele Muise, born in 1931 and the daughter of keeper Joseph Muise, spent her entire childhood on island stations in Maine. While at the Burnt Island Light Station, the family's evening ritual was to walk the perimeter in search of bottles that had washed ashore. These went to a local lobsterman to use as buoys for his traps, and he rewarded the family with lobsters.

Fishing was a popular way to pass time as well as provide variety to meals. Before the automobile and before adequate roads connected light stations, keepers had to walk or go by horse for mail and necessities. Those stationed in offshore lighthouses could use the station boat when the weather cooperated and the distance was not too great. At more isolated places, such as in Alaska or at offshore stations, keepers were totally dependent on the lighthouse tender for supplies. For such stations, tenders brought not only standard provisions, but also carried circulating libraries in specially made wooden boxes. Begun in 1876, the deliveries included books and magazines on history, science, and poetry. Some 350 of these portable libraries were in circulation by 1912.

Women Who Kept the Lights

Mary Louise Clifford & J. Candace Clifford

Keeping a light station was a twenty-four-hours-a-day, 365-days-a-year activity. Before the use of electricity, maintaining a light required the keeper to change or refill the oil or kerosene lamps at least once during the night. Fog might creep in at any hour of the day or night, or heavy rain or a snowstorm could make a ringing fog bell vital to mariners.

The 1902 edition of Instructions to Light-Keepers stated specifically that "A light-house must never be left wholly unattended. . . . If there is only one keeper, some competent member of his family, or other responsible person, must be at the station in his absence." All members of keeper families learned to keep the lights burning and ring the fog bell.

The first woman to keep a lighthouse in what would be the United States was Hannah Thomas, left in charge in 1776 by her husband, John Thomas, when he went off to war. The lighthouse, built in 1771 on land belonging to Hannah's husband, was on Gurnet Point, Massachusetts, and marked the entrance to Plymouth Harbor. John Thomas soon died of smallpox, and Hannah saw that the light was kept until its usefulness to British ships made it unwise to continue. It was relit in 1786 and remained Hannah's responsibility until 1790 when her son received the keeper appointment.

Keepers in the nineteenth century were often also responsible for tending minor lights, which took them away from their main stations. They were also permitted to pursue other jobs, such as fishing or piloting ships into harbors or farming so long as such supplemental work did not interfere with lighthouse duties. When the light station included suitable land, keepers' families tried to be self-sustaining. Josephine Freeman, keeper of Blackistone Island Light on the Chesapeake Bay (1876–1912), wrote in her diary that her husband and sons kept cows, pigs, turkeys, and chickens, fished, crabbed, and nippered oysters, hauled seines, hunted ducks, and tended a garden and fruit trees—all this to feed the six-member family. Any surplus was sold to supplement Josephine's $600 annual salary.

Kate Moore at Black Rock Harbor Light remembered her childhood playmates being chickens, ducks, lambs, and her two Newfoundland dogs. She also had a garden, but had to depend on rain because each time the family tried to dig a well they hit salt water. Kate was twelve when her father, an injured mariner, took up his keeper's appointment. He needed Kate's help from the beginning. She kept the light for him from 1817 until his death in 1871, then received the official appointment herself. She was eighty-three years old when she retired in 1878.

Stephen Pleasonton, who directed the lighthouse service from 1820 until 1852, wrote in 1851: "So necessary is it that the lights should be in the hands of experienced keepers, that I have, in order to effect that object as far as possible, recommended, on the death of a keeper, that his widow, if steady and respectable, should be appointed to succeed him." In all, 141 women received official appointments as keepers, with at least twice that number serving as paid assistant-keepers. There is no record of the hundreds of women who must have performed keeper's duties without remuneration. During the 1870s, the peak period for female appointments, forty-nine of the more than 600 light stations in the United States were in the hands of women.

Disabled war veterans had some claim to keeper's appointments. In 1824 Rebecca Flaherty wrote the Treasury Department to request a keeper's position for her husband John, a veteran of the War of 1812. Rebecca became keeper at Sand Key Light Station in Florida when Major Flaherty died. Charlotte Layton's husband was a veteran ordnance sergeant of a U.S. Army artillery regiment when he became the first keeper of Point Pinos Light

Idawalley Zorada Lewis, known as Ida, was one of a number of female lighthouse keepers. When she was a teenager her father, the keeper of Lime Rock Lighthouse off Rhode Island, suffered a stroke. She took over tending the light and caring for her father. The only access to the lighthouse was by rowboat, which she used numerous times to save lives. In her thirty-nine years as light keeper she was officially credited with saving eighteen lives. Some reports have her saving as many as twenty-five people. (John Witt, U.S. Coast Guard Art Collection)

in California (1855). When he was killed while serving as a member of a sheriff's posse chasing a notorious outlaw, his wife and four children would have been destitute had Charlotte not received the appointment to succeed him.

A number of widows of Civil War veterans were allowed by the Light-House Board to take over their husbands' appointments. Caroline Litigot was nominated to replace her husband as keeper of the Mamajuda Light (1874) on the Detroit River in Michigan after Barney Litigot died from wounds received while serving in the Union Army. Kate Marvin tended Squaw Point Light Station on the Upper Peninsula of Michigan after the death of her husband, a disabled Civil War veteran (1897). The same was true of Emma Tabberrah, who took charge of Cumberland Head Light Station on Lake Champlain after the death of veteran William Tabberrah in 1904.

Several women had remarkably long careers. Kate Moore was at Black Rock Harbor Light for sixty-one years. Barbara Mabrity kept the light at Key West from 1832 to 1862. Maria Younghans kept faithful watch at Biloxi, Mississippi, from 1867 to 1918. Catherine A. Murdock was at Rondout Creek on the Hudson River for half a century (1857–1907). Ida Lewis kept Lime Rock Light in Rhode Island from 1857 until 1911, although she did not receive the official appointment until 1879. Harriet Colfax was

keeper at Michigan City Light in Indiana from 1861 until 1904. Nancy Rose stayed at Stony Point Light on the Hudson River from 1871 until 1904. Kate McDougal was keeper at Mare Island Light Station in California from 1881 until 1916. Laura Hecox spent over thirty years at Santa Cruz Light in California (1883–1917).

Not all the women were wives or daughters of keepers. Harriet Colfax used a political connection to obtain her appointment at Michigan City (1861–1904). Emily Fish's naval son-in-law arranged her appointment at Point Pinos in California (1893–1914). Kate McDougal was the widow of a naval officer. He drowned while performing the duties of lighthouse inspector. Kate was grateful to have a keeper's post (1881–1916) at Mare Island Light because her pension was too small to support her family.

Lighthouse keepers in the eighteenth and nineteenth centuries, male and female, faced much danger and heavy physical labor. Ida Lewis, Kate Walker, and Margaret Norvell all had to launch boats to make daring rescues of shipwrecked mariners. Several women—Abbie Burgess at Matinicus Rock Light, Maria Younghans, Barbara Mabrity, and Harriet Colfax—stayed at their posts to keep the lights burning through terrifying storms and hurricanes. Catherine Murdock worked resolutely at the second Rondout Creek Light throughout a Hudson River flood. She could hear the roar of water and the crashing of boats and barges against the foundations, but the lighthouse stood firm, the beacon shining brightly in the tower.

The last civilian woman lighthouse keeper was Fannie Salter who took over Turkey Point Light on the Chesapeake Bay after the death of her husband in 1925. Because, according to Civil Service rules, she was too old to succeed him, she appealed to her senator, who went directly to President Coolidge to get approval for her appointment.

The few women lighthouse keepers after Salter's retirement in 1947 were all Coast Guard personnel. Eventually the nation's lights were automated and no longer needed keepers. The women who kept the lights performed their duties as faithfully as any of their male colleagues, and all should be remembered and honored for their courage and dedication.

Makapu'u Point lighthouse clings to the side of a lava flow high above the trade-wind-driven surf crashing below. Makapu'u Point Lighthouse on southeastern point of Oahu, Hawaii, built in 1909, is the site of America's largest Fresnel lens. Augustin-Jean Fresnel designed seven numbered orders, or sizes, of lighthouse lenses. The first order lens is designed for large seacoast lighthouses while the sixth order lens, the smallest, is designed for pier or breakwater lights in harbors (a third-and-one-half order makes up the seventh size). Because Makapu'u Point is an important landfall light for ships arriving in Honolulu from the West Coast, the Lighthouse Service ordered a newer, larger, fixture called a Hyper-Radiant lens. This twelve-foot-tall lens, nearly 8 feet in diameter, was purchased in 1887 and exhibited at Chicago's World Fair before being installed at Makapu'u. Makapu'u Point Lighthouse was automated in 1974. (U.S. Coast Guard)

Danger could also be part of the keeper's job. A band of Indians attacked and burned the Cape Florida Lighthouse in 1836. The keeper survived, but his assistant was killed. Both keepers of the Minots Ledge Lighthouse off Boston, Massachusetts, were drowned when the structure was destroyed in a severe storm in 1851. In 1857, before the Cape Flattery Lighthouse could be constructed on Tatoosh Island at the entrance to the Straits of Juan de Fuca, Washington, a blockhouse outfitted with twenty muskets had to be erected for protection against hostile Indians. During the Civil War lighthouses were attacked by both sides. The lighthouse at Hooper Strait, Chesapeake Bay, with its keepers inside, was literally plucked away by ice flows in 1877 and moved five miles south. A hurricane killed a keeper, his wife, and daughter at Horn Island Light Station in Mississippi in 1906. In 1925 one assistant keeper at Makapuu Lighthouse, Hawaii, was killed and another injured when alcohol they were using to fill the lamp exploded. A tsunami swept away the Scotch Cap Lighthouse in Alaska, drowning its five-man crew in 1946. Holland Island Lighthouse, Chesapeake Bay, was mistakenly fired upon with rockets from Navy planes during a training exercise in 1957. In 1983 the keepers at Cape Saint Elias, Alaska, were chased by bears.

In the midst of dangers it is not surprising that many lighthouse keepers performed acts of real heroism. Frederick T. Hatch, a member of a lifesaving crew on Lake Erie at Cleveland, Ohio, rescued twenty-nine persons from two vessels on two successive days during a terrible storm in 1888. Then two years later, as keeper of Cleveland Breakwater Lighthouse, he saved another life. A ship had wrecked just off the breakwater. All eight persons onboard had reached the breakwater, but several were swept back into the water by heavy waves, and one was killed. Hatch launched a small boat, but just after reaching one woman, the wife of the captain of the wrecked ship, his own craft swamped and capsized. Despite the waves, Hatch seized the woman, and though terribly exhausted himself, and after almost losing his own life, managed to reach a thrown line

Cape Florida, located on the southeastern tip of Key Biscayne across the bay from Miami, has a colorful history that includes an attack in 1836 by Seminoles. The light keeper and his assistant barricaded themselves inside and returned gunfire. The assistant was dead when the battle ended; the keeper was alive but suffered from six wounds. Fire following the explosion of a keg of gunpowder heavily damaged the lighthouse. (Paul C. Scotti)

Sandy Hook Lighthouse marks the southern entrance to New York Harbor. It is the only standing colonial lighthouse, with its origin going back to 1764. (Ralph E. Eshelman)

Above: *This view from the lantern room of Point Wilson Lighthouse is across Admiralty Inlet with its sometime swift and turbulent currents that can exceed six knots. This narrow neck between Strait of Juan de Fuca and Puget Sound is a major shipping passage. The red portion of the light shows only on a bearing to danger when seen from the sea. (U.S. Coast Guard)*

Above: *Cape Flattery Lighthouse, the westernmost lighthouse in the continental United States, is located on the rugged Tatoosh Island at the entrance to the Strait of Juan de Fuca in Washington. Access to the island for keepers and families, prior to helicopters in the 1960s, was via a large box hauled by a hoist suspended over a cliff lowered to a boat below, surging in the swells. In 1857, before the lighthouse could be constructed, a blockhouse was built and outfitted with twenty muskets for protection from hostile native tribes. The site for the lighthouse was on sacred grounds. (U.S. Coast Guard)*

Right: *In many small towns around the nation, small Coast Guard units—lighthouses and small boat stations—are homogeneous with the village. Here, nearly a thousand Chatham, Massachusetts, residents gather at Chatham Lighthouse and Coast Guard station for their annual town picture. Townspeople parade ninety-foot-long American flags to commemorate the lighthouse's 125th anniversary. (Amy Thomas, U.S. Coast Guard)*

and was dragged, still holding on to the woman, safely to the station. For his bravery Hatch twice received the Gold Lifesaving Medal, the highest honor the government can bestow for lifesaving heroism.

In 1896, Jefferson M. Brown, keeper of the Point Arena Lighthouse, California, along with two other men, attempted to rescue the crew of the wrecked steamer *San Benito*. The three went out in an un-seaworthy boat, but each time they were hurled back by the force of the seas until finally they succeeded. All were awarded the Gold Lifesaving Medal.

Nils Nelson, assistant keeper of Sakonnet Lighthouse, near West Island, Rhode Island, accomplished an equally daring rescue in 1906. After a boat swamped and was dashed to pieces, a man was left lying flat on the rocks, clinging to crevices to keep from being swept away by the turbulent seas. Breaking waves held off two rescue boats until Nelson, with great difficulty, pulled near the man and told him to throw himself toward the boat when the next wave passed. The man reached the boat, and the next wave carried it over the reef into shelter.

Lightships

Despite having sails, and later engines, lightships were designed to lie at anchor in one spot to mark a certain position. One writer referred to them as "traffic lights at sea." During times of harsh weather when other ships sought the safety of ports, lightships remained on station.

New South Shoal, twenty-four miles off Sankaty Head, Nantucket Island, Massachusetts, with the broad Atlantic to the east and rips and breakers around it, was considered the most desolate and dangerous lightship station in the United States. The ten men stationed aboard suffered from constant pitching and rolling—the only thing worse was the extreme isolation. Because of the treacherous shoals and rips, tenders could reach the New South Shoal only during good weather, and the crew

Opposite, top right: *The 1906 California earthquake severely damaged the first Point Arena Lighthouse, constructed in 1870. A rebuild of the 115-foot tower and keeper's buildings, completed in 1908, incorporated steel-reinforced concrete, the first used in any lighthouse tower in the U.S. Offshore navigators could see the first-order Fresnel lens at a distance of twenty miles. The modern replacement is visible out to sixteen miles. (Gary Todoroff)*

A lightship was established at the western entrance to Vineyard Sound in 1847. Located near the rocks known as Sow and Pigs—with the vessels often referred to as such—this station was discontinued in 1954 after 107 years of operation. Lightships were replaced with a lighted whistle-buoy. Duty at this exposed location was hazardous. Lightships were blown adrift or dragged off station twelve times. During a hurricane in 1944 Lightship No. 73 *sank with the loss of all twelve men aboard. Nineteen years later the bell was recovered from the sunken vessel and dedicated in a monument to all those who lost their lives on this fearsome post. (U.S. Coast Guard)*

Huron Lightship *was built in 1921 for duty on the Great Lakes with a planned fifty-year lifespan. Because it did not have to withstand the forces of ocean duty it was built smaller, at a length of ninety-seven feet. Ocean-duty lightships generally ran about twenty-five feet longer. Huron Station was established in 1893 to mark shoal water at the south end of Lake Huron off the entrance of the St. Clair River. Three ships wore the Huron name between 1893 and 1970. This ship, LV-103/WAL-526, was the last of the trio. The normal color of lightships is bright red. However, the color of the hull in this photograph is true. This lightship is the only one painted black; done in 1935 to denote the side of the channel, it was marked in accordance with the then color designations of channel aids to navigation. (U.S. Coast Guard)*

A lightship crew performing that eternal seafarer time-passer, card playing. (U.S. Coast Guard)

was expected to stay through the winter, sometimes from December until May. So far out to sea was the station, when the ship *City of Newcastle* wrecked on those shoals, all twenty-seven crew members were saved and kept on board the lightship for two weeks before a passing vessel was finally signaled.

The first lightship, placed on the shoal in 1855, parted its cable and wrecked on Nantucket Island. Its replacement lightship, however, was better designed. A one-ton lantern was built around each of its two masts. By lowering the lanterns down the masts into specially designed wooden houses with convertible roofs built on deck, the lamps could be trimmed and fueled in relative safety. Once ready, the deck-house roofs reopened and the lighted lanterns were hoisted up the masts. During one foggy stretch, the ship's fog bell operated continuously for twelve days and nights. When the fog lifted and the bell finally fell silent the crew had become so accustomed to the clanging they had trouble sleeping without it.

The captain of *Cross Rip Lightship* on Tuckernuck Shoal, near Nantucket, Massachusetts, admitted that "if it weren't for the disgrace it would bring on my family I'd rather go to State's prison. Yet I know there's no nobler duty to be served aboard any vessel anywhere." Life on a lightship was like solitary confinement only with *mal de mer* added. The crews of lightships called themselves "fish" because they spent so much of their lives at sea.

The first lightship in the United States was stationed in the lower Chesapeake Bay in 1820. Such ships played an important role in establishing navigation markers in locations where no permanent structures

Columbia *lightship as observed for many years when ships passed crossing the infamous Columbia River bar at the river's mouth between Washington and Oregon. (Coast Guard Museum Northwest)*

158

could be built. These lightships marked entrances to harbors, warned of dangerous shoals, and served as approach and departure marks for ocean and coastal traffic. The hulls of lightships were almost always painted red with large white letters identifying the name of the station. The last operational lightship was Nantucket Shoals, which was taken out of service in 1983. Between 1820 and 1983, 116 lightship stations stood duty, with 1909 the peak year when fifty-six were maintained.

Lightships, like lighthouses, had their dangers. When *Lightship No. 37* foundered off Delaware Bay in 1893, only two of six crewmembers survived. Buffalo *Lightship No. 22* went down with all its crew when swamped by a huge wave in Lake Erie in a November storm in 1913. In 1918, the first American lightship to be sunk by an enemy submarine, *Lightship No. 71*, was lost on Diamond Shoals, North Carolina, but her crew was able to take to their boats and reached shore without injury. *Lightship No. 105*, stationed off the same notorious Diamond Shoals, was hit by a powerful hurricane in 1933. With the engine running full speed against the violent winds and strong currents, the lightship was nevertheless dragged five miles into the breakers. The lifeboats, radio antennae, and engine room ventilators were carried away by the winds and waves. Water had began to rise above the deck plates of the engine fire-room when suddenly the wind shifted and pushed the vessel off the shoals. Miraculously the lightship was able to run into Portsmouth, Virginia, for repairs. President Franklin D. Roosevelt personally commended the crew for their efforts. In 1934, the steamship *Olympic* struck

In 1934 the four-year-old lightship Nantucket, *was anchored on station forty-one miles off-shore. A light and radio beacon beamed outward from the fixed vessel for ships to use for navigational reference. The lightship was clothed in thick fog when at mid-morning on 15 May without warning, the British cruise liner* Olympic, Titanic's *sister ship, struck it broadside at twenty knots and drove the lightship to the bottom of the Atlantic Ocean. Seven of the eleven Lighthouse Servicemen died. (Charles Mazoujian, U.S. Coast Guard Art Collection)*

Large, unmanned navigational buoys now mark some locations once held by the ever-present lightship with its lonely crew. Crewmen shown here are aboard only for routine maintenance. (Tracy Phillips)

159

Boston Lighthouse on Brewster Island in Massachusetts Bay sits at the site of the first lighthouse built in North America in 1716. The British blew this up during their withdrawal from Boston in 1776. The current lighthouse was constructed in 1783 and is the second oldest tower in North America after Sandy Hook Lighthouse, built in 1764. (Brent Erb, U.S. Coast Guard)

Lightship No. 11 in dense fog on Nantucket Shoals. The lightship was cut in two and sank with seven of its eleven crewmembers. Collisions were common: at least 150 lightships suffered such mishaps. The Scotland, New Jersey, station seemed particularly unlucky—lightships there were struck six times between 1892 and 1904.

The United States operated the largest aids to navigation system in the world by 1924. At the end of World War II the Coast Guard was responsible for 468 lighthouses. A Lighthouse Automation and Modernization Program (LAMP) started in 1968 to accelerate the automation of lighthouses and standardized the equipment at those previously automated. Over 300 billet reductions resulted by 1990 in automating every lighthouse in the United States. The sole exception was Boston Harbor Light Station. This historic site will continue to be staffed, commemorating lighthouse keepers following the Coast Guard Authorization Act of 1989. (U.S. Coast Guard)

Lighthouse Traditions Continue

While the role of the lighthouse and its keepers has diminished over time, largely due to new technology and cost saving measures, the tradition continues. Across the United States from the northern tip of Maine and Washington, to the southern tip of Florida and California, to the Great Lakes to the mouth of the Mississippi, to the shores of Alaska, to the islands of Guam, Hawaii, Cuba, Puerto Rico, and the U.S. Virgin Islands, lighthouses and other aids to navigation continue their work. A tradition dating from the American colonial period, lighthouses serve as constant reminders of the dedicated, loyal, sometimes heroic men and women of the U.S. Lighthouse Establishment, U.S. Lighthouse Bureau, and the Coast Guard, who served their fellow mankind regardless of hardship. Of all of these symbols, perhaps none is more fitting than Boston Harbor Lighthouse, the 1716 site of the first lighthouse in what today is the United States, and the last officially "manned" U.S. Coast Guard lighthouse in America. May Boston Harbor Lighthouse forever stand in honor and memory of all the men and woman who served the colonial and post-colonial lighthouses of the United States.

Cheeseburgers in Paradise

John Fitzgerald

Imagine arriving on a small, tropical island in the middle of the Pacific Ocean, one with only a handful of coconut trees and no fresh water. Your biggest worries are sharks in the lagoon or a tsunami that could submerge the whole island. Its highest elevation is only fourteen-feet above sea level. A walk around the entire island takes forty-five minutes, and you quickly discover there are twenty-two other people who have met the same fate as you—to spend a year here before returning to civilization and again enjoying restaurants, theaters, and all the modern conveniences taken for granted every day back in the United States. This Swiss-Family-Robinson life is real at an isolated Coast Guard loran station.

Based on the simple principle that a position can be determined by the intersection of electronic signals from different sources, Long Range Aids to Navigation, or loran, was responsible for safely guiding hundreds of millions of people and billions of tons of cargo around the world during the second half of the twentieth century.

Loran is both fast and reliable—it is accurate to within 100 yards—and once was at the leading edge of navigation technology. Loran chains consisting of multiple stations provided navigational aid around the globe, and while many overseas loran stations have now been shut down, some in the continental United States and Alaska are still in operation.

In order to maximize coverage, some units were located in desolate areas uninhabited except by the Coast Guard personnel assigned loran duty. One of those stations was on Kure Atoll, Hawaii. Approximately 1,400 miles northwest of Honolulu, Kure is the westernmost island in the Hawaiian Island chain and lies just forty miles west of Midway Island. One of three stations in the former Hawaiian loran chain, its remote location—just over 178 degrees west longitude—near the International Dateline justified the station's motto of "Dark Side of the Sun" as it was one of the last places on earth to see the dawning of a new day.

The most isolated station of the three (the others were on Johnston Atoll and the island of Hawaii), the unit was in operation from 1961 through 1992 on an atoll a little over a mile-and-a-half long and a half-mile across at its widest point. Its most prominent features were its coral runway, a 625-foot tower that transmitted the loran signal and thousands of breeding albatross. Its only residents were the twenty-three unaccompanied (no spouses or families) Coast Guard men and women assigned to the station for one full year.

The crew included a lieutenant (jg) as commanding officer and a chief warrant officer (Electronics) as executive officer. Eight electronic technicians maintained all the loran equipment. Three machinery technicians, a damage controlman, and one electrician's mate formed the engineering department that maintained the diesel-powered generators. They also relied on duct tape and a great deal of innovation to fix everything from the unit vehicles to the station's refrigerators and plumbing. Two cooks, one corpsman, a storekeeper, and four non-rated personnel completed the team.

The goal of these men and women was to attain the loran Operational Performance Award for 99.99 percent signal availability during a 180-day period. This meant providing 179 days, twenty-three hours and thirty-five minutes worth of usable loran signals over a six-month period. If the station suffered any mechanical or technical anomaly for more than twenty-five minutes, the unit would become ineligible for the award and have to start a new six-month period.

The loran signal was created in a small timer-room, and a twenty-four-hour watch stander ensured it was working in proper sequence with the other stations

in the chain. Since the electronic gear creating the signal was extremely sensitive and needed to be accurate to within millionths of a second, the room was kept immaculately clean and air conditioners constantly circulated cold air to prevent overheating.

Located near the base of the tower, the antenna building housed two large, vacuum-tube transmitters. One transmitter always broadcast the signal while maintenance was being done on the second. Maintenance on all electronic equipment and the generators was performed in such a manner that a spare unit could be brought on line transmitting in a matter of minutes if operating elements failed.

If an electrical blackout occurred or an animal found its way into a transmitter, if the timer failed or anything else caused the signal to fall out of required tolerance, a shrill alarm immediately alerted the watch stander—as well as everyone else on the island. While the signal was out of tolerance, the station was charged with "bad time." While the watch stander traced the cause of the alarm, engineers scrambled to ensure the generators were working properly, and electronic technicians ran to the antenna building to inspect the transmitters. Even support personnel such as the corpsman would hustle to the timer building to offer assistance and, if nothing else, moral support.

Eventually the problem would be fixed, the signal put back on the air and the "bad time clock" was stopped. On average, an alarm would sound every two

weeks. As a result, many loran personnel summed up their experience at a loran station as hours and hours of boredom interrupted by these few minutes of shear panic. Despite the obstacles posed by its desolate location, Loran Station Kure Island achieved a milestone in 1990 when it was awarded its sixth consecutive Operational Performance Award.

The layout of the station was simple: three main buildings formed a rough T-shape; at the top of the "T" was the barracks with living quarters, a galley, sickbay, and a billiards room. Each crewmember had a private room, approximately eight feet by ten, and shared the two communal bathrooms. Next to the barracks was a machinery building that housed the unit's three generators, a workshop, and the timer room. The antenna building formed the bottom of the "T."

There was a fuel-tank farm with diesel fuel for the generators and three station vehicles: a pickup truck, front-end loader, and forklift. Fuel was delivered once a year by barge through a pipeline extending to an anchorage approximately a half-mile off shore. All the buildings had gutters that drained rainwater into tanks. The rainwater and desalinated seawater were the only sources for drinking, cooking, and bathing water.

Above: Kure Island loran station, as it appeared in the 1970s, was located virtually in the middle of the North Pacific Ocean just west of Midway Island. A 625-foot tower that once transmitted the loran signal appears from the air as a toothpick stuck in a snack offered on a turquoise platter. The sandbar is the home to thousands of breeding albatross. For thirty-one years, its only other residents at any time were the twenty to twenty-five Coast Guard personnel. (John Fitzgerald)

The station's lifeline was Coast Guard Air Station Barber's Point, Hawaii, and its C-130 fleet. Every two weeks one aircraft would deliver food, parts, supplies, and mail. Of course several air crewmen brought pizzas and other special treats from Honolulu to trade for fresh lobsters caught in the lagoon. Usually a large pizza was worth between two and four tails, depending on the negotiating skills of the parties involved.

Living beyond the range of television and radio reception, crewmembers relied on the taped television shows and movies delivered on every flight. Telephone calls were a rarity. Used almost exclusively for urgent business or emergencies, the station phone depended on a microwave link from Kure to Midway. On Midway, an operator prioritized requests from both islands and connected the caller using a government phone line to Oahu, which limited the user to local calls. Coast Guard ingenuity helped station personnel circumvent the Navy's phone restrictions. The unit had a ham radio and developed a friendship with some local operators on Oahu Island, Hawaii. Each day both parties would coordinate their on-air time and station personnel would put in orders for magazines, sports equipment, and other personal items that were eventually delivered by the C-130s. On other occasions, operators arranged for personnel to make long distance phone calls over the radio to family members in the United States.

The atoll's natural beauty was truly awe-inspiring. Although scuba diving was not permitted—since the nearest decompression chamber was in Honolulu—snorkelers shared the crystal clear water with dolphins, sharks, sea rays, seals, turtles, and countless fish. Every year thousands of albatross, who crisscrossed the Pacific to feed on squid and other fish, would return to the island to raise their chicks. On the pristine beaches, glass Japanese fishnet floats would wash up beside Hawaiian Monk seals sleeping on the white sand while frigate birds and terns circled overhead.

Despite the tranquility and almost total isolation from the rest of the world, once a year the crew was treated to a small taste of civilization, literally. During

The Kure Island loran station crew poses with Santa for the eagerly anticipated annual holiday celebration with a cheeseburger feast in paradise. (John Fitzgerald)

the Christmas holidays, in what became a Kure tradition, a McDonald's franchise in Honolulu sent volunteers to the island on the five-hour C-130 logistics flight. As soon as they arrived, the McDonald's staff unloaded their supplies and started cooking fresh hamburgers. A small-gift exchange was held on the mess deck as the aroma of Big Macs and French fries filled the air. At the same time, crewmembers reminisced of Christmas traditions and families back home. Finally, after weeks of anticipation, a McDonald's feast was ready and the entire crew sat down to enjoy cheeseburgers in paradise.

Eventually, the Global Positioning System, GPS, utilizing satellites, was developed. GPS, more accurate than loran, provides greater coverage and requires no maintenance. It replaced loran as the primary means of navigation and a majority of loran stations throughout the world was decommissioned during the 1990s. As of 2003, there were eighteen operational loran stations in the United States, six in Alaska, and a few chains kept operational by foreign countries. In 1992, loran Station Kure Island was decommissioned and the island became a wildlife sanctuary. Almost all the equipment on the island, including electrical transformers and other large objects previously deposited in the station's garbage dump at the end of the runway, were removed in an effort to restore the island to its natural state. Today, aside from a few empty buildings there are almost no physical reminders of the Coast Guard's presence on Kure.

Into the Surf

Clayton Evans, Canadian Coast Guard

The morning of Saturday, 8 August 1987 at USCG Station Tillamook Bay on the rugged coast of Oregon began like most. Before breakfast the station crews were already checking their equipment and getting a head start on the daily routine. A diesel engine's low rumbling was heard as one of the station's thirty-foot surf rescue-boats, SRB *30619*, fired up. Compared to the slower forty-four-foot and fifty-two-foot heavy-weather motor lifeboats at Station Tillamook, the high-speed fiberglass surfboat was designed for dash-and-grab missions and generally carried a crew of two.

On board the SRB were Boatswain's Mate First Class Rick L. Spencer and Machinery Technician Third Class Steven P. Meshke. Spencer, or "Spence," a thirteen-year veteran of the Coast Guard, was on duty as the station's number-one surfman on this particular day. If any calls-outs were to occur on the treacherous river-mouth bar at the entrance to Tillamook Bay, Spencer would be the principal coxswain, or boat driver. His other duties as surfman included monitoring the conditions on the bar, such as the size of the seas and swell, whether there was the potential for any breaking waves, otherwise known as "breaks" or surf, and advising his commanding officer whether the bar should be closed to maritime traffic. For this very reason, the SRB had been fired up, and the two men proceeded to sea to get a feel for what the day's weather might bring.

Upon arrival at the Tillamook Bar, they discovered an abnormally large ground swell, created by distant Pacific storms, driving in from the west. Otherwise, the surface of the ocean was as calm as glass. It was an eerie combination. Spencer knew the tide was flooding that morning,

A crew braces themselves against the impact of a large wave crashing over their motor lifeboat. A breaking wave's force is measured in tons per square foot. A wave's power has broached lifeboats, blown out bulletproof windows, and ripped metal from hulls and pilothouses. Crewmembers train to understand wave tendencies and learn to avoid the fatal grab of breaking waves. Hypothermia protection suits are worn for added safety and crews are strapped in to avoid being flung overboard. (Barry Lane, U.S. Coast Guard)

Pages 164–165: The high-speed fiberglass surfboat, SRB, is designed for dash-and-grab situations. One summer day two Coast Guardsmen, in a boat similar to this thirty-foot surfboat, dashed into treacherous waters off the Oregon coast to rescue five people tossed into the sea from their capsized eighteen-foot runabout. These are common waters for this boat and crew; only the numbers of survivors and victims change with each case. (U.S. Coast Guard)

Opposite: The 30-footer goes ten miles up the coast, zigzagging among the breakers, just to reach the scene. Once there the Coast Guardsmen find and pull aboard the survivors—all the while maneuvering in ten-foot waves. (U.S. Coast Guard)

The Pacific Ocean of the Oregon coast is among the most treacherous water for Coast Guard rescue work. The builders of Tillamook Lighthouse attested to that when they constructed it on a rock a mile off Tillamook Head in northern Oregon. Waves battered the workers throughout their toil and later the keepers lived in terror through storms. During one, a stone weighing 135 pounds crashed through the roof of the keeper's quarters trashing a room and its contents. Giant waves, over the lighthouse's seventy-seven years of operation, hurled rocks and flotsam shattering the lens-room glass protecting the lantern 133 feet above sea level. (U.S. Coast Guard)

A motor lifeboat crashes through the Pacific surf. Such boats are built to withstand the terrific forces of violent seas. If capsized by waves, these specially designed boats have the ability to right themselves within seconds. While the vessels have to be tough, crews have to be clever to brawl with an ocean's unrelenting and overwhelming force. (U.S. Coast Guard)

pushing in from the ocean up the river, which meant that later in the day when it switched to an ebb, millions of tons of water, both fresh and salt, would begin flowing out over the bar in the opposite direction of these big incoming swells. As a result, they would slow down, expend their energy upward and begin to break and plunge in treacherous fashion. The crew hoped any mariners at sea would have returned to port by that time. With a spin of the wheel and a shove on the throttle, Spencer swung the SRB around and returned to the station.

After the SRB tied up, the two men made their report to the station's operations room and joined the rest of their colleagues for breakfast and the routines of boat station life. There were lifeboats to maintain, new personnel to train, and piles of paperwork to fill out. Both men realized that their early morning jaunt had probably been their "boat ride" for the day and that it was time to get on with the more mundane, albeit necessary, aspects of the job. For both Spencer and Meshke, this would not, however, be an ordinary day.

A short time after one in the afternoon, the station's operations room received a distress call from a pleasure craft reporting that an eighteen-foot runabout had capsized, not on the Tillamook Bar, but some ten miles to the north of the station at the mouth of the Nehalem River. This was an equally treacherous piece of water. Initial radio communications from another vessel on scene were chaotic and confusing. Eventually it was determined five people were in the water in large breaking seas, only two of whom were still clinging to the overturned boat.

Now the tide had changed. Spencer's worst fears of the morning were realized. He knew the only chance of rescuing the people in the water rested with getting there fast, but the Tillamook Bar, which they would have to cross on the way to the scene, was now being combed with ten-foot breaking waves. These seas were beyond the designated operational parameters of the thirty-foot SRB, but the beefier MLB's maximum speed was 12 knots, and with one of these vessels it would take twice as long to get there. A decision was made and the two men in the faster thirty-foot SRB *30619* soon found themselves crashing through the surf zone at the entrance to Tillamook Bay. The 30-footer was small, but fast (25 knots) and maneuverable, and Spencer zigzagged his way among the breakers, riding the "canyons" while Meshke kept an eye to seaward for any whitewater coming their way. Somehow, Spencer was able to cover the distance to the mouth of the Nehalem in less than forty minutes.

While the SRB wove and surfed its way north, other events were unfolding at the accident scene. A Coast Guard helicopter launched from Air Station Astoria and was flying to the capsized craft. In addition, a pleasure craft, *Slo Gin*, skippered by David Morrow, was attempting to enter the breakers and rescue the drowning men. Morrow's first attempt failed due to the immense seas, but undaunted, he tried again and somehow was able to recover two survivors from the overturned hull, but not before almost capsizing his own vessel in the process. The remaining three in the water were being swept into even larger seas closer to shore, and having tempted fate twice and succeeded, Morrow knew another attempt would be suicidal. Two lives had been saved through his heroic efforts, and once *30619* arrived on scene *Slo Gin* departed to rendezvous with an awaiting ambulance.

Immediately upon arrival, Spencer and Meshke stopped just outside the Nehalem bar to assess the conditions. The skies were clear, the wind blowing from the north at 20 knots, the seas about eight to ten feet high, but the breaks on the bar were even higher than those at Tillamook, with the occasional 14-footer.

They decided to poke *30619*'s nose in about the time the HH-3F arrived from Astoria. The helicopter quickly spotted the over-turned boat, and hovering above it, provided Spencer with a visual reference to the craft's location. From the low elevation of their small rescue boat, and with great walls of water constantly laying them over on the side and temporarily obliterating their field of vision, it was virtually impossible to spot small objects on the surface.

As Spencer quickly realized, the boat and any survivors around it had now drifted into the worst possible area, a maelstrom of surf known as the "jaws of the bar," directly between the ends of the north and south jetties. From their position, Spencer and Meshke could not see any survivors and, so far, none had been spotted by the helicopter either. Spencer knew there were three people out there somewhere and that they could have been scattered as pounding surf drove them toward shore. The question for the surfman was, "Which way were they?"

It was at this point that Spencer felt "things got really weird." Through the roar of the wind and surf and the gyrations of the turbo-charged diesel the boatswain's mate heard a voice say, "Turn to the left 10 degrees and go." Spencer knew it wasn't Meshke who had whispered in his ear, but he had enough experience to know not to question the source. He swung the SRB to port and hammered the throttle. Within sixty-seconds they spotted a head bobbing in the surf about a quarter-mile from the overturned boat.

Spencer changed his focus to the task at hand, recovering that person from the water. He skillfully maneuvered the SRB among the breaks, trying to get into the best position to come up-swell and recover the man with the seas on the SRB's nose, while at the same time watching for a "lull in the series," a brief window of opportunity when a few of the waves may be less severe. When the time was right he brought the man, who was clinging to a floating cushion, along the starboard side of the SRB's cockpit. Spencer had to let go of the wheel to help Meshke haul the man on board. While they were hanging over the side of the boat two large breakers struck the *30619*, knocking the rescue boat on its beam, partially submerging both the rescuers and the victim. Spencer and Meshke, strapped with harnesses to the SRB, never let go of the victim and brought on board a forty-seven-year-old man. He was still conscious, but suffering from hypothermia, and they quickly placed him in the survivor's compartment aft of the cockpit.

As soon as he was aboard, the man pleaded with the Coast Guardsmen to look for his son, also lost somewhere in the surf zone, but with no lifejacket or other floatation. The man said he believed the third person in the water, his father, had already succumbed to the breakers

A thirty-foot surfboat runs out through the incoming surf during training exercises. Not built as strong as the larger lifeboats, its assets are speed (25 knots) and maneuverability. The surfboat demonstrates high agility in working in heavy surf among rocks. (U.S. Coast Guard)

Coast Guard Petty Officer Kevin Post grabs a scared three-year-old Johnny Dudek from Petty Officer Cuester Bethelmie after rescuing the child from a sinking vessel. All human life is precious, but when a child is saved, rescuers' emotions soar even higher with joy. (Tom Sperduto, U.S. Coast Guard)

Days at sea are not always as cruise liner advertisers would have their potential customers believe. Cloudless blue sky and glass smooth seas are not the rule aboard Coast Guard cutters. More often, it is one of hanging on to keep one's footing as the vessel crashes through the waves. (Courtesy James Moerls)

The Coast Guard is equipped with small boats designed for many uses. When seen moving at high speed, typically there is business at hand needing instant attention. These boats, regardless of size or shape, are readily recognized by a red, white, and blue racing stripe located near the bow on a white or aluminum colored hull. Special use boats may be black, red, or gray but are still identified by the distinctive racing stripe. (U.S. Coast Guard)

and sunk beneath the surface just minutes before the SRB arrived. A brief lull in the waves occurred, and the crew of the SRB had a few moments to reassess the situation.

It didn't take long for Spencer and Meshke to locate another person in the water. It was the victim's son, about thirty yards away in the midst of the breakers close to shore. They tried to get in close but the boat was knocked over 110 degrees. Meshke found himself underwater. The self-righting ability of the SRB design kicked in and the boat leveled itself. They made another approach, only this time they were so close to shore Spencer worried about striking bottom in the trough of a wave— a certain catastrophe for all on board.

Spencer maneuvered the SRB within thirty feet of the second victim, who appeared to be losing consciousness. These suspicions were confirmed when Meshke skillfully tossed the rescue ball, a form of heaving line, right between the young man's outstretched arms. There was no reaction and the rescue ball was knocked out of the man's reach as another wave struck the 30-footer.

They'd have to move in closer to the victim and make another attempt. Once again Meshke tossed the rescue ball, only this time providence was on the victim's side. Somehow the ball skipped under an arm and in the motion caused by the rough seas, the line attached to the ball twisted around the arm, allowing Meshke to drag him slowly toward the SRB. As the young man was being drawn to the boat, Spencer tried to keep the SRB's bow facing the breaks while attempting to jockey the vessel sideways to close the distance even more. Timing would be everything. With the victim finally alongside the starboard cockpit and a brief lull in the wave series, Meshke yelled, "Spence, he's sinking!"

The life-line had come off and only a dim outline of the victim could be seen sinking beneath the foamy sea. Spencer left the wheel and the two men frantically reached into the water trying to grasp anything they could lay their hands on. Incredibly, just as another series of breaking waves was barreling down upon the rescue boat, they felt something and managed to drag the man's sixteen-year-old son over the gunwale by his hair.

It was now Spencer's job to get everyone out of there and Meshke, who was trained as an emergency medical technician, began trying to revive the unconscious victim. The youth was unresponsive and not breathing; air bubbles came out his nose. Providing medical attention to a drowning victim on level ground was difficult enough, but in the tiny cockpit of a thirty-foot SRB, being tossed by breaking waves almost half its length, verged on the impossible.

In the cramped cockpit, Spencer, who was standing between the victim's legs, used his skills as a surfman to make his way outside of the breaks while Meshke did his best on the heaving deck. Miraculously, his airway cleared and having been given artificial respiration, the young man coughed, expelled a great deal of sea water and—as his father watched through the sealed survivor-compartment port-light—returned to life.

The helicopter radioed *30619* offering to hoist the victims but Spencer replied that would be next to impossible given the sea conditions. It would also be equally difficult for *30619* to cross the Nehalem bar. The survivor's best chance for rapid medical attention would be back at Tillamook. Spencer swung the SRB to the south with Meshke continuing to administer first aid.

Even though Spencer would later describe the rescue in the surf as seeming to "occur in slow motion," the rescue, from the time the crew of SRB *30619* spotted the first man in the water until they departed the surf zone with both victims onboard, had taken less than three minutes.

Rescue crews need to be strong swimmers. To complement swimmer training, fun competitions are held among Coast Guard units. Here petty officer Terry Labombard makes a "save" during the rescue swim event at Coast Guard Group Milwaukee's boat rodeo. (Dean Jordan, U.S. Coast Guard)

A disabled sailing vessel is taken in tow. The appearance of the Coast Guard is a welcome sight to seafarers, both commercial and recreational, when they get into difficulty underway. (U.S. Coast Guard)

Coast Guard Station Miami Beach, Florida, proudly claims the title as the "World's Busiest Multi-Mission Station." Year after year this unit responds to more cases than any other Coast Guard station. The reason is location. Nearly always favorable weather, intense boating and aircraft activity, nearness to the many Bahamian islands, proximity to preferential drug smuggling routes, and lying in the path of tropical storms ushers in a constant flow of opportunities. With constant practice from the frequency of calls by the station's personnel, there is no slack in responding to near-continuous appeals for rescues and law enforcement incidents. (Ryan N. Doss, U.S. Coast Guard)

171

While the Coast Guard has a large mix of coastal and deepwater cutters, the service's ubiquitous vessel is the small boat. The Coast Guard is recognized worldwide for superb boat handling under most extraordinary conditions. (U.S. Coast Guard)

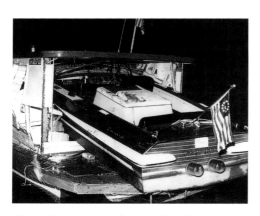

The safe operation of recreational boats is a serious matter to the Coast Guard. Boat collisions annually top the list of boating accidents. The Coast Guard's public education courses and inspection program are intended to prevent mishaps such as this. While much of safe boating is common sense, Coast Guard public education programs that instill boat handling and seamanship skills add immeasurably, making "pleasure boating" truly a pleasure. (U.S. Coast Guard)

Forty minutes later, when the SRB pulled up to the dock at Station Tillamook, the two men were transferred to an awaiting ambulance and taken to the local hospital. Both would live to tell the tale. Later the same day the father would return to the station for an emotional thank you. For both Spencer and Meshke all the years of training and experience had paid off; they had accomplished what they had joined the service to do—save lives.

For an individual to serve at a small boat station in the United States Coast Guard is to become part of a long tradition of extraordinary valor and accomplishment. Crews at over 130 Coast Guard small boat stations serve in some of the most hazardous sea conditions on earth. On these dangerous waters they are expected to perform a multitude of missions including law enforcement, marine and port security duties connected with homeland security, as well as conduct boating-safety and environmental-protection inspections. Their principal responsibility however, continues to be the saving of life at sea.

This is not a profession for the uninitiated or those lacking a strong nerve—247 small boat crewman have lost their lives in the line of duty since 1876. Calm nerves and cool heads are required, as is a sense of duty that overrides rational fear. Station crews are routinely called to go out in conditions when most mariners have retreated to safe refuge. They venture forth not in large sea-going vessels with dozens of personnel and multiple decks, but in relatively small boats, usually thirty to fifty feet in length, and with fewer than ten crew members. In some cases the height of the waves can exceed the length of the boat. They conduct this job quietly, professionally, and, in most instances, with little or no fanfare.

Left: *Coast Guard crew aboard the 110-foot Island Class Coast Guard patrol boat* Chandeleur *fights a fishing boat fire. This class boat is powered with two engines totaling 5,760 hp and has a maximum speed in excess of 26 knots for responses to emergencies such as this. (U.S. Coast Guard)*

Above: *Seaman Jason Kelly coils a line, a task that seems to crewpersons aboard small boats to be repeated 100 times a day. (Jacquelyn Zettles, U.S. Coast Guard)*

This has been the way of the small boat crews in the United States for over a century and a half since the establishment of the first lifesaving stations funded by the U.S. government in 1848.

In many ways, the men and women who crew the more than 1,500 small boats in the Coast Guard today, principally operating motor lifeboats (MLBs) and utility boats (UTBs,) can be considered victims of their own and their predecessors' success. So efficient have they become at saving those in peril along the coastal and inland waters of the United States that occupational circumstances that might be considered exceptional and incredibly hazardous by most have now been accepted as routine by all and, unfortunately, not always deemed entirely newsworthy. The reality is the men and women who crew the small boat stations of the Coast Guard have become so extraordinary at conquering adversity that success has become the expected norm. The Coast Guard responds to approximately 50,000 search-and-rescue cases every year and saves nearly 4,000 lives. Over 30,000 of these calls for help are handled by the Coast Guard's small

Above: *An osprey in a nest built atop a Coast Guard-installed and -maintained channel marker watches unruffled as Coast Guard small boats return to station from drills. Training, coupled with experience, improves proficiency. So efficient have Coast Guard crewmembers become at saving lives that many incredibly hazardous rescues have become accepted as routine, with these events not always deemed newsworthy. (Randy T. Ashmore, U.S. Coast Guard)*

Left: *Lifejackets are thrown to people in the water the moment the Coast Guard boat arrives at the scene of a sunken pleasure boat. (Joseph M. Patton, U.S. Coast Guard)*

173

A Coast Guard seaman splices a manila line. Marlinspike seamanship is a skill passed down from the ancient mariner to seamen as a right of passage over the centuries from the time when ropes and lines were first used aboard vessels. Mastering knot-making skills and splicing lines frequently moves beyond a need for hitching and binding to an art form. (Sarah Foster-Snell, U.S. Coast Guard)

boat units, the first line of defense in a constant war against the harshest elements of nature and the misadventures of mankind.

Such expertise in small-boat operations did not develop overnight. It is the product of history and traces its origins to the determination, bravery, and humanitarian initiative that induced the nation's earliest lifesavers to head out to sea in open pulling boats in the harshest of conditions. This spirit of survival in the face of overwhelming odds remains a guiding principle among those who crew the Coast Guard boat stations today. They must continually harness the same spirit to overcome an ever-expanding workload in the contemporary world of high-tech equipment and multiple roles and responsibilities as government attempts to do "more with less." To truly understand the force that drives many of the unique individuals who crew the small boats of the Coast Guard today, we must first look at the history of the small boat stations in the United States, how they developed, the crews who manned them, and the tools they used.

Origins

The present-day Coast Guard has its roots in two services: the United States Revenue Cutter Service founded in 1790 and the United States Life-Saving Service, or USLSS, created by Congress in 1871. These two were combined to form the Coast Guard in 1915. History shows the USLSS to have been one of the most well-organized and efficient state-funded coastal lifesaving organizations the world has ever seen. At its peak of operations in 1914, the USLSS had over 280 lifeboat and lifesaving stations around the outer coasts, on the Great Lakes, and along the principal inland waterways of the United States. At one time there was even a station at Nome, Alaska. The primary lifesaving tool of the service was the small boat, principally the lightweight surfboat and the heavier self-righting lifeboat.

Many Coast Guard small boat stations are compact units located in coastal, lake, and river communities such as this station located in Shinnecock on Long Island, New York. Other units are in large cities co-located on larger bases that are also home to a variety of units conducting other Coast Guard missions. (U.S. Coast Guard)

A Dobbins Boat, circa 1904, battles its way into the surf. This routine was practiced on all coasts of the United States where lifeboat stations launched directly into the surf. The railroad trestle in the background was constructed to carry rocks by train to assist in building the North Jetty at the mouth of the Coquille River, Oregon. Massive rock jetties later allowed the dredging of river-mouth sandbars, opening these rivers to navigation and enabling Coast Guard stations to leave the beaches for the protected waters up river. (U.S. Coast Guard)

In 1871 there were no turbo-charged diesels to propel rescuers to the scene of disaster. These original American lifesavers pulled oars, or rowed, their wooden surfboats through the breakers using brute manpower and sheer determination. If they were lucky enough to be in a lifeboat and the winds were right, they might be able to hoist a sail or two, but often these larger rescue craft had to be rowed as well. In some cases the toil of rowing out was preceded by a long trek down the beach, handling horses or manually pulling the boat and carriage through sand to the scene of the calamity.

Thousands of lives were also saved using line-throwing guns and rockets that shot ropes out to shipwrecks and the survivors being brought ashore by breeches buoys, or in a submarine-like device known as a life-car. In the roughly forty-three years of its existence the service was responsible for saving the lives of, or otherwise assisting, an astounding 178,741 persons from shipwrecks and other maritime calamities. In the same period approximately 1,455 unfortunate souls were lost along American shores, less than one percent of the total saved—a phenomenal statistic even in today's world of helicopters, high-tech rescue boats, and advanced communications. Most of these lives were saved using small boats and other lifesaving apparatus operated by highly trained and experienced small boat crews. The annals of the

The standard surfboat for many years was about twenty-five feet in length and weighed approximately 1,300 pounds. These boats, riding on a large-wheeled cart, were pulled to the launching area by the crewmembers or by horse, if available. (U.S. Coast Guard)

In the nineteenth and early twentieth centuries—before the development of the rescue helicopter—the only alternative to rescue by boat was pulling survivors from vessels wrecked near shore by the breeches buoy apparatus. Lines were connected from the beach to the vessel and people were hauled ashore in the ring and cutoff trousers device shown during this drill. (U.S. Coast Guard)

early lifesaving services are replete with hundreds of examples of heroic deeds in the face of extreme danger.

Such efficiency in these humanitarian endeavors had not always been the case. Prior to the introduction of organized lifesaving services, thousands of lives were lost along American shores, particularly along the Atlantic seaboard, on the coasts of New England, and on the approaches to the ports of Boston, New York, and Philadelphia. During the first half of the nineteenth century, hundreds of ships were wrecked en route to the New World, many of them crammed full of European immigrants eagerly awaiting a much different fate than that which befell them.

In response to this loss, private humane societies were formed. The first of these organizations in North America was the Massachusetts Humane Society (MHS), founded in 1785, which went on to establish the first small boat, or "lifeboat," station in the United States at Cohassett, Massachusetts, in 1807. The MHS would construct many more houses of refuge and small boat stations manned by volunteer crews, but, true to its name, the facilities of the society were confined to the commonwealth only. Other humanitarian and benevolent societies to aid shipwreck victims would eventually be formed in New York and Philadelphia, but not until New Jersey Congressman Dr. William A. Newell's famed "vigorous and victorious" plea to Congress in 1848 would the first public funds be allocated directly to the cause.

By the outbreak of the Civil War, these earliest government stations had stretched beyond the shores of New Jersey to New York, Maine, New Hampshire, the Carolinas, Georgia, Florida, and even Texas. In addition, boats and lifesaving gear were procured for dozens of harbor and customs authorities throughout the United States, including twenty-three locations on the Great Lakes. Public funds were also allocated to assist the various humane societies, including the MHS. These may not have been the most efficient lifesaving stations in terms of their maintenance and manning

structure, but thousands of lives were saved just the same. Most of these original stations and their gear did not survive the ravages of the Civil War. It would take the concerted efforts of the likes of Sumner Kimball and Captain John Faunce, both of the Revenue Cutter Service, to reinvigorate the cause of the small boat lifesaver along the coasts of the United States, the result of their efforts being the establishment of the USLSS.

The crew of a 47-footer fights blazing rail-road tank-cars after a runaway train piled up on the edge of the Genesee River near Rochester, New York, and exploded. Coast Guard boat crews are frequently involved in shore-side rescues and firefighting. At times, the route by water is the only access for firefighters to advance on a fire onshore. All Coast Guard small boats are equipped for fighting fires. (George R. Taylor, U.S. Coast Guard Auxilliary)

Small Boat Stations

The crews at the earliest lifesaving stations along the coasts of Massachusetts and New Jersey were drawn from the local population. Generally, these men were expert seamen with an extensive knowledge of the local area and sea conditions and well-honed skills in operating small boats in the surf. These strong and stalwart "surfmen" formed the core of the early lifesaving services in the United States and founded a tradition of excellence in small boat seamanship that continues in the Coast Guard to this day. These original crews were, in most cases, hand-picked by the local "keeper" of the lifesaving station. The keeper was the man-in-charge and was generally chosen from the best surfman for his skills of seamanship and his ability to lead. After the introduction of government funding for lifesaving in 1848, the lifesaving stations became the responsibility of an officer of the Revenue Cutter Service,

In the United States' early days, with much of the nation's thousands of miles of shoreline uninhabited, it became evident from the number of ships wrecking along the coast that lifesaving stations were needed. The crews of the earliest stations were drawn from skilled seamen in the local population. (Paul C. Scotti)

also known as a District Superintendent, to whom the keepers reported. Thus began a management style that carries on in the Coast Guard to this day, with the bulk of officers in charge at contemporary small boat stations coming from the enlisted ranks, principally chief petty and warrant officers from the deck ratings, with commissioned officers providing a supervisory role from the group and district offices.

The latter half of the nineteenth century saw the establishment of many other coastal lifesaving organizations around the world, principally in Europe. Almost without exception, all of these organizations operated with volunteer crews, drawn from the local community, who were paid for attending drills as well as for rescues. In the United States, a similar manning system was established by the MHS and at the pre-USLSS stations with the keepers receiving a small annual salary to manage the station. After 1871, however, this began to change and a uniquely American manning structure began to evolve.

Sumner Kimball, superintendent of the USLSS for its entire existence, soon recognized that paid crews were required for most of the service's lifesaving stations. Unlike much of Europe, the vast size of the relatively unpopulated coastline meant that human resources were often scarce. Also, this was the period of rapid territorial expansion in the United States and the opportunities envisioned by the words "Go west, young man," were a much stronger drawing card than the lifesaving service for most. By necessity the volunteer approach in the American lifesaving service would gradually vanish. Some stations, such as those on the Great Lakes, would remain seasonal, but all of the small boat crews would become employees of the service, the first large-scale paid public coastal lifesaving service in the world.

This permanency of employment helped establish another unique feature of the early American lifesaving stations, that of the station as a community unto itself. Originally, it was only the keeper, typically along with his wife and children, who could maintain a residence at the station. Gradually, however, as the boat crews themselves began to board in the station houses, some of them, particularly those with families, would start to construct their own residences in close proximity to the station. Given how remote some of these stations were, many of these "lifesaving communities" became self-sufficient entities where everyone banded together both for the sustenance of themselves and the salvation of others. Victims of shipwreck would commonly be shepherded by wives of keepers and surfmen into the individual residences and provided with food, clothing, and shelter.

Many small boat stations in the Coast Guard today carry on this tradition. Because search and rescue requires rapid response, crewmen and their families still often live at, or close to, the stations. Many young recruits, men and women, some away from home for the first time, also live on station in the crew dormitories. The station and fellow servicemen now formed their new home and support network. The stations also evolved as and remained integral parts of local communities, the nearby cities, towns, and villages.

At many of the stations, Coast Guard personnel are a key component of the community's emergency services, on both land and sea, helping local law enforcement, paramedics, and fire departments on a regular basis. In some of the more remote locations, the crews of the local Coast Guard station, as the only federal presence in the area, are practically the sole provider of these services. Such duty may be unofficial, but it is a reality of life at the small boat units.

Families eventually added to the size of isolated small boat stations. The original boathouse expanded with living quarters for only the keeper, along with his wife and children. Gradually as the boat crews began acquiring families, they would construct their own residences in close proximity to the station eventually creating a small community. (U.S. Coast Guard)

Small-boat station buildings range from modern brick structures to decade's old wood-frame buildings that, like the station Niagara in upstate New York, frequently blend architecturally with the local community. (Harry Craft, U.S. Coast Guard)

The Boat Station Team

Clayton Evans

Operating a small-boat station in the modern Coast Guard is like any military operation where high-tech equipment and hazardous duties are involved. It takes many people to get the job done safely and efficiently, not all of whom are in the limelight. In order to save the lives of those in peril at sea and to protect the lives of those trying to save them, an integrated team-approach has been developed at the stations where various ranks, ratings, and trades administer, train, maintain, and feed the machine that keeps the station running.

The person in charge of the machine is generally a noncommissioned petty officer, such as a boatswain's mate first class or master chief, or on occasion, a chief warrant or commissioned officer. Station crew generally come from the deck ratings, starting out after boot camp as seaman apprentice and working up to the various ranks of noncommissioned or petty officers known as boatswain's mates or simply "Boats."

Every station has a training officer and the training regimen is constant at small-boat units due to the steady stream of recruits and the almost constant upgrading of rank and qualifications. There are six ranks of boatswain's mates in the U.S. Coast Guard, from petty officer third class right on up to master chief. Boatswain's mates have to be competent seaman, navigators, and boat handlers, and most importantly, leaders. Each level requires that the candidate pass written examinations and a local review board, in addition to having completed the various training elements while underway. Most station boatswain's mates are required to become proficient as "coxswain" on each of the station's individual boat types, having completed further examinations both underway and onshore. The best "boat drivers" at the units are then hand-picked for further training at the National Motor Lifeboat School. Most of the officers in charge at Coast Guard boat stations today come from the boatswain's mate stream, many ending up as warrant officers. At the same time, it is not uncommon to have a commissioned lieutenant as commanding officer at a station since such experience at a small-boat unit proves invaluable for future details within the service.

The ultimate proficiency test for a small-boat coxswain is to receive qualification as a modern-day surfman, a carry-over from the days of the USLSS, but a qualification just as important in the modern Coast Guard. To achieve this designation, coxswains must already have spent considerable time underway in

command and at the helm of motor lifeboats. They must have completed a series of objectives; many of these conducted in surf and sea conditions of considerable magnitude. Once these are completed, the candidate must then pass a review board made up principally of experienced surfmen. The granting of this designation is not taken lightly by those on the board. Once qualified, these individuals become the expert boat handlers on station and are responsible for training aspiring boat coxswains. The Coast Guard also requires that in certain conditions of heavy weather, small-boats cannot be operated without a designated surfman present and he or she is considered an expert advisor to the officer on duty or the station's commanding officer.

Another crucial member of the station team is the machinery technician. These are the small boat engineers whose responsibility it is to keep the UTBs, MLBs, and other small-boats running smoothly and the myriad other station equipment such as generators and boat hoists in good condition. Starting out as a fireman apprentice, fresh from boot camp, engineers at the small-boat stations have to know their boats inside and out and be adept at fixing things on the fly. Like all small-boat crewmen, these individuals have to be prepared to fulfill other duties onboard, from tending towlines to the performance of blind navigation. It is not surprising therefore that many machinery technicians are qualified for other duties, including boat coxswains and emergency medical technicians.

Rounding off the boat station team, especially at the larger stations, are several other ratings with crucial responsibilities. Yeoman/storekeepers are the men and women who keep the station's administrative and logistical infrastructure running, ensuring supplies are kept up-to-date and maintaining station accounts. Food service

specialists are there to provide daily sustenance. They are the cooks and catering personnel that run the cafeterias and who make sure that boat crews have the human fuel they need to carry out the job.

Opposite, top: Training in rescue never lets up. Shipmates share the role of victims and rescuers. This gives them a more thorough understanding and a sensitivity to their role. (Tom Sperduto, U.S. Coast Guard)

Opposite, bottom left: Samoa Lifeboat Station near Eureka, California, is a classic example of older stations still serving the Coast Guard today. (Gary Todoroff)

Opposite, bottom right: Rescues are not always along the beach in oceans and lakes. Here Coast Guard personnel learn defensive and survivor recovery techniques during a swift-water rescue course, needed if ever called for river rescues. (Tiffany Powell, U.S. Coast Guard)

Above, left: A Coast Guard boat responds to the scene in present-day Seattle where this Boeing 307 Stratoliner, built in the late 1930s, ditched. The crew are recovered without injury. This restored relic ditched in Elliot Bay on a test flight. The valuable artifact was recovered and once more restored. Just over a year following this crash, the airliner resumed its cross-continent flight for display in the Smithsonian Museum. (Sarah Foster-Snell, U.S. Coast Guard)

Above, right: The Coast Guard has a large mix of small craft that includes specialty boats for specific situations. Petty Officer Third Class Chriss Rutt at Coast Guard Station Michigan City, Indiana, tries out a personal watercraft, commonly known as a "jet-ski." The Coast Guard sometimes acquires commercially produced boats to meet certain operational requirements not possible with their fleet. These boats once included captured rumrunners and in recent years the high-speed drug running boats. Even the less glamorous blunt bow "John boats" fill a need as workboats for navigation aids in rivers and lakes. (Chris Grooms, U.S. Coast Guard)

Below: A 41-footer sits pier-side ready for a Coast Guard crew to carry out whatever mission it is called upon to perform. The day for the "ready crew" never ends. Boats and crews at small-boat stations are ready to go at the sound of the search and rescue, or SAR, alarm around the clock. (Jeff Hall, U.S. Coast Guard)

Small Boats

The Coast Guard, and the Life-Saving Service before it, produced some of the most popular and innovative designs of rescue craft in the world. One of the principal reasons for this technological success over the last 130 and more years has been an ability to combine the technological expertise of the parent organization with the occupational expertise of the boat crews. When conducting the design process for new boats, the "system" has generally listened to those with experience operating small boats in hazardous conditions. By surveying operators at a multitude of stations within the organization as to the best facets of particular designs and design proposals, an intellectual resource of tens of thousands of underway hours can be tapped for educated suggestions. As a consequence, improvements to design, ergonomics, and technology can be made prior to full production. Over the decades, this approach has borne some impressive results. Although the small-boat fleet in the Coast Guard today fulfills a variety of responsibilities and missions, the evolution of small boat design in the United States since the 1870s has been principally influenced by the need to operate boats in hazardous conditions both to save the lives of those in danger and to minimize the risk to the small boat crews.

In the beginning, surfmen required surfboats and that was precisely the type of craft that was chosen for the early lifesaving stations along the Atlantic seaboard. Generally, these were relatively small, open boats in the twenty-five- to thirty-foot range such as the New Jersey surfboat, characterized by lapstrake hulls with a generous sheer, a narrow flat

Harbors keep Coast Guard boat crews busy. On any given day, they can be involved in stopping smugglers, escorting hazardous cargo vessels, inspecting anchorages, fighting fires, engaged in homeland security duties and making rescues, or just being there for the needy boater. (U.S. Coast Guard)

bottom with no keel, a pointed bow, and a square raked-stern. These boats were lightweight and easily handled both onshore and off—an advantage when being launched from shore into heavy surf, especially as the coast around many of the first lifesaving stations was characterized by exposed, sandy beaches with treacherous offshore sandbars running parallel to the coast. Lifesaving crews had not only to launch from the beach through an initial line of breakers, but to continue to do so as they passed over shallow after shallow while attempting to reach an offshore wreck.

These men trusted the boats they worked with on a regular basis in their other occupations as beachmen, fishermen, and salvagers, thus it only made sense to use the same type of boat for lifesaving. In reality, this was the only option for the service, as it would have been practically impossible to entice crews to head to sea in the worst of conditions in vessels with which they were not familiar and had no practical experience. Many early volunteer boat-stations also received a "metallic" version of the surfboat, constructed out of hydraulically pressed galvanized iron sheets. These boats were the invention of Joseph Francis of New York. Although dozens of the metal surfboats and lifeboats were constructed for the government stations over the first decade of their operations, some remaining in service until the 1870s, they do not appear to have retained much favor with the crews due to their heavier weight and susceptibility to corrosion and puncture.

In 1858 the Treasury Department, through the auspices of the Revenue Marine, established a three-man commission to experiment with various types of lifesaving vessels and to recommend to the department,

Coast Guardsmen search for signs of life around flooded barns. Spring floods that strike in the Midwest bring the Coast Guard to these regions to prevent loss of life among humans, pets, and livestock. They also assist in preventing property destruction. (Tom Gillespie)

183

Surfmen prepare to lift one end of the surf boat onto the beach cart. They, or a horse, then tug it over the beach to a launching site near the area of disaster. It could mean miles of towing over the sand before they unload it, then fight it into the surf and row to recover shipwreck victims. (Coast Guard Museum Northwest)

The Coast Guard is arriving—seen from a survivor's point of view. Tossing a life ring may appear a trifle act, but this small task is something Coast Guard crews practice—even holding contests. Attention to these small details leads to making the U.S. Coast Guard a premier, world lifesaving-service. (U.S. Coast Guard)

"for its consideration the life-boat which may be best adapted in all its conditions for the saving of human life from shipwreck on the coasts of the United States." Different designs of wooden and metal surfboats were tested in New Jersey at the Spermaceti Cove Life-Saving Station in October of that year. Although new, larger self-righting and self-bailing rescue craft, known as lifeboats, were gaining favor among lifesaving organizations overseas, at the end of the trials the favorite in the United States remained the surfboat, tried and true.

Following the establishment of the USLSS another review of the services' boats was conducted, this time at Seabright, New Jersey, in May of 1872. True to the traditions of the lifesaving service then and now, the commission consisted "of officers of the Treasury and Navy and experienced beachmen." Once again, the traditional wooden surfboat was the clear winner, with the Jersey, Excelsior, Monomoy, and Beebe styles being a few of the favorites. Although the commission leaned once again toward the tried and true, they were aware of recent advances in rescue craft design overseas, and efforts were made to produce a standard surfboat design that might incorporate some of these additional safety features.

The result was the Beebe-McLellan surfboat. Although not self-righting—surfboats were manually righted by the crew, who were constantly drilled in this practice—this surfboat was considered unsinkable, with a water-ballast system and side air-cases for added buoyancy. It was also self-bailing, having six square relieving tubes on either side of its keel to allow any water shipped to drain out. The surfboat crews could now remain at their oars instead of having to bail by hand.

Like the European lifeboat, the new surfboat was a double-ender rather than having a flat transom, another safety feature when operating in the surf. Many of these design alterations were initiated by Lieutenant Charles H. McLellan of the USLSS, a man who would be instrumental in the development of rescue craft designs for many years to come. The standard Beebe-McLellan surfboat was around twenty-five-feet long and weighed approximately 1,300 pounds. These boats were generally hauled to the wreck site on a lightweight carriage by horse or manpower then launched into the surf.

In some cases boats were launched off slipways directly from the station. By the turn of the century the Beebe-McLellan was the principal surfboat in the USLSS, with over 200 in service around the country. Thousands of victims of shipwreck would owe their lives to these simple, stalwart surfboats and the men who rowed them.

In 1873 another significant step in the development of American rescue craft was taken by the USLSS when it ordered the purchase and construction of a much larger Standard Self-Righting type pulling and sailing lifeboat from the Royal National Lifeboat Institution of Great Britain. Newer stations on the Great Lakes and the Pacific were located at greater distances from one another, casualties could be many miles from these stations and there were not always roads and beaches in proximity to the wreck-site. If a lifesaving crew was to row several miles, most probably in the same appalling conditions that created the calamity in the first place, they would be so fatigued from exertion and exposure upon arrival that they would be practically useless for lifesaving. The ability to sail to the wreck circumvented this problem. True to its namesake, the lifeboat was also designed to right itself using the buoyancy of large air cases at either end in combination with a relatively narrow beam and a heavy iron keel. All American lifeboats would be self-righting from this day forward.

The original English Lifeboat, as it was called, was thirty-feet long and designed to be launched from a fixed slipway or to lie afloat. This boat would become the predecessor of generations of lifeboats and motor lifeboats used by the Coast Guard well into the latter half of the next century, with seventy-seven more of its type constructed in the United States from 1876 to 1897.

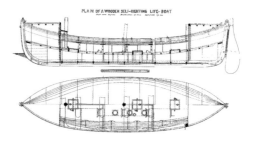

The spirit of innovation in rescue craft design thrived in the USLSS. After the introduction of the larger pulling and sailing lifeboats some keepers felt a compromise rescue craft should be developed, one that incorporated the lightweight versatility of the surfboat with the self-righting features of the much larger lifeboat. David Porter Dobbins, a district superintendent in the service, designed a smaller self-righting, self-bailing lifeboat during the 1880s in the twenty-four- to thirty-foot range averaging only 1,600 to 2,000 pounds. The Dobbins lifeboat was never popular at the Atlantic stations, but boats of this design were used considerably on the Great Lakes and at the Pacific Ocean stations. The concept of self-righting as an important feature in all rescue craft was taking hold and soon a self-righting design of the Beebe-McLellan surfboat was finding its way into the service.

In 1899 McLellan would set the stage for the next great era in rescue craft development when he began experimenting with the concept of installing an internal combustion engine in one of the service's lifeboats as auxiliary power to the oars and sails. McLellan's were the world's first tests of this type of motorized propulsion in lifeboats, and as a result, the USLSS, and later the Coast Guard, would be at the forefront of this revolution in lifesaving technology for decades to come. There had been previous experiments with steam-powered lifeboats in England, Holland, and Australia, but the sheer size and weight of the power plant severely limited their efficiency and usefulness. Initial tests of mechanized propulsion in the United States involved a twelve horsepower, two-cylinder Superior gasoline engine in a thirty-four-foot lifeboat stationed at Marquette, Michigan. Despite an original engine weight of a whopping 1,500 pounds, the experiment was a resounding success where it mattered—with the small boat crew. McLellan carried on and had another

thirty-four-foot pulling and sailing lifeboat constructed for further experiments with an auxiliary motor, this time with twin-propellers.

McLellan, unlike many of his European counterparts, soon realized that motorized lifeboats were here to stay and believed oars and sails should from then on be considered auxiliary to the engine. He was absolutely correct. In 1906 the service began construction of the first purpose-built motor lifeboats in the world, starting with a thirty-five-foot version and culminating in the famed 36-footer design of self-righting, self-bailing, pulling and sailing MLB. The first production models were launched out of the Electric Boat Company or popularly known as Elco in Bayonne, New Jersey, in 1907. Utilizing the basic lines of the English Lifeboat, McLellan designed a somewhat beamier version that utilized a single 25 H.P. "Standard Automotor" weighing less than half its 12 H.P. predecessor. The success of this design was almost immediate. In 1908 one of the new thirty-six-foot motor lifeboats from the USLSS Station at Monomoy Point on Cape Cod successfully rescued the crew of a sinking schooner in horrendous sea conditions and, according to a contemporary chronicler of the event, the lifesaving crew going "over the same cross seas in which a crew of six men from the Monomoy station were lost five years ago, when the life-savers had to rely upon their own strength at the oars. The motorboat reached the wreck in less than an hour."

The introduction of this first true motor lifeboat would start the "footer" terminology used to describe Coast Guard rescue craft to this day. The boat also incorporated another interesting first, a mercury switch circuit-breaker that automatically shut down the engine in the event of a capsize. Such switches, with little alteration from the original concept, are still used on modern self-righting rescue craft around the globe. By 1912 there were sixty-eight of the 36-footers in service with the USLSS. In addition, many of the Beebe-McLellan type were converted to motor surfboats. By the time the USLSS was amalgamated in 1915, to form the Coast Guard, more than half of the over 200 boats in the life-saving fleet were converted to motorized propulsion. By comparison, the RNLI in Great Britain, with a comparable number lifeboats, had only nineteen MLBs in service by the year 1919.

Several versions of the venerable 36-footer—the principal MLB for the Coast Guard right up until the 1960s—would be constructed at the Coast Guard's boatyard at Curtis Bay, Maryland, for about fifty years. The hull, based on the English Lifeboat of 1873, would remain essentially the same, with significant changes occurring mainly in engine and helm location, size of the flotation chambers and type, weight and size of the power plant. The boat was slow, averaging about eight knots, and was colorfully described by well-known surfman Thomas D. McAdams as having an affinity "to roll in a turtle's wake." The crew still stood outside in the weather, although later versions had a small windscreen to protect them from the elements. Despite these quirks, the boat was dear to all who served on it and thousands of lives were saved by the 36s. The last 36-footer was retired from service at the USCG Station at Depoe Bay, Oregon, in 1986 and is on display at the Mariner's Museum in Newport News, Virginia.

A Coast Guard motor lifeboat returns from a search for lost fishermen in the Great Lakes. The 36-footer was the Coast Guard's principal motor lifeboat for fifty years. The crew stood exposed in the open with only a small windscreen to protect them from the elements. (U.S. Coast Guard)

Four Coast Guardsmen in a thirty-six-foot motor lifeboat head out from Chatham, Massachusetts, into seventy-mile-per-hour winds on a stormy night in February 1952 looking for a tanker that split in half. In spite of the blinding snowfall and a broken compass they find the ship's stern portion, load the small boat with thirty-two survivors, and then find their way back to base. (Richard Kaiser, U.S. Coast Guard)

Above: *To meet the mission demands of small-boat stations, in addition to search and rescue, the multi-functional forty-foot utility boat went into operation in 1951. Designed and built by the Coast Guard, it replaced the worn out, wooden thirty-eight-foot picket boat adapted in the 1920s from the Navy. The French adopted these rugged, steel boats for use in the rivers and canals against the Viet Minh during the Indochina War. (U.S. Coast Guard)*

Above, right: *The aluminum 41-footer replaced the steel 40-footer and is probably the most recognized craft in today's Coast Guard small-boat fleet. (Eric Eggen, U.S. Coast Guard)*

The role of the small-boat stations began to change following creation of the Coast Guard in 1915, as crews began to evolve from a civilian to a military role that entailed a multitude of additional responsibilities and missions beyond the previous core duty of lifesaving. Coastal and port security as well as law enforcement were becoming increasingly prominent missions, particularly after the introduction of Prohibition in 1920, when preventing the smuggling of alcohol from Canada and Mexico became the order of the day.

To aid in these efforts a new type of small boat, referred to as a "picket boat," was adapted for the Coast Guard from the Navy. Averaging around thirty-eight feet in length, these wooden boats were fast and powerful for their time, capable of cruising along at a comfortable 18 knots. Picket boats were versatile, excellent for law enforcement, and their speed was quickly recognized as a distinct advantage for lifesaving when weather was not a critical factor and the self-righting thirty-six-foot MLB was not required. As a result, many picket boats were co-located with MLBs. Following the end of World War II, the Coast Guard small-boat design team began to draw up a replacement for the now worn-out picket boats, their efforts culminating in the multi-functional forty-foot Utility Boat, UTB.

Above: *Following a rescue, a victim is removed from a 41-footer and transferred to an ambulance. This is a scene that is repeated virtually every day somewhere along the U.S. coast where these 41-footers operate. (Lance Jones, U.S. Coast Guard)*

Right: *A fifty-two-foot motor lifeboat crests a wave in the Pacific Ocean. This is part of the routine these remarkable boats have gone through over their fifty years operating in the torturous seas along the Washington-Oregon coast. (U.S. Coast Guard)*

188

The introduction of the first production forty-foot UTB in 1951 signified a radical departure from previous USLSS and Coast Guard small boat designs in the decision to use steel construction. The Coast Guard's yard at Curtis Bay was one of the first boatyards to use a rotating jig for hull construction, a common method of welding boats today, and in short order they were producing one boat per day. With twin diesel propulsion, the forty-foot UTB cruised at over 20 knots and would remain the standard workhorse at most Coast Guard small boat stations for many years. In the 1960s, the Coast Guard began developing a newer version of the type, the all-aluminum—another first in rescue craft design—forty-one-foot UTB, of which 180 would be constructed. Most of these are still in service. Powered by twin 280 H.P. diesels, the 41-footer can cruise at 26 knots and remains one of the most well-used and well-recognized vessels in the Coast Guard small boat fleet today.

In 1928, the Coast Guard would begin experimenting with a larger version of MLB, adding limited onboard accommodations that allowed the vessel to be used for more extended patrols and calls offshore. The result was the first generation of the 52-footer, two prototypes being launched from Curtis Bay in 1933. These boats were of heavy wood construction and were the first American rescue craft to utilize diesel power. Named *Invincible* (CG-52300) and *Triumph* (CG-52301), these were the only two first-generation 52-footers ever built. Weighing thirty tons and having a range of 600 miles, these boats could either carry sixty survivors below decks or 100 topside. Both fifty-two-foot MLBs eventually found their way out to the Coast Guard's 13th District in Washington and Oregon, where they were put to good use on the rough bar conditions at Grays Harbor and the Mouth of the Columbia River.

In 1955, in response to the preference in the 13th District for the larger MLB at certain stations, the engineers at Curtis Bay began the drawings for a new twin-diesel version of the 52-footer, this time, like the relatively new forty-foot UTB, with a steel hull. Four of these second generation boats were constructed to replace the two earlier boats. The first *Triumph* was tragically lost in a hurricane-force storm at the mouth of the Columbia River in 1961. They also provided improved lifesaving coverage at Yaquina Bay and Coos Bay, Oregon.

A fifty-two-foot motor lifeboat heads out to sea from Coast Guard Station Cape Disappointment in Washington. (Kurt Fredrickson, U.S. Coast Guard)

Surf and surfboat are about to meet. Student coxswains are about to experience their first real wave. Classroom training may inform new boat crewmembers that a wave exerts so many tons of force. However, to truly grasp its consequences they must get slammed a few times. This experience comes when the indoor classroom transfers to the deck of a 44-footer in the ocean "schoolhouse." (Chris Rose, U.S. Coast Guard)

The steel-hulled fifty-two-foot motor lifeboat can withstand 100-mile-an-hour winds and seas to thirty-five feet. There are only four of these unique craft and they all operate in the rugged waters of the Pacific Northwest. These are the only Coast Guard craft under sixty-five feet that are named. Periodically, all four gather for "round up," where the crews hold friendly competitions in various rescue exercises. (U.S. Coast Guard)

The forty-four-foot motor lifeboat replaced the aging 36-footer starting in 1962. Unique design features allowed the MLB to self-right if rolled inverted. The "44" was one of the most successful lifesaving boats in history. The Coast Guard built 110 boats with—at the time of design—a unique construction utilizing extra-strength steel for the hull and aluminum for deckhouses. Most boats remained in service for over thirty years. The first built, 44300, served in the rugged Pacific Northwest waters for thirty-four years until it went out of service in 1996. This noteworthy 44-footer is on permanent display at the Columbia River Maritime Museum in Astoria, Oregon. (U.S. Coast Guard)

The 44-footer's time in rescue has gone into Coast Guard annals giving way to the new robust forty-seven-foot motor lifeboat. If the 47-footer rolls over it will come upright in eight seconds or less, compared with thirty seconds for the 44-footer. (Ryan Widdows, U.S. Coast Guard)

Master Chief Boatswain's Mate Lars Kent, taking a forty-seven-foot motor lifeboat into the surf, says of the 47-footer that it is a vast improvement over the 44-footer, but nonetheless it still behooves boat operators to learn its nuances. "The 47-footer can take a lot but can also hurt the crew if operated improperly." (Ryan Widdows, U.S. Coast Guard)

The new 52s were self-righting—unlike their predecessors—and could cruise for an incredible 1,071 nautical miles at 10 knots. Testament to their design, construction, effectiveness for lifesaving in practically all sea conditions—and general uniqueness—is the fact that all of these boats remain in service, even though they are approaching fifty years on the job.

By 1960 another mainstay of the Coast Guard small boat fleet was nearing the twilight of its existence. The fleet of 36-footers was aging and the rapidly expanding number of call-outs for pleasure craft in difficulty meant that a faster, more versatile heavy weather rescue resource was required. Thus began the development of the self-righting, self-bailing forty-four-foot MLB—or 44-footer. The 44-footer remains one of the most successful designs of lifesaving boats in history. The Coast Guard would build 110 of these stalwart vessels, many of which are still in service around the world today. Following the introduction of the type at the International Lifeboat Federation Conference in Edinburgh, Scotland, in 1963, the 44-footer would be adopted by Great Britain, Canada, Norway, Portugal, Italy and Iran.

The design of the 44-footer was unique in combining speed with an ability to self-right, a previously impossible combination given the limitations of the earlier displacement hulled lifeboats. Although the boats required considerable skill to operate in adverse conditions, they could also be quite forgiving of their operators and could withstand a phenomenal amount of punishment from wind, wave, and weather. With an initial top speed of 14 knots and a range of approximately 200 miles, the MLB incorporated an extremely strong Corten® steel hull with a lightweight, aluminum house-works and aft survivor's compartment affectionately referred to by many as the turtleback, or simply "the turtle."

For over thirty years the forty-four-foot MLB has held the title of the principal modern day surfboat in the Coast Guard. Many images the public associates with small boat stations are 44-footers smashing through giant walls of water, either on calls or training exercises. The Coast Guard's National Motor Lifeboat School at Cape Disappointment, Washington, was founded originally in 1976 as a type-training center for operating forty-four-foot MLBs in heavy weather. Today, the 44-footer has been replaced by a new generation of MLB, the all-aluminum 47-footer. This faster boat incorporates the speed and versatility of the UTB with the safety and seaworthiness of older MLBs.

Surf School

Chief Warrant Officer Mark H. Dobney, USCG (Ret)
Former Commanding Officer, U.S. Coast Guard National Motor Lifeboat School

The day is dark and gray as solid clouds blanket the area with a heavy mist. Waves that have traveled hundreds of storm-driven miles reach the Pacific Northwest shoreline rising then crashing with the sound of never-ending thunder. The strong engines of a boat roar as the helmsman pushes the throttles to the stops fighting the power of the Columbia River and the ebbing tide. Several lookouts shout warnings about buoys, ranges, logs, crab pots, and a person in the water.

Above it all the loud, steady, urgent voice of the surfman instructor penetrates the mind with, "Come right! Get around into this one! Get your bow over! Square up, square up! Easy on the power! Hang on, this one's gonna' hurt!" The forty-seven-foot motor lifeboat fights its way into the howling wind riding quickly up the face of the growing wave. The current and engines move it quickly, almost vertically, up the face of the steep sixteen-foot breaking wave. As the twenty tons of boat reach the top, everyone hangs on while waiting for the hard landing in the hole left by the speeding wall of water. It's another perfect day for the men and women of the Coast Guard's unique school.

The National Motor Lifeboat School is located at the mouth of the Columbia River on a point of land called Cape Disappointment. Since 1878 this area, also known as the "Graveyard of the Pacific," has been home for Coast Guard rescue facilities and its predecessor the U.S. Lifesaving Service. During the late 1960s and early 1970s, local Coast Guard units pooled their resources in order to conduct coxswain and crew training on forty-four-foot motor lifeboats. The steel-hulled boats were more capable than the wooden thirty-six-foot lifeboats they were replacing. The crews manning them were typically very experienced and under the leadership of seasoned veterans who passed on their seamanship skills directly to each new crewmember. The localized training, at motor lifeboat stations found at each river entrance, allowed small groups of Coast Guard crews to share experiences and techniques. The 13th Coast Guard District sought out a more consistent method of sharing the lessons learned through hard practical experience. The veteran surfmen established a training curriculum and routinely gathered their resources to put on classes focused at operating the forty-four-foot lifeboat in the surf environment. The success of these gatherings in passing on skills was soon recognized as potentially valuable for all lifeboat coxswains nationwide.

The U.S. Coast Guard's National Motor Lifeboat School was established in 1980 in Ilwaco, Washington, co-located with the existing rescue station at Cape Disappointment. Wind and sea state extremes—up to Beaufort Force 10—often cause surf conditions with ten- to twenty-foot breaking waves across the wide river

Boat crews learn the tendency of wave movements and how to maneuver craft to avoid getting caught under the curl of a breaking wave. (Larry Kellis, U.S. Coast Guard)

Above: Instructors discuss techniques in the classroom before taking boats into the surf. (Sarah Foster-Snell, U.S. Coast Guard)

Left: The Coast Guard's unique National Motor Lifeboat School and small boat station are located at Cape Disappointment at the mouth of the Columbia River in Washington. This location provides a classroom of towering waves needed to learn techniques for taking a boat into the worst of seas. This school serves not only the special needs of Coast Guard coxswains but students from other nations in the art of small-boat handling in raging surf. (Rich Muller, U.S. Coast Guard)

mouth making the location ideal for the lifeboat school. Resources and budget were identified to give dedicated lifeboats to the newborn school along with personnel to provide maintenance and seasoned surfmen as instructors. New maintenance facilities, offices, and classrooms were later built and dedicated in April 1993.

Students from all over the nation attend courses at the National Motor Lifeboat School in order to focus on practices that will keep them alive and teach them to make full use of the motor lifeboat's power and tough design. The dangers and challenge of working in the big surf and strong currents are foreign to many of these young men and women. Many seaworthy vessels have broached and capsized while crossing the breaking surf on these northwest bars, usually with injuries or loss of life.

Almost half the training at the school is done underway on motor lifeboats, with one student at the wheel, a surfman-instructor standing nearby, and the other students working the deck under the watchful eyes of a school engineer. Students are taught proven methods for rescuing a person from the water, towing or delivering salvage equipment to other boats, and navigation under adverse conditions. Though the motor lifeboat is designed to be self-righting—it can survive a complete 360-degree capsizing—the classes at the surf school do not intentionally roll the boats.

The force of breaking waves is measured in tons per square-foot and is powerful enough to broach the lifeboat, blow through bulletproof windows and tear metal. Lessons focus on understanding the wave movements and maneuvering the lifeboat to prevent getting caught under the curl of a breaking wave. Crews of even the newest forty-seven-foot motor lifeboat wear suits for hypothermia protection and strap in so they are not lost overboard as the boat carries students through one of the toughest classroom environments in the world. As one surfman-instructor observed, "The goal is not to beat Mother Nature, only to ensure crews come home safely, calling it a draw."

After 1915

The Act of Congress creating the Coast Guard in 1915 also contained provisions for the retirement of the USLSS and many of the men who had served so valiantly during the course of its incredible history. Those who remained found themselves instantly transferred from a civilian organization to a military one, and the crews began adapting to this new role as an armed service both at home and abroad. During the tumultuous years of Prohibition, many of the small boat units found themselves in their first law enforcement role. Coming face-to-face with alcohol smugglers became yet another unpredictable and dangerous duty.

Throughout both of the World Wars station crews never forgot their principal mission of saving life at sea. Thousands were rescued along United States coasts, particularly off the Atlantic seaboard where dozens of merchant ships fell prey to the German U-boat menace, at times within sight of the stations themselves.

During the Second World War the Coast Guard's expertise in small-boat operations was widely recognized by other services. Many experienced surfmen were utilized by the Navy to train their personnel in the operation of small boats and amphibious attack craft, most particularly in the use of landing craft in the surf, the principal tool of first-strike Allied Invasion forces throughout the war. Small-boat servicemen of the Coast Guard were also directly involved in almost all theaters of

The thirty-two-foot near-shore boat is custom-made for Coast Guard Station, Chatham, Massachusetts, by Halmatic Ltd. of Portsmouth, England. The self-righting lifeboat maneuvers easily in Chatham's shifting sandbars and shallow waters. (U.S. Coast Guard)

The classroom instruction moves out to sea. As one surfman-instructor observed, "The goal is not to beat Mother Nature, only to ensure crews come home safely, calling it a draw." (U.S. Coast Guard)

193

conflict. Crews of the Coast Guard small-boat stations also were instrumental in the provision of beach patrols as well as near-shore picket duty. Port security duties were added to the roster of duties at many stations during this period, a role that was reinstated during the Korean conflict.

Above: *Small-boat station life is not all speeding around in boats. Keeping boats clean and running properly is a never-ending chore. Moreover, building and grounds need tending. A scrub brush or paintbrush is an ever-present tool. The small group works together like a family, frequently each working as many as eighty or more hours a week often at a station in an area isolated from typical communities, with their movie theaters and shopping malls. (Adam Wine, U.S. Coast Guard)*

Small-Boat Station Life Today

Many aspects of life at a Coast Guard small-boat unit today remain relatively unchanged from the days of the USLSS. The routines of daily drills and maintenance have been altered only by technology. Although the fundamental aspects of the job remain the same, the ever-expanding role of the Coast Guard as the principal maritime arm of the United States Government on and around the nation's coasts means crews today have to be far more versatile than their predecessors. There are many new hats to wear in the "multi-tasked" world of the modern Coast Guard, and the people performing the missions have to be as "multi-functional" as the job itself.

Forming one of the five services of the Armed Forces of the United States, the Coast Guard was deeply involved in *Operation Noble Eagle*, the

U.S. military operations in homeland security after September 11. The Coast Guard's boat stations, being strategically located almost equidistant along the nation's coasts, on waterways and at principal ports, form an integral component of this protective force, protecting 361 ports and approximately 95,000 miles of coastline. In fulfilling this role, the small boat units are conducting extensive port security duties, including harbor surveillance, perimeter enforcement for high-risk vessels, and vessel boardings at sea. Hundreds of new high-speed interception and response craft have been ordered to fulfill this rapidly expanding mission.

As front-line foot soldiers for the Coast Guard, crews at small boat units are often first responders to major disasters and high profile incidents at sea. As a result, within hours and sometimes minutes of leaving their base, small boat crews can find themselves in the focus of the public spotlight. When the Twin Towers came crashing down, the Coast Guard's small boats were some of the first vessels on scene and were instrumental in coordinating and evacuating hundreds of thousands of people from lower Manhattan. The peaceful routine of daily life at a small boat station can often lead, at a moment's notice, to in-depth involvement in the most extraordinary of events.

Above, left: *A forty-four-foot MLB is towing a boat in a training session off Waikiki Beach, Cape Disappointment, Washington, near the Coast Guard's National Motor Lifeboat School located at the mouth of the Columbia River. Extremes in winds and seas combine for the ultimate in training conditions. (Lynda Wilcox, U.S.Coast Guard)*

Above: *On a stormy, 1997 February night, four crewmembers in a forty-four-foot MLB crossed the river bar from their La Push, Washington, Coast Guard station outbound into the Pacific Ocean responding to a distress call from a dismasted sailboat. The MLB lies aground on the rocky beach on James Island with the top crushed from crashing into the seabed while capsized. The boat's engines were still running when the lone Coast Guard survivor, a battered Benjamin Wingo, crawled off the boat into waist-deep water and waded ashore. (Della Price, U.S. Coast Guard)*

Opposite, bottom: *Members of the Quileute tribe conduct a memorial service in the Indian Village of La Push, Washington, for the Coast Guardsmen killed when their motor lifeboat capsized en route to a rescue. During the ritual, Master Chief Petty Officer G.A. La Forge, officer in charge (left) and Seaman Benjamin Wingo (right), the only survivor of the tragedy, are wrapped in blankets. Traditional belief is the blankets will protect the men throughout their lives. (Steve M. Aitkins, U.S. Coast Guard)*

Left: *Hundreds of boats similar to this 25-footer have been built to meet the Coast Guard's homeland security demands. The aluminum hull is surrounded by a plastic foam donut. Not only does the bulging bulwark provide stabilization but in combination with the metal hull, offers some protection to gunfire. The boat is also armed with automatic weapons. Powerful outboard engines offer high-speed response to incidences. (Louis Hebert, U.S. Coast Guard)*

The role of the Coast Guard as the primary enforcer of law and order on the water remains unchanged. At many small boat stations, particularly those around the Gulf of Mexico, the amount of time spent on law enforcement far exceeds that of search and rescue even though the caseload for rescues at these units is also quite substantial. Officers-in-charge and commanding officers at the stations must not only ensure firearms training is maintained, but also that suitable personnel with the appropriate law and enforcement qualifications are on site.

Like a police officer on land, designated law enforcement personnel at the stations must be adept at taking evidence and interviewing witnesses as well as understanding inter-jurisdictional court procedures. They must not only be able to enforce laws that apply both on land and water, such as the impaired operation of a car or vessel, but must also be conversant and familiar with very complex statutes and regulations, such as those

197

dealing with fisheries and environmental law. As a result, many trained law enforcement personnel at the stations have to be both seasoned small boat mariners and veritable lawyers of the sea. Law enforcement at many stations also entails federal customs and drug interdiction duties. This particular task involves its own high risks and hazards reminiscent of the Prohibition days of old.

Coast Guard small-boat units are considered a primary resource in the event of a marine environmental emergency within their particular zone of responsibility. Crews must react rapidly as first responders in the event of catastrophes such as an oil spill, as well as pursue and prosecute any mariners or shore-side facilities that break the law and pollute the nation's coasts and waterways.

Crews at small-boat units provide another important public safety function, namely boating safety enforcement, inspections, and lectures to local communities and the mariners with whom they interact. Such preventive measures and advice have their own long-term rewards. The station crews are well-suited to the provision of this task, knowing from experience just how important certain basic nautical skills and proper safety equipment are when operating boats. All of the aforementioned missions assigned to the station crews are in addition to their regular duties, and in many cases require qualifications and continuous upgrading beyond the standard job elements of a proficient small boat mariner, engineer, and rescue specialist.

Seaman Apprentice Ellen Holkenbink ties up a 44-footer at Coast Guard Station, Ocean City, Maryland. Women among the boat crews are a common sight today. (Dave Santos, U.S. Coast Guard)

A forty-four-foot motor lifeboat and crew enjoys an infrequent calm run offshore in the Pacific Ocean. (U.S. Coast Guard)

Epilogue

The men and women who crew the vessels in the Coast Guard small boat fleet today carry on in the finest traditions of their predecessors. Despite the many other roles and responsibilities assigned to them over the years, they remain steadfastly loyal to their principal objective and area of expertise, that of saving life at sea. This is why many joined the service in the first place and why many remain. Operating small-boats in extreme conditions is not a simple task, it takes generations of experience and knowledge passed down from small-boat crewman to small boat crewman. It is only through this kind of drive and determination, developed and harnessed over the last 150 years, that today's small-boat crews have been able to consistently make extraordinary acts of seamanship and self-sacrifice seem ordinary, and one can only hope they continue to do so for generations to come.

Above: *Bear, the station dog, trots after Petty Officer Michael Maher to give its moral support while Maher refuels the boat. Dogs are nearly as common to Coast Guard units as are the boats and some would argue, nearly as important. (Pete Milnes, U.S. Coast Guard)*

Left: *Boat construction materials and vessels' shapes today differ significantly from the early wooden surfboats propelled by oars. Here is the wild performance demonstrated from high-horsepower outboard engines combined with a rigid hull of either aluminum or fiberglass wrapped in an inflatable tube. These craft are called a rigid hull inflatable boat or RHIB. They come in many sizes and shapes. A variation on the inflatable tube is using a solid foam-plastic collar around the boat's bulwarks. (Coast Guard Museum Northwest)*

At Sea

José Hanson

To seafarers of earlier times a cutter was any single-masted, gaff-rigged vessel that carried two headsails. Since such a configuration proved to be handy and fast, it was adopted by England for ships used to thwart smuggling. Thus over time and through common usage, any vessel deployed for protecting the coasts, regardless of its rig, legitimately could be called a cutter.

This British designation, like so much maritime tradition, was handed down to the American colonies and passed to the first vessels of the newly born U.S. Treasury Department. Although the ships themselves might be sloops or schooners, because they collected taxes and guarded the coasts, in common parlance they had to be cutters. Today, in keeping with that tradition, any Coast Guard ship over sixty-five feet in length, be it a buoy tender, an icebreaker, or the three-masted barque *Eagle*, is officially designated a cutter.

Still, efficiency required a method of distinguishing different kinds of "cutters," and during World War II the Coast Guard adopted the Navy's classification system. So that Coast Guard craft wouldn't be confused with those of the Navy, the letter "W," which the Navy wasn't using, was placed before the class-designation and hull number of Coast Guard vessels. This system served well for twenty-five years before the current system, based on the cutter's endurance—the time it can keep at sea without support— was put in place.

The initial "W" has been maintained, but today large cutters are known as High Endurance Cutters or WHEC. Because of their extended cruising capability, such ships are said to be "long legged," while less capable cutters became Medium Endurance Cutters, or WMEC. Patrol boats continue to carry the letters WPB.

Cutter Escanaba *ploughs through seas en route to Ocean Station. From the 1940s to the 1970s cutters would spend twenty-one days at a time maneuvering within a ten-mile square plot of ocean collecting and transmitting weather data and giving position checks to transoceanic airliners. The time off-station included the transit time to and from station and shore-side maintenance to repair and replenish the ship for the next month at Ocean Station. If an airplane had to ditch, the Coast Guard was there. (U.S. Coast Guard)*

Opposite, top: *Coast Guard barque* Eagle *under full sail. (Telfair Brown, U.S. Coast Guard)*

Opposite, bottom: *The Coast Guard icebreaker* Polar Star *is capable of breaking through ice twenty-one feet thick. The Coast Guard operates the United States' only polar icebreakers. These special ships travel to the Arctic and Antarctic on supply and scientific-research missions. (U.S. Coast Guard)*

Buoy tender Buttonwood *services a "monster" buoy off the California coast. These large data collection buoys of the National Oceanic Atmospheric Administration have diameters of thirty-nine and forty-seven feet. Because of the buoys' size Coast Guard buoy tenders are used to tow them to their ocean stations. (Tracy Phillips)*

Above: *A Coast Guardsman goes over the side of a cutter refurbishing markings. On a ship, hard-to-reach places sometimes seem to need regular attention even more often than accessible ones. Unlike most other maintenance tasks, this one could wait for good weather and calm seas. (U.S. Coast Guard)*

Above, right: *The bridge is the eyes, ears, and brains of a cutter, the point where all possible information on the ship and its surroundings is constantly collected, updated, and evaluated, as is being done here on the bridge of CGC Dallas. The cutter itself and the lives of all on board depend on the close teamwork, training, and first-hand experience of those on the bridge. (George F. Schoenberger, U.S. Coast Guard)*

For most people, however, it's not the letters and numbers on the bow that set Coast Guard ships apart—it's the hull colors: red for icebreakers, black for "work-boats," white for everything else. Even this system doesn't always hold true, because experience has shown that any Coast Guard vessel may be called on any time for almost any job.

Just as astonishing as the wide variety of vessels that have been called cutters, is the diverse duties a vigorous maritime nation has assigned its Coast Guard. The service of course protects the country's coasts and waterways, but other missions take it worldwide. It must uphold U.S. laws, thwart smuggling, illegal immigration, and terrorism, but it also searches out, rescues, and aids victims of all kinds of disasters and mishaps, protects the environment and commercial fisheries, maintains

a vast navigational system, clears harbors and shipping channels of ice, provides public education and training programs, oversees licensing and vessel registration, assists scientific projects, and enforces international agreements—all of this in time of peace. When America is at war, as part of the Navy, the Coast Guard goes into combat.

On an average day the Coast Guard responds to over 100 search-and-rescue calls, assists nearly 200 people in distress, saves ten lives, helps contain twenty chemical spills, assists 2,500 vessels entering or leaving the U.S., boards nearly 150 vessels, seizes some $10-million worth of illegal drugs, and conducts 100 large-vessel checks—everyday events that can never be routine. At any moment something can go wrong; bravery, strength, and endurance are constants, as are seamanship, innovation, and fast thinking.

Although the strong qualities of Coast Guard personnel probably have not changed greatly in 200 years, the ships and boats they man today are vastly different. This evolution of the Coast Guard cutter goes well beyond just the technological advances of the last two centuries and is due in great part to the ever-expanding role of the Coast Guard. Probably the most pressing demands of the modern age are reflected in the enhancement of the cutters' sea-keeping abilities. Today even a relatively short-legged buoy tender may have a range—an ability to cope with what the sea dishes out—far beyond that expected of most early revenue cutters.

The cutter Midgett, *alongside a U.S. Navy aircraft carrier, takes on fuel from the carrier. Such close maneuvering of vessels at sea calls for first-class seamanship. (U.S. Coast Guard)*

Above: *At the approach of a Coast Guard cutter, a Haitian on a grossly overloaded craft leaps or falls into the water, and Coast Guardsmen jump in to save him. Those on the cutter have thrown a heap of life vests overboard so that should others fall from the unsafe craft, they too will be able to stay afloat until help reaches them. (U.S. Coast Guard)*

Opposite, bottom: *Migrants hoping to reach the United States often risk perilous passages in overloaded and un-seaworthy boats. The first concern of the Coast Guard is in preventing loss of life. Legal issues and immigration matters will be handled only after everyone is safe. (Steve Sapp, U.S. Coast Guard)*

Above: *Fuel oil service to a frozen-in Northeast is provided with assistance by Coast Guard cutters breaking way for tugs bringing needed heating fuel to homes and offices. The cutter* Mahoning *breaks way up a frozen Hudson River for a convoy to meet a late winter's need. (U.S. Coast Guard)*

Above, right: *Dwarfed by a U.S. Navy aircraft carrier and its escort, a Coast Guard cutter takes its place with a naval task force. During time of war, operational control of the Coast Guard passes to the Navy, but in peacetime as well, the two maritime services often work closely together. (Theodore Roberge, Coast Guard Museum Northwest)*

Right: *The entire ship's crew including mess-cooks and supply clerks turns-to to haul the line, keeping tension connecting two ships as supplies are high-lined across. (Coast Guard Museum Northwest)*

In time of hostilities the Coast Guard, under whatever name, has always taken on extra duties, but World War I demonstrated that future combat missions might lie well beyond home shores. World War II only confirmed this, and although no cutters were called into combat during the Korean conflict, they saw plenty of action in Vietnam. Subsequent altercations, including those with Iraq, where in 2003 eleven cutters served alongside Navy ships, have proven a Coast Guard cutter might well be ordered to combat duty anywhere in the world.

CGC Gallatin, *deployed with U.S. Navy forces, moves into position for taking on stores and fuel. The maneuver, called "underway replenishment," allows the resupplying of ships at sea so a flotilla can continue to operate in an area without having to return to port for supplies. (George F. Schoenberger, U.S. Coast Guard)*

Barque Eagle

Vice Admiral Paul Welling, USCG, (Ret)

Each summer since 1947, the year after *Eagle* arrived in New London, all Coast Guard Academy cadets have embarked to begin their training at sea. "WOW" is how most react as they first step aboard. *Eagle* seems huge at first sight from the deck: masts reaching to the sky; miles of line; halyards, sheets, clewlines, and other rigging leading up the masts to the yards; braces and tacks running fore and aft; square sails furled overhead. Once the cadets locate their bunks and stow their sea bags, they begin an intense introduction that within hours will include climbing the shrouds to the top and out on the footropes slung below the yards.

Some cadets have experience in small boats and a few have sailed offshore, but none have sailed on board a 295-foot, three-masted barque with twenty-three sails. In two days they are underway on their first tall-ship adventure that will last a week. This introduction to the sea is the beginning of a life-long affair for many, and for a few, it may raise doubts about their career choice.

The Coast Guard took possession of the German sailing barque *Horst Wessel* in 1945 in Kiel, Germany, as war reparation. Built in 1936 in Hamburg as a training vessel for German sailors, *Horst Wessel* was renamed *Eagle*, and in June 1946 under the command of Captain Gordon McGowan, sailed to the United States with a mix of Coast Guard seamen and remnants of the German crew. The first Atlantic crossing proved memorable as *Eagle* battled a ferocious hurricane, arriving in New York with most sails in shreds.

Each spring from the late 1940s through the 1950s, cadets carried *Eagle's* sails aboard from the Academy rigging loft. Under the supervision of a few permanent crewmembers, upper-class cadets led in swaying the sails aloft and bending them onto the yards and stays. As the day of departure neared, cadets loaded supplies and food for the three months of summer training.

By the 1960s, the academic curriculum left

Far left: Sails are furled and unfurled by crew on the yards aloft. The task is far more difficult hanging in the rigging of a heeling barque sailing in a squall with a bit in its teeth and needing to be reefed. Grasping cold, wet sails is like gripping onto throbbing sheet-steel with numb fingers. (U.S. Coast Guard)

Left: The first task for a lubber when boarding to crew a sailing ship is to climb the ratlines (ropes strung between shrouds) to the mast tops. As courage and experience builds, the task of climbing the rigging becomes a race to see who can touch the mast truck—the very top—first. Standing in the rigging gives a grand view of landfall. (U.S. Coast Guard)

little time for the cadets to participate in the spring outfitting and Eagle's small permanent crew was augmented earlier in preparation for sailing. The size of the full-time crew increased as the perspective shifted on how best to safely operate Eagle in light of decreased cadet shore-side training.

Today, operating all year long, Eagle's professional crew of fifty-four oversees the training of roughly 600 cadets and several hundred officer candidates annually.

In a world of nuclear power, smart bombs, and the Internet, it's not unreasonable to question the utility of a wind-driven ship whose average speed under sail is less than six knots. So why does the Coast Guard continue to use Eagle as a mainstay of its officer training?

As the main engine of a tall ship is its sails, cadets quickly come to develop a weather eye, alert for changes in the wind and sea. Handling lines safely under heavy strain becomes second nature. While such limited training and experience must leave them still well short of becoming professional seamen, cadets learn marlinspike seamanship that will serve them well when later in their careers they direct others engaged in rescue at sea, in aids to navigation operations, or in pollution control efforts.

The real value of Eagle is its environment, which allows around-the-clock leadership opportunities for cadets. Planning and directing the activities of small teams in all weather, often working aloft while experiencing some level of physical apprehension, requires the development and application of strong leadership skills. Granted, setting and dousing sail, and tacking and wearing ship may not be rocket science, yet they surely challenge young women and men who have to wisely allocate their people among several tasks, and coordinate and lead them in physically demanding work—often high above rolling and pitching decks.

Eagle sails with cadets from two classes separated by two years, e.g., first class and third class. Twenty-five upper class cadets will lead and direct the training and

Top: Eagle running free with yards squared to the wind. Downwind running in the trades is delightful aboard a square-rigger. The deck is nearly level and the motion is easy. Wind over the deck is tolerable as the ship is going with the wind. Shown here all twenty-three sails have a good draft of air and Eagle is making about eight knots with a heel of a few degrees. Heel is influenced by wind speed and the angle of the wind to the heading of the ship. With a beam wind of thirty knots, with all sails set, in a moderate sea, Eagle will charge along at about fifteen knots with nearly a twenty-degree heel. (Gary Todoroff)

Left: Eighteenth-century maritime-transportation carried forward to date seen framed in the doorway of a Coast Guard helicopter incorporating twenty-first-century technology. Coast Guard Academy graduates qualifying as Coast Guard aviators experience transportation science separated by two centuries. (Gary Todoroff)

work of a hundred or more lower class cadets. The upper class cadets will set the example and be responsible for the performance and demeanor of all cadets embarked. They learn and practice the duties of petty officers and then junior officers aboard a ship focused exclusively on developing leaders and seamen.

Today, Eagle sails to Europe, Canada, the Caribbean, and occasionally to the Pacific. Wherever Eagle calls, it is met by hundreds of sailing and motor craft and visited by tens of thousands of spectators who marvel at the barque's beauty and size. Visitors can only imagine the wonder of being aloft with the sun setting on a brilliant horizon—an Eagle experience the majority of Coast Guard Officers share.

Top: Oilskins dull the cutting wind on a long trick at the wheel. Here, one seaman alone steers the 295-foot, three-masted barque. Three wheels joined are for extra hands when needed. The proper balance of the sails fore and aft reduces the pressure on the helm and rudder drag. (U.S. Coast Guard)

Right: The Coast Guard's 295-foot, three-masted barque *Eagle* flies twenty-three sails with the trade winds at the port quarter—the most pleasant of times at sea. All sails are raised and trimmed with human power as in the golden age of sail a century and a half earlier. The then-nine-year-old German barque *Horst Wessel* was acquired by the Coast Guard in 1945 as war reparation and was renamed *Eagle*. It sailed to the United States in June 1946 under the command of Captain Gordon McGowan with a crew made up of Coast Guard seamen and some of the barque's former German sailors. It still sails in the twenty-first century as a training ship for Coast Guard Academy cadets. (Telfair H. Brown, U.S. Coast Guard)

A cutter rushing to reach a disabled American fishing vessel encounters twenty-five-foot seas during a winter fisheries patrol. Sub-freezing temperatures require the crew to use wooden bats to beat ice off the superstructure. The weight of such ice, if allowed to accumulate, could cause the cutter to capsize. (Jim McPherson, U.S. Coast Guard)

Ice Patrol

For the first 120 years of its history the Revenue Cutter Service generally kept its ships fairly close to home, considered appropriate for a young nation's coastal patrols. As was necessary before the Panama Canal, a few cutters had followed the normal sailing course around the Horn, skirting the North and South American continents, but it was not until the Spanish-American war that the first revenue cutter, *McCulloch*, crossed an ocean, in this case, to be on hand for Dewey's victory in Manila Bay. But the importance of long legs for a cutter was not really brought home until the sinking of *Titanic* in 1912. The dramatic loss of the luxury liner with about 1,500 lives focused world attention on the consequences of a collision with an iceberg.

A month after *Titanic* went down, a Navy scout cruiser, *Birmingham*, was sent to "Iceberg Alley" south of the Grand Banks to watch for dangerous icebergs entering the steamship lanes and to report their position. In hardly more than two weeks, *Birmingham* had to make for Halifax, Nova Scotia, to take on fuel and provisions and was replaced by its sister ship *Chester*. A fortnight later *Birmingham* was then again on its way back to the Grand Banks to allow *Chester* to be resupplied. After another short stay, and believing by July icebergs no longer presented much danger, *Birmingham* went home.

The following year, however, the Navy felt it could not spare any vessels for ice patrol, and the Revenue Cutter Service was called upon to send out *Seneca* and *Miami*. From then on, until the beginning of World War II, Coast Guard cutters would take up alternating duty from April to September on the International Ice Patrol. Even after the war, when aerial surveillance was able to take over, cutters would continue to go out to search for dangerous bergs during times of abundant ice or poor visibility. This new duty put a premium on endurance, for the cutters would be expected to keep at sea longer and under worse conditions than ever before.

Vice Admiral T. R. Sargent recalled Ice Patrol duty on board *Tahoe* in 1938–1939: "The 250-foot Lake Class Cutters . . . were wonderfully rugged ships with a flared bow and plenty of freeboard. Ice Patrol was always an adventure. With no radar and the usual dense fog in the northern Atlantic, the OD had to rely on his sense of smell, changes in temperature, and echoes from the blast of the fog horn—and don't get too close, the berg might capsize." How many people today can judge the nearness of an iceberg by the scent in the air?

Even without icebergs, patrolling the Grand Banks was fraught with danger. This was the area hit by the "weather bomb" of Halloween 1991, the subject of Sebastian Junger's *The Perfect Storm*. A Coast Guard cutter, *Tamaroa*, played a major role in that drama, fighting forty-foot waves and eighty-knot winds to rescue three people from a sailboat caught in the storm. As recounted in the cutter's official history, the rescue was just over, taps had died away, and suddenly ten minutes later reveille sounded. Having barely caught its breath, the crew of *Tamaroa* turned again into the full fury of the storm, this time to rescue the crew of a New York Air National Guard helicopter that had gone down on another rescue mission. Coast Guard vessels are nothing if not versatile, and *Tamaroa*, originally a Cherokee/Navajo-class salvage tug acquired from the Navy, saved the lives of four of the five Air National Guardsmen.

From its very beginnings the service had learned much about cold-water sailing off the coast of New England, and by the 1860s its cutters were finding out how to contend with ice and ferocious seas off Alaska. *Lincoln*, *Corwin*, *Thetis*, and the indomitable *Bear*, formerly a sealing and whaling ship, had shown what stoutly built wooden ships could accomplish in the inhospitable north.

During the First World War the Coast Guard felt confident enough in its ships and high-latitude seamanship to send *Unalaga* on patrol in the Gulf of Alaska in winter. The ship received its cold-water baptism almost immediately when temperatures dropped below zero-Fahrenheit and hurricane-force winds arose. The ice buildup became so great it was feared the ship would capsize, but by morning the storm abated and *Unalaga*, encased in as much as 175 tons of ice, riding three feet below maximum water-line and listing twenty degrees, was able to anchor safely.

An icebreaker cruises en route to the north polar cap passing an iceberg. (Lawson Brigham)

Buoy tender Juniper, *the first of the new breed of ocean buoy tender, can hold position within a thirty-nine-foot circle while setting a buoy in winds up to thirty knots and seas to eight feet. The sturdy vessel can also break fourteen-inch-thick ice at a continuous speed and break a maximum of three-foot-thick ice by ramming. (U.S. Coast Guard)*

Even without icebergs, patrolling the Grand Banks is fraught with danger. A "weather bomb" struck this area in October 1991, which was the subject of Sebastian Junger's book, The Perfect Storm. *The cutter* Tamaroa *played a major role in that drama off Nantucket Island. In forty-foot waves and eighty-knot winds, the cutter's rigid hull inflatable boat rescued three people from the sailing vessel* Satori. *Then a short time later, while battling the same storm, rescued four crewmembers from an Air National Guard rescue helicopter that ditched. (U.S. Coast Guard)*

Above: *The icebreaker follows a lead through ice-mountains. (Lawson Brigham).*

Right: *At sea, like nowhere else, man is constantly reminded of the awesome power of nature. It is not only during the worst storms, however, when violent weather brings disaster and desperate calls for rescue, that the Coast Guard puts to sea. Since the cutters routinely patrol some of the most storm-battered waters of the world, Coast Guard men and women regularly find themselves at the center of nature's fury, as here where the Bering Sea boards a cutter (Jerry Minchew U.S. Coast Guard)*

Above: *CGC* Storis, *a combination icebreaker and tender, escorts a convoy of fifteen tugs and barges loaded with construction equipment destined for the new North Slope oil fields near Prudhoe Bay, Alaska, in the fall of 1975. The arrival of the fleet of twenty-three tugs and forty-seven barges was delayed by pack ice surrounding Point Barrow. Delivery was successful, however, in the chopped-ice wake of* Storis. *(U.S. Coast Guard)*

Opposite, bottom: *The crew of a Coast Guard icebreaker stopped in the ice splits into teams to play football in what is termed the "Penguin Bowl." The once-white hulls were painted red beginning in the 1970s to make them easier to spot in the ice by their accompanying helicopters. The all-white helicopters too, took on the all-red paint scheme for the same reason. (U.S. Coast Guard)*

Icebreakers

Naturally, given the regions where they operated, Coast Guard cutters had always done their share of icebreaking, but this was usually in conjunction with other duties and carried out by vessels not designed especially for the task. A real icebreaker, one taking advantage of the latest technology, was needed.

Progress in icebreakers, however, like the ships themselves, must sometimes back up before pushing forward again. This was the case with the original *Northland*, commissioned in 1927. The 210-foot cutter was designed to replace the aging *Bear* on the Bering Sea Patrol. *Northland*, the most costly cutter up to that time, was a test ship for new ideas: the power of the ship's engines went, not directly to the propeller, but to generators that drove an electric motor that turned the prop shaft. *Northland* also swerved from tradition with a radically cut-away forefoot, a U-shaped hull—to allow it to rise up on the ice rather than be crushed by it—and no bilge keels. Yet, as if not quite ready to commit itself fully to the future, the ship also carried a sailing rig. Unfortunately, *Northland* did little well and was hardly an improvement on the old wooden whaling ship of the previous century it was designed to replace.

Not until the mid-1930s, in the interest of commerce, did the Coast Guard assume responsibility of keeping U.S. channels and harbors free from ice. Within three years the country's first true icebreakers, the 110-foot *Raritan*-class tugs, *Raritan*, *Arundel*, *Naugatuck*, and *Mahoning*, were ready for duty. These were followed by the 180-foot *Cactus*, *Mesquite*, and *Iris*-class tenders, and the building of the mighty *Storis*, an extraordinary 230-foot cutter.

The Coast Guard continued to perfect its icebreakers, and by the autumn of 1944, the 180-foot tenders carried, along with their other armaments, depth charges, barrage-rocket "mousetraps," and sonar for use against U-boats. These 180s were able to push through ice nearly two feet thick, and while their primary mission was tending aids to navigation,

they regularly would be called on to escort convoys, conduct search-and-rescue operations, tend anti-submarine nets, lay mines, and handle weather patrols.

In the last year of World War II, four 269-foot *Wind*-class icebreakers, *Northwind*, *Southwind*, *Eastwind*, and *Westwind*, were launched. In this design six Fairbanks Morse diesels drove generators that powered electric motors that turned three props. This system produced a whopping 12,000 horsepower—as compared to the 1,000 horsepower thought sufficient for *Northland* not so many years earlier.

Like the winds they were named after, these four cutters would travel widely. Three would be loaned to the Soviet Union and only be returned years after the war's end. Two would then serve in the Navy before finding their way back home to the Coast Guard some two decades later.

Eastwind, the only one of the four to remain with the Coast Guard, saw as much adventure as any ship of the era. Not only did *Eastwind*, together with *Southwind*, capture the only German ship taken as a prize at sea during the war, it somehow survived a deadly collision with a tanker a few years later and went on to participate in the first *Operation Deep Freeze*, the mission to provide supplies to bases in Antarctica. Then going from the bottom of the world to the top, the cutter cruised the Arctic supporting DEW Line outposts. In 1961 *Eastwind* became the first cutter to go around the world and six years later, the first to circumnavigate the North Pole. But then those sort of wanderings might be expected of any ship named for the wind.

In a similar vein, *Storis*, the Coast Guard's one-of-a-kind cutter, seems like *Eastwind* to have had its destiny determined by its name, which to the Vikings meant "big ice." Certainly no cutter has been more at home among the great floes and bergs than *Storis*, which at the time of writing is the Coast Guard's oldest ship and wears gold hull numbers marking it as "Queen of the Fleet."

After service on the Greenland Patrol during World War II, *Storis* transferred from Boston to Maryland, then served a stint breaking ice on

Icebreaking twins, Polar Star *and* Polar Sea, *create an access channel for supply ships to reach the scientific research station at McMurdo Sound in the Antarctic. (U.S. Coast Guard)*

Above: *Sledges move into position on the ice alongside CGC* Glacier *at McMurdo Base, Antarctica, delivering supplies during the short summer period in early December 1967.* Glacier *is a part of the Navy Task Force of forty-three ships engaging in* Operation Deep Freeze 1968 *supporting the U.S. Scientific Stations in the Antarctic. Following this delivery* Glacier *engaged in the Waddell Sea expedition. (U.S. Coast Guard)*

Opposite, bottom left: Polar Sea *stopped while a scientific party prepares for an examination on the ice. (Lawson Brigham)*

the Great Lakes before joining the Bering Sea Patrol. In 1957, together with cutters *Bramble* and *Spar*, Storis set out to find a northwest passage that could be used in time of war to support or evacuate DEW Line outposts. This voyage of discovery would take the three cutters from Seattle across the top of North America to the Atlantic, and before returning home again they would circumnavigate the continent. In honor of this, the Canadian government would name a distant, ice-choked strait Storis.

Sometimes the effort went smoothly, but often the ships were stymied and had to search out other routes. Occasionally all three became stuck, were trapped in the ice, and carried where the flow took them. Helicopters were launched to search out leads to open water and often returned without finding any.

In the mid-1960s the Navy decided to leave ice-breaking to those who were best at it and transferred all five of its icebreakers to the Coast Guard. Among these ships was *Glacier*, known as *Big G*, and at 309 feet, the country's largest icebreaker. This gave the service an ocean-going ice-breaking fleet of eight, somewhat elderly vessels, that nine years later was augmented further with two 399-foot ships, *Polar Star* and *Polar Sea*.

These new additions, like the *Hamilton*-class cutters, could choose from two power sources. Under normal conditions they steam through ice over six-feet thick at a steady three knots using a combination of diesel engines and electric motors producing 18,000 horsepower. When needed,

USCGC POLAR SEA (WAGB 11)
SEATTLE, WASHINGTON

Lawson W. Brigham 22 AUG 94
Captain, U. S. Coast Guard
Commanding Officer

Above: *Patch depicting the arrival at the North Pole of the first two North American icebreakers, USCGC* Polar Sea *and Canadian CGS* Louis S. St. Laurent. *(Lawson Brigham)*

Left: *Cancellation stamps from* Polar Sea's *post office cancelled at the North Pole on 22 August 1994. (Lawson Brigham)*

Above: *A modern ship relies on countless, incredibly complex systems that must be maintained, and sometimes repaired and replaced, far out at sea. Such self-sufficiency demands highly trained personnel, often with expertise in multiple areas, as well as a suitable and carefully managed parts inventory. Since no amount of planning can prepare for every contingency, most Coast Guard vessels also have a workshop able to make replacement parts if necessary. (U.S. Coast Guard)*

however, the ships can switch to three Pratt & Whitney gas turbines turning out 60,000 horsepower, and force their way through ice over three times as thick. This whopping power allowed *Polar Sea* in 1994 to become the first American surface ship to reach the North Pole.

By then, however, the Coast Guard had already phased out all its aging ocean-going icebreakers, leaving only *Polar Sea* and *Polar Star*. During this time it concentrated on increasing its fleet of lighter ice-breaking tugs by adding nine 140-footers from 1978 to 1987. As always, a good cutter had to be able to do many things well, and the versatile tugs could meet the country's routine ice-breaking needs.

The service's ice breakers had long been called on to support scientific research, and this work highlighted the need for a modern vessel able to take advantage of the latest technological advancements. In 2000, the Coast Guard's most advanced icebreaker, *Healy*, was commissioned and

Above: *The North Pole is just a mile and a quarter walk away as shown on the navigation read-out on the icebreaker's bridge. (Lawson Brigham)*

homeported in Seattle. At 420-feet *Healy* is also the service's largest ice-breaker ever, and uses the time-tested system of diesel engines driving electric generators to deliver 30,000 hp at the twin props.

Like every other cutter, *Healy* is expected to be able to fulfill an almost limitless range of duties from logistics support, search-and-rescue, and law enforcement to environmental protection, especially in polar seas. What makes *Healy* extraordinary, however, is its ability to perform as a self-contained, scientific research platform. The cutter carries nearly a dozen laboratories and research areas including biological and chemical facilities and meteorological, computer, and electronics labs. It also has an extensive bathymetric survey system for mapping the ocean floor, as well as special dive lockers and decompression chambers. Each year in the short time since the cutter was launched, *Healy* has seen sea duty at one or the other of the poles. Before the ship was a year old it set out for a six-month assignment in the eastern Arctic in the waters northwest of Norway. The next year found the cutter in the Bering Strait off Nome, Alaska. In 2003, as part of the annual *Operation Deep Freeze*, *Healy* and *Polar Sea* cleared a path through the ice for resupply vessels bound for McMurdo Station, center of the U.S. Antarctic missions.

Law Enforcement in All Waters

Since the days of the Revenue Cutter Service sea duty in extreme conditions always had come with the territory, but the cutters were seldom called on for true international missions until the final years of World War I. Not surprisingly in light of its full plate of domestic responsibilities, the Coast Guard had only six cutters prepared to patrol on the other side of an ocean. These six, *Ossipee, Seneca, Manning, Yamacraw, Algonquin*, and *Tampa*, were assigned escort duty for shipping between Gibraltar and England, served two years, and all except *Tampa*—sunk six weeks before the end of the war—were home again by the summer of 1919.

The world was becoming smaller, however, and even a home-grown experiment like Prohibition, following on the heels of the Great War, proved able to entangle the Coast Guard's ships in international squabbles and seemed to call for bigger vessels with longer legs. Since large rumrunners of foreign-flag stood well offshore and unloaded liquor onto fast smuggling boats that darted for the coast with their contraband, the best solution appeared to be to go after the source and try to catch the mother ships. The Coast Guard asked Congress for twenty new cutters of good endurance, but instead received twenty mothballed destroyers from the Navy. Averaging around 300 feet in length and with a top speed of up to thirty-five knots, these ships were certainly able to keep up with the largest smuggling vessels and follow them anywhere, but the destroyers were hard to maneuver and thus easy to evade, especially in poor visibility. They nonetheless gave Coast Guardsmen their first experience with ships of that kind. This training would stand the service in good stead in the years ahead, especially in World War II, when Coast Guard personnel would serve on Navy ships. Now operating its own destroyers, the Coast Guard could no longer be dismissed as a "shallow-water" Navy.

The destroyers were most useful outside the three-mile limit of territorial waters and the Coast Guard did not hesitate to chase and seize smugglers well beyond that line. This would lead to international disputes, new legislation, eventual reconciliation of all parties involved, expansion of U.S. territorial waters, and increased authority for the Coast Guard. As the Coast Guard's missions grew, so did the endurance of its ships and so did its operating area, which in turn brought the service new missions. This cycle was to be repeated.

As it happened, the destroyers were never as effective as hoped. The rum-ships only moved farther offshore and became more widely scattered. Also the Coast Guard, never flush with funding to begin with, realized it could not hope to afford the upkeep of such vessels indefinitely. More versatility was needed. This led the service on in the search for the perfect cutter, one tailor-made for all the duties required of it.

The search for the perfect cutter as an antidote to smuggling was still going on when Prohibition ended in 1933. The lucrative business of slipping contraband into the U.S. did not collapse with the relegalization of alcohol, however, and although the Coast Guard was able to return its borrowed destroyers to the Navy, it continued to look for a top-notch anti-smuggling cutter, yet one that could do everything else well too.

With the lessons of Prohibition still fresh in mind, the service decided a Navy design, the *Erie*-class gunboats, might be just what it was looking for. The narcotics trade was on the rise, and in 1936 the newly commissioned 327-foot *Secretary*-class cutters—each was named for a former secretary of the Treasury—set out to deal with the problem. Heavily modified from the original Navy plans, the 327s could reach nearly twenty knots, a good speed for anti-smuggling work, and yet were designed to carry additional heavy armaments should they be needed for combat. With a sharp eye to the political weather, in just a few years—well before the attack on Pearl Harbor—almost with their

Willing to risk death for the hope of freedom, four Cubans have set out to cross the unpredictable Straits of Florida in a frail, poorly hammered-together boat. Good weather and discovery by a patrolling Coast Guard cutter has likely saved their lives. (Adam Wine, U.S. Coast Guard)

Seaman Steven Decker aboard Valiant *unloads bales of marijuana onto the pier in Miami. The bales, totaling 3,360 pounds, were tossed overboard from a suspected smuggling boat during a chase near Cuba. (Gibran Soto, U.S. Coast Guard)*

A Coast Guard boarding-crew measures the mesh of a fishnet to make certain it meets the regulated size. Inspectors must be knowledgeable, not just in the regulations and legal requirements governing fishing vessels, but must also be alert for safety and environmental violations, as well as for signs of illegal immigration and smuggling, and be on the lookout for other suspicious activities. Through training and experience, the inspectors gain an in-depth understanding of the tricks and tools of the trade of a variety of maritime occupations. (U.S. Coast Guard)

Coast Guard inspectors radio a report from a fishing vessel to their waiting cutter. If violations are major, the vessel may be seized and its cargo sold. In addition, fines may be imposed and these must be paid before the vessel is released. (U.S. Coast Guard)

Above: *Crewmembers of CGC* Mellon *on fisheries law enforcement patrol near St Paul Island, Alaska, prepare towline to take the disabled fishing vessel* Aleutian Rover *in tow to prevent it from drifting into an ice shelf. (U.S. Coast Guard)*

Right: *A Coast Guard boarding team nears a foreign fishing vessel working within the United States' 200-mile Exclusive Economic Zone. The ship will have its catch and equipment inspected to assure it is operating within the law. (U.S. Coast Guard)*

paint still fresh, the 327s prudently began making their way to the Navy yards to take on those extra, bigger guns.

With all the rapid changes between the World Wars, it would be easy to overlook two small and often unheralded beginnings that held great, long-lasting ramifications for the service. The first of these, as mentioned above, was the commissioning of the handsome 327-foot *Secretary*-class cutters in the mid-1930s. These ships that served so well on Ocean Station duty had been designed with something else entirely in mind: intercepting narcotics traffickers. For that reason they had cranes for handling floatplanes carried aboard, something hardly necessary for working the Ocean Stations, but exactly in step with the future.

A second easily missed event was the enactment in 1936 of laws requiring enforcement of international regulations on whaling. Since 1868, when the Treasury Department first sent a cutter to stop the plundering of the Alaska's offshore sealing grounds, the service had played an ever larger role in protecting the nation's fisheries and pelagic wildlife. By the 1920s this authority had been expanded to include protection of virtually all living things in Alaska, from bears and mountain goats to sea birds. When, however, in the years before World War II, Coast Guard officers began serving as inspectors on whaling ships in the far-off Indian Ocean and the seas of Antarctica, a new era began. From then on the service would be called on to enforce not only American, but international regulations. Nothing of the sort could have been imagined for the ships of the tiny Revenue Cutter Service.

In following years, the Coast Guard would also represent the United States at whaling conferences, and the service's international role would continue expanding until today the cutters regularly work alongside foreign agencies. Such missions would increase dramatically after 1992 when a United Nations resolution calling for an end to all large-scale drift-net fishing on the world's oceans went into effect. Since drift-netters can stay at sea for eight months and more, challenging them would call for fast, long-legged ships.

Despite advances in technology, the rules of good seamanship and many chores of the sailor have not changed in hundreds of years. Cutters still have bells, brass has to be polished, hands still go aloft. As seen in the background, the need for belaying pins—and the skills to properly belay a line—did not pass away with the age of sail. (U.S. Coast Guard)

Fortunately, the Coast Guard's 378-foot *Hamilton*-class high-endurance cutters proved themselves a match to the task. Built from 1965 to 1972, these multipurpose vessels could choose power from either a pair of 36,000-hp Pratt & Whitney gas turbines, which provide speed, or two 7,000-hp Fairbanks-Morse diesel engines that allow economical, long-distance cruising. Driven by the gas turbines, the cutters can approach a speed of thirty knots; under more economical diesel power they cruise at around eleven knots. Two thirteen-foot-diameter, controllable-pitch propellers give the ships good maneuverability, as does a retractable bow propulsion system.

Success seldom comes easily, however. In a single year *Boutwell*, for example, spent 201 days at sea, and as cutter crews know, the chase to catch a lawless fishing ship can cover vast distances. In 1997, *Cao Yu 6025* was spotted by a Canadian Air Force fisheries airplane 1,300 miles northwest of Midway Island. As the plane circled, the ship's crew began hauling in a drift-net and prepared to escape. The pilot reported the sighting, and the information went to the U.S. Coast Guard.

When *Cao Yu*'s claimed registration in the People's Republic of China was denied by the Chinese government, the vessel was declared stateless and therefore under Coast Guard jurisdiction. No high-endurance cutter was available, but a Coast Guard HC-130H Hercules search aircraft was sent from Hawaii to keep track of the fishing ship until the 180-foot buoy tender *Basswood*, based in Guam, could arrive on the scene.

The fifty-four-year-old *Basswood*, however, had a maximum speed of twelve knots—not much greater than that of *Cao Yu*—and when the

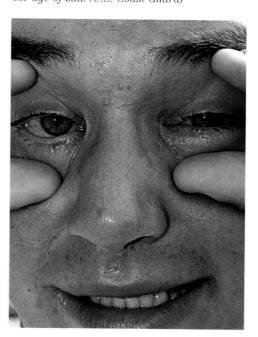

Seaman Adam Season, a crewman onboard the Coast Guard Cutter Bainbridge Island, gets fresh air into his eyes after being sprayed with OC pepper spray during law enforcement training. Coast Guard members are required to undergo the training in order to carry the spray. (Tom Sperduto, U.S. Coast Guard)

A Coast Guard cutter coming to the aid of a disabled fishing trawler in the Aleutians. (Lawson Brigham)

Above: In a setting that might be out of a science fiction movie, Coast Guardsmen stand ready at their battle stations. (U.S. Coast Guard)

Right: The crew of a Coast Guard cutter clean the barrel of 76mm deck gun after a firing exercise in the Pacific Ocean. Although seldom fired in anger, a cutter's guns are kept in top condition and crews drill with them frequently to keep skills sharp. (Alice Sennott, U.S. Coast Guard)

skipper of the fishing ship decided to flee rather than allow boarding, a two-week, 1,700-mile chase ensued. The long-running game of cat-and-mouse came to an end when the 378-foot, high-endurance cutter *Chase* arrived. Coast Guardsmen and Canadian fisheries department officials forcibly boarded *Cao Yu* and seized the vessel, along with its drift-net gear and some 120 tons of tuna and shark fins.

Such outlaw ships do not often surrender meekly. In May 2000, *Arctic Wind*, a fully operational fish-processing ship, was discovered drift-netting 600 miles off Adak, Alaska, and was pursued by the cutter *Sherman*. Trying to escape by taking an erratic course across the open ocean, *Arctic Wind* led *Sherman* on a five-day chase. Thinking the Coast Guardsmen would not risk an international incident by shooting at them, the vessel's Russian crew refused to stop even when overtaken by the cutter.

Above: *A lifeline is passed to crewmen of the sinking British ship* Ambassador. *By this means a life raft was moved to the ship. Five men jumped into the life raft but waves promptly tossed them into the ocean. Six Coast Guardsmen in wetsuits leaped into the water and rescued two. Remarkably a wave washed the other three back aboard their ship. Coast Guardsmen saved eleven of the twelve crew. The twelfth man drowned before he was located. (U.S. Coast Guard)*

Left: *Chief Gunner's Mate James G. Guerette checks the control console of the 76mm deck gun. Such a gun mount is unmanned and fired remotely. (Alice Sennott, U.S. Coast Guard)*

Sherman's skipper, Captain David Ryan, then requested—and received—permission to fire on *Arctic Wind*. When the Russians saw *Sherman*'s guns uncovered and turned on them they wisely decided not to push their luck and halted to allow their ship to be boarded.

Investigators found *Arctic Wind*'s nine-mile-long drift net held 700 salmon, eight sharks, fifty puffins, twelve albatross, and a porpoise—a modest catch by drift-net standards, but nonetheless a success for the Coast Guard cutters: another indication the days of ninety-mile-long nets seem to be over as drift-netters turn to short nets that can be hauled quickly for a fast getaway.

Because of international support for Coast Guard patrols, law-breakers are forced to take ever greater pains to hide their identity. *Arctic Wind*, owned by Koreans, tried to pass as a Honduran vessel; it was crewed by Russians and its catch was intended for buyers in Japan.

To help cut through the layers of subterfuge and also lessen the risk of international misunderstandings in drift-net busts, officials of foreign governments are now often on patrol with the cutters. This is increasingly common as, for example, in 1999 when the drift-netter *Yng Fa* was spotted by a Canadian CP-140 surveillance plane. As the cutter *Rush* came on the scene it launched its helicopter, and the *Yng Fa*, realizing it had been discovered, cut away its drift-net and tried to escape. *Rush* soon overtook *Yng Fa*, however, and boarded it. On *Rush*'s team was an official of the People's Republic of China fisheries department, assigned to the cutter specifically to help it battle high-seas, drift-net fishing.

Drift-net operations, of course, are only one of many missions for the high-endurance *Hamilton*-class cutters, and all twelve have action-filled histories recounting innumerable smuggling seizures and harrowing rescues, as well as mind-numbingly boring weeks in the bygone times of Ocean-Station duty, with their endless days of repetitive chores, card games, and reading.

A Coast Guard boarding officer squeezes down a hatch on a fishing vessel to inspect the catch. Boarding teams inspect every section and item on fishing vessels, including catch and fish-capturing equipment to determine compliance with vessel safety and fisheries regulations. (Ron Mench, U.S. Coast Guard)

Buoy Tenders

Tom Beard

Coast Guard cutter Walnut, *a 225-foot buoy tender— the second of this name—deployed in January 2003 from its home port in Honolulu to the Persian Gulf, joining Coast Guard units assisting coalition forces as the Iraqi War opened. Walnut, with its modern oil-spill recovery system—with a 400-gallon per minute skimming capacity—was sent to prevent pollution of Gulf waters from intentional environmental-terrorism acts. The ship's crew, in preparation, trained with weapons and force protections, and drilled in chemical, biological, and radiological attack responses.*

When these threats did not materialize after their arrival, Walnut shifted roles and engaged in law-enforcement activities assisting other Coast Guard and Navy units in halting smuggling.

Walnut then engaged in its third task, described by its title—buoy tender. The urgent need of humanitarian and war supplies called for secure and clearly marked shipping channels. Walnut's crew set buoys (discovered in an Iraqi warehouse and repaired by the ship's crew) along the 41-mile Khawr Abd Allah navigational channel leading to Iraq's port, Umm Qasr, thus opening a safe sea-lane for relief ships to begin supplying needed goods to Iraq.

This task was interrupted momentarily, when the buoy tender responded in its traditional Coast Guard search and rescue role, to search for survivors from two downed United Kingdom helicopters and later to rescue a boat's crew caught in heavy weather. In yet another of its roles, a military vessel, the ubiquitous buoy tender then assisted in the capture of Iraqi offshore oil terminals.

In an earlier generation, the previous Coast Guard buoy tender named Walnut, built in 1939 as a lighthouse tender for the U.S. Lighthouse Service, also came under the guns of war.

The Japanese forces attacking Hawaii on 7 December 1941 also had naval destroyers shelling Midway Island, 1,200 miles away, intent on neutralizing any opposing United States units. Crewmembers from the unarmed Walnut, at Midway working on aids to navigation, observed gun flashes in the night and then saw eruptions in the water where shells landed within 100 feet of the vessel. Earlier that day when word of the Pearl Harbor attack reached the buoy tender's crew, they extinguished all island navigation lights to prevent the enemy from using the aids as navigational or targeting references. The 175-footer escaped unharmed from the 30-minute bombardment. However, it was during this attack that a Navy PBY crashed in Midway Lagoon. Walnut's crew successfully recovered the injured crew.

For the remainder of the war, Walnut continued aids to navigation tasks, combat search and rescue, and convoy escort missions but with guns and depth charges added. Following the war, the multi-mission cutter continued to serve the manifold Coast Guard roles and missions until decommissioned in 1982—after 43 years of service.

Marinette, Wisconsin, has provided stout vessels for the naval service for three generations. The latest is the series of 16 buoy tenders coming off the ways of Marinette Marine Corporation into the Menominee River. The 225-foot buoy tender, of which the second Walnut is one, represent the latest in shipbuilding, propulsion, and ship control technology.

Cutters in the 225-foot WLB Juniper class, seagoing buoy tenders named for trees, are equipped with a single, controllable pitch propeller for main propulsion and both bow and stern thrusters for maneuvering. These three thrust elements give the cutters the maneuverability they need tending buoys in restricted waters. Sophisticated automatic controls for the propulsion machinery with an automatic monitoring system, combined with electronic navigational chart displays on the bridge, enable the 225-foot cutters to operate with a much reduced crew complement compared to earlier buoy tenders. Furthermore, a dynamic positioning system using both these

features with the Global Positioning System as a position reference, can automatically hold the vessel within a 10-meter circle. These features allow the crew to service and accurately position floating navigation aids in winds up to 30 knots and seas to eight feet. This piloting system also has the ability to navigate the vessel along a track line to specified positions with only data inputs and monitoring required by the helmsperson—no more hand steering to a swaying compass.

The Coast Guard's harbor and river buoy tenders, painted black like their seagoing big brothers, are virtually unknown and usually unnoticed as they ply the nation's rivers and lakes maintaining navigable waterways, protecting the environment, enforcing laws, and lending assistance wherever needed.

Inland waterways vital to the nation's economy are serviced by these buoy tenders. While ice in the nation's industrial regions stops commerce and destroys aids to navigation, these vessels keep sea-lanes open and enhance the economic health of the nation. Breaking open lanes in the ice on the Great Lakes early and late into the seasons adds extra months each year that are vital to moving commerce. Critical supplies of heating fuel-oil often find their way to an unexpectedly frozen Northeast in barges following a trail broken in ice by these workhorse vessels.

Not only do springtime thaws tear channel markers

and buoys from their stations, but also river channels often change with floods. These buoy tenders must be there replacing the guides for shipping to continue on the Mississippi, Ohio, and Missouri rivers. Like all units, the buoy tenders stand ready for all the roles and missions assigned to the Coast Guard. For example, floods frequently bring the need for disaster relief only possible with these tough, hard-working boats and crews. Coast Guard buoy tenders are true all-service cutters.

Top, left: Lighthouses on the Great Lakes can become ice sculptures, as St. Joseph Light is shown here. The tender *Amaranth* removed the keepers from Stannard Rock Lighthouse, on Lake Superior, in similar conditions resulting from a late November storm. (U.S. Coast Guard)

Top, right: Buoys fouled with smelly marine growth need to be hauled periodically, cleaned, repaired, and replaced. A newly overhauled bell buoy is going overboard replacing one just hauled sitting on deck (U.S. Coast Guard)

Below: Coast Guardsmen drop a "sinker" and buoy from the construction tender's deck alongside a waterway channel. The stack of concrete blocks, sinkers, and buoys on deck portends a busy schedule. (U.S. Coast Guard)

Support and Weather Missions

Search-and-rescue and even support operations might occur anywhere on the globe. Traditionally, the cutters of the Bering Sea patrol had long served as medical and dental clinics, provided emergency relief, and even legal services to the isolated villages of Alaska, and yet were always ready to drop everything to respond to sudden search-and-rescue missions. Similar assignments far from U.S. shores had begun requiring cutters. In the late 1930s *Itasca* was delivering supplies to mid-Pacific islands when it was called to search for the missing Amelia Earhart, and *Northland* was on its way to Antarctica to support the Byrd expedition when war broke out in Europe and *Northland* had to turn around.

It was in these between-wars years that a seemingly unrelated milestone delivered yet another offshore task for the cutters: airplanes suddenly achieved the range to easily cross oceans. If anything, this advancement should have lifted some burdens from the cutters, for there are many tasks aircraft can handle more efficiently than watercraft. Instead, transoceanic flights came to depend on ships scattered across the globe to provide navigational and weather information.

For a time the world's merchant fleets were able to furnish the necessary weather reports, but with the outbreak of World War II, these ships began maintaining radio silence. Since International Ice Patrol

Bow awash, Mendota *plunges ahead on ocean station "Delta" in the North Atlantic named for the letter designation from the phonetic alphabet of the period. An old hand on ocean station understands this shorthand when "Able" or "Sugar" is mentioned. In seas like this, each jolt vibrates through the steel, and the effort of just keeping on their feet wears down crews. For weeks on end, year-in, year-out, Coast Guard cutters held positions far out at sea on the Ocean Stations to provide information for international flights—and to be on hand should a rescue be necessary. (John S. Ryall, U.S. Coast Guard)*

USCGC Itasca

USS Bancroft, *built in 1890 for the Navy as a training ship, was transferred to the Revenue Cutter Service in 1906. It was renamed* Itasca *following modifications at the service's depot in Arundel Cove, Maryland.* Itasca *was commissioned as a School of Instruction for Cadets ship in 1907. This vessel was the forerunner of the Coast Guard Academy and the third vessel serving in this role following the schooner* Dobbin *beginning classes in 1877 and the barque* Chase *in 1878.*

The cadets' education was served underway. Itasca *visited European and Caribbean ports throughout the fair-weather months and wintered over in Curtis Bay, Maryland. This location later became the Coast Guard Yard for building and repairing vessels. Some winter cruising was done in the Chesapeake Bay, along the Atlantic coast, and into New York Station.*

The School of Instruction was moved from the ship to Fort Trumbull in New London, Connecticut, in 1910 with Itasca *still performing as a training vessel. Its last instructional voyage was in 1920 where it circled the Atlantic, visiting European ports. Idled after this trip, it sold out of service two years later.*

The 189-foot steel ship carried a beam of thirty-two feet with a displacement of 980 tons. Along with its steam power plant turning two screws, it had a masts rigged to hoist sails. The training ship was armed with four guns.

Itasca, cadet training ship from 1907 to 1920, is shown with masts fore and aft of its central smokestack, portending a time of transition from sail to steam power. (U.S. Coast Guard)

cutters had long been providing information on icebergs entering the shipping lanes, it followed that such vessels could also serve as weather stations. At the beginning of 1940, at the direction of President Roosevelt, four Coast Guard ships scattered themselves down the North Atlantic and began yet another new mission, one that would endure for well over a quarter of a century: weather patrol.

At the height of the war there would be altogether forty-six weather stations scattered across the Atlantic and Pacific. The tremendous burden of keeping these was borne primarily by the Navy, with the help of Britain, Brazil, and Canada. Such weather stations have been described as mid-ocean information booths, for they reported weather and sea conditions, relayed radio transmissions, and provided position readings, besides standing by for search and rescue. After the war, the Coast Guard would be charged with maintaining the stations, but fortunately, given the costs, only about a dozen were to be manned full-time.

This mission called for long-legged cutters that could comfortably and economically ride the swells near the center of a designated ten-mile square region far out to sea. There they would pass the time for three weeks and then be relieved by another cutter. Travel to and from location did not count, so often cutters were at sea well over half the time. The duty, as crewmembers described it, was "weeks of boredom interrupted by days of inactivity."

Opposite, top: *The Bering Sea is a rich fishing ground that attracts great numbers of foreign fishing vessels. Coast Guard inspectors, from the cutter* Jarvis, *shown here, board fishing vessels to enforce both national and international regulations to prevent the depletion of marine resources or the taking of protected species. (Russ Tippetts, U.S. Coast Guard)*

Ocean Station duty requires a vessel to remain within a defined area regardless of weather. CGC Pontchartrain *battles the North Atlantic on Ocean Station "Baker." Crews on station invariably have "one hand for the ship and one for themselves" with ships unable to run-off distances evading storm conditions. Eating a meal in these conditions often means sitting on a deck with one's back braced against a bulkhead. (U.S. Coast Guard)*

Periodic dry-docking is imperative to clean a ship's hull of clinging marine growth, which not only retards a vessel's speed but can cause other problems. This is also the time to accomplish major repair and maintenance that would be difficult or impossible to do when the ship is in the water. (U.S. Coast Guard)

Four types of cutters proved they were up to it and bore virtually all the Ocean Station burden. The first of these were the shallow-draft 311-foot, *Casco*-class seaplane tenders built by the Navy during World War II and meant to operate in protected waters. The Coast Guard got three of these, and incredibly, they proved to be excellent vessels for loitering far out at sea. They had good, long legs, but being flat bottomed, they tended to pound in a seaway, and the punishment took its toll on hull structures, necessitating expensive repairs. Still, the Coast Guard liked the ships and got fifteen more from the Navy.

The newly built USCGC Owasco *in July 1945 prepares to go to war. Unique to previous Coast Guard cutters built prior to World War II, the 255-foot class cutters, launched between 1944 and 1946, were constructed as heavily armed warships. As constructed, Owasco carried two, twin-mount 5"/38 dual-purpose guns as the main battery and was powerfully fortified with anti-aircraft weapons in the day of the kamikaze threat with two, quad-mount 40mm/60 cannons and four 20mm/80 cannons. Further battlement for anti-submarine warfare consisted of two depth charge tracks, six "Y" guns, and a hedgehog. Though 122 feet shorter and three feet wider, the 255s displacement was similar to a Fletcher-class destroyer. The cutter is shown here in its postwar configuration, with armament substantially reduced. (U.S. Coast Guard)*

224

The second type was the 327-foot *Secretary*-class cutters. The Service had come out of the war with six of these ten-year-old cutters, which were designed to counter narcotics smuggling, but were soon called to combat in World War II. They proved adaptable to keeping the Ocean Stations. Each, except for *Alexander Hamilton*, which was torpedoed and sunk by a U-boat, put in almost fifty-years service before retiring.

The third—and strangest—type were the stubby 255-footers. The original Coast Guard design called for a cutter 316 feet long, but expediency caused the vessels to be built sixty-one feet shorter than planned. Following Ocean Station duty, all served in Vietnam and were decommissioned soon afterward.

The final type, the 378-foot *Hamilton*-class, the all-around, high-endurance cutters, began coming down the skids in the mid-1960s. They were excellent performers on the Ocean Stations as this was their primary mission. When that duty came to an end only a few years later, all went on to earn their stripes in other missions, proving once again, that above all, cutters must be jacks of all trades.

Airplane Rescue

The idea of stationing cutters at sea began in 1938 with the crash of a Pan Am plane near American Samoa. Lieutenant Commander George B. Kelly was convinced the Service could do much to prevent such accidents and at the same time encourage the country's budding air commerce. The following years would prove Kelly correct, and those times when the Coast Guard could not prevent a plane from going down at sea, a cutter might be in the area at least to help rescue survivors.

Kelly's hope that cutters could support commercial air travel was confirmed in the fall of 1947 when *Bibb*, one of the 327s originally built to run down opium smugglers, was on Ocean Station Charlie off Newfoundland. The weather was awful, as usual in those waters, and a gale had been blowing for two days when a flying boat running out of fuel was forced down near *Bibb*, reportedly in thirty-foot seas. The winds were howling, the cutter rolling thirty-five degrees, and as the plane taxied toward *Bibb* it lost control and smashed bow first into the

Above, left: *Little has changed in custom from the days when sailors sat around the capstan entertaining themselves with fiddle and hornpipe. This is a holiday routine on the fantail of a cutter long at sea off Vietnam's coast. (Coast Guard Museum Northwest)*

Above: *A picnic aboard ship lacks only a park's ball-fields and green grass. In their place is the ever-present sea. (Coast Guard Museum Northwest)*

Above, top to bottom: *Engine failure forced a Pan American airliner to ditch in October 1956 at Ocean Station November, located between Honolulu and San Francisco. CGC* Ponchartrain *determined a ditching heading based on the most favorable wind and sea direction and spread a foam runway across the waves. When the plane hit the water it bounced once, seemed to dive into a swell then twisted a bit before pointing itself toward the cutter. In less than a minute passengers appeared on the floating aircraft's wings. (U.S. Coast Guard)*

Eight minutes after the Pan American airliner hit the water, lifeboats from Ponchartrain *were alongside. All twenty-four passengers and seven crewmembers were saved before the stricken airliner sunk moments later. (U.S. Coast Guard)*

Eighteen passengers from the cruise ship Prinsendam *in a lifeboat along with two Canadian paramedics not recovered by helicopter were rescued by a Coast Guard cutter. Believed one of the largest evacuation/rescues of a ship at sea, only one person was reported injured out of the more than 500 recovered. No one was lost. (U.S. Coast Guard)*

The cruise ship Prinsendam *was abandoned in October 1980 by 320 passengers and about 200 crewmembers following a fire at sea in the Gulf of Alaska, leaving the cruise ship adrift. Coast Guard and Air Force helicopters plus Canadian forces aided in evacuating passengers from lifeboats and transferring them to the nearby supertanker* Williamsburgh. *Three Coast Guard cutters responded and aided in the search for scattered lifeboats.* Prinsendam *sank after eight days of drifting. (U.S. Coast Guard)*

cutter's side. The rescue efforts went on through the dark and by morning, miraculously, all sixty-nine people from the airplane, including children and a baby, had been pulled on board the cutter.

This was dramatically illustrated once more in October 1956, a few hours before dawn. *Ponchartrain*, another of the 255-footers, was on Ocean Station November between San Francisco and Honolulu, when a Pan American Clipper, *Sovereign of the Sky*, radioed trouble with one of its four engines. Shortly afterward another engine failed. The plane, carrying twenty-four passengers and seven crewmembers, could not reach land, and had no choice but to ditch. The pilot, however, was able to maintain altitude until daylight when the plane, nearly out of fuel, ditched. This gave *Ponchartrain* a valuable five hours to get ready for the crash-landing. Keeping in close contact, Commander William K. Earle, skipper of the cutter, and the Clipper pilot, Richard Ogg, carefully laid out rescue plans.

Ponchartrain put a two-mile-long frosting of foam on the water, and just before 8:30 in the morning, *Sovereign of the Sky* came down, plowing into the swell, smashing its nose and breaking off its tail. Passengers and crew scrambled out onto a wing and launched liferafts. In quick passes *Ponchartrain*'s gig and whaleboat scooped up passengers and flight crew and delivered them to the cutter, just minutes before the Clipper disappeared beneath the waves. *Ponchartrain*'s small boats continued to search the surface and recovered mailbags and a good deal of luggage.

A rescue that at one time would have looked impossible had gone off so smoothly as to appear almost routine. Yes, conditions had been nearly ideal, there had been time to plan and prepare, but more important, hard training had paid off. The cutters on the Ocean Stations were working out just fine.

Environmental Protection

Dealing with environmental disasters has come to be a major mission of the cutters. Protecting nature is a responsibility reaching all the way back to the Revenue Cutter Service. Indeed, it even preceded the conservation duties of the Bering Sea Patrol with its protection of Alaskan wildlife, and had its beginnings in enforcing laws against cutting oaks in the southeastern United States.

In 1822, Congress ordered the Service to put a stop to the cutting of live-oaks on government land in Florida. The highly esteemed wood—considered the best in the world for building ships—had to be protected from thieves who were devastating the forests. This duty required navigating narrow, winding, inland waterways, which was just what the first steam-powered cutters, contracted to be built in 1839, were meant to do.

The Service's conservation missions would continue to expand, and before World War I, *Thetis* would be instrumental in maintaining a bird sanctuary on Laysan, an island 700 miles from Hawaii, and other cutters would be protecting sponges and shrimp from being exploited to extinction in the Gulf of Mexico.

Still, no environmental challenge could match that posed by the astonishing growth, both in size and number, of sea-going tankers. These vessels, "essentially huge, powered oil cans," as historian Donald Canney describes them, are some of the largest man-made objects afloat. The environmental threats they present are as great as their massive size. Just how devastating a mishap with one of these giants could be was found out in 1967 when *Torrey Canyon* leaked thirty million gallons of oil into the English Channel. Henceforth Coast Guard cutters would have to be prepared to deal with pollution on a catastrophic scale.

Two laws, the Water Pollution Control Act and the Ports and Waterways Safety Act, meant the service would be the first line of defense in pollution enforcement on waterways and at sea. Then in 1973, the International Convention for the Prevention of Pollution from Ships brought something of a worldwide standard for environmental protection of the oceans—and gave the cutters yet another global role. From then on the causing of environmental damage on any ocean of the world became their business.

In 1989 the U.S. suffered its worst oil spill when the *Exxon Valdez* ran aground and dumped over ten million gallons of oil into Alaska's Prince William Sound. In a little more than half-an-hour the Coast Guard was on the way. The subsequent cleanup involved more than 450 vessels, among them four Coast Guard cutters and four of its buoy tenders. *Rush* provided air-traffic control for the hundreds of planes in the skies above the spill every day, and *Morganthau* assisted in the cleanup. Despite a valiant effort, however, 350 miles of coastline were covered in oil.

Beaches are washed clean of crude oil lost in the tanker Exxon Valdez *collision with a reef in Alaska. Volunteers work alongside Coast Guardsmen in this unwholesome task. (U.S. Coast Guard)*

Crewmembers and Potangeras Island (Ulithi Atoll, Carolines) natives working in concert rolling fuel drums ashore from CGC Kukui *anchored off the reef. Next they must lift and lug the 400-pound barrels across rugged terrain and sharp rocks bringing fuel oil to keep the important loran station on line. This stalwart vessel is little more than the literary "tramp steamer" in the Pacific bringing building materials and fuel for generators stocking loran stations scattered through Pacific islands. (U.S. Coast Guard)*

Inflating a helium balloon to raise the Voice of America *radio antenna aboard CGC* Courier. Courier *remained on station as a transmitting station for* Voice of America *in the eastern Mediterranean near the Greek island of Rhodes for twelve years during the 1950s and 1960s, remaining outside the United States longer than any other cutter ever. (Coast Guard Museum Northwest)*

Although the number of accidents involving oil-carrying barges and tankers seems to have decreased recently, they still average some 1,000 a year. While cleaning most of these spills involves little more than deployment of skimmers and containment booms, some are full-blown disasters. In 1976 an explosion aboard the tanker *Sansinen* threw the ship's deckhouse 750 feet in the air and damaged hundreds of ships in Los Angeles harbor. The cutter *Venturous* responded, helped put out the fire and contain the oil—a three-week job.

In the winter of that same year, *Bittersweet*, *Sherman*, *Spar*, and *Vigilant* fought gale-force winds and fierce seas to come to the rescue of *Argo Merchant*, a Liberian-registered tanker grounded and breaking up off Massachusetts. The forces of nature were too great, however, and the cutters were unable to save the tanker or keep it from spilling its cargo of over seven million gallons of oil.

To crews of the cutters, the huge tankers might well seem more like gigantic bombs than floating oil cans. In 1990, the Norwegian tanker *Mega Borg* exploded off the coast of Texas and was left drifting helpless and on fire. The spanking-new, 110-foot patrol boat *Cushing* quickly reached the burning tanker and was soon joined by representatives of a wide spectrum of active Coast Guard cutters: the grandfatherly, World-War-II era tender *Buttonwood*, the eighty-two-foot, thirty-year-old patrol boat *Point Spencer*, and two medium-endurance cutters, *Steadfast* and *Valiant*. Even with this formidable array of power it took a good week to put out the fire, and only about 10 percent of the nearly four million gallons of oil that spread across the water could be contained and recovered.

Mascots

Tom Beard

Somehow a mascot, particularly a dog, aboard ship raises the level of camaraderie and generally makes for a "happy ship." A dog gives and receives affection regardless of the eminence of human companions. The lowest seaman is regarded by a dog with the same esteem as might be given the highest ranking officer. However, actions by some seagoing dogs suggest this statement might not be totally true. From some anecdotes it appears dogs aboard ship tend to favor the enlisted crew and make difficulties for the officers. This is to the unifying delight of the enlisted, perhaps, and usually with favorable results in shipboard morale. The mascot becomes a binder for fellowship.

Sinbad, a real seadog, a mixed-breed whose life-story became a legend, served as an accepted member of the crew aboard the cutter Campbell for eleven years from 1938 through World War II. He had his own service record, uniform, decorations, and bunk. For most of a half-century this dog was the only Coast Guardsman (sic) to have a published biography, Sinbad of the Coast Guard, by George R. Foley.

Sailors could identify with Sinbad especially on liberty. He reportedly created international incidents ashore from Greenland to Casablanca. Sinbad never quite rated "gold hash marks" or "good conduct medals" of a "four-oh" sailor for his behavior exhibited in liberty ports. This happy mongrel was a popular visitor in bars everywhere. And like the sailors he companioned, he might be a bit raucous when ashore—likely with some encouragement—but at sea he was the honorable, dutiful seaman (or seadog). He went AWOL once. His punishment was restriction from liberty in any foreign ports thereafter. Following his captain's mast for this infraction, he reportedly had "hearty distrust" for any-one in the crew wearing gold. Following battle damage from a German submarine, all nonessential crew were

ordered from Campbell during its tow from harms way. Sinbad remained with the damage-control party patching the ship.

Sinbad returned from the sea after spending more time than most sailors, retiring to Barnegat Light Station, New Jersey. A favorite off-duty hangout became the front steps of a local tavern. His grave lies beneath the station's flagstaff. Even in passing, Sinbad never left the Coast Guard.

Skunk, like hundreds of seadogs before and after his time—while not receiving the international reputation of Sinbad—had a full Coast Guard career. This shabby-looking crossbreed pup began his service in World War II following his birth in Greenland. Skunk romped along with his sire attached to the Greenland Sled Patrol. Coast Guard Rear Admiral Edward H. "Iceberg" Smith established this unit in September 1941 using Danish and Eskimo crews. The patrol's discovery, soon thereafter, led to the capture of a Norwegian sealer used by the Germans setting up radio stations along Greenland's coast. Later, the frisky pup located and uncovered caches left by German troops as he scampered, unleashed, accompanying the patrol's sledges. By the spring of 1943 a grown-up Skunk became a regular member of the dog-pack patrolling eastern Greenland looking for intruders. The wire-hair terrier/wolfhound cross uncovered more buried German supplies eventually

Above: Coast Guardsmen are known to enjoy liberty in foreign ports, and, Sinbad was no different. He was beloved by his shipmates who believed that as long as the mascot was on board nothing bad would happen to the cutter. Who can say otherwise? After all, Sinbad's cutter *Campbell* was the first Coast Guard cutter to go up against a German submarine wolf pack in World War II, and *Campbell* came out top dog. (U.S. Coast Guard)

tracking to a Nazi patrol. Skunk's sire was killed by gunfire in the encounter.

As a result of this find, the Coast Guard cutter Northland *destroyed a German weather station and captured soldiers. Yet more than another year passed with Skunk still patrolling the bleak Greenland coast when in October 1944 he witnessed the cutter* Eastwind *destroy a German radio station. At the first opportunity he abandoned his duties and stowed away on the ship. Then after being at sea only two days, Skunk, stationing himself doggedly at the ship's bow, barked constantly, and would not be shushed. Further, he refused to be taken below. Eventually the human watches spotted what Skunk was already well aware of, a Nazi trawler. This vessel was quickly captured.*

Skunk formally enlisted in the Coast Guard when the ship reached Boston. He was, according to one report, "given his 'man' tag, 000-00, and rated as Sea Dog 1/c. During a party of good American dog food and bones, Skunk was toasted as 'watch dog, mascot, and real American citizen, who had distinguished himself during the early war.'"

Skunk exhibited similar reactions as Sinbad toward ships' officers. He would not approach anyone wearing khaki uniforms, according to one crewman's account, and was wary of civilians. Aboard ship in "heavy weather Skunk would relieve himself in officer country. He was an enlisted man's dog and never took to the brass."

One day after a long North Atlantic patrol as the ship pulled alongside the pier with many visitors waiting, Skunk leaped off to the dock "before the gangway was set," according to a witnessing ship's crewman, "and walked over and peed on a lady's leg." Shortly after, Skunk was sent to a lifeboat station for a shore-

Top: Sinbad, the celebrity mascot of the cutter *Campbell* before, during, and after World War II. This salty canine was the subject of numerous magazine and newspaper articles. Even a book was written about his life. (George Gray U.S. Coast Guard)

Center: Skunk, an unglamorous combination of a wire-hair terrier and wolfhound was born in Greenland, where the mascot assisted the Coast Guard in uncovering German supply caches during World War II. (U.S. Coast Guard)

Bottom: Skunk aided the Coast Guard capturing German troops on Greenland. One of the most unfettered dogs to adopt himself into the Coast Guard might be responsible for this capture. (U.S. Coast Guard)

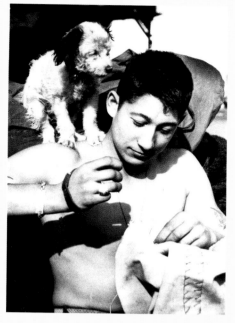

tour. However, "he just wasn't cut out for shore duty" and was back on the pier waiting for the ship when it arrived off the next patrol.

Skunk spent all his time on the bridge during emergency drills except the "Man overboard," his favorite. He was usually the first to leap into the small boat lowered from the ship to retrieve the practice dummy. That is, until later in his life, when he misjudged and missed the boat and ended in ice-filled waters—twice—making for realistic drills. Finally in 1951 this dog, then about a decade old with many years now at sea, was sent to Chatham Life Boat Station on Cape Cod for permanent shore duty. The station's security became his chosen task. Milk, bread, and paper deliveries were delayed and every person attempting to visit the station got his personal—intimidating—attention. He took his self-imposed responsibilities very seriously. Skunk, after only a month ashore, was assigned back to ships at sea.

These are but brief stories of two from thousands of dogs that contributed to the Coast Guard's success in accomplishing its tasks and bringing harmony to ships' and stations' crews.

More than mascots, dogs were trained for duty with the Coast Guard. During World War II, Coast Guard dogs were trained to find aircraft crash sites in mountains. They accompanied beach patrols. But mostly they were there for the moral support of human crews. Other animals were pets on board ship as well, even cats. Camouflage, a tiger cat, was on board a Coast-Guard-crewed LST in the World War II Bougainville landing. This cat's fascination was chasing tracer bullets fired from Japanese aircraft as they ricocheted across the deck. Kodiak, a friendly and frolicsome black bear, just walked aboard a Coast-Guard-crewed LST in Alaska,

where he made it his home. He was a favorite in the crew's quarters and, like some dogs, this bear shunned officers. Kodiak stayed aboard to engage in the Aleutian Islands invasion and later, Tarawa in the South Pacific.

Mascots can frequently still be found at Coast Guard units. Their contributions to good morale and leadership are unassailable—even to that occasional act of heroism—but the animals are best remembered for never-ending reminiscences of bigger than life accounts.

Top, left: Nosey, mascot of a World War II Coast-Guard-manned LST in the Pacific, brought the crew a good deal of happiness and laughter, providing welcome relief from the grim business of war and the bloody island-hopping assaults made by U.S. forces as they pushed toward Japan. (U.S. Coast Guard)

Above: Pete the Pooch, a mascot of a patrol boat that provided search and rescue during the Normandy invasion, was famous on the waterfront as an enthusiastic mooring-line handler. (U.S. Coast Guard)

Below: Aboard a World War II attack transport, T-Bone sits with Coast Guard Commander Jack Dempsey, former world heavyweight boxing champion, as the ship steams to Okinawa to support an amphibious invasion landing in April 1945. (U.S. Coast Guard)

Harbor Sentinel

Captain John Dwyer, USCGR

At eight o'clock in the evening, Lieutenant (jg) William Benn and Lieutenant (jg) Laila Grassley prepared to board their second foreign freighter of the day in Tacoma, Washington. They were leading a team of Coast Guard petty officers to check out the ship, its crew, and its cargo for potential security threats. The gangway had come down moments before, and Benn and Grassley had met the ship on its arrival before any of the crew disembarked, or the cargo off-loading began, or anyone else came aboard. The boarding team's home office had known about this ship coming in for over ninety-six hours, and had reviewed its history, cargo, and crew list for potential security concerns. When the vessel's history search revealed this was its first-ever port call in the United States, Benn and Grassley and their team were dispatched to check it out.

Tracked by the radars of the United States and Canadian Coast Guard Vessel Traffic System since it was over forty miles off the coast, the ship had behaved normally, and there was nothing to indicate there would be a problem. As the boarding proceeded it became apparent there was no security threat, so Benn and Grassley turned their attention to focusing on safety and pollution prevention issues instead. It took them about two hours to finish the boarding, then they faced an evening drive back to Seattle, where they still had to enter the data results of their boarding into the Coast Guard's computer system. Another long day, but since 11 September 2001, such days were nothing new for these two young officers.

Benn and Grassley previously headed up Coast Guard Reserve week-end foreign vessel boarding teams of three to four Reserve petty officers checking foreign vessels for safety and pollution problems. On 11 September 2001, their mission and their lives changed. Benn, a management trainee

Opposite, top: *Hull integrity is a crucial concern in vessel safety. Hull exteriors beneath the waterline normally can only be thoroughly examined by Coast Guard marine inspectors during ships' infrequent dry dockings. (U.S. Coast Guard)*

Above: *Coast Guard marine inspectors check a ship's hold. Renewal of American registered ships' licenses is based on passing critical Coast Guard examinations. (Tom Gillespie)*

Bottom, left: *A repair weld on the underside of a double-bottom tank barge is checked by Lieutenant (jg) Eric Allen. Coast Guard marine inspection officers conduct periodic ship inspections including such critical items as welded joints. For this they must crawl in spaces seldom or never intended to be occupied by people after the ship is built. (Mike Hvozda, U.S. Coast Guard)*

Bottom, right: *A football-size patch is welded to a small hole in the hull of the 950-foot-long tanker* Long Beach, *sister ship to the former* Exxon Valdez. *Coast Guard marine inspection teams inspect the ship's repairs to assure seaworthiness and especially its critical need to contain the oil cargo. The welder can be seen standing at the bow of the commercial 60-foot utility boat dwarfed beneath the hovering hulk. The arc from the welding glows just above his head. All the ship's oil cargo was removed and ballast transferred aft to raise the bow from the water in this highly unusual pose for a behemoth. (Tom Thompson,* Peninsula Daily News, *Port Angeles, WA)*

with Alaska Airlines, and Grassley, a financial analyst in Seattle, were mobilized to active duty to conduct port security inspections of foreign and U.S. vessels. Putting their civilian careers and lives on an indefinite hold, and both still fairly new to the Coast Guard, each with less than five years experience overall and none previously in port security, they were now on the front line in the nation's sudden transition to detecting terrorist security threats and defending itself against terrorist attacks.

Mission

While new to Benn and Grassley, as the Coast Guard's name obviously implies, protection of the coasts of the United States during times of war or from hostile or terrorist threats is a primary mission of the service. Providing that protection has long been a Coast Guard duty—not just along the coasts at sea, but within the ports and harbors and rivers of the United States as well. This protection of internal and coastal waters is known as Port Security.

The challenges of a rapidly growing mission and too few resources required the Coast Guardsmen's trademark ingenuity and perseverance to accomplish a daunting job. The nature of ensuring the security of ports and inland waterways makes it a typical Coast Guard mission, but one that has varied greatly in its scope and impact over the years. In peacetime, port security is a minor player in the array of missions given the Coast Guard, while in wartime or in the midst of a high terrorist threat it assumes a virtual preeminent importance. Called formally the Port Safety and Security, PSS, program, it provides for the protection of ports, harbors, vessels, and waterfront facilities from sabotage, terrorism, accidents, and negligence. In times of peace the latter elements take precedence, with Coast Guard officers like Benn and Grassley conducting safety inspections of vessels and facilities, monitoring petroleum, chemical and hazardous materials shipments, movements and storage, and ensuring the safe operation of vessels on the waterways of the United States. Coast Guard Marine Safety Offices, operating under the cognizance of their dual-hatted role as Captains of the Port and Officers in Charge, Marine Inspection, are the primary agents for performing these activities.

234

But in times of war, or when terrorist activity is likely, such as the current "post 9/11" era, the security aspects of the PSS program become a prime focus of the Coast Guard. The program expands from its peacetime somnolence to fully demonstrate the extensive authority of the Captains of the Port and their ability to control the activities of a port. When faced with implementing a full port security program, the Captain of the Port can pick from a wide array of options, including conducting vessel, vehicle, and aerial patrols of the waterfront and waterways, setting safety

Below: *The port of Houston, Texas, is one of many large water-land cargo transfer junctures where the Coast Guard oversees security and safety. Close scrutiny by Coast Guard units is maintained here due to the large number of petrochemical plants located along the confined waterway. (Robert D. Wyman, U.S. Coast Guard)*

or security zones to restrict traffic near sensitive vessels or facilities, inspecting facilities for security measures such as fences, lighting, and access control, and inspecting vessels and facilities for terrorist or sabotage activities. Most significantly, the Captain of the Port can fully control the movements of any non-military vessel in the port, whether withholding clearance to enter or depart U.S. waters or to control the vessel's movements anywhere within those waters. The Captain of the Port can do almost the same with any waterfront facility, even using a Captain of the Port order to suspend the facility's operations unless it complies with the Captain of the Port security requirements. Such authority is not taken lightly. Finally, the Coast Guard will often serve as the first responder to a report of a hostile threat or act of terrorism, coordinating with national defense or civil law enforcement agencies to "mitigate the threat."

History

The array of port security programs currently administered by the Coast Guard evolved, like the Coast Guard itself, from humble beginnings. Few of the challenges and complexities present in the highly evolved ports of the twenty-first century were present when Alexander Hamilton was thinking of creating the Coast Guard's forebears, nor were the threats to the United States as intricate as those posed by today's terrorist organizations. Yet, though limited in its early application, the need for port security was no less important, especially to the youthful United States.

Even before the Coast Guard was known as such, its antecedent United States Revenue Cutter Service was guarding the coasts and performing port security missions. Indeed, from 1790 until the Navy's reauthorization in 1794, the Revenue Cutter Service was the young nation's only maritime service. Revenue cutters continued to protect the ports and waterways of a growing America. They battled British ships along the East Coast during the War of 1812, pirates in the Gulf of Mexico and gulf coast, and coastal Indian tribes like the Seminoles in Florida. Cutters provided an American presence during border disputes with the British in Canada, the United States of Texas, and enforced payment of customs duties in South Carolina.

Civil War

In the Civil War, port security duties for the Revenue Cutter Service were common. Fifteen cutters were assigned to protect major East Coast ports, such as the cutter *Andrew Jackson* patrolling the port of Baltimore. These patrols were needed to protect the major ports as Confederate ships harassed northern shipping and ports as far north as Long Island and Maine. The Revenue Cutter Service's first ironclad, the USRC *E. A. Stevens*, patrolled the Verrazano Narrows in New York Harbor, and took part in an unsuccessful raid up the James River on Richmond. *Harriet Lane*, the cutter famous for its blockade of Charleston and firing the first naval vessel shots of the war, was defending the newly captured port of Galveston in 1863 when it was captured during a Confederate counter-attack, with its executive officer dying in the arms of his father, a major leading the Confederate forces.

Spanish-American War

The overall role of port security remained a Navy responsibility until World War II. Yet, foreshadowing World War II practice, in 1898 the Navy assigned coast watching duties to the U.S. Lifesaving Service. Fully two-thirds of the Navy's coastal observation stations were Lifesaving Stations. In a mission that would be repeated in the Maritime Defense Zone concept of the twentieth century, eleven cutters, under the Army's tactical control, patrolled U.S. west and east coast ports against possible attacks by the Spanish fleet.

Opposite, top: The Coast Guard operates vessel traffic services in major ports throughout the country patterned after aircraft control centers. Controllers, such as petty officer Travis Costigan seen here, through the combined use of cameras, radar, and radio communications, maintain watch on all vessel movements within port areas assuring safe separation. The VTS centers are a significant aid in preventing collisions and groundings. (Tom Beard)

Opposite, center: Vessel Traffic Service radar image showing the coverage area around San Francisco Bay. While dots show all minor vessels, ships under the controllers' watchful eyes are noted with data such as course and speed. (U.S. Coast Guard)

Opposite, bottom: A Coast Guard boarding team, the first to board a ship on entry into United States, scales the gangway of a container ship just arrived in New York Harbor. The inspection team examines ship's papers, crew, and cargo manifest and checks the ship's general condition determining—even if it is a foreign registered vessel—that it will meet certain American-imposed safety standards during its stay in U.S. waters. (Mike Hvozda, U.S. Coast Guard)

Below, left: The cutter Winona *defended the entrance to Mobile Bay During the Spanish-American War against potential intrusions by Spanish warships.* Winona *was used prior to the entrance of the United States into World War I for inspecting foreign vessels suspected of shipping illegal armaments. (U.S. Coast Guard)*

Below: The cutter McCulloch *is shown with its former barkentine-rig, later cut down leaving only two masts for minimal sail-carrying power, suggesting more reliance on steam power or the possibility of more coaling stations as the twentieth century began.* McCulloch, *outfitted with a bow torpedo tube and four 3-inch guns, served with Commodore Dewey's squadron in the Spanish-American war. The cutter helped blockade Manila Bay in warning off the German warship* Cormoran *with a shot across the bow. With the United States' entry into World War I,* McCulloch *transferred to the Navy and was lost in June 1917 when it collided with the Pacific Steamship Company's SS* Governor. *All on board were rescued. (U.S. Coast Guard Academy Art Collection)*

Scenes of devastation suffered in the port of Halifax, Nova Scotia, Canada, by the explosion of the French freighter Mont Blanc *in the collision with* Imo. *Nearly 2,000 people were killed and almost 10,000 injured. Because explosives were loaded aboard* Mont Blanc *in New York City, the United States increased its emphasis on port security and safety requirements, including creating a position of the Coast Guard Caption of the Port. (W.G. MacLaughlan, National Archives of Canada)*

In addition to critical areas like fuel handling docks, anchorages, and piers, Coast Guard patrol boats maintain security of popular tourist sites that might be targets for terrorist activities. (Mike Hvozda, U.S. Coast Guard)

Captain Godfrey L. Carden, the Coast Guard's first Captain of the Port. His office was created in World War I for the Port of New York. (U.S. Coast Guard)

238

World War I

With the entry of the United States into World War I, the Coast Guard was assigned to the Navy in 1917. Unlike previous wars where the Revenue cutters were under Navy direction but the Revenue-Cutter Service itself remained under Department of Treasury control, in World War I the entire Coast Guard was transferred to the Navy. As occurred in the Spanish-American War, lifesaving stations performed as coast watchers, with the added improvement that many of the stations were connected into the Navy's communication system to enable faster reporting of suspicious activities. Though not yet part of the Coast Guard, Lighthouse Service buoy tenders were assigned to the Navy, conducting patrols, tending anti-submarine nets, and even laying mines.

Most significant for the Coast Guard's future in port security, however, was the establishment of the Coast Guard Captain of the Port. Yet much of the drive to improve safety on the waterfront came from a disaster not in the United States but in Canada. In December 1917, the French freighter *Mont Blanc*, outbound from New York City, arrived in Halifax, Nova Scotia, with 2,300 tons of picric acid and 200 tons of TNT. While entering the port, *Mont Blanc* collided with the freighter *Imo*, starting a fire that ultimately ignited the TNT, causing an explosion that obliterated *Mont Blanc*, tossed *Imo* ashore, and sent *Mont Blanc*'s anchor shank, weighing over half a ton, almost two miles from the site—damage later judged equal to that of a small nuclear explosion. The blast killed almost 2,000 people, and the United States became alarmed over the potential danger of such a disaster occurring at home, especially since *Mont Blanc* had just left New York.

As a result of the *Mont Blanc* explosion, and in concert with the strong concern over the potential for sabotage—a munitions plant in Black Tom, New Jersey, had exploded the year before, with sabotage suspected—the Treasury Department and the Navy collaborated in establishing senior Coast Guard officers as Captains of the Port, setting up offices in New York, Norfolk, Philadelphia, and Sault St. Marie on the

CAPTAIN OF THE PORT — CAPTAIN JOHN DWYER, USCGR

Captain Jane Hartley is the Coast Guard's first woman to serve as Captain of the Port. She began her career in the Coast Guard in 1980 working as a Reserve program administrator. Thereafter, she alternated tours between Reserve administration and marine safety, finding a natural blend with the marine safety program's heavy reliance on Reservists before finally assuming the command of Marine Safety Office, Wilmington, North Carolina.

The port of Wilmington has a blend of maritime activities, with international vessel traffic, coastal barge operations, river passenger vessels, and a military out-load facility. United States military supplies are loaded here for shipment overseas. This last role proved particularly significant for Hartley, as Wilmington became a primary port for loading military supplies for the 2003 Iraq War. Twenty-nine ships were loaded in ten weeks. This activity caused the Marine Safety Office to grow from a staff of forty-three to almost 500 personnel in Hartley's command, adding more Regular Coast Guard active duty, Reserves, and Auxiliary members. Hartley coordinated a robust training program for arriving Reservists ensuring, among other tasks, fully qualified small-boat crews to provide security patrols for the port. Hartley also pioneered the use of the Incident Command System, for a military loadout operation, to coordinate multiple agencies' operations.

Hartley's tour was not just marked by accelerated wartime activities. Hurricane Isabel struck the North Carolina coast head-on, creating almost 1.7 billion dollars in damage along with damage to the coastal-transportation infrastructure. As a result, the COTP added an additional incident-command system for storm recovery. This command directed environmental response units to handle the numerous oil and hazardous material spills caused by the storm. Furthermore, in the tradition of Coast Guardsmen serving humanitarian needs, its members helped deliver medical supplies, food, and water to numerous communities on the Outer Banks.

While Hartley's tour at Wilmington was eventful, like other Captains of the Port, her previous tours around the nation prepared her well. From responding to ice-jammed rivers as the Marine Safety Office Executive Officer in Duluth to running Reserve officer personnel management in Coast Guard Headquarters, Hartley's career path demonstrated clearly the breadth of experience provided to the Coast Guard's "COTPs." This experience is central to the Captain of the Port's success; they truly embody the can-do spirit of **Semper Paratus.**

Captain Jane Hartley, the first woman to serve as Coast Guard Captain of the Port. (Courtesy, Jane Hartley)

Great Lakes. These Captains of the Port were responsible for many of the duties now associated with port security.

Most of their authority came from the Espionage Act, passed in June of 1917, six months prior to *Mont Blanc*'s explosion. In fact, the Coast Guard already had the authority to set anchorages, provided by the River and Harbor Act in 1915. However the *Mont Blanc* disaster demonstrated the critical importance of ensuring that the explosives were properly loaded and safeguarded. This job was given to the newly established Captains of the Port, or COTP.

The largest COTP in the Coast Guard in World War I was at the port of New York City, where Captain Godfrey L. Carden, commander of the Coast Guard's New York Division, was the first given the title of Captain of the Port. Carden's staff quickly grew to where his command became the largest in the Coast Guard, with over 1,400 personnel, and a fleet of nine Coast Guard and Army Corps of Engineer vessels under his control. Over 345 million tons of explosives sailed out of New York on over 1,600 ships during his eighteen-month tenure in World War I without serious mishap.

Coast Guardsmen Justin Likens and William Groosman monitor New York City Fire Department operations in the aftermath of a barge explosion at an oil facility. A large piece of the destroyed barge was hurled into the facility. Port security and safety under the office of the Coast Guard Captain of the Port have made harbor disasters an infrequent occurrence since the position was created in 1917 following a ship collision, fire, and explosion in Halifax, Nova Scotia, that killed nearly 2,000 people. (Mike Hvozda, U.S. Coast Guard)

A current variation on this World War II scene, where railroad boxcars are inspected, today is the opening and inspection of shipping containers arriving in ports around the country. (U.S. Coast Guard)

Ammunition for the Korean War was not only transported by ships. From the Umatilla Ordnance Depot in eastern Oregon, ammunition was moved by railcar to the Columbia River where it was loaded in barges and taken 200 miles downriver to transfer to ships for the ocean crossing to Korea. Coast Guardsmen supervised the loading and unloading of the dangerous cargo at each step. They were also the security guards. This is why Coast Guardsmen might be found in the desert of eastern Oregon or other ammunition-loading facilities far from the sea. (U.S. Coast Guard)

Years Between Wars

The importance of the Port Security program continued in the years between the two World Wars. The U.S. Lighthouse Service was amalgamated into the Coast Guard in 1939, adding a large component to the organization that would later aid port security efforts. In 1939, as the threat of war increased, the Coast Guard was charged with helping enforce America's neutrality. One task involved sealing radios of foreign vessels while in U.S. ports to ensure they did not broadcast intelligence information or the locations and sailing times of vessels. This proved a demanding mission: one eight-man detail in Philadelphia sealed over 10,000 radios in three years.

Another mission required the Coast Guard to inspect vessels' armaments, to determine if they were loaded with offensive or defensive weapons, and were thus either warships or merchantmen—much like checking for the construction of privateers in the Quasi-War with France over 100 years earlier.

In June of 1940 President Roosevelt reinvoked the Espionage Act of 1917, giving the Coast Guard full authority to protect harbors and coastal and inland waterways, and renewed authority to direct the movement and control of vessels; at this time the Coast Guard's port security forces were put in a wartime status.

The authority of the Captain of the Port continued to grow. In October 1940 the Dangerous Cargo Act was passed, addressing the safety component of port security, vesting in the COTP the authority to oversee the safe loading of explosives and hazardous materials aboard ship. By November of 1940 the number of COTP offices had grown to twenty-nine; by war's end there would be nearly 200 COTP and assistant COTP offices.

Despite the growth in both COTP offices and responsibilities, there were still gaps in authority. The Coast Guard had the authority to protect waterways, but not waterfront facilities; that power would not come until 1942. Fire prevention, facility security, and explosive loading at docks were serious port security program gaps that were not fully addressed until during the war itself. Yet the pace of additional duties continued to rise. Coast Guard coastal security patrols also increased. For example in Alaska, cutters stopped and checked Japanese fishing boats for spying and other threatening activities. In November 1941 the Coast Guard was transferred to the Navy and the formal transfer of the port security program—presaged by many of the authorities already given to the Coast Guard—followed in June of 1942.

World War II

Once the U.S. entered the war, changes in the authority and responsibilities of the Coast Guard's port security program accelerated. Four days after Pearl Harbor, the Coast Guard was given the authority to guard national defense waterfront facilities. The lack of sufficient personnel, however, meant that only the most vulnerable and critical facilities could be protected. The full authority to mandate the security of commercial or port waterfront facilities was not to come until 1944.

While the authority for dockside security was limited in some ways for much of the war, in other areas the Coast Guard was able to wield

tighter control. The Coast Guard declared certain sensitive areas of the waterfront to be within "Security Zones," cordoning them off and patrolling them with armed Coast Guardsmen. The Coast Guard issued ID cards to dockworkers and others needing access to these areas of the waterfront.

February 1942 saw the Coast Guard grow further, with the Bureau of Marine Inspection and Navigation, BMIN, added. This placed the civilian ship inspectors and merchant personnel licensing officers within the

A Coast Guard officer in World War II passes out orders to port-security jeep patrols. These patrols were made up largely of volunteers, most of whom had full-time civilians jobs but spent their free time guarding harbors and ports for the Coast Guard. Many, at the beginning of the war, even provided their own uniforms. (U.S. Coast Guard)

Coast Guardsmen conducted full-time port security patrols at all the nation's wartime harbors where ships were loaded with munitions and supplies for the Allied efforts. In addition to harbor boat and dockside jeep patrols, a Coast Guardsman guarded each ship's gangway in this World War II effort at homeland security. (U.S. Coast Guard)

A Coast Guard helicopter hovers over a gasoline barge shortly after it explodes at a petroleum storage site in New York City. While city firefighters battle the fire, Coast Guard crews in the helicopter assess the potential for contamination to adjacent waterways and determine the need for additional fire-fighting and pollution control resources. (Mike Hvozda, U.S. Coast Guard)

A common wartime harbor craft in World War II was the thirty-foot Hanley fireboat with its four 500-gallon-a-minute fire pumps. This boat was used for security patrols and firefighting. This specialty craft arrived as a welcome asset as port authorities typically had few maritime fire-fighting resources early in World War II. (U.S. Coast Guard)

Coast Guard, giving it central authority over the waterfront. The civilian BMIN members were mostly ex-mariners. The Coast Guard offered them, and almost all accepted, military officer commissions in the Coast Guard to bolster their authority on the waterfront. These officers now enhanced the safety aspects of the port security program, ensuring that the ships themselves were safe to load the wartime cargoes.

Of all the safety programs inherent in port security, fire prevention and response was one of the most critical, both for the harbor facilities and the vessels that used them. But the program did not achieve significant results before the loss in January 1942, in New York City, of *Normandie*, a French passenger liner being converted to a troop ship. The loss of *Normandie* had a positive result, however, as President Roosevelt in February issued an executive order requiring the Coast Guard, through the Navy, to assume the role of safeguarding the American waterfront from such disasters.

The Coast Guard responded by beginning construction or conversion of hundreds of vessels into fire boats. On the West Coast, Coast Guard fire boat barges were stationed at the most hazardous port locations, and on both coasts, picket and patrol boats were outfitted with fire-fighting pumps. By war's end the Coast Guard had detected over 25 percent of all fires that occurred on ships or waterfront facilities and had responded to over 90 percent of them.

While the efforts to improve fire prevention were underway, equal attention was focused on the loading of explosives. Designated "explosive anchorages" for loaded munitions-ships were established. Coast Guard personnel trained in explosives-handling techniques to reduce accidental

explosions. The incorporation of the Bureau of Marine Inspection and Navigation personnel improved the Coast Guard's position of authority, as the BMIN had responsibility for the overall safe loading of ships. Gaps in responsibility on waterfront facilities for explosives shipments to the vessels were addressed in meetings with the Army and Navy. While the Coast Guard held sway on commercial facilities, at Army and Navy facilities where munitions or military vessels were loaded, the Coast Guard could not stop dangerous practices if these were performed wholly under Army or Navy authority.

The Coast Guard's port security efforts were equally active on the water. Buoy tenders set anti-submarine nets and lightships guarded harbor entrances. For example, *Nantucket Shoals* became the examination vessel for Portland, Maine, checking all vessel traffic. Hundreds of civilian yachts, fishing boats, and other craft were conscripted into the Coast Guard—with owners signed on as crew—to patrol waterways for enemy submarines and saboteurs. In Florida alone, by June 1943, 276 vessels thirty to 100 feet in length patrolled the state's coastline. Called the "Hooligan Navy" or the Corsair Fleet—with a Walt Disney logo—due to their unusual and diverse crews, these vessels served officially as the coastal picket patrol, and provided valuable support for port security during the early years of the war.

The Coast Guard lived its name on foot, too. Setting up beach patrols in concert with the lifesaving stations and the lighthouses, the Coast Guard patrolled beaches and docks with armed Coast Guardsmen, using

Above: *Being a farrier is a strange task for a twentieth-century seaman and is an indication that unusual tasks challenge Coast Guardsmen even into the present century. Coast Guardsman Joe Opalka is a blacksmith shoeing horses at a World War II beach patrol station. An ever-present duty-canine assists. (U.S. Coast Guard)*

Right: *A mounted beach-patrol returns at dawn from a night's tour of duty sweeping long expanses of deserted sandy stretches, beaches susceptible to enemy landings or the graveyards for seaman cast ashore from torpedoed ships. (U.S. Coast Guard)*

Right: *Coast Guardsman John Cullen discovered Nazi saboteurs on New York's Long Island shore shortly after they landed from a German submarine. The four intruders first threatened Cullen and when this failed, attempted to bribe him. Cullen, armed only with a flare gun, pretended to agree to the bribe and went for help. Cullen returned with an armed squad and found the saboteurs gone, but the patrol uncovered a cache of explosives. The saboteurs were captured soon after by FBI agents before they could carry out their mission. (U.S. Coast Guard)*

Far right: *Beach patrols might arrive at the scene by boat as men and dogs leap ashore in a World War II exercise on a South Carolina beach. (U.S. Coast Guard)*

dogs and even riding horseback in some areas. Over 24,000 personnel covered some 50,000 miles of coastline using over 2,000 dogs and more than 3,000 horses—an unusual sight for a maritime service! The beach patrol was coordinated with Army shore defenses at coastal forts, and Navy offshore patrols.

Although phased out as the war moved away from America's shores and men were needed increasingly overseas, the beach patrols did figure in anti-saboteur incidents; most notably, the discovery of Nazi saboteurs on New York's Long Island by Coast Guardsman John Cullen. The patrols' usefulness continued in unexpected ways even as their forces dwindled, reporting downed airplanes, assisting boats in distress, reporting forest fires, and aiding in local disasters.

In action predating similar circumstances in the Gulf War almost fifty years later, a Coast Guard commander was put in charge of securing the port of Cherbourg, France, shortly after D-Day in 1944. Commander Quentin R. Walsh was awarded the Navy Cross for his leadership of a Navy reconnaissance party that took over the port from the remnants of the German occupation force and then set about clearing the port to receive critical war supplies.

World War II would see the largest number of Coast Guard personnel dedicated to port security to date. The demand for people to execute this program was enormous. By one count, New York Harbor alone needed

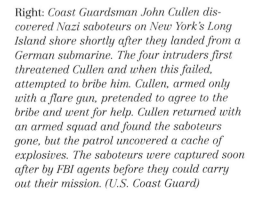

244

Left: *The Russian freighter* Lamut, *wrecked in a storm off the Washington coast, was discovered by a Coast Guardsman during his beach patrol in March 1943. Coast Guardsmen gathered on the cliff above and toss a line to the ship. This line, too short to reach, was reportedly extended to span the distance with bandage rolls and shoestrings. With this improvised line they were able to retrieve lines from the ship and pull the surviving fifty-four crewmembers to safety. (U.S. Coast Guard)*

Above: *Close security was maintained in all harbors during World War II as a ship's crewman is checked for identification by a Coast Guardsman. A role in homeland security is not a recent effort by the Coast Guard, but a revitalized practice dating back over 200 years. (U.S. Coast Guard)*

almost 17,000 to provide full port security—a number, however, never reached. Recruiting efforts were bringing in thousands of new recruits. However, the numbers needed mandated new sources for workers.

The Coast Guard formed the full-time Women's Reserve, known as the SPARs. Over 10,000 women served, many in port security-related duties. The demand for port security personnel still exceeded the supply, so the Coast Guard created a Temporary Reserve, with over 20,000 part-time members dedicated to Volunteer Port Security Forces at twenty-two major ports. Over 172,000 served in the Coast Guard port security program at the height of World War II.

Korean War

In Korea it was a different enemy, but for the Coast Guard, many of the same responsibilities. The Coast Guard had shrunk to 23,000 members by 1950, with almost no Coast Guard Reserve. Yet, many of the same wartime duties returned. As was done in World War I and World War II, the Coast Guard's port security authority had to be reinstated; this time it was done in 1950 with the signing of the Magnuson Act. This act amended the Espionage Act and created the Title 33, Code of Federal Regulations "Super Six" powers, that gave Captains of the Port the authority to ensure "adequate security" of vessels and waterfront facilities, and to have full control of the movement of vessels. Unlike in previous wars this authority was never relinquished. It still exists today as an essential tool of the Captain of the Port.

Members of a well-practiced Coast Guard beach-patrol unit journeyed to China in 1944 to train members in the Nationalist Chinese Army in the use of dogs and horses for patrol and counterinsurgency duty. (U.S. Coast Guard)

One of the more controversial authorities extended under the Magnuson Act was to give the Coast Guard the responsibility to issue Port Security Cards to sailors, ship pilots, dockworkers, and other waterfront personnel, based on background checks conducted by the FBI. Although similar to what the Coast Guard did in World War II, the intensity of concern over the Communist menace added much controversy to this program. By 1952 the Coast Guard had screened about 500,000 applicants for the Port Security Cards; only 2,000 were denied clearance.

The port security program was faced with a new concern not seen in World War II: the potential smuggling of an atomic bomb into the United

A lonely Coast Guardsman armed with a bayoneted rifle guards a loaded ship awaiting a convoy to Europe. The ship has a deck load seen here of a P-38 fighter and fuel bowser for the U.S. Army Air Forces. (U.S. Coast Guard)

The cutter Tahoma *was on guard in its homeland security role stationed at the entrance to Chesapeake Bay in 1952. With its hull painted bright yellow and further identified with the word "Guard" painted in black letters, the cutter identified and cleared all incoming vessels. Coast Guard cutters patrolled harbor entrances to all major ports during some of the intense years of the Cold War following World War II. Crews armed with Geiger counters searched for smuggled atomic weapons and checked inbound ships for general explosives and bacteriological weapons. (U.S. Coast Guard)*

Above: *Coast Guard Explosives Loading Detachments were in Vietnam at the Army's request to supervise the safe unloading of ammunitions ships. Ninety-eight percent of all supplies for the Vietnam War arrived by ship. (U.S. Coast Guard)*

Coast Guardsmen inspect a waterfront explosives warehouse in 1959. The close proximity of these explosives-filled storage buildings to military cargo ships was a constant concern. The Coast Guard checked that the shells and bombs are properly stowed to prevent accidental detonations. (U.S. Coast Guard)

Right: *Shipboard cargo-lifting equipment is checked for wear by Coast Guardsmen as a part of their task of supervising the handling and moving of dangerous cargo from ships in Vietnam. (U.S. Coast Guard)*

States via ship. Noted by Senator Magnuson when he introduced his legislation to amend the Espionage Act, the threat of a nuclear incident became a prime concern of the Coast Guard. Vessels were required to give advance notice of their arrival, and suspicious vessels and their cargo were checked by Coast Guardsmen using radioactivity detectors. "Guard" boats were stationed at all the entrances to major ports; at New York two cutters were used, each checking over forty vessels per month.

The years of the Korean War also saw the introduction of the helicopter by the other military services. As the same time, the Coast Guard set up its first helicopter detachment in New York City, using three aircraft to do aerial port security surveillance.

Vietnam

Unlike in the Korean War, the Coast Guard saw significant coastal and riverine operations in the war in South Vietnam. The area's many small vessels and diverse coastline made it a prime target for the smuggling of weapons by sea from North Vietnam. Coastal patrol craft were needed to provide security, and in 1965 the Coast Guard sent eighty-two-foot patrol boats to Vietnam to form Coast Guard Squadron One as part of operation *Market Time*. In just the first year of operation alone the cutters boarded over 35,000 Vietnamese junks and seized over 100 tons of enemy military material.

While naval engagements with the enemy were infrequent, other operations such as support of various land missions, search-and-rescue missions, and good-will efforts with local villages filled the gaps. The force grew to twenty-six patrol boats, establishing a record of effective operations. Ultimately, after training by their Coast Guard personnel, the Coast Guard patrol boats were taken over by the South Vietnamese.

Also unlike in the Korean War, the need for port security overseas was made a Coast Guard mission. From 1965 to 1973 the Coast Guard

provided port security and explosives loading detachment personnel in Vietnam. The staff started—and stayed—small, with only a four-person office—the Port Security and Waterways Detail. In addition to the Port Security Detachment, four full-time and one part-time Explosive Loading Detachments were ultimately assigned. The detachments found problems with safety rampant, with people smoking a continual occurrence aboard explosive-laden vessels and barges.

Attacks on these vessels by the Viet Cong were common, and fighting fires, caused by the attacks, often involved detachment members. In one occurrence in 1968, after a Viet Cong attack on an ammunition barge, a lone Coast Guard engineman put the fire out by himself using buckets of water and his bare hands, even while six pallets of mortar shells burned during his efforts.

One other Coast Guard element that contributed to port security in Vietnam was the merchant marine inspection detail. With much authority to detain vessels due to unsafe conditions or operation, the marine inspectors provided a key link to the overall safe and secure operation of merchant vessels there. They served as a primary Coast Guard authority on the many merchant vessels carrying war supplies, acting and ruling on everything from sabotage to drug use to equipment problems.

Gunner's Mate First Class Joseph R. Glenn, USCG, receives the Bronze Star Medal for single-handedly capturing five Viet Cong attempting to sabotage an ammunition ship at anchor in Da Nang harbor. Glenn was armed only with a .45 caliber pistol. (Captain David L. Powell, USCGR (Ret.))

Operation Market Time *was the name given to the mission of denying combatants and supplies from reaching South Vietnam by sea. A large amount of patrol time with the twenty-six Coast Guard 82-footers involved inspecting the thousands of fishing junks along South Vietnam's shoreline and rivers. (U.S. Coast Guard)*

Port Dangers

Paul C. Scotti (*Condensed by author from* COAST GUARD ACTION IN VIETNAM)

The U.S. Army in Vietnam had the vital chore of moving war supplies off the daily conveyor belt of merchant ships arriving into ports and into temporary storage until needed for the troops in the field. Recognizing that it knew little about protecting waterfront complexes, it sent a message to the Joint Chiefs of Staff that "an urgent requirement exists for Coast Guard personnel trained in port security." This call brought Coast Guard explosive loading detachments, ELD, to oversee the safe unloading of ammunition ships and a port security and waterways detail, PSWD, to advise the Army on port protection.

On 15 October 1966, the first PSWD arrived in Saigon. Captain Robert J. Loforte, commander, Coast Guard Activities, Vietnam, met the detail and afterward wrote in the unit diary, "after they had their first look at the port they were ready to ship out—not over. Well, as I told them, there's no other way to go but up on that job."

Three savvy Coast Guard veterans composed the first PSWD, headed up by Commander Raymond C. Hertica, fourty-four, who survived the World War II torpedo sinking of his cutter by a German submarine. His thorough port security knowledge, backstopped with a sturdy build and a hardset countenance, conveyed the impression that if his advice was heeded calamity could be averted.

His assistant, brawny Lieutenant Donald G. Kneip, thirty-seven, whose promotion to lieutenant commander came through a month later, like Hertica, treated port security as earnest business. Chief Boatswain's Mate Charles D. Wise rounded out the team. His main job was ensuring that cargo was properly stored.

At their initial meeting with Major General Charles W. Eifler, commander, 1st Logistical Command, the general told them that they were to improve security at all coastal and river ports, barge sites, and anyplace else where munitions were put ashore in the command's jurisdiction. They were amazed at the general's confidence in them, because that meant they had responsibility for 70 percent of South Vietnam.

In reality, it became the entire country when the Navy, in I Corps, learned of their effectiveness. To begin, however, their first priority was the port of Saigon, which at the time inhaled most of the cargo coming into the country. They were given open-ended travel orders and status as direct representatives of the general. If local port commanders, or others, tended to shrug them off because they were not U.S. Army, they carried a personal letter from Eifler that left no doubt that any suggestions offered by these Coast Guardsmen were to be accepted as coming from him.

To better understand how to secure Saigon Port they commenced a rigorous scrutiny by foot, jeep, and helicopter. The chaos dismayed them. Clusters of junks and sampans hugged docked ships. Storage facilities were dilapidated and wharves rundown, while mixed cargos made little mountains along the waterfront without regard for their harmony.

The 1st Logistical Command, having the unfamiliar port security job only four months, instituted roving patrols ashore and afloat, but from the Coast Guardsmen's perspective they were not preventing anything. Furthermore, no fencing existed between the port and the city, allowing anyone to meander about unchallenged.

Studying the layout as if they were saboteurs, the Coast Guardsmen unanimously agreed that simply starting a fire in the dry season could destroy the entire installation. Moreover, rather than the enemy causing a conflagration, they feared that with so much disregard of safety measures, the odds were greater that fire would start accidentally. Without pause, flames would consume the haphazard array of combustibles because of a feeble fire-fighting defense.

Docks lacked handy fire-fighting equipment and the port had one fire truck, a pumper with a 400-gallon water supply crewed by Vietnamese and an American advisor. The few tugs available for fighting a fire had only single monitors of limited use. As a consequence, Hertica passed the word to all ship captains to have their vessel's fire-fighting equipment in a "go" state, as they will get little, if any, shore-side assistance in event of a fire on board.

Their critical survey of the port took weeks of exhaustive study and legwork. They even examined waterfront blueprints and traced the city's storm drain network, from which Saigon expelled its slime into the harbor out of three-foot-wide openings. Concerned that someone would crawl into these befouled passages with demolitions, the PSWD inspected each one to see that they were barred.

Seven and a half weeks after arriving, Hertica turned in his written report for securing the port. He detailed where fences, guard towers, lights, and guards should be placed. He called for a clear zone between An Khanh and the mooring buoys because anyone could walk from shore to the ships over the sampans, junks, and lighters crammed together. Eifler was pleased with the document's comprehensiveness and ordered the recommendations carried out.

South of Saigon, along the river at Nha Be, only a mile separated the huge petroleum-oil-lubricant, POL,

Above: Coast Guard Lieutenant Ted Deming (right) and Army Captain John Anglin confer while ammunition is unloaded from ship in Vietnam. The U.S. Army offloaded munitions from ships, stored, and moved it into the field of combat. At the Army's request, Coast Guardsmen were assigned to the Army as advisors in dangerous cargo handling. This led to four Coast Guard Explosive Loading Detachments and a Port Security & Waterways Detail being sent to Vietnam. (Courtesy James P. Ruff)

Left: Aboard an ammunition ship in Vietnam, Lieutenant James P. Ruff, Coast Guard hazardous cargo expert, meets with the vessel's captain. Ruff briefs the ship's officers in the process for unloading of munitions safely. Occasional breaches of safety measures might lead to exceptional punishment for errant crewmen not entirely aware of the dire consequences of seemingly minor infractions while handling munitions. Some who defied orders and continued to smoke cigarettes frequently found themselves handcuffed to a ship's rail. (Courtesy James P. Ruff)

A 10,000-pound bomb up from the hold of a merchant cargo-ship in Vietnam. Special attention to details required in munitions handling called for the Army to engage the Coast Guard as advisors for dangerous cargo handling.

tank farm that supplied virtually all of III and IV Corps from the ammunition ship offload anchorage. An earlier Coast Guard survey recommended shifting the anchorage up to Cat Lai because an exploding ammunition-carrier would begin a chain reaction that would destroy the tank farm. When Hertica realized that nothing was being done, he pushed hard for the relocation. Despite Hertica's professional judgment, some agencies involved disagreed, believing Cat Lai less secure. Nonetheless, the move did take place after the discovery of aiming stakes lining up the ammunition anchorage for Viet Cong mortarmen. Not long afterward, two intense attacks on the tank farm in the span of three days caused severe damage. Many believed that had the ammunition ships still been there, the entire POL terminal would have been leveled.

At the same time that the PSWD was trying to make Saigon Port secure, a new multi-million-dollar cargo facility was under development upriver. When finished, it would handle most of the military cargo clogging Saigon's docks. Commonly referred to as the new port, this title stuck and became its name. Persistent inspections enabled the PSWD to get many security and safety measures built into Newport. As a result, Newport grew into a well-protected installation. This was proven during the failed Tet Offensive of 1968, about which Kneip boasted that at Newport the machine gun emplacements "rolled them [the enemy] up ten deep."

Port protection is a marriage between security and safety. Shielding against subversion is futile if the destructive end is accomplished through accident or negligence. The necessity to empty the ships backed up in the harbor as fast as possible contributed to turning every clear spot into a cargo heap. In Saigon, Wise saw corrosive liquid-filled drums stacked atop flammable liquid-filled drums pressed against a lumber pile. Had the corrosive fluid leaked into contact with the flammable liquid the result would have been explosive and fiery. This is why 80 percent of Wise's job was proper cargo storage, which he taught to soldiers running the warehouses and docks.

The men of the PSWD applied themselves in places other than Saigon. Security breaches elsewhere wailed for correction, such as at Cam Ranh Bay, where a Vietnamese boy had slipped aboard SS Old Westbury and was trying to set fire to a napalm bomb. Barge sites were especially vulnerable. These were usually small wharfs where a barge could lay to be offloaded by a mobile crane. At the Coast Guard's urging the Army supplied these isolated dropoff points with 500-gallon-per-minute, trailer-mounted firefighting pumps. They developed tactics to stop North Vietnamese swimmer commandoes from slipping into ports to attach explosives to the hulls of ships and presented the persuasive argument to the Department of the Army, in behalf of the Army in Vietnam, of the critical need for thirty-nine PBRs (thirty-one-foot, river patrol boats) to detect and defeat the enemy in the harbors. Not only did they succeed in getting the boats, but they trained the army crews in boat handling and surveillance tactics.

The Coast Guard's port security men in Vietnam were few in number, but what they accomplished saved countless lives and prevented the loss of critical military supplies. Port catastrophe that would have happened— did not—simply because the Coast Guard was there.

The Cold War

Coast Guard port security duties continued domestically after America's involvement in Vietnam ended, but were gradually scaled back. However, in the 1980s much attention was placed on developing a more robust doctrine to improve Navy and Coast Guard port security and naval coastal warfare interaction. The lessons of operation *Market Time* demonstrated the value of the Navy and Coast Guard working together in coastal and port security missions. In the mid 1980s the concept of Maritime Defense Zones was established, giving the responsibility for the defense of coastal areas to Coast Guard Atlantic and Pacific Area commanders, while operating within a Navy chain of command. The National Port Readiness Committee Network was established, with the Captains of the Port chairing local committees of Department of Defense and Department of Transportation agencies to ensure the safe and secure transportation of military cargoes at U.S. ports. The Special Interest Vessel program continued, where vessels of Communist and other persona-non-grata countries were tracked and their entries and departures to and from U.S. ports were tightly controlled.

In parallel with the development of domestic port security efforts, the application of Coast Guard and Navy forces in overseas port security roles was also being revised. Coast Guard Reserve units dedicated to overseas port security missions were developed. These port security units, PSUs, were designed to have approximately 140 personnel, operating twenty-five-foot, heavily armed fast-boats to protect harbors, and are integrated into Navy/Coast Guard Harbor Defense Commands providing protection of overseas ports loading military supplies.

The value of this preparation paid off in operations *Desert Shield* and *Desert Storm*. When Iraq invaded Kuwait, domestic Coast Guard forces were put in a heightened port security status. Marine safety offices and groups set up port security detachments to oversee shore and water-side security at facilities loading war supplies aboard ships that supported the U.S. efforts to free Kuwait.

Coast Guard law enforcement detachments were embarked aboard naval vessels blockading Iraq to inspect all Iraq-bound vessels for contraband cargoes. Three Coast Guard port security units, PSUs, were deployed, the first in September 1990 to Saudi Arabia—this marked the first-ever deployment of a Reserve port security unit overseas. The port security units were mainly pulled from East Coast locations, but to fill out their ranks and provide rotation of deployed members required the inclusion of Reservists from all over the country. They were trained at Camp Blanding, Florida, then shipped out in successive deployments over the course of the war. Once *Operation Desert Storm* started in January 1991, at home the marine safety offices worked with the groups and stations to increase water and shoreside patrols of critical waterfront facilities. Overseas the PSUs performed their missions well—their contribution highlighted by a Coast Guard boat leading the first Allied watercraft into the newly liberated port of Kuwait City.

Port security measures even extend to an efficient bike patrol. Petty Officer Matthew Boulay (left) and Petty Officer Michael Schober glance at the water surrounding a boat at Martha's Vineyard, Massachusetts, looking for signs of pollution. The Coast Guard Marine Safety Field Office on Cape Cod debuted bike patrols in the summer of 2001 to promote pollution prevention awareness and to encourage safe boating practices. Bike patrols are the primary means of promoting maritime domain awareness along the 1,000-mile Cape Cod, Nantucket, and Martha's Vineyard shoreline during the heavy boating season. Public reaction to cycling mariners was immediately positive. During the first year of bike patrols, the Coast Guard received a 50 percent increase in pollution reports. Prior to bike patrols, the public's interaction with the Coast Guard was generally limited to enforcement activities. The patrols now offer boaters the opportunity to talk casually with the Coast Guardsmen, gaining information ranging from boating safety to marine protection. (Amy Thomas, U.S. Coast Guard)

A Coast Guard twenty-five-foot port security boat provides escort for a ship loaded with military cargo arriving in the Middle East during Operation Desert Storm. *While much was reported of air transport bringing supplies in for this war, large ships carried the majority of the materials. These ships required security for escort in the harbor areas and at the dock for unloading, which Coast Guard port security units provided working as part of Navy harbor defense command units. (U.S. Coast Guard)*

Petty Officer Yered

Paul C. Scotti *(From excerpts in* Coast Guard Action in Vietnam*)*

The explosives loading detachment, ELD, Coast Guardsman did not fit in any clique; he was an outsider, always "an X among Os." On the waterfront he engaged merchant mariner belligerence, within the Army he dealt with soldier coolness, among the foreign populace he coped with enemy violence, and surrounded by explosives, he lived within a spark of annihilation. Engineman First Class Robert J. Yered's experiences sketch this environment. A New Englander, Yered possessed the stalwart regional traits that ideally suited him to dangerous cargo duty. His ability to get along with diverse personalities, his sound judgment, and his fearlessness served him well during his 1967–1968 tour with ELD #1.

Yered would not forget February 1968. On the night of the 18th, off Cat Lai and under a bright moon, three ammunition ships loafed at anchor on the quiet river while their cargo was transferred into barges. Along the weedy river's edge, 300 yards away, the Viet Cong slipped into position. The port side of SS Neva West and the ammunition barges alongside faced the enemy. It was 0100 and the Vietnamese stevedores and Army checkers were enjoying a meal break. Yered was in his cabin cleaning up when explosions erupted around the ship. He ran on deck making a rapid search for damage. The vessel seemed all right until he looked over the port rail and saw a 130-foot barge, which was three-quarters full of 81-mm mortar rounds, on fire.

Through the smoke he could see flashes of small explosions caused by heat. Using a hose laid out by number three hatch, he gushed water onto the blaze, oblivious of the incoming shooting—unlike the stevedores and crews, who stayed in hiding. In the wheelhouse, an Army sergeant kept the base informed by radio and reported enemy positions.

For fifteen minutes Yered soaked the barge. Then to get at the flickering beneath the wooden pallets, he dragged the hose along as he made the vertical climb down to the barge. Finding that he still could not reach the obscured flames with the hose, Yered shouted to the sergeant that he wanted a bucket. He then stepped among the ruptured mortar shells picking up burning fragments and sixty-pound cases and threw them overboard.

The sergeant came down from the bridge, picked up Yered's hose, and continued dousing the barge. Shortly someone dropped Yered a bucket. He began hurried trips from the side of the ship, where he filled the pail with water draining from the main engine cooling discharge. He carried the water in repeated trips back to the burning cargo.

He did not know how many buckets of water it took to drown the fire, but an hour had passed since the enemy began shooting. The attack ceased after military police, transported by landing craft, chased the Viet Cong from the riverbank. With the fire out and the enemy gone, Yered had a chance to take in the ship's appearance and saw it blackened and holed from wheelhouse to waterline.

Later, he withdrew to the fantail and smoked a cigarette to calm his lingering excitement. Yered reflected briefly on how close a call this had been, then turned his thoughts to his wife and two children back in Massachusetts. The U.S. Army had their thoughts, too—of Yered's valor—and awarded him a Silver Star.

Above: Engineman First Class Robert J. Yered, USCG, is awarded the Silver Star Medal for heroism during a Viet Cong attack in Vietnam. When a barge receiving mortar ammunition from a ship at anchor began to burn, Yered jumped onto the barge where he first tossed burning shells overboard. Discovering the fire hoses too short, Yered then extinguished the remaining fires—in wooden pallets beneath the ammunition—with water he toted in buckets filled from an overboard drain on the ship's side. (U.S. Coast Guard)

The Coast Guard issues licenses for professional seamen. Mariners at all levels are required to pass Coast-Guard-administered tests before being qualified to act in any capacity aboard ship. These are samples of license certificates issued by the Coast Guard to merchant mariners. (U.S. Coast Guard)

Haiti, Olympics, & WTO

After *Desert Storm*, the role of domestic and overseas port security continued to be refined, especially after the collapse of the Soviet Union. The use of port security forces began to broaden, from an overseas, large scale military war like *Desert Storm*, to include more specialized duties. In 1994 the Coast Guard supported operation *Able Manner/Uphold Democracy in Haiti*, where Coast Guard members of a harbor defense command aboard the cutter *Chase* were deployed, eventually setting up two harbor defense commands with attached PSUs at two Haitian ports. In 1996, elements of Port Security Unit 305 were used to help provide protection at the Atlanta Olympics.

The most significant domestic use of Coast Guardsmen in a port security role in the years between the Vietnam war and 11 September, 2001 came in 1999. The World Trade Organization, WTO, conference was held in Seattle, Washington, with President Clinton and hundreds of heads of state and senior finance ministers from around the world attending. Riots by protesters against international monetary policies prompted high-security efforts on the waterfront, where a number of WTO conferences were planned. Active duty and Reserve marine safety office, group, and port security unit forces were integrated into an incident command structure, a response organization typically used for

Coast Guard boats rafted in Los Angeles, California, ready to provide security for the 1984 Olympics. The Coast Guard provides on-the-water security for major public events such as the Olympics and Operation Sail. (Tom Gillespie)

During intense security measures taken in United States' seaports in the wake of the September 11 attack, Coast Guard port security, marine safety, Navy harbor defense, and intelligence agency members assemble at Coast Guard Incident Command Puget Sound, for daily port security briefing. (Tom Beard)

A Coast Guard helicopter crew conducts a security over-flight of petrochemical facilities. In addition to security patrols, airplane and helicopter crews routinely monitor for oil leaking or breaches in dams or levees leading to possible petroleum or other contaminants escaping into waters adjacent to petrochemical handling facilities. Coast Guard aircraft crews also examine off-shore drilling rigs looking for escaping pollution and security threats. (Robert D. Wyman, U.S. Coast Guard)

A forty-one-foot patrol boat assigned to escort a cruise liner meets its assignment prior to the ship entering port. This is a security measure undertaken by Coast Guard boat crews during periods of high terrorist threats to the nation's ports. The armed patrol boat remains with the ship until shoreside security takes over. (Mike Hvozda, U.S. Coast Guard)

wildfires and pollution incidents and natural disaster events. This represented the first time this organization was mobilized on such a scale for a port security effort. The presence of the Coast Guard patrols ensured that the protests did not affect the waterside venues. The use of port security units overseas did not stop either, as they were sent to Bahrain to support ongoing U.S. operations there.

September 11

The Coast Guard's growing ability to use port security forces and tactics domestically proved critical to the country's maritime response to the terrorist attacks of 11 September 2001. Although the attacks came through the air against landside targets, the threat of attacks using alternative means became an instant concern. Immediately after the attacks, the Coast Guard went into a heightened state of readiness to protect the ports and harbors of the United States. Four port security units were activated, and marine safety offices and groups began continuous shore, water, and aerial patrols. Many marine safety offices set up Coast Guard incident commands. These incident command system-derived organizations were headed by the Captain of the Port and incorporated a variety of Coast Guard and Navy commands into a single team.

Port Security Today

The threats to port security today are many. The potential exists for taking hostages on cruise ships or ferries, as demonstrated on the cruise ship *Achille Lauro* in 1984 in the Mediterranean Sea, where Arab terrorists took over the vessel and killed an American passenger. While over 6,500,000

Above: *The terrorist-bomb-damaged USS Cole aboard the heavy-lift ship* Blue Marlin *receives a Coast Guard escort upon its arrival in U.S. waters en route to the ship-repair yard. (Patrick Montgomery, U.S. Coast Guard)*

Left: *The buoy tender* Maple *lowers a security zone buoy into position near the southern terminus of the Alaska oil pipeline. (U.S. Coast Guard)*

passengers are carried on cruise ships in the United States, Washington State ferries alone carry over 26,000,000 passengers annually.

Weapons of mass destruction are threats to both vessels and waterfront facilities. Shipping containers that arrive at the rate of over 6,000,000 per year, with over 8,000 ships making 51,000 port calls, offer the opportunity to smuggle in radioactive, biological, or chemical bombs that could be detonated elsewhere in the country.

The Coast Guard's port security mission will continue to be crucial to the United States, whether defending the coasts at home from terrorists or protecting U.S. forces during armed conflicts abroad. Though often requiring the ingenuity and dedication of its commanders and personnel to make it work despite a routine lack of resources, the Coast Guard has proven throughout its long history its skill and success at providing port security. In this mission more than virtually any of the many others assigned, the Coast Guard truly lives its name. Port security is an essential part of "Guarding the Coast."

Above: *Access to cargo containers aboard ship by Coast Guard inspectors is not always a simple matter. Here a few of the more than six million shipping containers coming into this country each year reach high above the Coast Guard inspectors on the deck of a large container-carrier. Only a cursory examination is conducted aboard ship primarily for damaged, open containers or those leaking substances. A foul-smelling noxious fluid seeping from one container aboard this ship turned out to be raw animal-hides soaked in seawater en route from Asia to Seattle. (Tom Beard)*

Left: *A Navy nuclear submarine arrives back in port under the protective guns of the Coast Guard. The Coast Guard has authority to impose and enforce protective security zones around vessels and port facilities. (James Moerls)*

Secret Wars

Commander Theodore. A. Bull, USCG

The Coast Guard does a little gardening in the Sacramento River delta by loading fifty marijuana plants harvested on an island from a garden hidden in the rushes. Information for such seizures typically comes through intelligence sources. (Veronica Bandrowsky, U.S. Coast Guard)

The key to victory against drug and other contraband smuggling is reliable intelligence. Information from many sources is forwarded to cutters at sea where suspect vessels are intercepted, boarded, and searched. (Ferdinand Petrie, U.S. Coast Guard Art Collection)

I t is no secret that many in the intelligence community of the United States consider our first president the greatest intelligence officer that our country has ever known. General George Washington clearly understood what he termed "the necessity of intelligence," and his expert use of it during the American Revolution is widely known. In fact, his effective use of intelligence may very well have made the ultimate difference between victory and defeat for the Continental Army against a far superior force.

A relatively diminutive armed force, charged with protecting the prosperity and security of an entire nation, must rely on intelligence to achieve its objectives. The intelligence program of the United States Coast Guard is based precisely on that premise. Throughout the Coast Guard's history, the necessity of intelligence has been apparent, but it has never been more evident than in the last twenty years—especially so in the last several years, in the wake of terrorist attacks on our nation's major cities. The unleashing of terrorism on our nation has brought home some very old lessons about just how necessary intelligence really is, lessons that go back to the early days of our republic.

When Washington was inaugurated as our first president, the new nation had no standing army or navy. Likewise, there was no effective means of enforcing the customs laws, which provided the main source of revenue for the economy of the fledgling nation. Smuggling, which had been rampant since long before the revolution, continued nearly unabated long afterward. In 1789, the newly appointed Secretary of the Treasury, Alexander Hamilton, was given the difficult and very daunting task of

The Coast Guard must rely on a combination of intelligence and capable assets, such as this rigid-hull inflatable boat seen here being retrieved aboard the cutter Cochito *through its stern ramp. (Patrick Montgomery, U.S. Coast Guard)*

Arresting hands confine a man taken in custody for possession of contraband. The Coast Guard is unique in having the dual power of a military committed to the defense of the country and a maritime police force dedicated to enforcement of all federal laws. (David M. Santos, U.S. Coast Guard)

With four 4-pounders and two 2-pounders taken from the grounded Eagle *and hauled up a bluff, Captain Frederick Lee and his crew continued to battle from a makeshift fortress the armed barges sent in by the British* Dispatch *to capture* Eagle. *With ammunition running out,* Eagle's *crew began firing shot already fired on them from* Dispatch's *barges with cartridges made from pages torn from the ship's logbook. The initiative of* Eagle's *crew and their tenacity in battle characterizes a trait carried forward to this day in Coast Guardsman. (U.S. Coast Guard Art Collection)*

collecting import revenues and halting the smuggling that threatened to undermine the new—and very experimental—government.

Hamilton looked to his regional Collectors of the Customs for answers. All of them reported that the seaports were rife with smuggling. For example, the Customs Collector in the major port of Philadelphia, Mr. Sharp Delany, responded with reports of information that even coffee and other sundry items were being smuggled regularly and with ease into his port. He urged the use of armed vessels to stop the illicit activity. Hamilton took that information in hand when he went to Congress to propose a solution to the growing problem.

The Revenue Cutter Service, one of the predecessors of the modern-day Coast Guard, was created in 1790 when Congress appropriated enough money for Hamilton to build a fleet of ten cutters intended to enforce the customs laws. It is worth noting that the justification for spending money on this new fleet was not a simple matter for a nation with very little ready cash. The decision was based principally on the reliability of trusted information about illicit activity—or intelligence—from the Collectors of Customs.

Since those early days, the Coast Guard has relied on many types and sources of information to provide intelligence for the purpose of improving its operations and the performance of its wide array of missions, which have continued to broaden from 1790 until the present day. The Coast Guard's efforts to collect, validate, analyze, and disseminate intelligence have not always been highly centralized or sophisticated, and its effectiveness in maximizing the use of intelligence certainly has waxed and waned over the years.

From the early days of the Revenue Cutter Service through the First World War, the intelligence available to cutters offshore did not amount to anything more than scant verbal reports and visual sightings. A functional intelligence program did not really exist until the end of the twentieth century. Cutters on patrol remained largely self-reliant until then; the vigilance of the crews determined their success.

The War of 1812 illustrates that point. A famous encounter between a British warship, *Dispatch*, and the Revenue Cutter *Eagle* took place just off the coast of New York in Long Island Sound in October of 1814. It was a fight that has become the stuff of legend and lore—it is even celebrated in the Coast Guard anthem, *Semper Paratus*.

Eagle had been on patrol for several weeks, watching for any sign of an elusive foreign enemy that had previously attacked some of the major cities of the United States, including our nation's capital. The ship had received reports that the enemy might attempt to capture commercial vessels involved in coastwise trade as prizes and use them as weapons to terrorize and attack the port of New Haven, Connecticut, and other cities and ships along the eastern seaboard.

Alerted to the presence of *Dispatch*, which had been sighted offshore after conducting several raids along the coast, *Eagle* ghosted along in the early morning hours of 11 October. The mission of *Eagle* was to hinder any attack. The crew had no idea, however, as to the exact whereabouts of the enemy ship.

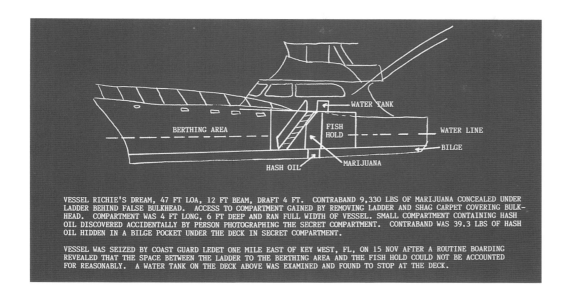

Coast Guard search teams find 9,330 pounds of marijuana in a hidden compartment under a ladder on this forty-seven-foot sports-fisherman, following a routine boarding. An investigation of the large compartment uncovers a secret compartment containing 39.3 pounds of hash oil in a bilge pocket under the deck. Drawings like this aid in instructing future boarding teams. (U.S. Coast Guard)

VESSEL RICHIE'S DREAM, 47 FT LOA, 12 FT BEAM, DRAFT 4 FT. CONTRABAND 9,330 LBS OF MARIJUANA CONCEALED UNDER LADDER BEHIND FALSE BULKHEAD. ACCESS TO COMPARTMENT GAINED BY REMOVING LADDER AND SHAG CARPET COVERING BULK-HEAD. COMPARTMENT WAS 4 FT LONG, 6 FT DEEP AND RAN FULL WIDTH OF VESSEL. SMALL COMPARTMENT CONTAINING HASH OIL DISCOVERED ACCIDENTALLY BY PERSON PHOTOGRAPHING THE SECRET COMPARTMENT. CONTRABAND WAS 39.3 LBS OF HASH OIL HIDDEN IN A BILGE POCKET UNDER THE DECK IN SECRET COMPARTMENT.

VESSEL WAS SEIZED BY COAST GUARD LEDET ONE MILE EAST OF KEY WEST, FL, ON 15 NOV AFTER A ROUTINE BOARDING REVEALED THAT THE SPACE BETWEEN THE LADDER TO THE BERTHING AREA AND THE FISH HOLD COULD NOT BE ACCOUNTED FOR REASONABLY. A WATER TANK ON THE DECK ABOVE WAS EXAMINED AND FOUND TO STOP AT THE DECK.

Left: Four members of a Coast Guard tactical law enforcement team are aboard a Panamanian-flagged ship as it pulls into Tampa, Florida, following its seizure. More than a ton of cocaine was discovered in its cargo. (Paul Rhyard, U.S. Coast Guard)

Below: The cutter Eagle built in Georgia in 1793 and reportedly about the same size as the revenue cutter Massachusetts—at sixty feet—took on the French fleet off the U.S. coast during the Quasi-War with France between 1798 and 1801. Eagle and the other seven revenue cutters conscripted by the Navy, each without assistance, accounted for the capture of fifteen French vessels and aided other ships in capturing five more. These cutters also freed twenty American vessels captured by French ships. They were a part of the Navy's fleet that accounted for the capture of ninety-nine French vessels. (John Tilley, U.S. Coast Guard)

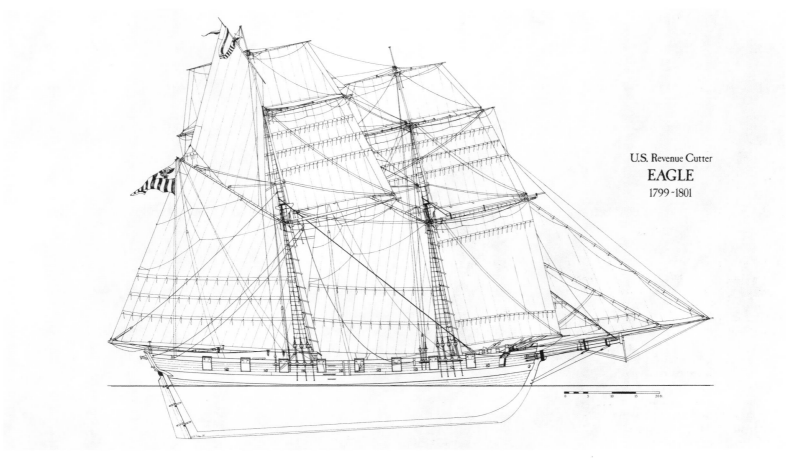

U.S. Revenue Cutter
EAGLE
1799-1801

So they waited, and they watched. A few hours later, the sun came up, but visibility was obscured with a heavy blanket of fog. As the sun rose higher in the sky, the fog began to burn off. Then, about mid-morning, it vanished altogether. Suddenly, right in front of *Eagle*, the enemy appeared under full sail, bearing directly down on it out of the fog.

A fierce fight broke out between the two ships. *Dispatch* was a British brig of far superior firepower. *Eagle* was outgunned. Seeing the futility of the fight, Captain Frederick Lee tried to save the ship by sailing into shallow water, finally beaching *Eagle* near a 160-foot bluff, fifteen miles northeast of Port Jefferson, New York. Then, he ordered his crew to strip the ship of sails and rigging, and to haul the guns ashore and up the steep bluff. Taking up a position at the top of the bluff, the daring crew fired down on the British ship, keeping the enemy from coming ashore or capturing their ship.

Throughout that day and into the next morning, the crew bravely defended their position. When their supply of ammunition ran out, they began retrieving the shot the British had fired at them. This shot they loaded into their own guns and returned it in a maelstrom of fire to the enemy. Consequently, *Dispatch* was forced to withdraw that day, although the brig eventually captured the hapless *Eagle* as the ship attempted to return to port for repairs.

This inspiring story, along with countless others, sharply illustrates the courage and tenacity that have characterized the history of Coast Guard actions through the past two centuries. However, it also clearly

demonstrates the hazardous extremes that often are of necessary resort when good intelligence is scarce.

It is quite astonishing to think that, in terms of intelligence capability, Coast Guard ships operated under very similar conditions for almost 200 years, with the exclusion of the two world wars, when the Coast Guard benefited directly from the wartime resources of the United States Navy. Of course, the later advent of modern electronic sensors, such as radio and radar, together with modern aviation, have made significant improvements in the ability of cutters to detect what is sailing in the waters around them. However, before the last twenty years of the twentieth century, despite the benefits of modern technology, the Coast Guard was really limited to scarce human intelligence and visual sightings as the main sources of information for conducting its entire array of missions, from search and rescue to maritime security. The reason for that limitation was the absence of a formal intelligence program.

Among several factors contributing to the lack of a well-established intelligence program, two stand out in particular. They usually worked in consonance. The first was a continuously strained budget. Since the early days of the Revenue Cutter Service, frugality has been a hallmark of Coast Guard service. Far more often than not, the Coast Guard and its predecessors nearly always have been expected to do more with less. The second factor was the strong emphasis on search and rescue as a major mission, which has grown since the U. S. Lifesaving Service and the Revenue Cutter Service merged to form the Coast Guard. That emphasis has lasted until the present day.

Ingenuity by both the smuggler and the Coast Guard frequently offers excitement and sometimes a tough, dirty job. Coast Guardsmen discover cocaine bales artfully buried beneath a ship's cargo of iron ore. (U.S. Coast Guard)

A Coast Guard HITRON squadron Stingray moving in to begin a firing run with warning shots across the bow from its machine gun to stop a suspected drug-running go-fast boat. If the boat fails to stop at the warning, the helicopter's gunner will shoot with a .50-caliber rifle, targeting to disable the boat's engines. (William R. Greer)

The very nature of the search-and rescue-mission tends to diminish the need for an intelligence function in the minds of most people. Albeit an oversimplification, the prevailing notion has been that search-and-rescue victims typically will make every effort to make their situations and locations very obvious and conspicuous; therefore, given the preeminence of the search-and-rescue mission, it would seem more important to spend scarce resources on building emergency response capability than to spend it on collecting information about possible illicit or enemy activity. It has been only in the last decade or so that the Coast Guard has come to recognize the real potential for intelligence systems to be a kind of force multiplier in all of its missions—as much to locate the site of a maritime emergency, as well as to find a suspect smuggling vessel headed for the coastline. That potential has yet to be fully realized, but it is being developed.

There are two notable events in history, however, that helped establish the need and the basis for a capable, modern intelligence program in the Coast Guard. The first came between the world wars, in the early decades of the twentieth century, during the so-called Rum Wars of Prohibition. The second was the war on drugs, which came a half-century later.

Rumrunners were notoriously brazen in flouting the laws of Prohibition. In the 1920s, they established what was widely known as "Rum Row" off the coast of New York, which was a somewhat remote gathering place for ships engaged in smuggling rum from the islands of the Caribbean and other illegal liquor from all over the world. Smuggling vessels flocked there to await the clandestine approach of offload boats, which would rendezvous to pick up their illicit cargo. The same kind of activity occurred along the west coast. The Coast Guard was given the difficult task of putting a halt to the smuggling.

Maritime law enforcement has always been extremely challenging. The enormous expanse of ocean extending from both coasts of the United States and the thousands of miles of sometimes sparsely populated coastline and hidden coves, not to mention frequent changes in

A 41-footer crew moves a captured thirty-five-foot go-fast to Station Key West, brought in by CGC Nantucket. *The smugglers were captured after a 300-mile chase. Meanwhile CGCs* Bear *and* Nantucket, *in the background, transfer 2,139 pounds of marijuana and the suspected smugglers to the base. (Dana Warr, U.S. Coast Guard)*

Boarding officer Chief Petty Officer Luke Bethel, of the Royal Bahamas Defense Force, is inspecting a suspect vessel, assisted by U.S. Coast Guardsmen in Bahamian waters. (David M. Santos, U.S. Coast Guard)

263

Coast Guard crews weigh Marijuana taken from a shrimp boat near Brownsville, Texas. The total comes to 8,975 pounds with an estimated street value of seven million dollars. Weapons carried by the Coast Guard members and bullet-proof jackets worn suggest the potentially dangerous nature of this law enforcement mission. (U.S. Coast Guard)

Marijuana, due to its bulky bales, is difficult to disguise or hide. This ship is caught with its illicit cargo openly visible to Coast Guard aircraft flying overhead. (U.S. Coast Guard)

Petty Officer William Brooks examines an ion swipe during a routine boarding to determine if traces of cocaine are aboard the vessel. Results from this quick test may determine the need for a more comprehensive search. This technology makes for an expeditious routine boarding. (Jacquelyn Zettles, U.S. Coast Guard)

weather conditions, present a host of forbidding impediments to success in detecting and identifying illicit activity in the constant flow of maritime commercial traffic that enters and leaves our ports every single day. Smugglers have always taken full advantage of those difficult conditions. Such was the case as well in 1924, when the Coast Guard was directed to put a halt to the activities on Rum Row. By then, the use of marine radios had made smuggling easier than ever before, because a clandestine rendezvous could be arranged quickly and without notice, thereby making detection very unlikely. The use of codes and encrypted messages was very common, for obvious reasons.

The Commandant of the Coast Guard at that time, Rear Admiral Frederick C. Billard, realized that extraordinary measures would be needed to accomplish the daunting task of detecting, locating, and identifying the rumrunners at sea. Rear Admiral Billard established the first formal Office of Intelligence in the Coast Guard for that very purpose. For a short time, the office consisted of a lone intelligence officer, but the complexity and enormity of the task was clearly too much for one person. The staff grew within a year to a grand total of five. The team, though small, was extremely effective in employing a variety of different types of intelligence to accomplish their mission, including the use of domestic sources, foreign spies, imagery, and cryptanalysis. Due to his influence and leadership in establishing this much-needed capability, Admiral Billard has long been recognized as the father of the Coast Guard intelligence program.

After the end of Prohibition, the Coast Guard returned to other pressing duties, and subsequently the importance of intelligence waned. It was not until the 1980s that the program began to flourish once more. The reason for its resurgence was, again, smuggling. This time it was marijuana transported by ship from the Caribbean and South America, mainly Jamaica and Colombia. Since the late 1970s, smugglers had been using small cargo ships and old fishing vessels to ship multi-ton loads of marijuana, baled like hay and stacked in rows on deck—often

in plain sight. These mother-ships would rendezvous to offload the marijuana to smaller vessels, usually under the cover of darkness, either at pre-arranged locations along the coast, or at open-water sites hastily arranged through the use of high frequency radio.

The Coast Guard adopted a choke-point strategy to stem the flow, stationing cutters on patrol in the Windward Pass, between Haiti and Cuba; in the Mona Passage, between the Dominican Republic and Puerto Rico; and in the Anegada Pass, east of Puerto Rico. Cutters and aircraft also patrolled the waters between the Yucatan Peninsula and Cuba, guarding the entrance to the Gulf of Mexico. This strategy required nearly a constant presence at each place, but it proved to be very effective, forcing the smugglers to alter their methods and devise more careful means of hiding their illicit cargo.

The chokepoint strategy, however, did not require sophisticated intelligence gathering. Rather, its success came from being at the right place at the right time from taking into account growing seasons, weather patterns, and known smuggling routes. Most seizures at that time were "cold hits," that is, apprehensions unaided by intelligence.

Coast Guard air crewmen from an HH-60J assist in offloading cocaine in Nassau, Bahamas, seized from a motor vessel. Members of a joint-country operation assigned to Operations Bahamas, Turks and Caicos, or OPBAT, discovered this cocaine worth $80 million in a secret compartment inside the 200-foot vessel. Eight crewmen from the seized motor vessel were arrested. OPBAT was created in 1982 to assist in reducing the flow of smuggled drugs through the Caribbean from Columbia and Panama. (Alvin Dalmida, Jr., U.S. Coast Guard)

Rum War Intelligence

Lieutenant Commander Eric Ensign, USCG

The roots of modern-day Coast Guard intelligence can be traced back to the Prohibition era. After four years of largely ineffective enforcement measures and the development of a large "Rum Row" of smuggling ships off the New York coastline, in May 1924, the Secretary of the Treasury tasked the Coast Guard with stopping the influx of liquor into the United States by sea. Rear Admiral Frederick. C. Billard, the Coast Guard Commandant, rallied the Service, reminding all Coast Guardsmen that "neither the old Revenue Cutter Service nor the old Life Saving Service ever failed in any duty given it to do." He then set the tone for the task at hand: "The Coast Guard has never failed, and it will not fail in its performance of this big task." Yet when faced with the monumental responsibility of protecting the nation's thousands of miles of coastline, it was clear existing resources would not be enough. So the Coast Guard turned to intelligence gathering to help bridge the gap between well-organized smugglers and under-resourced law enforcement.

The task of orchestrating the Coast Guard's intelligence effort fell to Lieutenant Commander Charles S. Root, the Service's sole intelligence officer, who reported directly to the Commandant. As the founding father of Coast Guard intelligence, Root organized a global intelligence effort using a multi-source approach to magnify the effectiveness of the Coast Guard's fighting force. Root's early efforts focused on the collection and analysis of various intelligence information reported by patrolling cutters, and the dissemination of finished "Intelligence Circulars" back to the fleet. Root also organized intelligence sharing efforts between the Coast Guard and other federal agencies to ensure a coordinated federal enforcement effort.

The immensity of the job soon exhausted Root's abilities to keep up with the need for timely, accurate intelligence and the extensive liaison duties required of his position. Acutely aware of the value intelligence had to the enforcement effort, in the summer of 1925 Commandant Billard designated a Coast Guard Intelligence Section and placed it under the Chief of Operations at Coast Guard Headquarters. In addition, Root, promoted to commander, was given clerical assistance and a deputy to help with the large amount of secret correspondence required of his section.

With a staff of three, Commander Root was now able to focus on additional intelligence collection methods. He placed spies in Cuba and other countries to report on the names of rum-running ships and companies transporting liquor to the United States. He sent a Coast Guard officer to Nova Scotia to gather intelligence on the latest engine and ship designs being built for the rum-runners—so that Coast Guard cutters could be designed to outrun them. He also enlisted the assistance of the U.S. State Department and foreign governments to supply him with information on the status of vessels being built in foreign countries for the expressed purpose of smuggling liquor into the United States.

With the use of radio commonplace among rum-runners by 1927, Commander Root expanded his intelligence collection efforts to include the interception of coded radio messages passed between rum-running vessels and their shore-based controllers. In order to succeed in the world of code breaking, or communications intelligence, the Coast Guard garnered the assistance of world-renowned code breaker Major William F. Friedman, of the War Department's Signal Corps. In addition, the Coast Guard hired two cryptologists, one being Friedman's wife, Elizebeth Friedman, who worked for the Coast Guard for several years during the height of Prohibition, breaking rum-runners' codes and allowing Coast Guard cutters to intercept the smugglers well offshore.

The Coast Guard also employed new high-frequency direction-finding equipment as part of its communications intercept efforts. In the summer of 1930, now Captain Root, with the cooperation of the Department of Justice, used the new "X Type" portable HF radio direction-finders to locate and shut down six illicit amateur radio stations operating in the New York area. X Type direction finders were also placed on Coast Guard cutters to help them locate rum-running vessels at sea. In September 1930 the War Department released Friedman for two weeks to work aboard CG-210, a seventy-five-foot patrol boat specially outfitted for detecting and identifying rum-runners. While operating off the New York coast, Friedman deciphered various codes and identified smuggling ships operating in and around New York Harbor. He then read the decoded messages back to the rum ships, which had the effect of halting delivery of all alcohol along the New York coastline for several days.

Even imagery had a place in the effort to identify rum-runners. With the arrival of the first five amphibian aircraft purchased by the Coast Guard beginning in October 1926, the Coast Guard was able to obtain photographs of suspected rum-runners operating over a wide ocean area. The photographs were compiled to produce an identification book of rum-runners for use by patrolling cutters in identifying and stopping ships involved in the illegal liquor trade.

Other, less clandestine methods of collecting intelligence included reviewing daily newspapers from key rum-running ports to glean information on ships and individuals involved in the rum trade. The use of newspapers to keep abreast of developments in the smuggling business became a staple in the Coast Guard's intelli-

gence arsenal and provided much of the analysis that went into the production of intelligence circulars.

The Coast Guard Intelligence Section, having grown from a one-man operation in 1924 to a force of five by 1927, continued to expand its responsibilities and its support to operations until the repeal of Prohibition in 1933. By the end of the Rum War, the liquor assault that began with blatant law-breaking in plain view of enforcement officials along New York's Rum Row had been reduced. Smugglers were being forced to make risky, clandestine rendezvous, sometimes effected hundreds of miles offshore, in attempting to evade Coast Guard defenses; liquor traffickers never regained an effective stronghold anywhere along the United States coastline. By using intelligence to multiply the effectiveness of its operational forces, the Coast Guard created a unified front that allowed for a refined and successful enforcement strategy as the Rum War came to a close.

In 1924, one officer with a vision for how intelligence could benefit the Coast Guard began a campaign to integrate all types of intelligence into every aspect of Prohibition enforcement. Relying on his intellect and foresight, and by keeping in focus a worthy goal, Captain Charles S. Root created an orchestrated support effort so important that it made the difference between the Coast Guard winning the Rum War and just treading water.

Above, left: The Coast Guard borrowed a Navy surplus Loening UO-1 for a search aircraft in the Rum War and paid the Army one dollar for a large tent to use as a hanger. The success of this aircraft in gathering intelligence led, a year later in 1926, to Admiral Billard's success with Congress to obtain money to purchase five airplanes for the Coast Guard. (U.S. Coast Guard)

Above, right: The use by the Coast Guard of the high-frequency direction finder such as this portable Type X RDF proved highly successful in prosecuting the rum-running activities. These radios could take bearings on rumrunners' radio transmissions, revealing their positions leading to their capture. (U.S. Coast Guard)

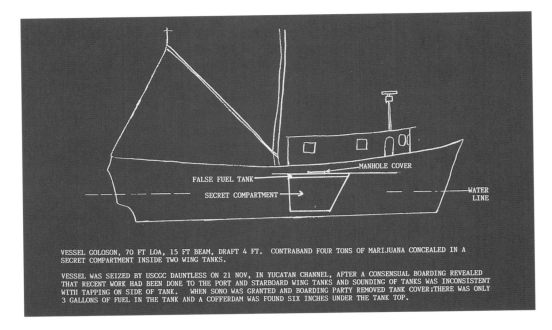

VESSEL GOLOSON, 70 FT LOA, 15 FT BEAM, DRAFT 4 FT. CONTRABAND FOUR TONS OF MARIJUANA CONCEALED IN A SECRET COMPARTMENT INSIDE TWO WING TANKS.

VESSEL WAS SEIZED BY USCGC DAUNTLESS ON 21 NOV, IN YUCATAN CHANNEL, AFTER A CONSENSUAL BOARDING REVEALED THAT RECENT WORK HAD BEEN DONE TO THE PORT AND STARBOARD WING TANKS AND SOUNDING OF TANKS WAS INCONSISTENT WITH TAPPING ON SIDE OF TANK. WHEN SONO WAS GRANTED AND BOARDING PARTY REMOVED TANK COVER;THERE WAS ONLY 3 GALLONS OF FUEL IN THE TANK AND A COFFERDAM WAS FOUND SIX INCHES UNDER THE TANK TOP.

Fishing vessels with large fuel capacities can have a false tank or void built within a conventional fuel tank. A tip for boarding officers frequently is evidence of recent repairs on or near these built-in fuel tanks. Four tons of marijuana were discovered hidden in cavities built inside the fuel tanks on this Gulf shrimper by a Coast Guard boarding crew. (U.S. Coast Guard)

Coast Guard expertise in law enforcement extends beyond America's waters. A boarding team from the cutter Adak *boards a cargo dhow in the Persian Gulf searching for smuggled Iraqi oil. Coast guard cutters supported coalition forces during* Operation Iraqi Freedom *to stop oil smuggling and search for terrorists. (Matthew Belson, U.S. Coast Guard)*

Drug-sniffing dogs are trained for the Coast Guard by the Auburn University Canine Detection Center. The instructor here is placing two small bags of marijuana in a suitcase for this training sequence. These skilled dogs accompany Coast Guard tactical law enforcement teams. (Donnie Brzuska, U.S. Coast Guard)

In 1982, The Coast Guard asked the Navy to provide more help, as well as better intelligence, in the Caribbean, which proved to be a real boon to enforcement efforts, due to the Navy's far more capable sensors. Smugglers adjusted to the improved interdiction tactics of the United States by altering their smuggling routes, using sophisticated hidden compartments on ships, as well as cargo aircraft.

It was by and large a cat-and-mouse game. For example, rather than taking direct routes through the narrow passages to Florida, some smuggling organizations began using larger vessels and making end runs, eastward through the Leeward Islands and then north to the coast of New Jersey or New England.

Soon afterward, President Ronald Reagan authorized establishment of a task force on counter-narcotics, which created an inter-agency command center, consisting of both federal law enforcement agencies and military intelligence officials. Called the Interdiction Operations and Intelligence Center, IOIC, it began operations in 1982 at the Coast Guard Seventh District headquarters in Miami, Florida. Together with other agencies, the Coast Guard began to marshal the best means of intelligence collection and exploitation available to respond to the growing threat.

This, however, was by no means the Coast Guard's first attempt to cooperate in sharing intelligence. For example, a decade earlier, in 1975, the Coast Guard had joined the El Paso, Texas, Intelligence Center, becoming one of the first members of a consortium of thirteen federal agencies in a partnership against the smuggling of drugs, illegal migrants, and weapons.

The Coast Guard soon realized, however, that relying on other agencies to provide information was not sufficient, and that the service, as the lead federal agency for maritime law enforcement, was in an excellent position to gather intelligence to share with other agencies. Consequently, during the mid-1980s, while continuing to develop partnerships with other federal, state, and local intelligence and law enforcement agencies, the Coast Guard began building its own intelligence program in earnest, primarily to cope with the ever-changing methods and tactics of smugglers on the high seas.

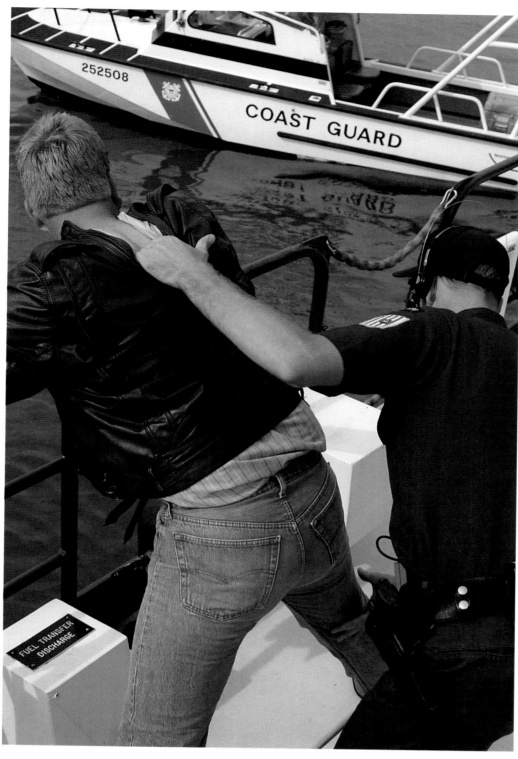

In his role as a law enforcement officer, this Coast Guard petty officer restrains a smuggling suspect while checking for concealed weapons. (Jerry L. Snyder, U.S. Coast Guard)

At one time during the war on drug smuggling, Coast Guard personnel extended their anti-drug activities deep into Colombia's jungle rivers assisting the Colombian government in operations to disrupt smuggling activities. (Dave Silva, U.S. Coast Guard)

Law enforcement boarding teams have tried many forms of detection tools. Here, petty officer Al Olsen prepares a boat scope that works on the periscope principle. It offers the ability for inspectors to peek into inaccessible voids and tanks. (David M. Santos, U.S. Coast Guard)

As the program grew, the Coast Guard saw the need for a centralized clearinghouse for maritime intelligence information, leading to the establishment in 1984 of the Intelligence Coordination Center, ICC, at Coast Guard Headquarters in Washington, D.C. The ICC increased the utility of intelligence available, but just as importantly, it provided the commandant with a better view of intelligence trends.

Previously, individual district and area staffs were responsible for collecting, analyzing, producing, and disseminating intelligence. The lack of a coordinated effort often left gaps in awareness about trans-regional activity. Typically, the district staffs consisted of one or two full-time intelligence officers, who might be responsible for analysis and dissemination of intelligence information for a multi-state region. The staffs at the area commands were not much larger. A single analyst might be required to monitor activity for the entire Gulf of Maine, or the mid-Atlantic Coast, for

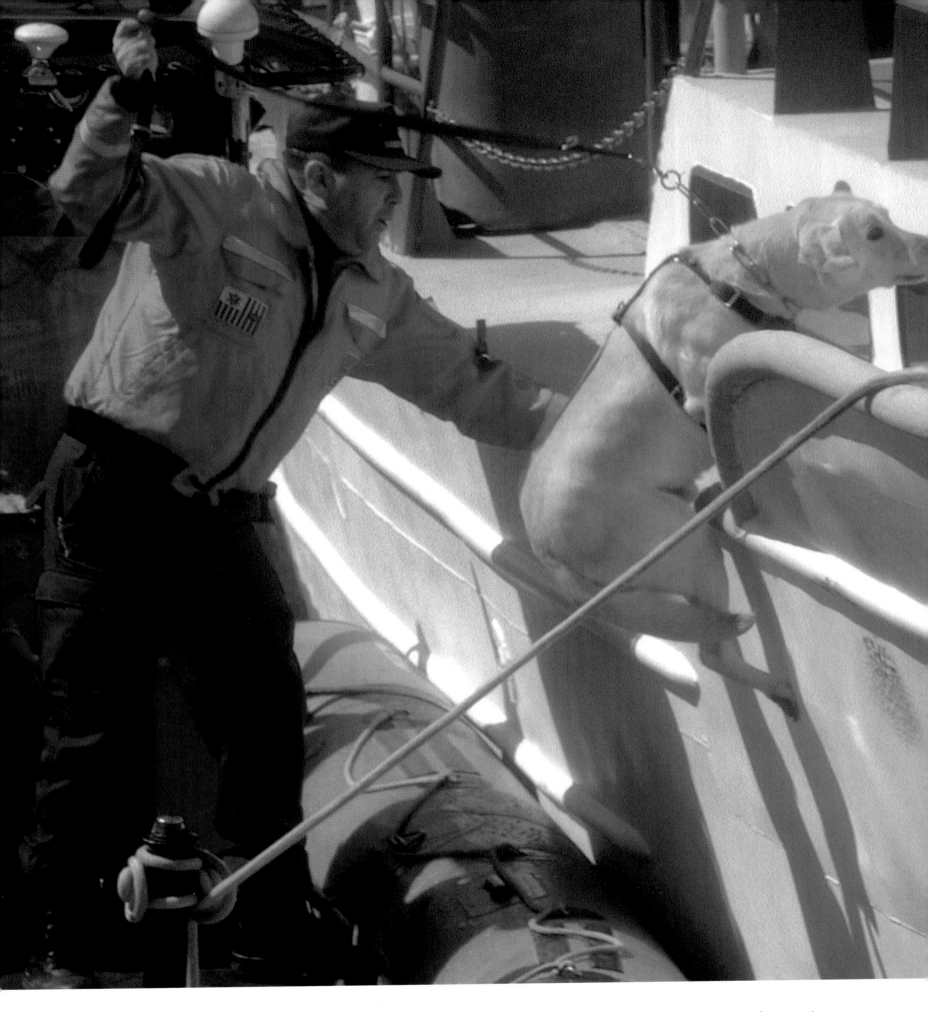

Dogs, effective workers for the Coast Guard in World War II for security, return in the war on drugs using their unique detecting abilities. Chief Petty Officer Diego Herrera assists his partner, Max, a four-year-old, aboard a boat. (Tom Sperduto, U.S. Coast Guard)

example. The quantity and quality of intelligence analysis and reporting was somewhat limited.

The exception among the various districts was to be found in Miami, Florida, at the Seventh Coast Guard District, where more resources and people were concentrated due to higher levels of activity. Drug smuggling was not the only law enforcement problem in that region. In the early 1980s, illegal migration into the United States surged enormously. The *Mariel Boatlift*, for example, inundated the South Florida coast with an unprecedented wave of 125,000 refugees from Cuba, arriving almost without warning between April and September of 1980.

Since then, the influx of illegal migration from Cuba and other Caribbean nations slowed to a comparative trickle, but today it still challenges those charged with enforcement of the immigration policy of the United States, particularly the Coast Guard's Seventh District, where intelligence has become absolutely essential to that effort. As drug smuggling along the southeastern coastline has increased, the Seventh District staff has been reinforced steadily through the years, leading to establishment of the Maritime Intelligence Center in Miami, which now provides tactical intelligence on a wide variety of threats, including drug smuggling, illegal migration, fisheries violations, and, most recently, terrorism.

From the late 1980s until the start of the new millennium, cocaine smuggling was deemed the single largest threat and presented the biggest challenge to the Coast Guard intelligence program. Cocaine is less bulky and far more profitable by weight than marijuana, and it is much easier to conceal in legitimate cargo. Sorting lawful from illicit freight was extremely difficult. Gone were the days when a circling aircraft could spot bales of contraband on the deck of a rusty coastal freighter. Smugglers had become much craftier in their methods, and they expanded their routes to include the eastern Pacific Ocean, a much wider expanse of open water in which to conceal their activity.

As the Cold War ended, the threat of drug trafficking, along with other so-called asymmetric threats, was considered so significant that the Department of Defense was given primary responsibility for detection and monitoring of both air and maritime smuggling in the transit zones. Although the full force of the department was focused elsewhere in the world, nevertheless the powerful intelligence resources of the other armed forces were brought to bear on the drug war, and the Coast Guard's own limited intelligence capabilities were augmented substantially, especially in the areas of human intelligence reporting and signals intelligence collection.

Coast Guard Marine Safety Detachment Dutch Harbor, Alaska, personnel use an infrared video-scope to scan for heat signatures emanating from a cargo container just offloaded from a container ship. These containers in the past have accommodated smuggled Chinese migrants into the United States. Based on intelligence, this inspection team had more than thirty containers removed from the ship's load to reach this suspect container to search for smuggled émigrés. (Marshalena Delaney, U.S. Coast Guard)

Above: Petty officer Jeff Strickland passes a bale of cocaine to a federal agent on board the Navy ship, USS Boone. The Coast Guard and Navy team seized more than 110 bales of cocaine from one fishing vessel. These seizures are the culmination of efforts by several federal, state, and foreign governments working together by sharing intelligence. (Dana Warr, U.S. Coast Guard)

Left: Drug running is a round-the-clock enterprise. The Coast Guard's task is likewise. CGC Diligence is on homeland security and drug interdiction patrol during the 2003 Christmas holidays. (U.S. Coast Guard)

HITRON Box Score—Captain Jeffrey Karonis, USCG

For Charlie Hopkins, Richard Forbes, Roscoe Torres, Steve Branham, Corey Nissen, and several hundred of their Coast Guard shipmates and planners in Washington, D.C., armed helicopters were not just a new chapter in Coast Guard history, but a new game with new rules, and now the good guys were winning.

The original Helicopter Interdiction Tactical Squadron 10—HITRON-10—proof of concept squadron scored a perfect five stops for five pursuits. Proving all the proposals, the squadron terminated operations after ten months. The ships, boats, and helicopters in this experimental group had stopped all intercepted "go-fast" boats—requiring the use of force. These smugglers carried 2.3 tons of cocaine and 3.5 tons of marijuana with a street value of just over $100 million. The team took seventeen suspects into custody.

Successes from the experiment led to the formation of a permanent squadron, HITRON Jacksonville, with new aircraft, the MH-68A. Organization and training, along with delays in receiving the new helicopters created a twenty-three-month hiatus until the squadron's first mission in February 2002. In the following twenty months, HITRON Jacksonville reportedly stopped thirty smuggling boats carrying 35.2 tons of cocaine and 2.2 tons of marijuana. The contraband's street value was over $2.3 billion. Ninety suspects were taken into custody.

This success and their unique abilities with armed helicopters and law enforcement authority, led to further roles for the squadron. Secretary of Homeland Security Tom Ridge, in adding the mission of national security to the initial role of drug interdiction for HITRON, said, "The use of Coast Guard HITRON for armed patrols will increase the level of security in our ports, provide an additional layer of defense, ensure continued safe flow of commerce, and deter possible acts of terrorism in our nation's key ports."

This small band of brothers meets each day as another day at war. Created to fight the drug smugglers they soon also became a first line of defense in the nation's security by providing armed helicopters anywhere from the Caribbean to Alaska and all ports between. (U.S. Coast Guard)

During this time the Department of Defense helped create several joint task-forces, later turned into joint inter-agency task-forces, JIATF, incorporating federal law-enforcement agencies and the armed forces in a cooperative effort to stem the smuggling tide. These command centers, which were far more capable than the former Interdiction Operations and Intelligence Center, placed operational and intelligence resources side by side. At JIATF East, in Key West, Florida, and JIATF West, in Alameda, California, a Coast Guard flag officer was placed in command to coordinate efforts.

Subsequently, the numbers and sizes of bulk cocaine seizures at sea rose considerably, although estimates on actual seizure rates were extremely difficult to determine. The ratio of seizures that were attributed to intelligence increased to around seven out of ten, as well. Human intelligence sources carefully placed throughout the Caribbean region proved very effective, and signals intelligence produced electronic targets that were much easier to track. At that time, if a suspected target got through the dragnet of military sensors, it was usually because the number of

targets exceeded the number of ships and aircraft available to pursue them, rather than due to a lack of intelligence information.

Though the counter-drug mission remained preeminent throughout the 1990s, other threats continued to loom on the horizon. Illegal migration increased greatly, and occasionally shiploads of illegal immigrants literally waded ashore, as happened in the case involving more than 300 people on the cargo vessel *Golden Venture* when it ran aground in 1993 on Long Island, New York. Ten people died trying to swim the 200 yards to shore. That incident, which occurred almost without warning, spotlighted the need for better intelligence more broadly applied across the missions of the Coast Guard.

Foreign fishing vessels encroached on the fishing grounds of the United States, as well, threatening to destroy the already depleted stocks of migratory fish. The continuing dispute over the Maritime Boundary Line in the Bering Sea, for example, resulted in frequent incursions by Russian fishing vessels, as well as others, sometimes producing tense confrontations between foreign fishing vessels and Coast Guard cutters. Usually the Coast Guard could spare just a single cutter to patrol those rough waters at any given time, so it was often on the line alone, which made the need for timely and accurate intelligence imperative. The same was true in other areas, such as Georges Banks, off the coast of New England.

The necessity of good intelligence has often outpaced the Coast Guard's capability to provide it, but that disparity has simply inspired the men and women of the intelligence program to Herculean efforts to meet the demand. Though the program has flourished during the past twenty years, its success has been accomplished largely by a workforce lacking in any specific expertise. There has never been an intelligence specialist rating in the Coast Guard; likewise, there has been no definitive career path for intelligence officers. Recruits to the program were plucked from other ratings and specialties to receive limited training in the world of intelligence. Even so, those who joined the ranks usually found the work exciting and challenging, and there was always plenty of work at hand to maintain interest. After successive tours, many returned for more.

A departure from the usual all-white color of Coast Guard equipment is this green vehicle in pursuit of smugglers along Gulf Coast beaches in Operation Gulf Shield. *What does not change is the distinctive racing stripe marking. (Joe Dye, U.S. Coast Guard)*

CGC Jarvis *in company with Chinese Fisheries law enforcement vessel* Zhong Guo Yu Zheng 118, *patrol as a team seeking fishermen using environmentally destructive drift fishing nets in addition to violators of United States' Exclusive Economic Zones. (U.S. Coast Guard)*

273

Members of Pacific Area Coast Guard Tactical Law Enforcement Team Bravo keep in physical shape by taking on one of the Marine Corps' grueling mud obstacles courses. Team members must also be physically fit to meet unexpected challenges during seizures, on occasions when they might also be outnumbered by not-so-friendly opponents. (U.S. Coast Guard)

The coming of the new millennium brought renewed awareness of the need for a more capable intelligence program in the Coast Guard. Forecasts of coming threats, which promised only to increase during the ensuing decades, made it clear that limited resources only would allow the Coast Guard to respond effectively if it had the advantage of sharing information more quickly and accurately. Cutters and aircraft could not expect to succeed on patrol without significantly more capable sensors and communication systems. Those systems had to feed into a network of information available instantaneously on demand.

The Coast Guard was in the process of building a stronger, more capable intelligence program when the terrorist attacks occurred on 11 September 2001. The Commandant, Admiral James M. Loy, had just named a new Director of Intelligence. The program also was receiving greater funding, both from the Coast Guard budget process and from the Department of Defense, to improve its sensor systems and increase its collection and analysis capabilities.

Soon after the attacks on New York City and Washington, D.C., the National Security Act of 1947 was amended, making the Coast Guard a member of the National Foreign Intelligence Program. Membership in this intelligence community permits the Coast Guard Intelligence Program to make unique contributions, it being the only member that is both an armed force and a federal law enforcement agency with broad legal authority. That special status allows the Coast Guard to bridge the gulf between the law enforcement and military communities as no other agency can.

With the advent of membership in the intelligence community, the size and importance of the Coast Guard's intelligence program is now

A weapons cache seized by a Coast Guard anti-smuggling law enforcement team. Such seizures are not the result of random searches but based on intelligence gathered through many sources. (U.S. Coast Guard)

274

growing. While the director of Central Intelligence will continue to shape the Coast Guard's intelligence mission, this will likely be in keeping with traditional Coast Guard responsibilities of international scope such as military-related foreign intelligence and counter-intelligence dealing with narcotics trafficking, terrorism, fisheries, and environmental threats.

The Coast Guard will also continue to receive funding from the General Defense Intelligence Program through the Navy. Maintaining this support will be crucial to the Coast Guard's ability to achieve what is now being called Maritime Domain Awareness.

Simply put, Maritime Domain Awareness calls for total awareness of vulnerabilities, threats, and targets of interest on the water. This is not a new idea. It is a new name being applied to a more aggressive, more effective means of gathering, using, and sharing information and intelligence than has ever been possible in the past.

Such expertise requires extensive knowledge of geography, weather, position of friendly and unfriendly forces, trends, key indicators, and so forth. New data-mining techniques will be needed, as will be databases shared across traditional boundaries to the extent the law allows. An even more powerful system of centralized intelligence centers is necessary to collate and analyze intelligence. Most importantly, Maritime Domain Awareness means providing operating forces, both afloat and ashore, with a single integrated operating picture that is timely, accurate, and reliable.

The Coast Guard's Intelligence Coordination Center is playing a central role in developing Maritime Domain Awareness. The ICC is the Coast Guard's point of entry access to the highly classified national systems operated by the intelligence community. Such access allows maritime security threats to be identified well out to sea, or even while still in a foreign port, long before they can reach the shores of the United States.

In the years ahead, the Coast Guard will become increasingly better able to detect, intercept, and interdict potential threats on the high seas. This will be accomplished through a layered system of systems; new cutters, patrol boats, and aircraft, called the *Integrated Deepwater System*, or *Deepwater*. This project will also provide the state-of-the-art sensor and communication systems needed to collect the intelligence needed to defend our nation's maritime interests.

Above, left: *A Coast Guardsman in Miami tests a discovered suspect substance to determine if it is a narcotic. (Telfair Brown, U.S. Coast Guard)*

Above: *Reducing the demand for illegal drugs is a part of the Coast Guard's War on Drugs. Petty Officer Carlos Cruz hands out anti-drug knick-knacks to teenagers following his anti-drug-use presentation at a high school in Miami. (Danielle DeMarino, U.S. Coast Guard)*

Spending time with kids is a high priority for Chief Petty Officer James Walker. The children are a part of an eight-day Drug Education for Youth summer camp at Coast Guard Group St. Petersburg, Florida. (Eric Eggen, U.S. Coast Guard)

Suspected smugglers surrender to an armed Coast Guard crew ending another chase and the seizure of more contraband drugs and the vessel. (U.S. Coast Guard)

Helicopter Interdiction Tactical Squadron—HITRON

Captain Jeffrey Karonis, USCG

Cuba's East Coast. 3 September 1999.

Prepare to be boarded? I don't think so.

The drug smuggler driving a "go-fast" looks at the large ships around him on this sunny Caribbean morning, smiles, and pushes his throttles forward. His plan is to once again deliver his load of illegal drugs through the Windward Passage, that busy ocean highway between Cuba and Haiti, to waiting traffickers in the Bahamas. One of the nearby ships is a tanker that the boat's skipper uses to mask his approach. The other ships are the Coast Guard cutters Gallatin and Seneca. Seizing the chance to flaunt his tremendous speed advantage, he roars his go-fast through the mile-wide gap between the two cutters. It is a decision he will soon regret, as this is not the typical Coast Guard counter-drug patrol.

"Set the go-fast response bill!" Loudspeakers and alarms on the cutters echo across the calm water as the ships' crews—and a new law enforcement tactic—are now set into motion. Aircrews rush to suit up with body armor and make pre-flight checks. Combat information center personnel on both cutters track the target with radar. In stifling hot engine rooms on both ships, watch standers rush to bring all engines and turbines on line for flank speed. Boat crews dash to install and load their boats' machine guns and suit out for another spine-jarring pursuit. Work is quick and professional, having done this twice before in just the last eighteen days.

Captain Steve Branham, Operation New Frontier task force commander, issues orders and within minutes armed Coast Guard helicopters leap off flight decks in hot pursuit. More backup is on the way, as each cutter launches its Over the Horizon Rigid Hull Boat, a high-speed pursuit craft. To Branham and the several hundred Coast Guardsmen on the cutters and aircrews flying overhead, the "end game"—as drug warriors call the final apprehension—is never in doubt.

Commander Roscoe Torres, aircraft commander on the lead MD900 helicopter embarked in Gallatin, and squadron commander of Helicopter Interdiction Tactical Squadron Ten—or HITRON 10—goes through a detailed checklist. Petty Officer Richard Forbes, the aerial gunner, trains his M-240 .30-caliber machine gun ahead of the racing go-fast and fires "stitches" or bursts of warning shots into the water to convince the trafficker to stop. This fails, so Torres orders Forbes to shoot out the go-fast's engines. Precisely aimed shots from a .50-caliber sniper rifle leave the go-fast with its one-ton cargo of marijuana dead in the water and immediately surrounded by armed Coast Guard boarding officers from the pursuing Coast Guard boats.

As he is handcuffed and begins to ponder the likelihood of many years in a United States federal prison, the go-fast operator is heard to mutter in disgust, "Those damn birds."

Frustration, and the New Threat

Since the late 1970s the Coast Guard and the drug traffickers have engaged in a constant struggle both on the high seas and in coastal regions between North and South America. This struggle has seen successes, failures, and frustrations on both sides. At first, the Coast Guard was able to deter the large bulk marijuana shipments carried by small foreign freighters, but the pendulum swung in the late 1980s when the traffickers started moving multi-ton quantities of cocaine to meet

A suspect drug-running boat encounters a warning "stitch" of machine-gun fire from a Coast Guard HITRON helicopter. A gunner aboard the helicopter will selectively shoot each of the go-fast's outboard engines if the boat fails to stop. (William R. Greer)

the growing demand in the United States and to reap greater profits from an increasingly popular drug.

Traffickers used airplanes. They used sailboats. They used large and small freighters, all with varying degrees of success. But each method had limitations. Increased radar coverage, in-flight interceptions by specially configured U.S. Customs Service and Coast Guard aircraft, and multi-national efforts all hindered air shipments. Hidden compartments were built into sailboats and in voids or fuel tanks on merchant ships, but Coast Guard boarding teams used hi-tech fiber optic equipment, intelligence information, and thorough searches to counter these methods. The cartel leaders sought even faster, reliable, and economical means to deliver their product. A result was the go-fast boat.

Go-fast is a common description for a thirty- to fifty-foot boat with a low profile and two or more large outboard engines. Capable of carrying over a ton of contraband and extra fuel, and with a two- to four-person crew, these boats can move their cargo from Colombia to the Bahamas or to other Caribbean islands in less than two days. Guided by navigation information from the Global Positioning System, they are all but invisible to search planes in daylight and present a minimal radar target. Most importantly, their high speed of forty plus

knots gives them the ability to escape any surface craft operated by the Coast Guard.

Admiral James M. Loy, then Commandant of the Coast Guard, knew something had to be done.

A New Solution

Coast Guard law enforcement planners had a difficult task. Defeating the go-fast threat was not going to be easy. The objective was to stop the boat without injuring crewmembers. This had to be done safely, had to use non-lethal delivery methods, and most importantly, it had to be successful. After balancing all of those factors, and following extensive consultation with other federal law enforcement authorities, it became clear new tools, new tactics, and stronger measures were needed. Airborne use of force was the solution. Admiral Loy made it a top priority and ordered an operational test.

Selecting the right people was critical, so Torres and his executive officer, Commander Pat Merrigan, handpicked aircrew members with key qualifications. First, he wanted pilots with instructor experience, since this initial team of squadron personnel would eventually have to teach new aircrew members. Second, he wanted experienced, shipboard-qualified helicopter pilots, since they needed to deploy aboard ship from the start. And finally, he wanted Coast Guard aircrews with prior Defense Department service experience in armed helicopters that met the first two criteria. Once he created this final list it took Torres only a few hours on the phone to get six pilot-volunteers. Lieutenant Jason Church was a typical member of the "first team"; a

Accurate shooting by a gunner, in a HITRON helicopter using a .50-caliber rifle, places a close pattern in each outboard engine on go-fast boats. Some boats with as many as four engines have attempted to continue their escape with three engines shot out. (Jeff Hall, U.S. Coast Guard)

former Army instructor-aviator with thousands of hours flying both the Army's Apache heavily armed attack helicopter and Coast Guard HH-65A Dolphin.

For a helicopter, the Coast Guard selected the civilian model MD900 Explorer helicopter. A successful airframe in the commercial market, it was safer for flight deck crews since it has no tail rotor. Pilots liked to fly it, and it was easy to maintain. Roomy inside, it had everything Torres and his pilots felt necessary to handle this challenging mission: armor in key locations, good operating range, two engines, and a mounting for a .30-caliber machine gun.

From coping with weather and sea conditions not always of their own choosing, Coast Guard people know how to adapt and improvise. The HITRON team exemplified this flexibility at its best. Commander Torres and his squadron talked to the Army's elite special operations aviation forces. They talked to Navy helicopter units. And finally, they talked to the Marines.

Merrigan was a former Marine who had flown in combat in both Lebanon and Grenada. In his 5,000 hours of flying helicopters he liked to note that he had "shot, shot at, and been shot up." Merrigan recommended training with the Marines at Camp Lejeune. The base offered training for sharpshooters and Marine helicopters to support aerial gunnery training.

With months of training now behind his team, HITRON aerial gunner Charlie Hopkins, a former member of the "Nightstalker" Army special operations aviation regiment and veteran of both the Gulf War and Panama, was under a lot of pressure. It was March 1999 and this was to be HITRON's graduation exercise.

Vice Admiral John Shkor, commander of the Coast Guard Atlantic Area, and other top leaders were at Camp Lejeune to observe the final training event and make the "go-no go" recommendation to the Commandant. Marksman Hopkins handled pressure well. Kneeling in the door of the helicopter—flying alongside the speeding target— he fixed his sight on the target, a towed go-fast boat, steadied his heavy .50-caliber rifle, and put three rounds inside a four-inch group on an outboard engine. With a sly grin, an observing Marine general remarked, "Couldn't you get them a little tighter?"

The test was a complete success. Vice Admiral Shkor said, "Go!"

Above: Sting Ray helicopters are armed with M240, 7.62mm machine guns. "Aviation gunner" Petty Officer Edward Marrufo holds a RC50 laser-sighted .50-caliber "disabling rifle." The Coast Guard armed aircraft again in 2002, the first since World War II. (William R. Greer)

Operation New Frontier—One Team

The plan was coming together fast. But something was missing. Captain Bruce Stubbs, a senior planner and one of the program's creators, realized that once a go-fast was stopped, apprehension teams needed to get on the scene quickly. He pressed to have Gallatin *and* Seneca, *the two cutters selected for* Operation New Frontier, *equipped with long-range pursuit boats.*

The tools were found, the people were trained, and the green light was given. Admiral Loy ordered deployment of Operation New Frontier, *proof of the concept for non-lethal use of force at sea.*

New Frontier represented a new vision in the Coast Guard: one standing, integrated mission team. The team had to do everything together, and the three unit commanding officers made it a constant imperative. Helicopter launch orders were given simultaneously. Air and boat crews had to be inseparable and complementary teams as they operated together far over the horizon. Executive officers on the two cutters even synchronized the ships' internal routines to accommodate extensive joint operations.*

Going Hunting

On a hot August afternoon, one of the most potent law enforcement forces the United States has ever deployed at sea slid quietly out of a Florida base. One team was going hunting—cutters, helicopters, and pursuit boats— and life for the go-fasts would never be the same.

On 16 August 1999, at less than 100 feet above the sea, Hopkins was under pressure—again. His helicopter, piloted by Merrigan and Church, with another MD900 flying nearby as cover, chased down a speeding, heavily loaded go-fast trying to escape into the sanctuary of Cuban waters. Smugglers knew they were just short of Cuban waters and were confident pursuing Coast Guard forces would have to stop in several minutes. And as far as the smugglers knew, Coast Guard helicopters did not shoot at drug boats.

But for these smugglers luck had run out. Rounds fired from the .30-caliber machine gun from Hopkins'

M-240 hurled up columns of seawater just yards ahead of the smugglers. As unexpected as the warning shots were, they did not deter them. The boat still flew on at high speed through the bullets' water bursts. Merrigan was worried they would get away. He knew it had all come down to this—months of training, secrecy, innovation, and the hope of the U.S. counter-drug community that this small Coast Guard team could finally stop these go-fasts with their drug cargoes. It was now time to turn up the heat.

Two .50-caliber shots from Hopkin's rifle and one go-fast engine was disabled. The smugglers were determined, however, and kept going even when their speed diminished substantially. The go-fast crew was just 1,000 yards from Cuban waters and only seconds from pursuit when Hopkins steadied his rifle once more, aimed and shot out the remaining engine on their fleeing boat.

The pursuit boats from Gallatin *and* Seneca *pounded at high speed through eight-foot seas and were on scene in minutes. The boat carried over one ton of illegal drugs. With the extra fuel found on board, the smugglers could have been in the Bahamas the next morning to deliver their million-dollar cargo. The* New Frontier *forces were ecstatic—they did it!*

An armed long-range pursuit boat launched from the same cutters deploying the armed helicopters pursues a go-fast boat. These special Coast Guard boats, working as a team with the ship and helicopters, make the seizure and retrieve contraband after the helicopter's gunner disables the drug-runner's boat, holding all until the arrival of the cutter. (William R. Greer)

New Dimensions

Tom Beard

"It all began—as usual for a military service—though scuttlebutt," explains helicopter pilot Lieutenant Bruce Decker. "I first heard of the possibility of sending a helo to the Adriatic on Wednesday morning." By Friday afternoon in May 1999, Decker was a ship's department-head in charge of a helicopter and crew aboard Coast Guard Cutter *Bear* en route to the Adriatic to join the Navy's combat fleet in the Kosovo war zone. Decker had just returned home to Atlantic City from two months in the Caribbean where he and his crew engaged in skirmishes against drug smugglers.

These sudden, unpredicted moves are all in a day's work for Coast Guard aircrews. All Coast Guard crews are in a military force—relentlessly occupied—in a different kind of warfare. Activities might include search and rescue, disaster relief, pursuing drug smugglers, capturing

Above: *Two Coast Guard HH-65As on the ice at Cape Crozier, the most easterly point of Ross Island in the Antarctic. This cape is noted for being the farthest south that emperor penguins have a breeding colony. Coast Guard helicopters form a part of the ship's company for all icebreakers making the annual trek to the Antarctic. These Coast Guard ships, guided by helicopters, break the paths for supply ships bringing supplies for the country's Antarctic research efforts. (U.S. Coast Guard)*

Above: *A rescue swimmer dangles in space from a helicopter hoist approaching a cliff for the rescue of a stranded climber. (Gary Todoroff)*

Left: *High winds and ice-filled waves forced the disabled crabber* Alaskan Monarch *toward the rocks off St. Paul Island in the Bering Sea. The Coast Guard cutter could not reach the crabber—trapped in an icepack—to tow it to safety. A Coast Guard helicopter, instead, hoisted the crew from the stricken boat's bow. The master and mate, struggling from the pilothouse forward to the vessel's bow for a helicopter pick-up, were struck as a towering wave of ice-filled seawater rolled over the vessel washing them overboard. The helicopter immediately shifted its hover and recovered the men from the sea. Ice and unceasing waves pounding* Alaskan Monarch *against the rocks soon destroyed the crabber. (Ralph B. Starr, U.S. Coast Guard Art Collection)*

Opposite: *Heading for the flight line in the early morning light to "strap on" a helicopter is a typical way for flight crews to begin a day aboard a Coast Guard air station. (Gary Todoroff)*

281

A helicopter air crewman lowers a rescue basket, attached to the end of the cable, to two survivors clinging to the bottom of a capsized boat. The survivors are without life-jackets, but do have a life ring, making their chance of survival quite low if the helicopter does not arrive before the boat sinks. The wind-whipped waves are from the helicopter rotor-downwash, which can be seventy miles per hour. (U.S. Coast Guard)

Above: Coast Guard helicopter crews are called on to rescue people from seaside cliffs. This operation requires perfect teamwork among the aircrew. The pilots must control their aircraft within feet of shear rock walls, sometimes in gusty wind conditions, while the rescue swimmer, maneuvered on the hoist by the SAR air crewman, works the cliff-face with all of its dangers from falling rocks and potential slides to retrieve victims. (Gary Todoroff)

Right: Coast Guard aircraft may be spotted at isolated locations anywhere worldwide. Always apparent, even where few might see the aircraft, is the evidence of pride taken by the crew. The crew of this C-130 takes that extra moment, even in harsh arctic weather, to hand turn all the propellers, aligning them with a "squared away look." (U.S. Coast Guard)

282

illegal aliens, meeting environmental crises, or conducting arctic scientific operations. Geography and nature frequently collide adding to mission hazards. All these encounters by flight crews can continue unexpectedly and randomly over a thirty-year career. They might start on the first day.

This happened to Lieutenant (jg) Randy Meador on his first mission out of flight training. Meador was the co-pilot of an HH-60J helicopter involved in the rescue of crews from four sailboats sinking in a May 2000 storm off the Carolina coast. His first mission—successful—lasted fourteen hours.

Whether it is a major flood, hurricane, drug interdiction, sinking ship, war, or a trapped hiker on a cliff, Coast Guard aircrews are there when needed, frequently with just moments' notice.

Two Coast Guard HU-25B fixed-wing jets specially equipped with surface, oil scanning AIREYE radars flew from the U.S. to the Persian Gulf for *Desert Storm*. Preparation time for the crews was just three weeks. This included training in chemical, biological, and nuclear warfare, desert survival, theater intelligence, and small arms firing. They, in this brief period, also grabbed moments for shots, passports, and personal paper-work and yet another goodbye to families.

These random and diverse missions anywhere in the world are possible for Coast Guard aircrews because of a time-honored tradition established at the beginning of Coast Guard aviation: "The crew that flies the aircraft also fixes it"; therefore, the typical or necessary deep support-line utilized by other military services, for the Coast Guard is thin or non-existent. This independence makes for rapid deployments anywhere, justly reflecting the Coast Guard's motto, *Semper Paratus*. Coast Guard aircrews greet each day with anticipation of an unexpected battle on unfamiliar fields.

This aviation legacy began in April 1916 when Third Lieutenant Elmer F. Stone and Second Lieutenant Charles E. Sugden entered the Naval Aeronautic Station, Pensacola, for flight training. Stone became the Coast Guard's first aviator, Sugden followed as number two. For both men, interest in aviation began the moment they saw their first aeroplanes. The

young officers were among the crew in CGC *Onondaga* berthed adjacent to Glenn L. Curtiss' aerodrome in Newport News, Virginia, where pilots were training for the new war in Europe, and they watched with intense interest the many daily flights from the nearby aerodrome. An aeroplane might, they speculated, be a good spotter and a rescue device.

A flamboyant Thomas F. Baldwin, former nineteenth-century balloon aerialist, entrepreneur, and aeroplane salesman for Curtiss, seeing an opportunity with the curiosity expressed by the young Coast Guard officers, offered the loan of a Curtiss "F" flying boat—with a pilot—for tests to see if it was capable of aerial searching and other tasks useful to the Coast Guard.

The Curtiss demonstration convinced Captain Benjamin M. Chiswell, *Onondaga*'s commanding officer, of the value of aircraft to the service, and today Chiswell is accorded the title of "Father of Coast Guard Aviation"— though he himself was never an aviator.

That same month, Chiswell, Byron R. Newton, Assistant Secretary of the Treasury, and Curtiss met in *Onondaga*'s wardroom to plan an airplane for the Coast Guard. Their ideas were profound, and as a result, far-reaching. The group initially sketched out a plan—now appearing quite naive—later recorded in a letter, for an aircraft utilizing a common Coast Guard surfboat "with wings and motor so arranged that they could be quickly eliminated when the boat lighted on the water . . . and would be, instead of a flying boat, an ordinary motor surfboat."

This particular scheme, while obviously impractical, did lead to a concept for flying lifeboats. Chiswell, moreover went on to predict, "I believe [the aircraft] would be the biggest find for the Coast Guard of the century and might be the means of saving hundreds of lives." The idea for seaplanes for use by the Coast Guard was born.

Vestiges of ideas from this meeting were incorporated in seaplanes used through World War II. The Navy's NC-4—piloted by the Coast Guard's Stone—the first aircraft to span the Atlantic, was a variation on this group's original flying surfboat concept.

Commander Elmer Stone, Coast Guard Aviator #1, was the pilot of the Navy's NC-4 in 1919 during the first transatlantic flight by any aircraft, for which he was awarded the Navy Cross. Stone was the Navy's seaplane test pilot and set the world speed record for amphibious planes in 1934. He was a pioneer in the use of aircraft for rescue and patrol missions. (U.S. Coast Guard)

A PBY Catalina maneuvers on the water as a mechanic on the wing checks the port engine as a J2F Duck passes overhead. These two aircraft are typical of the fleet for the Coast Guard through World War II. (National Museum of Naval Aviation)

For anti-submarine patrols in World War II, a .50-caliber flexible gun installation was locally manufactured at CGAS Brooklyn "simply because we had nothing better," according to Gunner's Mate Robert O'Leary—as with so many tasks accomplished by Coast Guardsmen. Metalsmith Carl Simon and Gunner's Mate Ralph Judkins made the installation in the bow hatch, which was normally used for mooring-line handling when the airplane was on the water. (Robert J. O'Leary)

The notion of using "flying lifeboats" or various versions of seaplanes and amphibians continued thereafter for nearly six decades with some isolated but remarkable successes. During the early years of World War II along the Atlantic coast, seaplanes located over 1,000 survivors of torpedoed ships and rescued more than 100 victims by landing in open seas. On one occasion, a seaplane overloaded with survivors had to taxi miles of open-ocean to reach shore, somewhat mitigating the *Onondaga*'s bizarre boat/airplane concepts created more than a quarter century before.

But it was the flying boat's shortcomings that later shaped an irreparable fissure between Coast Guard officers, with seaplane supporters ultimately losing a deeply emotional, sometimes acrimonious battle. An

The crew readies a PH-3 for a wartime patrol off the Atlantic seaboard. Seaplanes and amphibians dominated the Coast Guard's aircraft fleet until the arrival of the helicopter. A need came near the end of the 1930s for a seaplane for offshore work to replace the aging craft then in use. This was at a time of the modern seaplane. The Coast Guard, however, purchased twelve Hall Aluminum Company flying boats reminiscent of aircraft development of an earlier generation. The Hall Flying Boat was of stick, wire, and fabric construction emulating a basic design reaching back to the end of World War I. These aircraft were purchased in 1940 for $170,000 and went out of service in 1944. Today's aircraft can expect to remain in service from twenty to forty or more years. The HU-25 Falcon began service in 1982 and the HH-65 in 1984. Both are expected to provide service well into the twenty-first century. (Robert J. O'Leary)

entirely new and remarkable aircraft emerged, itself eventually becoming an icon to worldwide lifesaving.

Dr. Igor Sikorsky flew his experimental VS-300 helicopter in a public demonstration on 13 May 1940. Useful helicopters were still years away, but with a possible war just ahead, the Coast Guard with its added aerial responsibilities supporting the Coast Neutrality Patrol needed a large number of aircraft. Two visionary officers saw the potential of Sikorsky's revolutionary aircraft.

Lieutenant Frank A. Erickson moved with his ship-borne seaplane from CGC *Taney*, then in Honolulu, to the Navy's air base in Pearl Harbor on Ford Island in early fall of 1941. He was in charge of the patrol and utility aircraft operating from that island's runways and sea-lanes. It is also about the same time, coincidentally, when Erickson read an article about the flight by Sikorsky's new helicopter. He realized almost instantly this unique flying machine was the future aircraft for rescue and essential to the Coast Guard's role. Profound events shortly would sear this idea into a lifelong passion.

A Jayhawk is moving in to make a hoist from the stern of a Coast Guard 41-footer. The pilot in command sits on the right-hand side, flying the helicopter sideways as shown, in order to keep the boat in sight. The hoist and its operator are also on the aircraft's right side. Once over the boat and possibly out of the pilot's sight, the crewman standing at the open doorway aft, calls for the pilot to move "right," "left," "forward," "aft," "up," and "down" as necessary for the pilot to maneuver, maintaining a steady position above the boat. The boat can be moving at any speed for this maneuver. If a Coast Guard small boat recovers a survivor in need of critical medical attention, the victim can be hoisted in a basket or litter for quick transport to a hospital. Equipment such as pumps and fire-fighting equipment can be quickly passed between helicopter and vessel with this method using the helicopter's hoist. (Joe Dye, U.S. Coast Guard)

Above: *The memorial to the victims of the attack on Pearl Harbor sits astraddle the battleship USS* Arizona. *More than a half-century following the day that gave birth to the idea of a rescue helicopter a HH-65A flies overhead. On 7 December 1941 Lieutenant Frank A. Erickson viewed the carnage from his aerie in the airplane control tower located on Ford Island just ahead the helicopter's nose. Erickson was frustrated he had no way to rescue the hundreds of crewmen he watched struggling in the water from the burning and sinking ships along battleship row. From recent knowledge he had then of a new device built by Dr. Igor Sikorsky, Erickson already envisioned a new craft that would be the perfect rescue vehicle for the Coast Guard. The vision he witnessed of the carnage drove his efforts over the next decade to develop that helicopter. (U.S. Coast Guard)*

Right: *A Coast Guard HH-60J lands on Flamingo Cay, Bahamas, to evacuate those needing medical attention and bringing aid. A vessel smuggling eighty Haitians ran aground on the cay leaving the passengers to survive on the beach without food or water. (John Gaffney, U.S. Coast Guard)*

Erickson, with extensive experience flying seaplanes from sead-romes and ships, was acutely aware of their severe limitations. Recent crashes, along with the death of a friend in an offshore seaplane-crash, and the subsequent tragic crash in Greenland killing Lieutenant John H. Pritchard, drove Erickson with a single-minded endeavor to seek safer

LIEUTENANT JOHN H. PRITCHARD — TOM BEARD

Coast Guard aircraft brought their rescue role to the Greenland icescape in World War II. With their amphibians, pilots could land on the snow-covered ice to recover downed allied aircrews who crashed ferrying aircraft to Europe. One tragic event occurred when a J2F-5, flown by Lieutenant John H. Pritchard, Jr., launched from

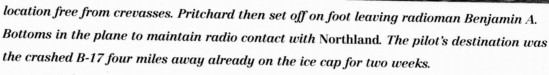

the sea next to CGC Northland *to recover survivors of a downed B-17. He landed the amphibian aircraft safely in the snow, with the landing gear retracted, on a*

location free from crevasses. Pritchard then set off on foot leaving radioman Benjamin A. Bottoms in the plane to maintain radio contact with Northland. *The pilot's destination was the crashed B-17 four miles away already on the ice cap for two weeks.*

Pritchard returned through the snow to his plane with three of the most severely injured men, planning to fly them to Northland. *With the added weight of three survivors on board the overloaded aircraft could not get airborne. The next attempt was successful—with one Army man left behind alone on the ice to face the coming night. The short arctic day soon ended and it was dark when Pritchard reached the ship. Aided by the ship's searchlights, he landed the amphibian in the icy waters alongside* Northland.

The weather the following day was too bad to consider retrieving the abandoned airman. Pritchard attempted the flight anyway and successfully landed in a snowstorm then sweeping the icecap. He located and picked up the lone survivor but his airplane crashed during takeoff in the blinding blizzard. His amphibian's wreckage was found later. Pritchard, Bottoms, and the passenger died in the crash. Both crewmen were awarded the Distinguished Flying Cross posthumously.

Above: Lieutenant John A. Pritchard, Jr., watches as the Grumman J2F amphibian he is about to fly is lifted by crane from its cradle aboard CGC *Northland* just before his fateful flight. A crane lowered the airplane overboard for a water takeoff and raised it back aboard after a water landing. This method of ship/aircraft operations was used extensively in Arctic waters. (U.S. Coast Guard)

Top: Lieutenant John A. Pritchard, Jr., with crewman Benjamin A. Bottoms begins the take-off run through icy waters to rescue the crew of an Army Air Corp B-17 on a Greenland icecap in 1942. The aircraft and crew never returned from this flight. (U.S. Coast Guard)

ways to rescue people from the sea. Erickson's dream to start a helicopter project came to life on 7 December 1941 with the first Japanese bomb striking Ford Island. He was base duty-officer at the moment of attack. Erickson spent the first hours during the raid at his general quarter's station in the aircraft control tower at the epicenter of the Japanese assault. He watched, helpless, as thousands died within his view, unrecoverable in flaming harbor waters except through gallant efforts by a few brave souls manning small boats. Ignominiously, the next few days, he flew the only surviving aircraft—unarmed Coast Guard amphibians—toting shotguns and rifles, looking for the Japanese fleet.

Five weeks following the Pearl Harbor attack, while Erickson searched the Pacific for the Japanese task force, removed from his dream of creating a life-saving aircraft, Sikorsky's first operational helicopter, the XR-4, made its pioneer flight. The novel craft flew only a short-lived, six-month Army Air Corps evaluation project. But having demonstrated no real use to the Army for the war effort, it was returned to Sikorsky.

Following the Air Corp's testing of the XR-4, Sikorsky demonstrated it to the public in April 1942, hoping to encourage interest from any government agency, including the post office, that might find use for this

The amphibious HU-16E appears to waddle from the water up a seaplane ramp. The Albatross was the end of an era for the Coast Guard of airplanes operating from the water for over sixty years. "The ramp," being a rare vestige from the very beginning of naval aviation, is still found at older Coast Guard air stations, where they are still being used to launch trailer-borne Coast Guard port-security boats. (U.S. Coast Guard)

Dr. Igor Sikorsky dangling in an early successful helicopter hoist with Commander Frank Erickson flying the HNS at the Coast Guard Air Station Brooklyn in 1944. The hoist was one of many "firsts" created by Erickson and his crew, leading to the helicopter's successes in many areas years later. (U.S. Coast Guard)

Captain William J. Kossler was the silent power behind Erickson, pushing the often disdained helicopter project. Kossler, as head of aircraft engineering at Coast Guard Headquarters, was the visionary as far back as 1941 behind the potential of helicopters for most of their eventual uses, which included such diverse tasks as anti-submarine warfare, forest fire-fighting, and insect spraying. He used his influence and communication skills to sidestep or overcome near-continuous opposition to the helicopter's development from within the Coast Guard and without. His sudden death in 1946 left a vacuum that nearly stopped helicopter development or acceptance in the Coast Guard for almost a decade. (U.S. Coast Guard)

Early helicopter experiments were rudimentary and courageous. The landing gear on an HNS is being exchanged for skids fabricated in the unit's shop by Commander Frank Erickson's group at CGAS Brooklyn in 1944. This experiment determined if a helicopter could operate with skids instead of wheels, a device common on helicopters sixty years later. The maintenance crew shows confidence, not only in a questionable and unproven machine but also in its pilot, Lieutenant Stewart Graham, as they work on the helicopter in flight. (U.S. Coast Guard)

unusual vehicle. Commander William J. Kossler, USCG, then chief of the Coast Guard's aviation engineering, and Erickson's close friend, witnessed this flight along with representatives from several government agencies. This exhibition convinced Kossler the helicopter would meet many Coast Guard and Navy mission requirements, so he enthusiastically recommended its purchase. Assistant commandant, Rear Admiral Lloyd Chalker, thinking the quarter-million-dollar price for three machines excessive, hesitated until Kossler expressed an obvious reality—understood by nearly all: although this aircraft did not appear essential for the war, it did hold a far grander potential.

Shortly afterward, Erickson received unexpected orders to the Coast Guard's air station in New York—Kossler had arranged the move to have Erickson near the Sikorsky factory to execute his plan. The first step was to get Erickson to witness a flight at the Sikorsky plant in Bridgeport, Connecticut. "It was the 26th of June, 1942, a day I will never forget," Erickson wrote. "I was fascinated with both the VS-300 and Mr. Sikorsky, and jotted down every bit of information that I could during the few hours that we were there. At home that night I started drafting a report to Headquarters. It took me most of two nights to outline my proposals. Since efforts to sell the helicopter as a life-saving device had not been successful, I stressed the application of the helicopter as an anti-submarine weapon which could be operated from ships in convoys."

Erickson and Kossler knew from their conversations with Sikorsky that the Navy, which purchased aircraft for the Coast Guard in wartime, would not consider helicopters for rescue purposes. Navy officials might consider the machine for anti-submarine warfare, ASW. Erickson was convinced, if he controlled the development of helicopters for any Navy program, he could run a simultaneous development project surreptitiously, enabling him to produce the ideal Coast Guard rescue craft.

Response to Erickson's request was quick. One month later, the Navy's Bureau of Aeronautics acquired four helicopters for study and development for anti-submarine duties by Navy and Coast Guard aviation forces. These results came about primarily through Kossler's nearly single-handed efforts. The Navy did not display any enthusiasm for helicopters but did allow the Coast Guard to dabble in its development without support. The Navy official most knowledgeable and influential claimed "that this type of craft could not be built large enough to carry a load to be of any value." But it was the British who provided the major break needed by Kossler and Erickson. In January 1943 they offered to purchase one thousand helicopters.

Kossler, using this news, urged Coast Guard Commandant Admiral Russell R. Waesche to assign Coast Guard helicopter crews as convoy escorts as a part of the organization's ASW responsibilities. Kossler further recommended the Coast Guard establish a school to train British helicopter pilots. This offer came despite the fact that neither the Coast Guard nor Navy had any helicopter pilots at the time; the Army only had one. Erickson summed up the day Waesche viewed a helicopter demonstration, urged as a result of the British interest, by saying, "'Igor's Nightmare,' which had been something of a joke around Bridgeport, even among the workers in his plant, was at last being given serious consideration." The Navy backed the Coast Guard's helicopter school scheme plus experiments to determine shipboard suitability for use of the helicopter in hunting submarines.

Erickson received his checkout from Charles L. Morris, Sikorsky's chief test pilot. He qualified as the naval service's first helicopter pilot in June 1943 by flying three hours at the Sikorsky factory in the XR-4. Lieutenant (jg) Stewart R. Graham, USCG, qualified in October 1943 as the Coast Guard's second helicopter pilot after three and a half hours flight-time. The novice, Erickson, was Graham's instructor. Graham worked with Erickson throughout the development period, later going on to become the Navy's first helicopter test pilot and developer of the Navy's helicopter anti-submarine warfare. Graham flew the world's first ASW mission in a British helicopter from a British merchant ship in mid-Atlantic in January 1944.

Commander Frank Erickson in 1944 experimenting with early hoisting equipment designed and built by his unit, developing techniques by using "live" volunteers. The horseshoe-shaped collar is still used as a device for recovery of military personnel trained in its use. However, Erickson also designed and developed a basket that has served more successfully for all types of recoveries. (U.S. Coast Guard)

Commander Frank Erickson, in his endeavor to sell the idea of the helicopter to others, invited General William "Wild Bill" Donovan, U.S. Army (center), in 1944 to observe the special capabilities of this little-known flying machine for possible use by the OSS. General Frank Lowe, U.S. Army (right), was an enthusiastic Erickson supporter and was the first military officer not trained or qualified as an aviator to learn to fly the helicopter. He was taught by Erickson at the Coast Guard's school. Lowe was on the Truman Committee, named for its head investigator, Senator Harry S Truman, for the National Defense Program searching for weapons to pursue the war. Lowe's enthusiastic influence likely led to the Army's early acceptance of helicopters. (Naval Historical Foundation)

Lieutenant Stewart R. Graham, a former Coast Guard surfman, at the moment of liftoff on an anti-submarine mission in the first flight from a ship in convoy. The helicopter is a British R-4 (HNS), the first helicopter to go to England, and the ship is the British freighter Daghestan. This flight commenced near the Azores in January 1944, proving the helicopter could go to sea. (Stewart R. Graham)

Right: *Captain David Gershowitz flew the helicopter for* Operation High Jump, *the military's first excursion to the Antarctic and Little America in 1946. Since Gershowitz "had attended an agriculture college," according to him he was selected as the keeper of live specimens on the expedition's return. He had penguins swimming in his bathtub in his New York apartment before delivering all to labs and zoos. (David Gershowitz estate)*

Far right: *Lieutenant Stewart R. Graham and Brownie aboard a Sikorsky HO3S-2 during test flights in 1947 at the Coast Guard Rotary Wing Development Unit at Elizabeth City. Brownie at the time had more helicopter flight time than most pilots in the world. The dog regularly accompanied Graham on test flights. (Stewart R. Graham)*

Opposite, top left: *The Coast Guard led in the development of helicopter flight simulators. Erickson sought training devices to aid in teaching the unique task performed by helicopter pilots. The complexities of helicopter flight were duplicated in this mechanical helicopter synthetic-trainer built in the hangar at the Coast Guard Air Station Brooklyn in 1944 by Donald Dodge of the Atlantic Elevator company and Lieutenant (jg) E. K. Smith, USN, attached to the Navy's Bureau of Aeronautics Special Devices Division. Like the helicopter, there was no precedent established on which to base this work. A device replicating helicopter flight was not built again until nearly two decades later with the advent of computer-based simulators. (U.S. Coast Guard)*

The novel aircraft was virtually unknown when Commander Frank A. Erickson began training pilots and testing aircraft with a small cadre of volunteers in late 1943. Most in the Coast Guard were against any proposals to develop this aircraft, as it was deemed useless. Erickson had to wage a constant campaign for public acceptance as well as create a machine that had useful properties. In addition he had to surmount overwhelming criticism from seniors and contemporaries. Here, Lieutenant (jg) Stewart R. Graham, Coast Guard helicopter pilot #2, is demonstrating a helicopter on the Capitol steps for congressional representatives. The crewman dangling midair from the hoist is in uniform complete with white hat. For all legislators, this is their first view of this novel contraption. Proud crewmembers inserted a period between the digits 4 and 0 of the aircraft's abbreviated serial number seen on the fuselage as their expression of excellence, "4.0" being a Navy term for a perfect score. (U.S. Coast Guard)

But just as suddenly as the promise arose, the urgency for helicopters as weapons against the Axis's submarine threat was dashed by a seemingly unrelated event in May 1943. A Navy torpedo bomber, flying from an escort carrier, sank a German submarine in the North Atlantic. This already-in-place, effective potential signaled the end of the German submarine threat in the North Atlantic. ASW helicopters were no longer needed for World War II, nor would they be capable in that capacity for many years following.

Erickson's first task in New York was to train fixed-wing pilots as helicopter pilots, and then, within a few weeks, as instructors in order to meet an expected influx of British pilots suddenly transitioning to helicopters. At the beginning, Coast Guard headquarters would not assign

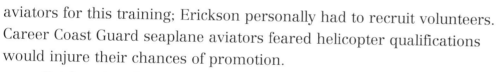

Above: *An external view of the HH-60J simulation trainer where the virtual world from inside is "world-wide." The Coast Guard, a pioneer in this field, began using the modern trainers at the Aviation Training Center in Mobile, Alabama, in 1972. The training complex containing several trainers, and classrooms are in Erickson Hall, named for Captain Frank Erickson. Every rotary-wing aviator in the Coast Guard trains in these computer-generated motion simulators at least once a year to achieve that extra edge needed in the critical flight regimes challenging Coast Guard crews every day. (U.S. Coast Guard)*

aviators for this training; Erickson personally had to recruit volunteers. Career Coast Guard seaplane aviators feared helicopter qualifications would injure their chances of promotion.

Erickson's only success was assigning present or former enlisted pilots as the first helicopter instructors. Graham, a former enlisted pilot, was the only instructor Erickson had for his school. Graham, too, attempted recruiting pilots but could not interest anyone. He later disclosed, "I was looked upon as not having all my marbles, was ridiculed beyond belief among my fellow flyers, that I would jeopardize my well-being to fly such a contraption." Erickson complained further, "There were many aviators who still insisted that the Coast Guard's future in aviation required the operation of seaplanes from the open seas."

It was just one month after the school opened, with two instructors and one student, that the then little known helicopter received national attention. Erickson delivered needed blood plasma to victims of an explosion in a Navy destroyer. A winter's storm grounded all airplanes and blocked highways to the hospital in the New York area where the plasma was needed. The helicopter was the only transport that could get through.

Suddenly in mid-1944 with signs of a victory in Europe, the British order for helicopters dwindled from the hundreds anticipated to just a few aircraft. Erickson's school was closed after only operating a few months. Of the 103 pilots trained by the world's first helicopter school, seventy-one were Coast Guard enlisted and officers, and eight were U.S. Naval aviators. Others were British, Army, FAA, and manufacturer test pilots.

The Coast Guard was a pioneer with the modern flight simulator. A flight crew can train and maintain flight skills without ever burning a pound of jet fuel in a real aircraft. Computer-controlled simulation-trainers feature motion and visual stimulation along with factual recreation of actual flight control and instrument responses through the full spectrum of flight conditions. After very few minutes in the "trainer" there is no sense of simulation for the crew—it is real—the sweat is real! The pilot here is making an approach to a virtual Coast Guard cutter seen through a virtual window with the virtual rotor blades flashing by overhead. The sounds and shaking he experiences are "real." (U.S. Coast Guard)

The war's anticipated ending by 1945 forced the cancellation of all helicopter production. Naysayers appeared correct. There was no place in real aviation for the helicopter. High-level support in the Coast Guard for continuation with any development programs ceased with Kossler's unexpected death in 1946. Erickson, who irritated many superiors in his dogged pursuit, was unprotected now from vociferous, powerful adversaries.

Helicopter development by the Coast Guard languished into the early 1950s. Erickson did, however, with a small devoted group, continue research and development, but his successes were largely ignored. The other military services continued from Erickson's earlier research and aggressively developed the helicopter to meet their missions. By the early 1950s all military services except the Coast Guard were operational with a major dedication to helicopters. Revival of the Coast Guard rescue helicopter came slowly.

However, crews flying Coast Guard helicopters made noteworthy rescues, bringing a second look to this demeaned craft and its humbled backers. A rare event occurred that helped boost the helicopter's early public popularity, and it did not come from stratagems contrived by Kossler or Erickson. Serendipity sometimes did a better job. This time the exposure came in the form of a complex rescue.

A near tragedy averted only by the unique abilities of the helicopter garnered international press coverage for the unlikely little training aircraft. Eleven Canadian flyers were marooned on a northern Labrador mountaintop in early spring of 1945 by an airplane crash that brought new attention to the unique lifesaving abilities of the much-maligned helicopter.

The Canadian airmen could not be recovered by conventional methods. Ski-equipped rescue airplanes bogged down in the mushy spring-thaw snow. One airplane crashed attempting to extract survivors leaving its crew behind also to be rescued. The adjacent lake remained frozen through the summer preventing landings by float-equipped airplanes. Waiting months until winter returned, allowing use of ski-equipped land vehicles, remained the only possibility for recovery. That is until Erickson heard about the airmen's plight.

Erickson had a HNS-1, two-seat trainer, disassembled and loaded aboard a C-54 transport to fly to Gander, Newfoundland. The crash site was about 125 miles away over snow-covered mountains. Lieutenant August Kleisch loaded the reassembled machine with seven, five-gallon jerry cans of gasoline lashed outside to the floats for the round trip. En route, he landed on a snow-covered lake to refuel from the gas cans. Kleisch then flew on to the camp where he picked up one survivor, all the aircraft could hold, for the return trip.

As Kleisch landed the first time at the crash site, he recalled, "The sight of the machine brought cheers." The survivors gathered around the strange new aircraft and invited Kleisch into their shelter, built from brush, snow, and parachutes, for coffee. They already had waited two weeks for rescue knowing up to that moment, without the heretofore unknown helicopter, it would be the next winter before new attempts might be made with conventional snow-traveling equipment. The little

Opposite: *An HH-65A is seen from above landing on the stone threshold at the base of the St Georges Reef lighthouse. Helicopters offer quick and easy service to isolated lighthouses compared to the difficulties and hazards for the same assistance by ship or boats. The automation of lighthouses eventually left this as a rare task for helicopters. (Gary Todoroff)*

Initial test by Commander Frank A. Erickson in 1944 using a hoist to rescue a person. All early testing involved using volunteer Coast Guardsmen. This confidence by the crew in the new, untested aircraft and systems reflected their faith in Erickson's belief that the helicopter was, as Erickson constantly extolled, "the road ahead." This phrase soon led to the derogatory comment, "Rotorhead," by many of Erickson's critics. (U.S. Coast Guard)

Modern Coast Guard helicopters offer medical assistance to an expanded maritime community. Here a pregnant woman, in critical condition, is about to be removed from a cruise ship with a modern version of a hoist and basket designed and created sixty years before by Captain Frank Erickson. Note the hundreds of viewers around the periphery observing a rare scene usually only seen by rescuers and survivors. (William R. Greer)

helicopter, pushed by its crew, persevered; the last survivor finally came out three days and nine trips later on the afternoon of 2 May 1945.

Another miracle with helicopters was repeated a little over a year later in a similar arctic rescue by Erickson and his crew when they rescued survivors from a Sabina Airliner crash in Newfoundland. Once again, the unique account was heralded with worldwide news coverage.

The handful of helicopters maintained by the Coast Guard for proficiency of pilots already trained soon started making isolated but noteworthy rescues. Accounts of these unique events crept into newspapers nationwide. Renewed looks at the prospects of this largely ignored vehicle began by the Coast Guard after series of remarkable rescues occurred during the 1950s. Two Coast Guard officers were about to change aviation history.

MacDee & Swede

Tom Beard

*T*he Coast Guard had two dreamers emerge from World War II. Each bore a vision for the future of Coast Guard aviation. Both joined the Navy as seamen in the 1920s, served aboard battleships, and later were Coast Guard Academy graduates, but each led Coast Guard aviation in a different direction. One had an immediate solution; the other still believed in a dream of a little machine that one day could do the job.

The Coast Guard aviation officer corps divided as the aviation program itself moved into uncertainty following World War II. Battles ensued between the two groups, at times with bitter acrimony. Most officers, following service tradition, accepted the seaplane and its inherent problems of being unable to land in the open sea.

Commander Frank A. Erickson's helicopter school had just started. A handful of pilots were beginning to learn to fly this newfangled contraption. Also in that month of July 1944, the end of the Coast Guard's use of seaplanes began, although no one was yet aware.

The Chief of Naval Operations assigned the Coast Guard a task of conducting off-shore landing tests for seaplanes with Captain Donald Bartram MacDiarmid, USCG, in charge.

Landing aircraft on runways is typically done into the wind for a minimum touchdown speed. At sea, winds drive a wave system before it, making landing into the wind like crashing into a series of onrushing walls. Early seaplanes' speeds were low enough that small lightweight aircraft could land and take off between the waves' crests. For larger seaplanes, MacDiarmid developed procedures based on an earlier technique Pan Am clipper pilots utilized by landing in the troughs parallel with the major swell system. This overcame the dangers of crashing into the face of onrushing waves but had the problem of landing crosswind and on an un-level surface.

MacDiarmid believed the PBM Mariner offered a far better service for Coast Guard rescue missions, if using its long-range ability, the airplane could land at sea anywhere to retrieve downed flyers and shipping-disaster victims. He was going to prove it. The consensus among Coast Guard aviators was that the future of Coast Guard aviation continued to require the operation of seaplanes anywhere—on any protected waters or open ocean. His experiments encouraged this supposition.

MacDiarmid's unwavering pursuit toward maintaining the past glories of the "flying lifeboat" was driven by an alarm. He believed, based only on suspicions, the Navy would assume the Coast Guard's aviation search and rescue responsibilities at war's termination, ending what, after three decades, was a rag-tag attempt by the Coast Guard at maintaining a viable air force. And the Navy without a war needed justification for maintaining its mightily wartime-expanded air force.

Meanwhile, Erickson, with unremitting arrogance and single-mindedness, believed some officers—with a definite nod toward MacDiarmid—distracted the Coast Guard from dedicating attention to developing the helicopter, which he deemed was rightly the aircraft of the future for Coast Guard aviation.

Top: Experiments to destroy icebergs were attempted as a part of the *International Ice Patrol.* Bombs were dropped from a HU-16E Albatross with little or no effect and the effort was soon abandoned. (U.S. Coast Guard)

Above: Captain Donald B. MacDiarmid championed seaplanes to the end. His hubris led his admirers and rivals—there were no fence sitters—to elevate "Captain Mac" or "Mac Dee," for those intimately familiar with him, to a legendary status in his lifetime. Stories of his sometimes outlandish endeavors persist in the retelling a half-century later. His career-long efforts to establish the seaplane as the principal tool for rescue at sea failed. However, out of all his research, MacDiarmid established safe methods for landplanes to ditch successfully at sea. (U.S. Coast Guard)

Above: *The "office" in the HU-16E where pilots frequently spent a dozen hours at a stretch flying search patterns over empty oceans. Though the aircraft could land on water, it was restricted to landings and takeoffs only in relatively protected waters. The Coast Guard operated the Albatross primarily as a landplane except for rare occasions where it did land at sea to save survivors. The Navy and Air Force also flew the HU-16. (U.S. Coast Guard)*

Above, right: *On occasion, Coast Guard helicopters climb into the mountains to rescue wayward hikers or victims who fall into swift rivers where only a helicopter with trained rescue personnel might offer assistance. (William R. Greer)*

Lieutenant Bruce Melnick—later the Coast Guard's first astronaut—with his crew flew a twelve-hour mission in the HH-3F Pelican rescuing crew and passengers from the burning cruise-ship Prinsendam *in the Gulf of Alaska. During one two-hour period, Melnick and his crew hoisted 109 ship's passengers delivering them to safety aboard a nearby tanker. They were able to squeeze twenty-four survivors into the Pelican's cabin on one trip. That feat amazed Lieutenant (jg) Terry Sinclair after observing one load in his Pelican. He had never seen more than six passengers previously on any mission in the HH-3F. He noted on this evacuation of* Prinsendam, *"Eighteen was a sight and they were huddled so close together I think five more would have fit. But we were up to maximum power due to the added weight and so moved off." (U.S. Coast Guard)*

Coast Guard officers split in loyalties between these two men—most following MacDiarmid—creating a rift that was evident even two generations later. As the war wound down, Coast Guard aviation suffered a schism in aircraft philosophy and wandered off in two self-destructive ways. The helicopter was not ready and would not be for years, until the turbine engine, and the seaplane was a dinosaur collapsing under its own massiveness. Limited seadromes further restricted its ongoing usefulness. A proliferation of airports created around the world developed for the war effort gave rise to major developments in land planes. They had the ability to skip around oceans.

For three years, MacDiarmid experimented with the Mariner in offshore conditions in the ocean near San Diego. He developed techniques utilizing reversing propellers for stopping and maneuvering on the water and JATO rocket motors attached to accelerate the seaplane's takeoff. MacDiarmid's dogged pursuit, Erickson believed, distracted the Coast Guard from developing the helicopter.

Bitterness within the Coast Guard still held Erickson at bay. Yet seaplanes were slowly becoming expensive behemoths to operate, while wholesale postwar personnel cutbacks substantially reduced the number of crews available at Coast Guard air stations—adding further hardships on the limited crews.

MacDiarmid in the early 1950s was still firmly convinced of the seaplane's future. Erickson and his followers were equally certain of the helicopter's superiority. At CGAS Elizabeth City, with MacDiarmid in command and where Erickson commanded a small helicopter test unit following the war, the Officers' Mess became a battleground for the two quite dynamic, clashing personalities and philosophies. Many pilots, trained under Erickson and now serving under MacDiarmid, walked a narrow line while hedging on their opinions. The battle was finally decided by events rather than by arguments.

During the late 1940s and into the early 1950s while the other services were moving rapidly ahead in this new field by building their helicopter fleets and training flight crews simultaneously, the Coast Guard acquired but a few helicopters and conducted no formal training to qualify new pilots. Some stations had a helicopter for pilot proficiency for those crewmembers already qualified. Typically, these helicopters

were not the "ready aircraft" for rescue. They might be used, however, if the situation could use a helicopter and a pilot happened to be available.

Two major rescues occurred in the 1950s. The first destroyed hopes of further considerations for seaplanes. The second demonstrated a remarkable ability for the helicopter to save lives. Both left an indelible mark on the future. The first episode to change the direction of Coast Guard aviation occurred on 18 January 1953. Lieutenant John Vukic piloting a Coast Guard PBM seaplane crashed in open-seas during takeoff after having rescued eleven survivors from a Navy P2V-5 shot down by Communist Chinese anti-aircraft fire off the China coast. Seven members of the Navy crew were lost along with five Coast Guard crewmen. Though the cause of the accident was engine failure during a critical phase of the takeoff run and not the fault of the highly skilled Vukic or of the technique he used based on MacDiarmid's teachings, open-ocean landings were rarely, if ever, tried again.

The second episode occurred on Christmas Eve 1955 in Yuba City, California.

The Yuba City case marked the end of Coast Guard aviation dating from 1916, and opened up a new "road ahead." The late 1950s and early 1960s saw a major change to Coast Guard aviation. Flying boats still dominated the fleet. PBYs of World War II success prevailed until the mid-1950s with the Coast Guard having more than 120. The larger, war surplus PBMs filled in the declining PBY flying-boat force until 1956 and this was replaced by the huge Navy P5M seaplane. This costly aircraft, in terms of manpower, saw service until 1961 when the Coast Guard finally abandoned seaplanes. The amphibian, HU-16E became the longtime holdover until 1977 but in later years was not used as a seaplane.

A PBY is making a mail delivery and pickup for the CGC Northwind *from an ice island in the arctic, circa 1952. This routine occurred in regions where landings by airplane or seaplane were not possible like northern loran sites. Mail delivery was done by dropping a mailbag from the aircraft's waist hatch. Outgoing mail then was snatched during a low-level fly-by with a hook attached to a line trailing beneath the aircraft. This hook snagged a looped line strung between two poles. The line was attached to the mailbag. Crewmen aboard the airplane hauled in the line bringing the mail aboard for the outgoing trip. (Guion M. Prince)*

The HC-130 has served the Coast Guard since December 1959. The latest version, the "J" model, began use in 2003. This formidable aircraft's future in the Coast Guard might yet be measured in decades even after a forty-five-year career. (Gary Todoroff)

Yuba City

Tom Beard

The episode pushing the rescue helicopter into the limelight occurred on Christmas Eve 1955. This case firmly bonded the helicopter to the Coast Guard in the public's mind and laid the groundwork for future Coast Guard aircraft purchases. It took only one helicopter and four stalwart crewmen to change the future of Coast Guard aviation. A storm-weakened river dike unexpectedly burst during the night of 23 December 1955. This immediately unleashed a volume of water greater than tumbles over Niagara Falls and sent it gushing directly into low-lying Yuba City, California. Soon after, one Coast Guard helicopter, a HO4S from the air station in San Francisco, with a hoist-and-rescue basket, lifted 138 victims to safety.

The first fifty-eight victims were spotted in the beam of a small hand-held searchlight and hauled aboard the helicopter in darkness. These waterlogged victims, many dressed for bed or some not at all, were snatched from their perilous rooftop retreats, found clinging to chimneys, television antennas, power poles, car-tops and trees. By Christmas Eve, with one helicopter and small boats brought into the area, the Coast Guard assisted in saving over 500 distressed survivors. The floods forced more than 100,000 people from homes, injured nearly 5,000, and killed almost 100.

Two days previously, forty-year-old Lieutenant Henry J. Pfeiffer flew a Coast Guard C-54, four-engine transport, from Honolulu to San Francisco in the same storm that devastated northern California. The following day, with no rest from the dozen-hour flight, he flew a helicopter for over twelve hours aiding flood victims in Jenner and Guerneville, California, along the coast seventy miles north of San Francisco. From here, he got a late-night diversion eighty miles inland to the northeast in response to a call for help in Yuba City.

Pfeiffer began his search in darkness in the early morning hours of Christmas Eve, skimming low over the housetops where floodwaters touched eaves. Some trapped victims escaped by chopping holes in roofs. Flying the helicopter in the storm-darkened night between trees, high-tension lines, television antennas, and telephone wires, Pfeiffer hovered just feet above a roof where a stranded mother cuddled her two children. Crewman, Chief Machinist's Mate Joseph Accamo, in the helicopter's cabin, lowered the basket and began the routine that would repeat itself through the night and throughout the next day from housetop to housetop. Pfeiffer then rushed the sodden survivors to the nearby airport high-ground and returned for yet one more trip. Children and mothers in wet nightgowns, bundled in soaked blankets, and clutching wrapped Christmas presents, were loaded into the helicopter.

Still in darkness, Pfeiffer took one more trip. He learned from the rescued husband that his wife, a paralyzed woman, was trapped in a flooded mobile home. Pfeiffer insisted on taking the trip immediately though it was nearly time with the soon-coming dawn to trade off with the only other pilot, Lieutenant Commander George F. Thometz, Jr. Thometz was recently qualified in the helicopter and not night qualified. Only Pfeiffer knew exactly where and how to reach the stranded woman. Once more Pfeiffer boarded the still running helicopter. The helicopter's engine was not shut down during the night and following day, even for fueling, for fear they could not restart it, so critical was its need.

In the pre-dawn Pfeiffer eased the helicopter into a hover directly above the partially submerged, floating mobile home. Accamo lowered Machinist Mate Victor Roulund—carried along on this trip just for this purpose— to the trailer's roof using the helicopter's hoist. Roulund later wrote, "only a pilot [and] hoist operator [were carried] on board to save weight [and] get more survivors to safety, except when one of us had to go down into the flood to get a person out."

Roulund, with ax in hand, chopped a ventilator from the roof and discovered the paralyzed victim floating on a mattress trapped in the bedroom. While Roulund was figuring out how to extract the woman from the trailer, Pfeiffer, using the precious helicopter time, flew off

to rescue others. "You can't imagine the feeling of standing on the floating trailer," recounted Roulund, "watching your helicopter fly away [and] leave you in the dark, not knowing what to expect or how in the world to get down into the trailer." Roulund succeeded in climbing down into the trailer and plunged into cold water. "That little old crippled lady was scared to death floating on a mattress in the dark."

Meanwhile, Pfeiffer maneuvered the lone helicopter through the trees to snatch yet more victims from a roof of a two-story building nearby. As he approached, he saw where muddy waters had nearly washed away an image of Santa Claus's face painted on a second-floor window. With the refugees hoisted from the rooftop, Pfeiffer, flying between poles for the third time, returned to the trailer to pick up the woman and Roulund.

Before the helicopter returned to the trailer, Roulund waded in waist-high "muddy water," as he wrote, "down a hallway to the back bedroom" and "calm[ed] her down [and got] her to trust me to get her out. I had to lift her up [and] carry her up to the front to get to a door [and] wait until the helicopter came back for us. I had to signal Joe Accamo with my flashlight to let him know where to lower the rescue basket [and] get the lady in the basket."

Flying without a co-pilot, Pfeiffer grew weary from the strain and accumulated hours of torturous work, but waited until daylight to switch flying duties with Thometz, which allowed for a short rest. Thometz had only a few months' experience in helicopters and had never before hoisted a person.

The two pilots, making alternate flights throughout the remainder of the day, rescued thirty-two adults, eighteen children, two dogs, a kitten, two teddy bears, and five dolls. Women clutching children were lifted

from treetops where the problem was to lower the basket without getting tangled in the branches. A woman naked, her nightdress ripped away by the rushing water, was rescued from an attic dormer. A man was hoisted from the top of an electric power pole where he had tied himself with the broken wires. Three children were saved from behind a sheltering wooden cutout of Santa Claus on his sled drawn by eight reindeer erected on a rooftop.

Pfeiffer continued until late Christmas Eve afternoon hoisting the cold and the wet and sick from the shambles of a city. He worked twenty-nine consecutive hours. He, Thometz, Accamo, and Roulund rescued 138 victims. When Pfeiffer landed at the San Francisco Coast Guard Air station, his left hand and arm were badly swollen from the constant shifting of the collective and cyclic controls and he limped on his left leg from ceaselessly adjusting for the helicopter torque by pushing on the rudder pedals. Shortly before midnight he dropped exhausted into bed, planning to sleep forever, as he related, but the next morning at dawn he was awakened by four-year-old Gary pounding on his chest shouting. "It's Christmas, Daddy, it's Christmas!"

Top: The helicopter crew that pulled 138 people to safety on Christmas Eve in the 1955 Yuba City, California, floods and changed Coast Guard aviation (left to right): Chief Petty Officer Joseph Accamo, Lieutenant Henry J. Pfeiffer, Lieutenant Commander George F. Thometz, Jr., and Petty Officer Victor Roulund. (Victor Roulund)

The "Pocket Rocket" was the Coast Guard's leap into the jet age and away from airplanes capable of landing on the water. The HU-25 Falcon is a medium-range surveillance, fixed-wing aircraft replacing the HU-16E Albatross. The Falcon flies missions in search and rescue, law enforcement, marine environmental protection, and military support. A study determined the service life of the HU-25—based on the Coast Guard's use and superb maintenance—would double from the originally calculated 20,000 flights and 30,000 landings to 40,000 flights and 60,000 landings, extending the airplane's useful life to about sixty years. (Jerry L. Snyder, U.S. Coast Guard)

Above: Chief Petty Officer Mark O'Brien performs a visual search and identification of icebergs from an HC-130 aircraft. The track lines flown by the aircraft are evident on the chart along with the bergs' locations. This information is relayed to ships transiting the dangerous waters of the North Atlantic. The service was initiated under international agreement resulting from Titanic's disaster. (U.S. Coast Guard)

Right: The Coast Guard acquired three RG-8A Condor "spy planes" as a part of their efforts at drug-runner surveillance in the Caribbean. The airplane—a powered glider—was virtually silent, undetectable above 600 feet over the ocean. The manufacturer, Schweitzer, was converting the Coast Guard airframes to twin-engine airplanes when one, not converted, suffered an engine failure during a night-time mission and was lost at sea. The crew bailed out and escaped unhurt. (U.S. Coast Guard)

MacDiarmid's dream faded and in 1957, a landplane and helicopter combination replaced the seaplane. So successful was the new HC-130 Hercules for long-range support and the HU-25 for medium-range missions that both still serve today after forty-five and twenty years respectively. With the recent purchases of the new fleet of HC-130J models, their use is projected well into the twenty-first century.

With the reciprocating aircraft engines available to power the helicopter prior to the introduction of turbine engines, all of Erickson's visions could not be realized. The frail craft, originally made of steel-tube and fabric, was too limited in power and capabilities. Finally in the late 1950s, Sikorsky adapted the lightweight, powerful turboshaft engine to the helicopter following some success with large, but heavy, reciprocating aircraft engines. This abundance of lightweight turbine-power allowed for sturdy airframe construction resulting in a rugged and versatile aircraft. Night and all-weather capabilities came shortly and the helicopter could meet the challenges of nearly all flight conditions—including the Coast Guard's time-honored ability to alight on water as well as on land and ships.

The helicopter suddenly moved to the forefront as the rescue vehicle with the introduction in January 1963 of Sikorsky's all-weather, amphibious HH-52A, Seaguard. Erickson's dream of two decades past came true. This was the beginning of today's Coast Guard aviation; one of the world's largest air forces.

The HH-52A was the most successful rescue aircraft of its time. Through its twenty-six years of service, it saved over 15,000 lives. This figure does not begin to disclose the unrecorded numbers of people and animals helped, or the property saved by this venerable aircraft. The "52" was in service less than four years when in September 1965, Hurricane Betsy struck New Orleans. In three days Seaguards (a name, strangely, even pilots flying it could never remember—it was forever the "52") carried 1,192 people to safety. This was hailed as the greatest airlift and rescue operation ever performed by Coast Guard helicopters. The turboshaft-powered helicopter leaves a legacy of thousands of tales of dramatic rescues.

The HH-52A was retired on 12 September 1989, not only with a remarkable record, but with having shaped all Coast Guard aviation. Its replacement, the HH-65A has gone on to achieve even greater triumphs in its record of saving lives. Because of the large number of HH-52As

La Conte

Captain Theodore C. Le Feuvre, USCG

"What do you mean no one has heard from them? For how long?" I exclaimed. I was commanding officer of Air Station Sitka, Alaska, and my heart sank as I heard the answer to my question: "Forty minutes."

Coast Guard helicopters are required to maintain a radio guard and make position reports every fifteen minutes. If two reports are missed a search is begun. I decided to go to the air station to monitor this search and rescue. Lieutenant Guy Pearce also had come to the air station to help. He located an Alaska Airlines flight overhead able to relay communications, which in turn located our missing helicopter flying safely in a Gulf of Alaska winter storm.

We both stood near the radio to listen to the relayed message and were aghast at what we heard, "Fifty-foot seas and fifty-knot winds!" I told Pearce we were going to need a third helicopter crew to cover the second crew that we had launched.

It was nearly 2300 hours as the third crew gathered to be briefed. I checked off the information we had. The first helicopter had found four men in the water but was returning to Sitka without them. It was forced to abandon its effort because a frayed cable had jammed the hoist. No survivors of the sunken fishing vessel La Conte were recovered by this helicopter. Seas were fifty feet high, winds over fifty knots and gusty. Visibility on scene was less than 300 yards. The thirty-four-degree air temperature forced the helicopters to stay below 1,000 feet to avoid icing. The second helicopter, the one believed missing earlier, was now on scene.

We then turned our attention to improving chances of rescuing the La Conte survivors from fifty-foot seas at night. In 1985 I had rescued four people from a fishing vessel near the center of Hurricane Juan in the Gulf of Mexico. That was in daylight with seventy-knot winds and forty-foot seas. In winds that high the hoist cable, with the rescue basket attached, deflects aft or downwind at up to a fifty-degree angle. The forty-pound rescue basket on

the cable's end then trails 150 feet behind the helicopter and flails around like a bat chasing a moth.

We would be attempting this rescue at night in extremely gusty winds and fifty-foot seas. We later wished the seas had remained at only fifty feet!

The visibility was so bad on our flight out we could not see the surface of the water from 600 feet. While the instruments indicated an airspeed of 140 knots, the computer showed the helicopter rocketing along at more than 200 knots groundspeed due to a strong tailwind. The closer we got to the scene the more the helicopter was knocked around by the turbulence from the gusting winds. The winds were so powerful that they were blowing the wave-tops off and throwing the salt spray hundreds of feet into the air. Most of the time, because of the snow, rain, and blowing salt spray, we were only able to see the surface of the water when we were below 150 feet.

As we approached the survivors' last known position we descended to 300 feet with the hope of seeing them and assessing the seas. We located them and began our approach pattern. The sixty-knot tailwind set us seven miles downwind during our turn-around. As we approached the survivors, deployed our first seven flares, and lowered the basket, we found that not only were the winds blowing in excess of fifty knots, but they would suddenly jump to seventy knots in an instant and abruptly change direction twenty degrees. These sudden gusts would hurtle the helicopter from the survivors, jerking the basket away. The gust would abate just as suddenly as it had started and the helicopter would shoot past the survivors in the opposite direction.

In a typical open-water hoisting situation pilots rarely use more than five degrees of attitude correction to maintain position, and the flight mechanics would never

use conning commands of more than "ten feet." This night on the Fairweather Grounds the conditions required the pilot to throw thirty degrees of nose up and nose down and bank left and right thirty degrees routinely. It also required the flight mechanic to use conning commands of "left 150 feet" and "back 200 feet," all in an attempt to hold position over the survivors in the erratically gusting winds and raging seas. After a few minutes in a hover, the aircraft commander, Lieutenant Steve Torpey, and I recognized that he was overwhelmed in these conditions, so I suggested that we split the controls. Torpey would manipulate the cyclic (stick) and rudder-pedals for lateral control and I would take the collective for altitude control. This was not at all an orthodox arrangement, but it worked for us. As Torpey whipped the cyclic about to hold position for the delivery of the rescue basket, I tugged and pushed rapidly as needed at the collective to hold the helicopter at a consistent altitude to facilitate the rescue.

As I scanned the few hundred yards I could see out in front of the helicopter, I could see the line of flares we dropped. We now were drifting downwind of them and would ride up these enormous waves long before

I could ever see the wave approaching.

Then suddenly I noticed that the flares rose much farther above the nose of the helicopter than before. In anticipation of this much larger wave I applied what I thought would be enough collective to easily clear it, but something was not right.

As this nearly eighty-foot wave approached we were suddenly hit by a vicious downdraft that forced the helicopter down into the path of this monster. As I watched this enormous wave move nearer yet, the radar altimeter continued to unwind indicating we were getting closer and closer to the surface. Our descent finally stopped at forty feet. Yet with full power on both engines, the helicopter was not climbing! We were still looking up at this onrushing wave ahead through the windscreen. Both flight mechanics were yelling "Up! Up! Up!"

I thought to myself then, "We are going into the water and I can't stop it." Reality sank in, and very rationally I thought to myself, we are going to crash. And then I prayed, "Lord, I am coming to meet you . . . but, do I have to go out cold and wet? Lord, you know how much I hate being cold and wet."

Photos: (Gary Todoroff)

Aircraft Repair & Supply Center

Tom Beard

The Coast Guard "operates a billion-dollar industry" overhauling aircraft, says Captain Bruce Drahos, commanding officer of the Aircraft Repair and Supply Center, AR & SC, at Elizabeth City, North Carolina. This facility, encompassing over a half-million square feet of floor space in fourteen buildings, employs over 1,000 military, civilian, and contract employees. Not only is this the Coast Guard's center of aircraft overhaul and repairs but is the central inventory-control location for all parts and supplies for the entire organization's nearly 200-aircraft fleet spread across twenty-four air stations, aboard ships going from pole to pole, and circling the globe.

All helicopters and fixed-winged aircraft go through a periodic overhaul, which means a virtual rebuilding. Also included in the aircraft's life are upgrades in equipment and powerplants to improve their performance, meet altered mission requirements, and extend their effective lifespan. AR & SC performs all these tasks. Coast Guard engineers long ago found that doing the work themselves meant a better job, resulting in a more reliable aircraft that lasted longer. Further, all this was accomplished with a significant reduction in costs when compared to work by outside contractors.

Following World War II and its separation from the Navy, the Coast Guard once again became responsible for its own aircraft purchases, and a small cadre of engineering officers and enlisted maintenance personnel established an airplane overhaul depot at Elizabeth City. This headquarters' unit was commissioned on 3 January 1947. Though the facility has grown significantly since, it remains at the original location.

The plant today can—virtually with bits and pieces—build a complete aircraft. It also has the ability to repair and restore damaged airframes allowing them to be returned to flying status. Shops include repair or overhaul for airframe components, engine, avionics, accessories, electrical, painting, and upholstery. Due to its long-regarded reputation for efficiency in rebuilding aircraft at very low costs with high-quality results, AR & SC takes on selected overhauls or aircraft modifications for other branches of the military services.

The monetary savings by in-house aircraft overhauls is significant, reflected not only in lower costs, but also through assured quality work, which is seen in the extended useful life of aircraft. For example, Drahos reported that due to the quality of the original HU-25 airframe and subject to the critical overhaul measures taken by AR & SC, this aircraft is capable of continuing in service beyond forty years. According to Draho's assessment, "[Aircraft Repair and Supply Center's] ability to provide all engineering and logistics services under one roof is unprecedented in Government."

The common axiom in Coast Guard aviation, "Those who fly them also fix them," is as old as Coast Guard aviation and is an assurance to all aircrews that they fly the best maintained aircraft in the world.

Top: James Spence, one of the nearly 1,000 civilian employees of the Coast Guard's Aircraft Repair and Supply Center, puts the final touch to a newly overhauled HH-65A. (U.S. Coast Guard)

Above: Materials engineer Sam Benavides performs a failure investigation of an HH-65A tail rotor blade in the AR & SC metallurgical laboratory. (U.S. Coast Guard)

purchased—ninety-nine—many pilots had to be qualified quickly. As a result, the Coast Guard established its own training command with the founding of the Coast Guard Aviation Training Center at Mobile, Alabama, in 1967. This school today is a worldwide leader in the aviation field through its influence on military and civilian flight crews in advanced crew management concepts.

The helicopter was the product of a few men with visions for the future. These farsighted individuals were not overwhelmed at the beginning by the realities of mere mechanical boundaries or limits to their knowledge. Neither were they intimidated or humiliated by their peers into giving up on an outwardly unrealistic dream. They lacked neither

Above: *Ronald James, a civilian employee at the Coast Guard Aircraft Repair and Supply Center, works on a constant speed motor. With a small fleet of aircraft spread nearly worldwide, each aircraft is expected to be ready to fly on any mission anytime. A supply of reliable parts for any aircraft instantly available anywhere is critical. The life of a person tumbling from a boat, for example, may rest here in the hands of James. (U.S. Coast Guard)*

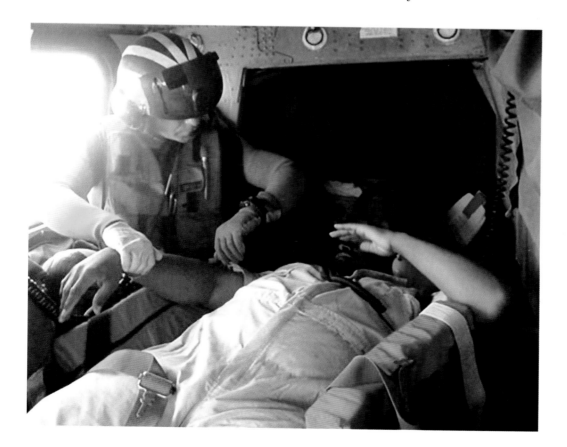

Left: *SAR air crewmen and rescue swimmers are trained in emergency medical procedures and can offer immediate lifesaving assistance once a victim is in the helicopter for transport. A crewman takes vital signs of a victim in the confines of the helicopter's cabin during a medical evacuation flight. (U.S. Coast Guard)*

The Coast Guard's second astronaut, Commander Dan Burbank, aboard space shuttle Atlantis on the STS-106 mission, on his first space flight in September 2000. The object of his mission, the International Space Station, appears just below the horizon. (NASA)

courage nor a willingness to risk their lives in this quest. The genius of these visionaries enabled them to see a future where those about them witnessed only time-wasting, foolish dreamers.

Because of these visions and sacrifices by a few, today the Coast Guard no longer has aircraft that can land on water. Gone are the "Flying Lifeboats." But in their place is an international icon of survival, the helicopter.

Today's formidable Coast Guard air force of 1,000 aviators, including over fifty women, and more than sixty enlisted women crewpersons, fly over 200 aircraft in a fleet containing 150 helicopters from twenty-four air stations, five air facilities, one squadron, one aviation training center, and forty-three flight-deck-equipped cutters, which includes four icebreakers.

Furthermore, Coast Guard aviation is unique among the five military services even with its history. This organization's involvement in aviation began with the first moments of manned flight. Life-Saving Service personnel, John T. Daniels, W. S. Dough and A. D. Etheridge, from Kill Devil Hills Life-Saving Station, assisted the Wright Brothers with the handling and launching of their gliders and airplanes at the turn of last century. The famous photograph, portraying the world's first manned flight on 17 December 1903, was taken by Surfman Daniels using the Wrights' camera. From this beginning through the following century, the fledgling service expanded the use of seaplanes, developed the naval helicopter, and eventually saw its aviators in space.

The Coast Guard operates a complex air force operating world wide and from Pole to Pole. Aircraft crews are involved in search and rescue, homeland security, logistics, law enforcement, environmental monitoring, scientific research, and military combat flights. The future is likely also to bring unmanned aerial vehicles for new roles in homeland security and maritime domain awareness. The familiar aircraft with the distinctive paint scheme will continue to be spotted globally, wherever there is that unique task for the especially skilled aircrews.

Above: Commander Bruce E. Melnick was the Coast Guard's first astronaut. Melnick, a former helicopter search-and-rescue aircraft commander, completed two space shuttle flights as mission specialist. (NASA)

Right: As a part of the Coast Guard's role in homeland security, armed airborne harbor-patrols are possible with MH-68A Sting Ray helicopters. (William R. Greer)

306

Vietnam Combat Air Rescue

Tom Beard with John Moseley

Unanticipated aircrew losses early in the Vietnam War forced the Air Force to activate their neglected Air Rescue Service with ill-suited aircraft and inexperienced crews. By 1966 they had acquired modern helicopters but still lacked experienced aviators. An exchange pilot program, to solve this problem, began with twelve Coast Guard aviators flying with Air Force crews. Ten flew helicopters; two flew HC-130Ps. One was killed in combat. Their task was to fly into enemy territory, frequently under opposing gunfire, and rescue downed aircrews. The HC-130Ps provided in-flight helicopter refueling and mission control.

Lieutenant Jack C. Rittichier was a dedicated lifesaver. Eleven days after reporting to the 37th ARRS, he was awarded a Distinguished Flying Cross for rescuing, under hostile fire, four Army helicopter pilots from two downed aircraft.

He had earned two DFCs while making thirteen saves in his two months with the squadron, and was going for number fourteen. A Marine attack pilot had ejected from his jet and radioed that a leg and arm were broken. He was unable to evade. Air strikes swept the area around him to keep a strong enemy force at bay. However, it was a trap; the injured Marine was bait.

The first HH-3E to attempt the pick-up made three approaches. Each time enemy fire drove it away. Finally, that Jolly Green had to depart to refuel, leaving Rittichier's as the only rescue helicopter. Rittichier went through concentrated fire, then pulled into the vulnerable hover, stopping in-flight over the injured pilot. Enemy fire became so intense the pilot waved off the first attempt. After Sandies, A-1 Skyraiders, Air Force propeller-driven attack aircraft, strafed the area, Rittichier moved back over the injured Marine pilot again. He entered another hover and lowered the forest penetrator, a folding seat on the end of the cable that could drop—without fouling—through the jungle canopy. Then enemy troops on the ground pounded

the motionless helicopter with massive amounts of gunfire. The airframe shuddered from impacts of multiple hits. One Sandy radioed Rittichier saying, "Your left side is on fire Jolly Green. Get out of there!"

Rittichier pulled off. Observers then noted the rotor blades visibly slowing. The stricken helicopter did not rise. It burst into flames then slammed to earth, where an instant fireball consumed it within thirty seconds. Rittichier and his crew became among the "missing in action in Southeast Asia."

Rittichier's remains were finally discovered, recovered, and identified in 2003 through tireless efforts by teams from Joint POW/MIA Accounting, the military agency that searches for and identifies remains of missing warriors.

Rittichier and his crew received the Silver Star posthumously for gallantry in action.

Top: Lieutenant James A. Quinn receives an Air Medal—one of eight plus a Distinguished Flying Cross—as an exchange pilot with the Air Force in Vietnam flying the HC-130P. (James A. Quinn)

Right: Coast Guard Lieutenant Jack C. Rittichier (left), Lieutenant Lance A. Eagan, and Lieutenant Commander Lonnie L. Mixon, assigned to the Air Force's 37th ARRS at Da Nang, Vietnam, for combat rescue duty. (Lonnie L. Mixon)

Devotion

Transitions:
The U.S. Coast Guard on and after September 11

P. J. Capelotti, Ph.D.

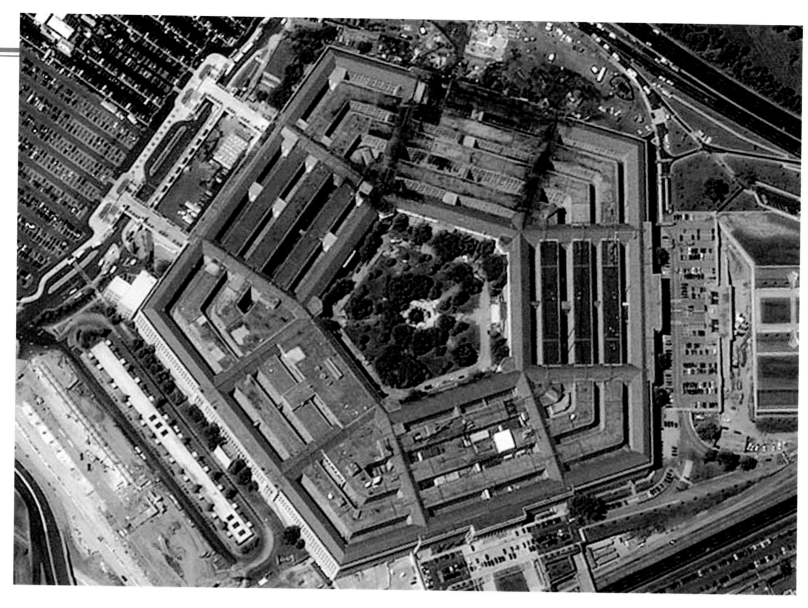

Pentagon

Lieutenant Commander Jeffrey Hathaway remembered well the best job he ever had in the Coast Guard. It was his first command on board the 180-foot buoy tender *Citrus* out of Coos Bay, Oregon. *Citrus* was scheduled home for Thanksgiving when a storm struck the Oregon-Washington coast, catching the fishing fleet offshore. So Hathaway kept *Citrus* at sea, ready to help. His crew would celebrate a memorable holiday.

Riding out the storm, a rogue wave, twice the height of *Citrus'* masthead, struck.

Next came a report hatches had blown open and water was pouring in. This was followed by the most dreaded report of all: fire. At that moment Hathaway realized his crew had only one question: What is the captain going to do?

"I looked at the helmsman," said Hathaway, "who had just qualified as a helmsman right out of boot camp, and he was looking at me with a look of abject terror and he said, 'Captain, are we going to die?' What raced through my mind at that moment was the thought that everything I do, everything I've learned about being a leader, I had to do it right— right now—because there was a whole group of people looking to me."

"Transitions" is based on condensed excerpts from Rogue Wave: The U.S. Coast Guard on and after 9/11, *Capelotti, P. J., Ph.D., Washington, D.C.; U.S. Coast Guard Historians Office, 2003.*

Coast Guard Rear Admiral Jeffrey J. Hathaway lost forty-two of fifty-one members from his command in the Pentagon's U.S. Navy Command Center. The terrorist attack on the Pentagon took the lives of 189 people. In the days immediately following, Admiral Hathaway walked at the head of dozens of caissons winding the roads through Arlington National Cemetery. (Telfair Brown, U.S. Coast Guard)

Pages 308–309: A boat on patrol around Guantánamo Bay, Cuba, where suspected terrorists are interred in Camp X-Ray. (Krystyna Johnson, U.S. Coast Guard)

Opposite: Coast Guard small boats rush to lower Manhattan Island to offer what immediate aid they can provide. These boat crewpersons soon begin the week-long maritime-security patrols to prevent further terrorist attacks via waterways, not only in New York but other major ports around the nation as well. (Tom Sperduto, U.S. Coast Guard)

Nearly fifteen years later, on the morning of 11 September 2001 terrorists piloted an airliner into the Pentagon, killing 189 people, including 42 of the 51 working in the destroyed U.S. Navy Command Center. In the following days, Hathaway, now a rear admiral and commanding officer of a section at the Center, found himself at the head of the funeral procession. As the caissons wound through Arlington National Cemetery, the memory of the rogue wave returned. In the moments after the terrorist attack, just as on board *Citrus*, people were scared. And once more a crew was looking to him for assurance, needing him to say "Here's what we're going to do," then to lead the way. Hathaway knew how to rally a frightened team, how to draw a command back together—to survive. It was something he learned from a rogue wave.

New York Harbor

It was a fine September day, and from his office, Boatswains Mate Third Class Carlos Perez looked out on New York Harbor. Its waters were like glass. Then Perez noticed smoke coming from one of the towers of the World Trade Center and in moments he had orders to take the 41-footer *41497* to the lower-Manhattan waterfront.

As his boat neared the tip of Governor's Island, Perez looked up to see the underbelly of a commercial airliner. Watching it as he sped toward the Battery, Perez saw the ball of flame as the plane smashed into the Trade Center.

As smoke and debris filled the air, Perez dashed on toward lower Manhattan and patrolled along its waterfront to look for people in the water and for debris that might be used as evidence. Later, moving past the Staten Island ferry terminals, the crew of *41497* heard a low rumble from the Trade Center. As the noise intensified they watched the South Tower splinter apart and shower down upon itself.

Through the weeks that followed, Perez and other Coast Guard coxswains drove themselves to the limits of endurance patrolling the

Many diverse Coast Guard craft from major cutters to tugs, patrol craft, and even Jon boats were immediately placed into action in New York Harbor to prevent further terrorist acts. Included in this assortment were two thirty-eight-foot Deployable Pursuit Boats, the Coast Guard's version of drug smugglers' "go-fast" boats, with speeds exceeding sixty knots, and no longer in service, were brought out of storage to patrol the New York harbor. These high-speed ocean racing boats formerly used to run down drug-running craft were operating in the harbor within days. (Tom Sperduto, U.S. Coast Guard)

Opposite: *The twin towers of the World Trade Center posted against a serene blue sky serves as an imposing backdrop to a Coast Guard helicopter performing a routine harbor patrol on a morning like that of 11 September 2001. (U.S. Coast Guard)*

Above: *Dozens of Coast Guard patrol boats enforced the security established throughout the New York harbor following the attack. A sightseeing boat is turned away from a security zone in the Hudson River. (Tom Sperduto, U.S. Coast Guard)*

Left: *From left, David Strickland, Eddie Rivera, Joe Harrington, and Gregory Thompson are showing an equal somberness in expression reflecting perhaps the horrific experience and long, tense hours patrolling New York Harbor. In the aftermath of the World Trade Center attacks Coast Guard boat crews worked twelve-hour shifts. (Dave French, U.S. Coast Guard)*

313

Above: *Rear Admiral Richard E. Bennis receives a distinguished service award at his retirement ceremony. Bennis had commanded Coast Guard units in New York Harbor and directed actions to protect citizens and secure the port. Just before the attack on the World Trade Center, the admiral underwent brain surgery and was back on the job a day and a half later. The surgery staples were removed a day before the attack. (Tom Sperduto, U.S. Coast Guard)*

Above, right: *Rear Admiral Richard E. Bennis, USCG, on medical leave and driving south from New York to seek a retirement home, received a call that a terrorist attack was happening in New York City. He immediately started back to his office in Coast Guard Activities New York located on Staten Island. When approaching Washington, D.C., Bennis observed smoke rising from the Pentagon. He knew his vacation was over. (Telfair Brown, U.S. Coast Guard)*

With dust filling the air from the rubble of the World Trade Center, a Coast Guardsman bows his head in silent tribute to those who died. The tragedy of the attack is shared in private moments even by those whose boldness is depended on in the aftermath. (Tom Sperduto, U.S. Coast Guard)

harbors, racking up the equivalent of twenty-two-years' wear on their boats in two months. In these same months, the Coast Guard, the nation's fifth armed force, would be the principal defender of America's maritime homeland.

Activities New York

Rear Admiral Richard E. Bennis, USCG, knew a great deal about emergencies and how to handle them. He had been in three of the country's largest ports, Charleston, Norfolk, and New York, and had served as Chief of Response at Coast Guard headquarters and co-chair of the national response team, an interagency coordinating body of all federal response organizations. As head of policies for the Coast Guard's response to explosions, fires, natural disasters, and oil spills, he dealt with catastrophes such as the *Exxon Valdez* spill and was on the security team for the 1996 summer Olympics. He was also Captain of the Port in New York for *OpSail 2000*, the largest peacetime gathering of ships in history. For Bennis, *OpSail 2000* became a rehearsal for this security nightmare one year later.

While anticipating a new Coast Guard assignment, Bennis looked forward to taking a year to put in writing the lessons learned from *OpSail*—until diagnosed with an "incurable" melanoma in his lungs and brain. Not accepting the prognosis that he had only six months to live, Bennis underwent brain surgery, and a day-and-a-half afterwards was back at the office.

Near the end of a full career, and now with unexpected health problems, Bennis changed his plans. On 10 September 2001 the surgical staples were removed from his head, and early the next morning Bennis and his wife drove south from New York City to seek a retirement home.

Captain Patrick Harris, Bennis' deputy, convened the morning staff briefing in the Coast Guard Activities New York crisis action-center located on Staten Island. A career aviator, with thirty-four Air Medals from his

Vietnam service as an Army helicopter pilot, Harris commanded all Coast Guard New York Harbor units, which included marine inspection, operations divisions, Vessel Traffic Service (VTS), all small boat stations, and two icebreaking tugboats.

As the morning briefing ended, Harris' attention was directed to the commercial television screen in the operations center. As an aviator, Harris was immediately skeptical about initial reports that a light plane accidentally hit the World Trade Center. Although the incident was land-based—not maritime related—he took the initiative to immediately activate Coast Guard forces.

Bennis was driving south through northern Virginia when Harris telephoned him. "You've left town again, Admiral," Harris said, "and something always happens when you leave town."

Bennis started back to New York. Crossing the Potomac River, he looked upriver and saw smoke coming from the Pentagon. He accelerated to 95 mph, often using the breakdown lane, and drove straight to Station Sandy Hook, where Harris arranged for a boat to meet him.

Harris was in front of the television screens and saw the second plane hit. "At that point," recalled Harris, "we knew what we had!" Seven minutes later, he closed the port of New York. "All our vessels immediately moved in toward the scene. Any [Coast Guard] vessels not underway were put underway within minutes. Very shortly, we had launched everything . . . We had volunteers start showing up within minutes of the second plane hitting . . . We turned into a true response organization for about six weeks."

Having now lost telephone communications, Harris ordered a cutter to the scene to provide command and control. Wanting a Coast Guard presence to show any terrorists that the harbor was closed, Harris also ordered forty-two Tactical Law Enforcement (TACLET) team members—boarding officers—from Florida and Virginia to join crews on Coast Guard boats. He then had all inbound commercial shipping stopped at Ambrose Light, where TACLET teams were to board every vessel.

Smoke rises from the rubble of the World Trade Center shortly after the towers collapse. Coast Guard units had already responded by this time though this was a land-based terrorist act. Coast Guard authorities were preparing for any follow-on attack on harbor and port facilities, plus they began making immediate efforts to evacuate victims from lower Manhattan. (Tom Sperduto, U.S. Coast Guard)

Above: *Four days following the World Trade Center attack, fires continued to burn. By this time, Coast Guard Reservists from the three Coast Guard strike teams were prowling through the ruins of buildings surrounding Ground Zero conducting air quality tests for the EPA to confirm a safe breathing environment prior to allowing rescue and recover efforts to continue in lower Manhattan. (Brandon Brewer, U.S. Coast Guard)*

Left: *Coast Guard boarding team members in New York hone defensive actions skills. Boarding teams must prepare for the unexpected when going aboard commercial ships from many nations. Small arms qualifications are also a part of this training. Developing skills in diplomacy perhaps is their greatest weapon in disarming sometimes tense situations. (Mike Hvozda, U.S. Coast Guard)*

Without specific plans for handling terrorist attacks in New York harbor, Harris retrieved the operation plans Activities had created for harbor security during *OpSail 2000*, and which covered the evacuation of lower Manhattan.

"It was a very concentrated evacuation," remembered Harris, "with everything coming from Lower Manhattan. We hadn't planned it that way. That day we had buildings falling down, debris coming down, and dust and soot in the air. We had people running for the first piece of shoreline."

Waterfront

Lieutenant Sean MacKenzie had just begun his first command assignment as skipper of the 110-foot patrol boat *Adak*. As *Adak* rushed at full speed to take up a position off the Battery, Quartermaster First Class Matthew James and MacKenzie began plotting positions of all Coast Guard cutters and small boats converging on lower Manhattan. From that moment until the arrival after midnight of the 270-foot Coast Guard Cutter *Tahoma* from New Bedford, Massachusetts, *Adak* acted as a command and control center and on-scene commander for all Coast Guard vessels in New York Harbor.

By mid-morning the Coast Guard had forty boats, supported by a volunteer fleet of civilian vessels, operating in the harbor. The Coast Guard tug *Hawser*, just back from the previous evening's duty, was being refueled, and its skipper, Chief Boatswains Mate James A. Todd, a fourteen-year Coast Guard veteran, was having breakfast ashore. Hearing the news that a plane hit the Trade Center and not waiting for orders, Todd

Petty Officer Nicholas Hallmark of Maritime Safety & Security Team 91103 conducts an inspection of the many spaces and voids below decks of a merchant ship during a boarding inspection prior to the Coast Guard clearing the vessel into the harbor. (Louis Hebert, U.S. Coast Guard)

immediately returned to the tug and recalled its crew who had just left on liberty. Within minutes, the tug and its crew of seven were on their way to lower Manhattan.

"We headed right for the buildings," Todd recalled. "We knew that there would have to be a security zone set, we knew there would be a need for medical facilities to be set up and people to be taken off the island. We knew we had a job even before being contacted. There was a mass of people on the shoreline . . . We took some people off, passed out gas masks, and unloaded our water, so people had potable water. We directed people to the medical centers that were set up, and tried to maintain some sort of order with the [commercial] tugs coming in to take people off."

Responding to reports of a frantic evacuation underway, Harris sent Coast Guard marine inspectors "with good strong command voices" from the Fort Wadsworth operations center. The inspectors took up positions at pier heads in Manhattan or boarded a pilot boat and ferries to gain control of the crowds, calm passengers, and direct the evacuation.

One inspector, Lieutenant Michael Day, had previously worked for the Port Authority of New York and New Jersey in 1 World Trade Center. He had also served on board Coast Guard Cutter *Seneca* during operations *Able Manner* (the Haitian migration of 1993) and *Able Vigil* (the Cuban migration of 1994). These experiences would provide valuable preparation for what he faced in Manhattan.

Day, along with Chief Petty Officer Fred Wilson and other Coast Guardsmen, boarded the Sandy Hook Pilot Boat *New York*, offered to them by its pilot, Andrew McGovern.

Above: *The 110-foot cutter* Adak *on patrol passes beneath the Brooklyn Bridge. A rifle-armed Coast Guardsman stands watch at the bow. The 25mm chain-gun on the foredeck is uncovered, ready for use. (Tom Sperduto, U.S. Coast Guard)*

Opposite, bottom: *Among the multitude of tasks for the ubiquitous buoy tenders,* Katherine Walker *accomplishes another and maintains a security zone around sailboats participating in "Sail for America." The event serves as a memorial for all those who died on September 11 and pays tribute to the spirit of America. (Mike Hzvoda, U.S. Coast Guard)*

Two weeks later, on 26 September, Coast Guard strike team members still prowled wrecked buildings monitoring air quality for the EPA, determining fitness for workers toiling in the wake of the disaster. They would continue this task for weeks. (Brandon Brewer, U.S. Coast Guard)

317

Petty Officer Charles Wells and his father, a New York Fire Department deputy chief, Charles R. Wells, mourn the loss of a family member at Ground Zero. The Wells lost a brother and uncle attached to Ladder Company 118. (Tom Sperduto, U.S. Coast Guard)

Coast Guard helicopter crews, trained in cliff rescues, rushed from their base at Cape Cod to New York planning to evacuate people trapped atop the Trade Towers. They even considered the possibility of rescuing those unable to make it to the rooftops by lowering the rescue basket down the side of the building, recovering people through windows. Their efforts were thwarted by emergency flight-restrictions into the area and the eventual collapse of both towers.(Tom Sperduto, U.S. Coast Guard)

Day hoisted a Coast Guard ensign on *New York*, and using its radio, began directing vessel traffic in the harbor and the evacuation of people fleeing lower Manhattan. He also pressed into service a civilian marine inspector with expert knowledge of the harbor ferries, "frocking" him in Coast Guard coveralls, ball cap, and float coat. By directing vessels to newly arranged routes, Day and Wilson soon brought order to the jumble of tugs and ferries rushing to the evacuation.

New York then eased up to the lower Manhattan docks and disembarked Coast Guard petty officers to assist the police in keeping the evacuation orderly. Day remembered people cheering as the ferries left the docks, a response he found strangely unsettling. By 5 p.m. Day and Wilson had helped an estimated 750,000 people depart from Manhattan.

Yet there was still more to do. When firefighters couldn't get fuel to pump trucks, water-cooler bottles were filled with diesel fuel from *New York*'s fuel tanks and a half-mile-long bucket brigade was created.

Near Ground Zero, Day saw a foot in a shoe. He stood transfixed, his thoughts flashing back to the pallets he saw being dropped off at North Cove—pallets holding 20,000 body bags for the anticipated casualties.

Rescue Helicopters

Captain Richard P. Yatto, commanding officer of Coast Guard Air Station Cape Cod, received a call just before 9 a.m. summoning him to the operations center. Yatto, a twenty-five-year Coast Guard veteran, looked at the TV-screen image of the burning North Tower. Another of the station's pilots, Lieutenant Kurt R. Kupersmith, was standing near Yatto and saw the captain's whole face change when the second plane went in.

Yatto remembered a hotel fire in San Juan, Puerto Rico, where people were trapped and died on the roof because they couldn't get off. "My first thought was that we needed to get a helicopter down there to take people off the roof."

Canadian Air Force Captain Joseph R. Palfy, assigned to CGAS Cape Cod as an exchange pilot, had already flown more than sixty SAR missions with the station's HH-60J four Jayhawks. On the morning of 11 September Palfy and Lieutenant Christopher L. Kluckhuhn were conducting a "ground turn"—maintenance test—in one at the station. Palfy and Kluckhuhn watched from the helicopter cockpit as two F-15 Eagle fighters from the adjacent Otis Air National Guard base scrambled. The two helicopter pilots, unaware of events unfolding in New York, knew something was up.

Yatto ordered his three helicopters to return immediately and to prepare to fly to New York. Two needed refueling. Palfy and Kluckhuhn were ready to go. They had sufficient fuel, and at full speed they could be in New York in an hour.

Kluckhuhn drove the helicopter at maximum continuous power, shuttering across Rhode Island Sound at 157 knots. Kupersmith followed soon after in a second HH-60J. Still without fully understanding the nature of the disaster, crews began planning the rescue. They discussed fuel consumption and where they might get fuel if they had to hover over New

York for any length of time. They considered options of how they might snatch people off the towers: their standard rescue load of six people had been exceeded previously—one HH-60J pulled twenty-eight from a sinking ship—and as many as 40,000 to 50,000 people could be in the buildings.

Palfy speculated they could pick people from windows: "Worse case scenario, if people were stuck, we could lower our basket down to the upwind side of the building. The winds were out of the north, so we would

Lieutenant Christopher Kluckhuhn, a twelve-year Coast Guard veteran, talks on the radio to the pilot of an arriving HH-60 Jayhawk at Air Station Cape Cod. Kluckhuhn and Canadian Air Force Captain Joseph R. Palfy were the first Coast Guard pilots ordered to fly a Jayhawk to New York City immediately following the attacks on the Twin Towers. Kluckhuhn and Palfy intended to land atop the buildings to evacuate people trapped there and use the helicopter's rescue basket and hoist to save people from the floors below. (Amy Thomas, U.S. Coast Guard)

A HH-60 Jayhawk departs from Coast Guard Air Station Cape Cod. The air station has four Jayhawks and four HU-25 Falcons to meet Coast Guard operational commitments along the Northeast coast. (Amy Thomas, U.S. Coast Guard)

have approached the north side of the north tower, kept the helicopter in clean air, with the smoke drifting away from us, and lower the basket."

As the Jayhawk reached Long Island Sound, the pilot tuned the radio to the New York Fire and Police frequency and heard that the South Tower had just collapsed. They raced on—a half hour from the city—determined to reach the still-standing North Tower and do what they could. They tried calling New York's FAA air traffic controllers but the radio was cluttered with chatter. Finally, when approaching Gabreski Field on Long Island, air controllers ordered the two rescue helicopters to land immediately.

"We said 'We're the rescue helicopter,'" Palfy recalled. Both helicopters were again ordered to land—immediately. He told the controllers once more that these were Coast Guard helicopters en route to the Trade Center for a rescue mission. The reply was: all air traffic was grounded. No aircraft were being allowed into New York. The Air Force F-15s, they were told, were clearing the skies and they wanted no additional air traffic near New York. Palfy pressed the issue. They were rescue helicopters. Once again they were ordered out of the sky.

As the crew stood by to refuel the helicopter, Palfry and Kluckhuhn ran into the control center at Gabreski, determined to curse their way to New York if necessary. For the first time, they saw the burning North Tower on television. As they watched, it collapsed.

The air crew was devastated. Kluckhuhn felt like he had been punched in the stomach. They believed had they been allowed to reach the towers they might have rescued at least some of the victims.

The cutter Bainbridge Island's *crew takes a breather from near constant New York Harbor patrols by taking their family members on an outing. The cutter flies the battle ensign, a regular sight during the height of security patrols following September 11. Lieutenant Christopher Randolph, the vessel's commanding officer, acquired the oversized flag to display during its New York Harbor patrols to raise crew morale. This action also had the effect of boosting New Yorkers' spirits wherever it was observed. Viewers, for example, along the East River seeing this oversized flag cheered and honked horns as* Bainbridge Island *passed. (U.S. Coast Guard)*

Yatto believed the two Jayhawks could have made several runs between the towers and safety. "There's a helicopter landing pad—the Wall Street pad—on the East River and that's just a two-minute flight from the top of the World Trade Center. We do cliff rescue training, we send our flight crews out to Coast Guard Air Station Astoria where they have advanced rescue swimmer training, and they practice things like cliff rescues where you send a rescue swimmer down on a harness and he can pick up a survivor. So it was potentially feasible for our crews to lower their rescue swimmers down fifty, sixty, eighty feet down the side of the building, with the helicopter hovering over the rooftop, to pick someone out of a window."

Palfy too, thought he would have used the Wall Street pad, but he even considered the flight-deck of the nearby aircraft carrier USS *Intrepid*, now a museum, as a landing pad. "If anybody was going to be doing any rescuing that day," said Palfy, "it was going to be us."

Operations Center

As soon as Bennis recognized the scope of the catastrophe, he put a call out to the rest of the Coast Guard to send everything. Communications, except sporadic cell-phone channels, were out nearly everywhere. Bennis, temporarily at Sandy Hook and unable to get through to Harris at Fort Wadsworth's operations center, improvised.

"I would take my little bitty cell phone, and I'd take it outside the command suite at Activities New York, and I'd lean against the bicycle rack near the galley, because that was where I had the best reception. I had a button that said 'Loy,' [Commandant James Loy] which I'd programmed in . . . and I'd call on this tiny cell phone and give the status report, telling what we were doing. . . . I said to the Commandant, 'You need to know that everything we need to be doing, we are doing. We're doing it well.

Opposite, top: *Lieutenant Christopher Kluckhuhn, (far right, sitting) scans electronic charts as Lieutenant (jg) Sean Krueger (right, standing) talks to the pilots of an incoming HH-60 Jayhawk rescue helicopter. Kluckhuhn was a pilot on the Jayhawk that took off for New York City on September 11. Falcon pilots Lieutenant Brad Apitz (far left) and Lieutenant (jg) Adam Cochrane are briefing for a mission. (Amy Thomas, U.S. Coast Guard)*

Coast Guard Commandant Admiral James Loy and Master Chief Petty Officer of the Coast Guard Vincent W. Patton are examining details of an aerial map of Ground Zero. (Tom Sperduto, U.S. Coast Guard)

Above: *Petty Officer Kevin Pritt, a Coast Guard firefighter from Coast Guard Station Cape May assisting at Ground Zero. (Tom Sperduto, U.S. Coast Guard)*

Left: *A Coast Guard crew flying a helicopter along Cape Fear River bank in North Carolina examines a suspicious contact near a port in Wilmington. (Krystyna Hannum, U.S. Coast Guard)*

Petty Officer Tim Frazier inspects his M60 machine gun before returning to patrol on the Hudson River. The guns on all boats in all harbors were fully loaded and ready for instant use every day. (Tom Sperduto, U.S. Coast Guard)

But we need more people, and more logistics support. But everything you think the Coast Guard should be doing, or needs to be doing, we are doing it. The only thing we're not doing, is demonstrating it to those of you outside of New York.'"

The Coast Guard began reestablishing communications using a trailer delivered from Atlantic Area's Communication Area Master Station Atlantic, CAMSLANT, in Virginia, which was set up in Fort

Right: *Secretary of Transportation Norman Y. Mineta presents Petty Officer Robin Shipley with the Transportation 9/11 Medal for her heroic efforts in the immediate aftermath of September 11. She, along with shipmates also receiving the award, demonstrated extraordinary leadership while patrolling harbors, securing critical infrastructure facilities, escorting high interest vessels, and conducting boardings of vessels entering U.S. waters. (Amy Thomas, U.S. Coast Guard)*

Opposite, bottom left: *The cutter* Escanaba *enforces a harbor safety zone by detaining a container ship six miles off the New Jersey shore. The cutter's small boat approaches the ship for a security boarding by bringing a multi-agency inspection team. During the crises in New York, all vessels were pre-cleared before being allowed into the harbor. (Eric Hedaa, U.S. Coast Guard)*

322

Wadsworth overlooking the harbor. The Atlantic Strike Team's Mobile Incident Command Post, MICP, arrived at Bayonne, New Jersey, boosting the communications net. Maintenance and Logistics Command, MLC, Atlantic sent 150 cell phones.

Bennis' foremost concern in the twenty-four hours following the evacuation of Manhattan was the possibility of more attacks, where they might come from, and how could he could prevent them. Harris likewise had no intention of letting anything into the harbor that hadn't been searched and declared safe. These concerns led to a series of evaluations: what had the terrorists done and, more importantly, what had they failed to do that they might try to finish with a second or third wave of attacks.

Before September 11 the Coast Guard analyzed scenarios and identified approximately 150 critical targets within the New York port area.

Above: *Master Chief of the Coast Guard, Vince Patton, reads messages attached to a first-responder fire truck near Ground Zero. In the aftermath of the tragedy, Patton visited Coast Guard members working the lower Manhattan disaster area and those units securing New York Harbor. (Mark Mackowiak, U.S. Coast Guard)*

Above: *Petty officer Thomas Duffy (left), Jason Miele, and Nicholas McConnell patrol near the Statue of Liberty carrying out the continued effort of harbor security begun as a result of September 11. (Tom Sperduto, U.S. Coast Guard)*

Above: *Coast Guardsmen Colin Redy (left) and Brett Davidson (right) watch the sunrise over New York City, the dawn ending their night security patrol. (Tom Sperduto, U.S. Coast Guard)*

Using a triage approach, priorities were established for potential targets: the destruction of a single bridge could close the entire harbor; damage to the Indian Point nuclear power plant might release radiation; an attack on an American symbol like the Statue of Liberty could have devastating psychological impact. Furthermore, the ports of New York and New Jersey, national economic nerve centers, needed protection. This led to some quick improvisation. "Against somebody who is intent on not allowing us to board, we wouldn't have a good way to do it," said Harris, "unless we assaulted from aircraft or disabled the vessel. The best thing we thought we could do was keep tugs near vessels, so if it looked like they were doing something that was unexpected we could deflect their aim." Closing the waterways to recreational traffic and stationing a cutter at each end allowed Activities to consolidate many potential targets under a single maritime security force.

Harbor

Bennis felt the New York harbor required more security units full time. Two thirty-eight-foot Deployable Pursuit Boats, the Coast Guard's "go-fast" boats—their speed exceeding sixty knots—built to counter fast drug-running boats in the Caribbean, came from the Tactical Law Enforcement Team in Yorktown, Virginia. No longer in use, these boats were taken out of storage and found their element in New York Harbor.

"Without knowing it, that is what those boats were designed to do," Bennis explained. "They were a very good tool for a public that respects and appreciates the Coast Guard while at the same time believing that the Coast Guard can't catch a Boston Whaler. We got the Deployable Pursuit Boats early on, and I would have them run from the George Washington Bridge to the Verrazano Narrows Bridge at speed several times a day, just so people could go, 'What the hell was that? It's the Coast Guard.' Just knowing we had that capability gave a lot of people pause, be they tourists or people intent on violating a security zone." The Coast Guard presence also offered emotional comfort to the public, Bennis noted. While awaiting a visit by President Bush, Bennis talked with a firefighter from Ground Zero whose company lost sixteen men. Later he repeated the fireman's comment: "You know how you feel when a fire truck comes through the neighborhood and you feel reassured? That's the way my family feels when they see the racing stripe out on the water."

Above: *A twenty-five-foot Coast Guard Raider boat races to intercept a vessel in the Hudson River. These armed Boston Whalers are designed for Coast Guard port security units to use in foreign ports. In an unprecedented move, the port security units manned by Reservists were called to active duty for protection at some major United States' ports following the September 11 attacks. These boats are painted dull gray with black slashes atypical to the high visibility paint schemes seen on most Coast Guard boats. For the first time, these special craft were seen patrolling in domestic waters. Sighting these heavily armed—with three machine guns—indistinctly marked boats did initially cause some alarm and confusion. (Tom Sperduto, U.S. Coast Guard)*

Opposite, top: *Petty Officer Jason Miele, a Maritime Safety & Security Team member, on guard in New York Harbor. (Tom Sperduto, U.S. Coast Guard)*

Opposite, bottom: *Chaplain Brian Haley from the Coast Guard Academy in New London, Connecticut, gives a moment of comfort to one of the many volunteers working at the site of the fallen towers. (William Barry, U.S. Coast Guard)*

Right: *With only their heads showing, two Coast Guardsmen play the role of terrorist infiltrators as they skirt the edge of a pier avoiding detection during security exercises. (Crystal Norman, U.S. Coast Guard)*

Above: *Coast Guard Petty Officer Patrick Oxenreider attends the Special Missions Training Center at the Marine Corps' Camp Lejeune, North Carolina. Oxenreider is looking around the corner of a barricade seeking enemy role-players while under simulated fire. Marines frequently train Coast Guard tactical operations personnel. (Zachary A. Crawford, U.S. Coast Guard)*

An armed port security twenty-five-foot boat from the Coast Guard Reserve unit at Fort Eustis, Virginia, deployed to New York Harbor in the aftermath of September 11. The port security Coast Guard Reserve unit, which is normally only deployed overseas, provided U.S. Naval Hospital Ship Comfort *an armed escort and continued round the clock protection while the ship lay in New York Harbor. (Brandon Brewer, U.S. Coast Guard)*

Opposite: *Petty Officer Peter Brooks volunteered to stand eight-hour guard shifts aboard a vessel loaded with military materials in transit from a Florida port to a port in Georgia. (Danielle DeMarino, U.S. Coast Guard)*

This echoed Bennis' belief. He had recommended not using Department of Defense forces in New York Harbor. He wanted the Navy battle group that was already offshore to remain offshore. "Striped hulls" offered reassurance to the public, while a DoD presence might be unsettling within U.S. boundaries.

"Rather than the one or two racing stripes [Coast Guard boats] the public was used to seeing on the water, they now saw forty-five or fifty. The public is used to seeing us work in tandem with the NYPD, so blue boats with white stripes are often alongside [the white boats with] the orange stripes. That being said, we made sure that the media carried as many pictures as we could get of our gray-hulled, black-striped PSU [Port Security Unit] boats, to let them know that this was a different operation. We never deploy those folks domestically, but now we did, so people knew we had a heightened level of security, beyond what the Coast Guard usually has on patrol." Bennis believed a second wave of attacks, if it came to the maritime domain, would not get far.

Port Security Units

Some Coast Guard Reserves, such as Port Security Units, remained on stand-by when not on active duty after September 11. One group, PSU 305, had 135 Reservists and five active-duty members. Unlike other members of the Coast Guard, they wore battle-dress uniforms, and their heavily armed Boston Whaler gunboats were painted flat-gray with black slashes rather than the familiar white boat with the orange and blue diagonal stripes.

PSU units were trained to work outside the United States providing security in foreign harbors used by U.S. forces. The commanding officer of PSU 305, Commander Robert W. Grabb, a former enlisted marine science

Below: *Maritime Safety & Security Team, MSST, boat in harbor action. The MSST units were created in direct response to the domestic attacks on 11 September 2001. These units are composed of active duty Coast Guard members primarily for the nation's home ports' security, whereas the Port Security Units, or PSUs, are composed of Coast Guard Reservists doing the same task but beyond the nation's borders. For example, PSUs operate with U.S. armed forces in the Persian Gulf along the coasts of Iraq and Kuwait. (Robert D. Wyman, U.S. Coast Guard)*

technician, was an original member of PSU 305. Grabb's people tended to keep one eye on their civilian jobs and another on CNN.

"On 9/11," Grabb recalled, "even before we got the recall, people assigned to the unit were already calling in. What we advertise is that, within ninety-six hours of receiving a recall notice, we can have everyone recalled, [equipment] fully loaded, fully palletized, and have everything on the tarmac ready for airlift, wheels-up, anywhere in the world. So our people pay attention to world events."

After their withering day combating the Pentagon fire, District of Columbia firefighters and Coast Guard Reservists Eric Bower and Michael

Left: *The Coast Guard provides coastal security at Camp X-Ray in Guantánamo Bay, Cuba, where detainees captured during the war against terrorism in Afghanistan are incarcerated. (Megan Casey, U.S. Coast Guard)*

Above: *Coast Guard Reservist Daniel Hinojosa of Port Security Unit 311 displays a memento he'll clutch tightly while deployed overseas. (Daniel Tremper, U.S. Coast Guard)*

Opposite, top: *A Navy forward-deployment ship is escorted through harbor areas by a Coast Guard craft. All movements by U.S. Naval vessels are monitored and frequently provided armed escort while in port or harbor regions. (Krystyna Hannum, U.S. Coast Guard)*

Walker were awakened on the morning of 12 September by phone calls summoning them to active duty. By Thursday evening all PSU 305 members were encamped in the gymnasium of Activities New York. Their boats had arrived by truck the day before, and their first task was to escort the Navy hospital ship *Comfort* into New York Harbor and guard it while it lay moored in the Hudson River.

After forty-five days on patrol in New York Harbor, PSU 305 Reservists were released from active duty. But after only two months as civilians they were recalled once again to active duty. Originally scheduled for a six-month deployment to the Middle East beginning in March 2002, they found themselves instead deployed in early January to Guantánamo Bay, Cuba, to provide harbor security for Camp X-Ray.

Strike Team

Ellen Vorhees, a Coast Guard Auxiliary member, worked as a volunteer in the Coast Guard's Atlantic Strike Team office in Fort Dix, New Jersey. She came in once a week, on Tuesdays. Tuesday, 11 September, began as an extra busy morning for Vorhees. New members of all three strike teams—Atlantic, Pacific, and Gulf of Mexico—came together and were in attendance for an indoctrination.

When a phone call alerted her that a plane had hit one of the World Trade Center towers, Vorhees went to the conference room to watch the event on television. She was old enough to remember Pearl Harbor and how frightened all the adults were then. Now she felt the same way. The following Tuesday, Vorhees returned to Fort Dix and her job, but the headquarters of the Atlantic Strike Team was quiet. Nearly the entire unit was gone—to Ground Zero.

Chief Petty Officer Dan Dugery, a marine science technician for more than a quarter-century, worked in a former aircraft hangar at Fort Dix, the staging point for the Atlantic Strike Team. Stored and maintained here

A port Security Unit 305 raider boat between patrols in Guantánamo Bay gets preventative maintenance for its engines from Petty Officer Ken King. (Megan Casey, U.S. Coast Guard)

were aircraft pallets loaded with anti-pollution equipment ready to be trucked or air-lifted by C-130s to any environmental emergency world-wide.

Each of the three Coast Guard Strike Teams is fitted out with identical gear and operates on the assumption it will receive no outside support wherever it is sent. In recent years, the Atlantic Strike Team's services were needed so frequently that real-life emergencies often replaced practice, and Dugery routinely saw the AST load up its flatbed trucks with tons of equipment and move from the hangar in less than forty-five minutes.

When a request for assistance comes in, whether from the Environmental Protection Agency, Federal Emergency Management Agency, or Coast Guard, Strike Team's Operations Officer, Lieutenant Scott Linsky, puts together a response team. He now ordered Warrant Boatswain Leo Deon to double the size of the watch section. Damage Controlman Chief Bernard Johnson, senior truck driver, was instructed to get three drivers, and equipment bags, prep the mobile command post, and get ready to go to New York.

"It's pretty common," said Linsky, "that we will see things on CNN and say, 'We're going to be there in twelve hours.' Even before the towers collapsed, I had a pretty good idea that Activities New York was going to want us there to set up the Incident Command System. Once the towers collapsed, I was pretty certain that the EPA was going to bring us in on the hazardous materials side."

When the second tower fell, Commander Gail Kulisch, Atlantic Strike Team commanding officer, phoned the unit. Like Lieutenant Commander Nathan Knapp, executive officer of the AST, she was an experienced port-operations and marine-safety response officer. She ordered the strike team's boats, coxswains, and engineers to prepare for deployment. Having just traveled the road near Staten Island, she was able to brief the truck drivers leaving Fort Dix on where highways were closed or clogged. The strike team's thirty-two-foot Sea Ark utility boat, as well as its twenty-three-foot boat, were loaded onto a flatbed and left for Station Sandy Hook.

Above: *Coast Guard active duty and Reserve members from the Atlantic Strike Team from Fort Dix, New Jersey, continued to monitor air quality while establishing personnel decontamination stations for workers and equipment polluted by dust raised in the rubble. (William Berry, U.S. Coast Guard)*

Left: *Ensuring that the air is safe for search and recovery crews, structural engineers, and office workers to return for their belongings is a task performed by Petty Officer Todd Wardwell. This charge, as many that come under the roles performed by the Coast Guard, places Coast Guardsmen once more first at the scene of a disaster—even on land. (Tom Sperduto, U.S. Coast Guard)*

Petty Officer Tom Telehaney finds a clear space among a forest of computers to log an air quality entry. The air is certified clean, allowing workers to return to begin the massive cleanup so companies can quickly recover and begin functioning again. (Tom Sperduto, U.S. Coast Guard)

Admiral Bennis directed Kulisch to bring the strike team's mobile command post, resembling mobile homes, which Activities New York wanted set up at the Military Ocean Terminal at Bayonne, New Jersey. This was to provide a support base for the dozens of Coast Guard small boats gathering in New York Harbor. The Mobile Incident Command Post consisted of two individual self-supporting elements: one for administration and the other for communications. A sleeve fitted to each side created a conference room and more office space. Designed to operate in areas without electrical power, each 40,000-pound command post could be assembled on-site by six people in three hours.

The Atlantic Strike Team's MICP was out the door by 11:05 a.m. and was later joined by a similar unit from the Gulf Strike Team. Together, they formed a remote base-of-operations for the strike team boats, Activities boats and later, the armed Boston Whalers of PSU 305, by providing food, water, fuel, crew rest facilities, and communications with Activities New York.

After talking with crews at Sandy Hook, Linsky realized this operation was going to differ from a typical port security mission. As casualty figures out of New York rose throughout the day, so did the likelihood of a massive medical evacuation from Manhattan.

"Before the boats went out the door," Linsky noted, "I structured the boat crews a little bit different. I sent a coxswain, an engineer, and a boat crewman, but I also sent an EMT [emergency medical technician] with each boat crew, assuming that we were going to be responsible for some medevacs."

Each of the nation's three strike teams ordinarily carried a roster of about three dozen active duty personnel. Linsky, however, assembled a team of some ninety members from all three units—who happened to be at Fort Dix for their indoctrination. This placed about 85 percent of the Coast Guard's entire National Strike Force in one unit for the New York emergency. Since they were trained to the same standards and equipped the same, Linsky was confident the three teams would integrate seamlessly. Furthermore, the operations officers from each team had worked together before and were able to move quickly. By the night of 11 September, the entire augmented AST had arrived in New York and were ready to monitor air-quality and worker-safety as rescue operations began at Ground Zero. The following morning a strike team platoon began monitoring air quality in the Manhattan financial district. Dugery led teams that entered the buildings, some sliced in half by the World Trade Center's collapse.

"Once we had ensured the safety of the air," he recounted, "we escorted representatives of these financial companies into their work spaces." As he moved about in the wreckage, Dugery felt his work boot scuff on something in the debris pile. Looking down he saw a human forearm. "You shook off your feelings like a chill." Another time Dugery found himself in a bank vault filling a rolling trash can with templates for the printing of gold and silver certificates. "It was vital that these banks retrieve their records, computer disks, and other materials that would get their operations back on line as soon as possible," he explained. "We needed to get the stock market and the economy back on a stable footing." As he made his way through the devastation in lower Manhattan, he was struck by the irony of a Coast Guard chief pushing a trash can holding the keys to an entire nation's economy.

Checking the building at 64 Wall Street for carbon monoxide, MST First Class Robert Schrader, a Coast Guard Reservist, remembered his group being the only people there. "We were all alone. Wall Street was empty. Broadway was empty. We could go into any building we wanted to, and anywhere in that building. Ground Zero was one block away. There was no electricity, no sound except for sirens in the background." At 2 World Financial Center, teams hauled their gear up twenty-five floors, then worked their way down through office spaces filled with a gray dust that sifted over the rescue teams and everything else. The chief noted several cups of coffee on a conference table, and underneath, a pair of women's shoes, "as if everyone had just got up and went to lunch, or that they were expected back shortly. Then you'd walk to the other side of the building and everything would be completely wiped out."

A week later Dugery was at Ground Zero with other strike team members monitoring air quality in the massive debris pile. The list of hazardous materials produced when the two trade center towers crumbled was overwhelming.

Opposite, top: *Petty Officer Tom Telehaney notes the air quality on the twentieth floor of World Financial Center Building Two. Coast Guard Strike Team members crawled through the carnage left in damaged and abandoned office buildings surrounding Ground Zero, testing air quality for the Environmental Protection Agency. (Tom Sperduto, U.S. Coast Guard)*

Success by combining the Coast Guard's three strike teams in direct response to September 11 led to the creation of special Maritime Safety and Security Teams. Members of this new 104-member tactical team, MSST 91106 in New York, are shown during their commissioning ceremony two years following the attack. Teams are trained as first responders to operate in the threat of chemical, biological, or radiological attacks, and to deal with everything from law enforcement and maritime interdiction to anti-terrorism and weapons of mass destruction. They can be sent anywhere in the nation within twelve hours. Other teams operate out of Seattle, Los Angeles, Hampton Roads, Virginia, and Galveston, Texas. Ports of Boston, Jacksonville, Honolulu, San Juan, San Diego, and New Orleans are receiving new units. (Mike Lutz, U.S. Coast Guard)

The Coast Guard Honor Guard prepares to fold the flag at a memorial service at the Merchant Marine Academy in Kings Point, New York, for a retired Coast Guard member who lost his life at the World Trade Center. (Tom Sperduto, U.S. Coast Guard)

A twenty-five-foot Defender-class *boat accompanies a New York Police Department boat on patrol demonstrating interagency cooperation under* Operation Liberty Shield, *the Department of Homeland Security's national plan to ensure the safety of ports, waterways, and facilities. The* Defender-class *boat offers a standard boat for all Maritime Safety and Security Teams. (Mike Hvozda, U.S. Coast Guard)*

An impromptu memorial created in the immediate aftermath of September 11 to venerate World Trade Center rescue workers. It was located in lower Manhattan's Battery Park. (Brandon Brewer, U.S. Coast Guard)

Tom Ridge, the first Secretary of the Department of Homeland Security, chats with Coast Guard members. The Coast Guard was transferred from the Department of Transportation to the newly created department in February 2003. This is the third department in which the Coast Guard has served during its 214-year history. (Telfair Brown, U.S. Coast Guard)

"We talked for days at the beginning [about site safety concerns]," said Linsky. "How much asbestos was actually in the air? Thousands of gallons of dry cleaning fluid were burning. There was gasoline and anti-freeze and motor oil and office furniture on fire. It reminded me of going to a metal plating plant fire or an industrial park fire where you spend the first two days just trying to figure out what hazards you're up against."

For Dugery it was a matter of tripping down a well-established list. "You start with the basics. Is there enough oxygen? Are there explosives in the air? If you get past those, then you start dealing with specifics, like airborne particulates."

Chief Warrant Officer Leo Deon, a boatswains mate, and one of the National Strike Force's leading experts in oil-spill response, noted that it was several days before people started considering the potential dangers to long-term health that might emanate from Ground Zero. Contract and volunteer rescue and response workers plunged into the "pile" at Ground Zero with little or no thought to personal protective gear. Deon was charged with setting up stations where these workers and their vehicles could be cleaned after working on the pile.

Deon also had to find locations where truckloads of debris could be searched for criminal evidence by FBI agents before being washed and removed to the landfill site on Staten Island. There the debris would be subject to even more sorting, investigation, and decontamination. Those desperate to locate loved ones and colleagues disregarded their own safety and hampered the strike team by entering what the team determined was a hazardous waste site.

Another of the unit's biggest concerns was rescuers putting themselves at great risk among the multifarious hazards the Coast Guardsmen knew to exist at Ground Zero. "Being charged with establishing these wash-stations, and vehicle washing areas," Deon recalled, "we could not mandate that these rescue workers, whose shifts had just concluded, go through and decontaminate. We were not allowed to even use the word 'decontaminate,' which is the proper term for a site of this nature. So we had the wash-stations available, yet they were not mandated for

Two Coast Guardsmen completing their work in the vicinity around Ground Zero sign their names on the last beam of the World Trade Center before it is removed. (Tom Sperduto, U.S. Coast Guard)

Above: *Coast Guard chaplains watch carefully at Ground Zero for emotionally distressed recovery workers and volunteers, not just Coast Guard, to offer their assistance as crews escape periodically from their hours toiling in the rubble. (Tom Sperduto, U.S. Coast Guard)*

Pages 336–337: *Coast Guard Maritime Safety & Security Team boat patrols New York City's East River near fireworks barges for a 4th of July celebration. (Tom Sperduto, U.S. Coast Guard)*

Page 337, bottom: *Commander Gail Kulisch and Petty Officer John Kapsimalis from the Coast Guard's Atlantic Strike Team at Fort Dix, New Jersey, explain the use of environmental protection equipment to President George W. Bush. Norman Y. Mineta, Secretary of Transportation, and presidential advisor Tom Ridge observe. The Atlantic Strike Team deployed to New York City after the attack on the World Trade Center to monitor air quality determining potential environmental hazards to people in the area. Soon after, a crew from this strike team went to the Capital to test air quality in the congressional buildings contaminated with anthrax. (Tom Sperduto, U.S. Coast Guard)*

use. Through some entrepreneurship, we were able to entice people to the wash-stations, with cold drinks, with rehab areas where they could actually sit down. Through this aggressive approach, a visit to the wash-station eventually caught on. When word got out that there were some nasty materials that you could potentially be inhaling or absorbing through your skin or left on your clothing, then it became very prudent for people to go through and wash down once they left. It took a long time to transition from a rescue and recovery site to a hazardous materials site."

"We're Coast Guardsmen first," said Knapp. "We think about the safety of human life. That was everybody's primary concern, including ours, just to get in and save people. But unlike the majority of the Coast Guard, our unit is focused on the nasties; what are we going up against here? What could we be called in to do?"

By 20 September, Chief Warrant Officer Leonard Rich had written a site safety plan for Coast Guard and EPA personnel working at both Ground Zero and at the Fresh Kills Landfill site, but he admitted designing

a comprehensive site safety plan for either spot was "like a child wrestling a bull." At the Fresh Kills site, a treeless mound 130 feet above sea level, Rich and his strike team set up air-monitoring and site-safety protocols. The city of New York was transporting not just debris from Ground Zero to Fresh Kills—there were separate piles for wreckage from Tower 1 and Tower 2, as well as for the other collapsed Trade Center buildings—but crushed rescue vehicles, police cars, and fire trucks as well. A temporary morgue was created for body parts discovered in the continuously arriving debris.

Yet all through this, team members knew their work was deeply appreciated. Lieutenant (jg) David Reinhard, the unit's assistant operations officer, remembered his teams being offered unimaginable gifts: "They tried to give us money, they tried to give us furniture and one guy tried to give us a painting by Picasso. They kept telling us 'that is our way,' and we had to repeatedly explain that we couldn't accept any gifts."

In early October, anthrax spores appeared in Washington, D.C., and in Florida. Kulisch, already exhausted by three weeks of continuous physically and emotionally draining work at Activities New York and Ground Zero, drove south to become deputy incident commander on Capitol Hill. As soon as the first anthrax reports surfaced, Kulisch knew the Atlantic Strike Force would be responding immediately either to real cases or hoaxes, and she had already gathered her response officers to formulate policy and evaluate how the team's capabilities matched the estimated threat. The team knew within the first week the anthrax on Capitol Hill had been "weaponized," that is, was a lethal, airborne killer.

"We were ramping up our weapons of mass destruction capabilities even before 9/11," said Chief Dugery. "We had some test kits. Unfortunately, for [a biological threat like] anthrax, you need a good lab, until the technology catches up [for field sampling]. If you're trying to identify the pathogen you need to grow it in a medium to find out what you have. It takes time."

337

A New Commandant, A New Direction

In 1998, James Loy, once a young combat officer in Vietnam commanding an eighty-two-foot patrol boat, became the twenty-first Commandant of the Coast Guard. Sensing the United States faced new and unpredictable "asymmetrical" threats from around the globe, Admiral Loy developed a doctrine for the Coast Guard as "a unique instrument of national security."

He recognized the Coast Guard's flexibility was key to rapid responses in national emergencies. Nowhere was this put to greater test than on the morning of 11 September 2001. Seeing the first televised images from Manhattan and suspecting terrorism, Loy rallied his staff to think through the service's response. The second aircraft confirmed his fears. Instantly Loy knew he needed the Reserves. He telephoned the White House and got authorization for a call-up of 5,000 Coast Guard Reservists.

Loy may have been surprised at the proximity of the attack, but the attack itself was hardly unexpected. In a remarkably prescient article for the *Homeland Defense Journal* before the September 11 attacks, co-authored with Captain Robert G. Ross, USCG, Loy argued that rather than provide a new era of peace and security, the end of the Cold War had brought about just the opposite:

"In this era of globalization, the world reach of America's economy and culture are creating powerful resentments in some sectors. Even without regional conflicts providing motivation, it is highly likely that Osama bin Laden or a similarly reactionary guardian of traditional ways would have arisen in reaction to the dominance of modern America's economic power and culture, some aspects of which are admittedly negative. Those with a dislike for the effects of globalization, as well as those who

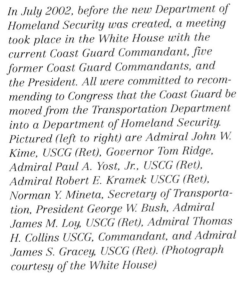

In July 2002, before the new Department of Homeland Security was created, a meeting took place in the White House with the current Coast Guard Commandant, five former Coast Guard Commandants, and the President. All were committed to recommending to Congress that the Coast Guard be moved from the Transportation Department into a Department of Homeland Security. Pictured (left to right) are Admiral John W. Kime, USCG (Ret), Governor Tom Ridge, Admiral Paul A. Yost, Jr., USCG (Ret), Admiral Robert E. Kramek USCG (Ret), Norman Y. Mineta, Secretary of Transportation, President George W. Bush, Admiral James M. Loy, USCG (Ret), Admiral Thomas H. Collins USCG, Commandant, and Admiral James S. Gracey, USCG (Ret). (Photograph courtesy of the White House)

merely feel threatened or left out by an economy and technology they do not understand, have strong motives for lashing out at the most highly visible source of their discontent: the United States."

Loy well understood that threats of economic disruption by the terrorists had to be taken as seriously as threats of violence. The challenge to the Coast Guard would be to secure the ports while maintaining the free flow of goods essential to the nation's economy. While providing security for 361 American ports, 95,000 miles of shoreline, and 25,000 miles of waterways, the service would still have to handle its other operations including search and rescue, protecting fisheries, counter-drug patrols, migrant interdiction, polar icebreaking, environmental protection, and support of scientific research. This, Loy knew, would be his first challenge. His second would be developing a vision of what the Coast Guard would look like in the year 2020. That future would be shaped by decisions made today.

Soon after the September 11 attacks, Loy went to New York to thank his people for their service. His time at Ground Zero and with Coast Guard personnel around New York Harbor became a spiritual experience. He saw the same combat shock and fatigue he remembered from Vietnam, with an important difference: "Vietnam was long periods of almost boredom interspersed with moments of sheer panic. Nine-eleven, and for weeks thereafter, was a constant, unrelenting requirement for service, at all levels of our service, humanitarian, operational, military."

For Loy, a single September day proved the Coast Guard was still the nation's premiere response team. No other federal agency could shift its focus so quickly or respond so effectively to a disaster of such proportions.

Standing security on a cruise ship entering New York Harbor, Petty Officer Kevin Murphy gazes on the skyline that is "not the same anymore." The best word to describe America and the Coast Guard before 11 September 2001 and after is—"Transition." (Mike Hvozda, United States Coast Guard)

Petty officers Jason Walker, Elliot Robles, and Master Chief Petty Officer Harry Moore participate in a joint services formation during a September 11 commemorative ceremony in Norfolk, Virginia, on the first anniversary of the attacks. (Krystyna Hannum, U.S. Coast Guard)

Pages 340–341: *(Tom Sperduto, U.S. Coast Guard)*

339

Semper Paratus
Today and Tomorrow

Admiral Thomas H. Collins, USCG,
Commandant of the Coast Guard

This 47-footer is making a dawn run out the "Gate." The 47-footer, now patrolling coastal regions, is a part of the new fleet of Coast Guard small boats. This self-righting boat can operate in hurricane-force winds and breaking seas in excess of twenty feet. Furthermore, with its superior abilities, it can still allow the crew to provide assistance in severe wind and sea conditions. (Gary Todoroff)

Above: *Chief Petty Officer Kevin T. Shaughnessy on Thanksgiving Day outside his living quarters, a tent in Umm Quasr, Iraq. Shaughnessy, with thirty-four years Coast Guard service, is the son of a former Coast Guard gunner's mate who served with Medal of Honor winner Douglas Munro at Guadalcanal. (Tom Sperduto, U.S. Coast Guard)*

Left: *The eighty-seven-foot patrol boat* Barracuda *is the first of the Coast Guard's new fleet of coastal patrol boats. It is designed for near-shore operations and for up to 200 miles offshore. A feature common to all new patrol boats is the stern launch-and-recovery system for an onboard small-boat. Note the well aft with a high-speed pursuit boat nestled in. This new class of patrol boat is also designed to work closely with the Coast Guard's future* Deepwater *assets, including all of its aircraft, to meet the nation's maritime needs well into the new century for search and rescue, law enforcement, environmental protection, and national security. (Gary Todoroff)*

"*The United States Coast Guard has been refined and shaped by the heat of battle and through trial by fire during more than two centuries of outstanding service.*"

—Tom Ridge, Secretary of Homeland Security
25 February 2003

As our nation's oldest continuous maritime service, the Coast Guard takes justifiable pride in its 214-year history of operational excellence. It is a history marked by a steady expansion of U.S. maritime interests at home and overseas. With each emerging need and crisis during peace and war over the past two centuries, the Coast Guard adapted its capabilities to accommodate or confront them—leading to the military, maritime, and multi-mission service we know today.

In company with the citizens it serves and protects, the Coast Guard now faces a dynamic future filled with great challenge and uncertainty. The dawn of the twenty-first century brought with it unprecedented terrorist attacks against our homeland and new threats to our nation's safety, security, and sovereignty. The Coast Guard responded with alacrity,

The future of the Coast Guard will be a reflection of its two-century history. This pattern of reliability and devotion to duty by the men and women of the Coast Guard created a foundation of excellence for those to follow into the future. (U.S. Coast Guard)

343

Above: *Petty Officer Chad Walder, boarding officer from Coast Guard Activities New York, verifies crewmembers' passports during a random boarding of a tanker. These boarding are a part of* Operation Liberty Shield, *which integrates selective national protective measures involving federal, state, local, and private security authorities throughout the nation. (Mike Hvozda, U.S. Coast Guard)*

Right: *An "over horizon boat" and Stingray armed helicopter each launched from the same cutter work as a team to pursue and apprehend drug-running "go-fast" boats. The helicopter uses its speed to overtake the boat and firepower to stop it. The Coast Guard boat moves in for the arrest and confiscation. It can also retrieve the jettisoned contraband floating in the wake of the pursued smuggler. (William R. Greer)*

Lieutenant Jack Rittichier was interred in October 2003 on Coast Guard Hill near Commander Elmer Stone's gravesite in a service at Arlington National Cemetery. His remains lay undiscovered for thirty-five years on the field of battle following his fatal crash in Vietnam in June 1968 trying to save another. The sixty-three-member Coast Guard Ceremonial Honor Guard assists in military funerals at Arlington National Cemetery. (Ray Copin, top, and Fa'Iq El-Amin, bottom, U.S. Coast Guard)

moving swiftly to safeguard the nation's ports, waterways, and coastal areas even as it continued to perform its other missions in the areas of maritime safety, maritime mobility, protection of natural resources, and national defense.

As part of the nation's response to September 11 and the ensuing global war on terrorism, the Coast Guard was realigned under the new Department of Homeland Security in 2003—the most extensive reorganization of the federal government's executive branch since the National Security Act more than fifty years ago.

Following September 11, more than half of Coast Guard selected Reservists were activated in support of *Operations Neptune Shield, Liberty Shield, Enduring Freedom,* and *Iraqi Freedom.* Coast Guard cutters, patrol boats, and port security units performed with distinction supporting U.S. combatant commanders in the Persian Gulf and Mediterranean Sea during the coalition's liberation of Iraq. Members of the Coast Guard Auxiliary performed yeoman service in domestic ports and waterways.

In 2001, the Coast Guard also launched two of the largest modernization and recapitalization programs in its history—*Rescue 21* and the *Integrated Deepwater System.*

Make no mistake. The Coast Guard is undergoing monumental changes. We are recapitalizing our forces with modern boats, ships, aircraft, systems, and technologies. We are adopting imaginative new concepts and accelerating our rate of change in ways unimaginable even a decade ago.

With our history as a guide, I know that the men and women of the entire Coast Guard team—active, Reserve, Auxiliary, and civilian employees—are equal to the tasks at hand and will seize the exciting opportunities that lie before us. Tomorrow's Coast Guard will differ from today's in many important respects, but our people—guided by our enduring core values of honor, respect, and devotion to duty—will perpetuate our heritage of operational excellence as America's maritime shield of freedom. The Coast Guard's past is truly a prologue to an exciting future.

A Sea of Change

Today's Coast Guard is navigating a sea of change unlike any in its history. The events of September 11 and their aftermath represent a seismic shift in the multi-faceted security risks confronting the United States. In keeping with its duty to provide maritime security to the nation, the Coast Guard must not only respond to today's threats, but also position itself to deal with the full range of potential threats anticipated in the future.

Because the United States is a seafaring nation dependent upon the oceans for its economic prosperity, the scope of our challenge is profound. Thousands of ships and millions of containers enter our 361 major seaports each year. Our maritime border consists of 95,000 miles of open shoreline, 25,000 miles of navigable waterways, and 3.4 million square miles of exclusive economic zones bordering coastal regions.

Threats to the nation may take several forms. Terrorists might seek to advance their nefarious plots by means of the cargo that enters U.S. ports each year or by commandeering a vessel—much like the hijacked commercial airliners. A successful terrorist attack against the country's maritime transportation system would wreak economic havoc. The Paris-based Organization for Economic Cooperation and Development estimated that a terrorist strike against the U.S. cargo-shipping system could cost our economy as much as $58 billion.

Challenges to our security will evolve and multiply as the twenty-first century unfolds. Threats might appear in unconventional and asymmetric forms, posing significant complications for the Coast Guard. Terrorism is a clear and present danger, but many other threats—drug smuggling, illegal immigration, circumvention of environmental law, and violations of the U.S. exclusive economic zone, for example—further jeopardize our citizens' quality of life, safety, and well-being. Moreover, these acts affect the nation's economic vitality. Several years ago the Coast Guard and the Navy produced a landmark joint intelligence forecast

Petty Officer Meghan Fischer tests air in a shipping container just removed from a ship. The multi-gas meter probe checks for flammable, oxygen-rich, or depleted atmospheres before inspectors fully open doors and enter for inspection of contents. The strap above Fischer's head holds the doors only slightly ajar to prevent them from slamming open into the inspectors should the gasses inside suddenly explode when the door is opened. (Dave Hardesty, U.S. Coast Guard)

For many years smugglers have used advanced technology to succeed. One moderately successful vehicle for them has been a high-speed ocean-going boat commonly referred to as a "go fast." This type of craft, formerly using then-modern aircraft engines, was also successful during Prohibition in the 1920s. The modern smugglers' boats are nearly impossible to detect on the vastness of the open ocean and in the past have outmaneuvered both unarmed helicopters and Coast Guard boats used to chase them. This photo shows a typical "go-fast" boat after capture. The outboard engines used by smugglers range from 150 to 250 horsepower each. Some boats may have several engines. Fuel for the run across the Caribbean is in the blue drums while the bales of drugs make up a cargo of 4,400 pounds of cocaine. Frequently go-fast boat crews will jettison drug bales during the chase. The Coast Guard's detection abilities, along with its high-speed open-sea boats and armed helicopters, have made this method of transport far less successful. (William R. Greer)

A MH-68A co-pilot with night-vision goggles preparing to search for "go-fast" smuggling boats in the oncoming darkness. A tactic drug smugglers use is to stop during daylight and camouflage their boats by covering them with blue tarps, then make their high-speed runs in darkness. The use of FLIR or infrared search technology and night-vision goggles on Coast Guard aircraft is successfully thwarting these tactics. (William R. Greer)

An armed MH-68A helicopter stands guard over oil tankers heading into and out of Prince William Sound, Alaska, following a threat to this vital American lifeline. A Coast Guard C-130 transported a helicopter and crew from its base in Jacksonville, Florida, to Cordova, Alaska. The Stingray was on patrol within twenty hours of receiving an alert. Near total self-sufficiency of units plus a unifying command structure offers the flexibility for Coast Guard units— land-based, afloat, and airborne—to operate jointly or independently in any combination for effective execution. This flexibility gives the Coast Guard its capacity to meet atypical challenges, immediately, nearly everywhere in carrying out its homeland security responsibilities. (William R. Greer)

of the maritime-security environment by projecting two decades into the future. This assessment still serves as a guide to anticipate future trends and to understand how our increasingly interconnected world will continue to be highly reliant upon the oceans for food, commerce, and energy. The study concluded that legal maritime trade, driven by global economic growth and international trade, would triple by 2020, with the most explosive growth in the container-shipping industry.

Organized crime also will increase through 2020 as demand for and profits from the illicit transportation of people, drugs, and contraband multiply. Criminals will be seen to take advantage of growing maritime trade to transport their products. Completed two years before September 11, the joint intelligence forecast described how adversaries of the United States will be more likely to engage in asymmetric warfare such as terrorism, sabotage, information operations, and chemical or biological attacks. The potential for proliferation of nuclear weapons will remain a concern. People migration, fueled by tremendous population increases in developing countries and uneven global economic growth, will be another important factor in the future U.S. maritime-security environment.

The Coast Guard/Navy study also forecasts that worldwide demand for fish will increase through 2020, stressing already fully fished and overexploited stocks. The large U.S. exclusive economic zone contains

Left: *Petty Officer Michael Smith (left) helps turtle rehabilitative specialists release a hawksbill turtle. The turtle named "Very Lucky" was discovered still alive trapped in a net off Galveston, Texas. (Patrick Montgomery, U.S. Coast Guard)*

Above: *A FLIR, or infrared image recorded on a forward-looking radar screen, in a circling Coast Guard aircraft can, day or night, pick up and record details of the smugglers. Three crew on board the boat are looking at the Coast Guard aircraft while a forth appears to be bending over and looking away. (U.S. Coast Guard)*

an estimated 20 percent of the world's fishery resources, suggesting growing competition for scarce fisheries resources.

While it is impossible to predict twenty years into the future, the foregoing trends suggest how the nation's protection envelope will evolve. Clearly, as the threats continue to increase in scope and complexity, the demand for the Coast Guard's multi-mission, military services also will escalate during the years ahead.

"One Team, One Fight"

External developments associated with our turbulent times are affecting the Coast Guard in many other ways. Our move from the Department of Transportation to the Department of Homeland Security on 1 March 2003 was a change of historic proportions. This realignment—accomplished smoothly and efficiently thanks in large measure to the hard

Coast Guard first responders aboard the damaged Staten Island ferry Andrew J. Barberi *shortly after it struck a pier slicing open the lower passenger level. Captain Craig E. Bone, USCG (right), commander of Coast Guard Activities New York, discusses emergency operations with the Coast Guard team at the scene. (Mike Hvozda, U.S. Coast Guard)*

Port security teams at the 361 seaports throughout the country are using the new twenty-five-foot armed Defender-class boat to meet elevated security requirements brought about since the Coast Guard moved to the Department of Homeland Security on 1 March 2003. (Mike Hvozda, U.S. Coast Guard)

work and professionalism of twenty-two agencies involved—was set in motion the preceding November when President George W. Bush signed the Homeland Security Act of 2002.

The president, that same day, signed the Maritime Transportation Security Act of 2002, MTSA. This is an extremely important law—both for the security of the global maritime transportation system and for the impact it will have on the Department of Homeland Security, and by extension the Coast Guard. The MTSA addresses the critical need to focus on the security of America's 361 seaports and the marine transportation system. This act creates a comprehensive legislative framework to enhance security through a methodological approach by defining responsibilities, creating standards, assessing vulnerabilities, and authorizing funds to address those vulnerabilities. The MTSA also provides a clear legislative mandate for the Coast Guard to initiate new rulemaking. In addition to its increased focus on the transportation system, the MTSA grants new authority and extends the Coast Guard's coastal jurisdiction over foreign-flag ships from three to twelve miles offshore.

Taken together, the Homeland Security Act and the Maritime Transportation Safety Act reinforce the Coast Guard's law enforcement authority. They mandate the Coast Guard to safeguard its traditional missions, improve maritime and seaport security, and protect the extension of the country's territorial waters.

Working in close cooperation with the Department of Homeland Security, the Coast Guard developed a maritime strategy for homeland security. Its provisions for a layered defense provide Coast Guard operating forces with a time-proven approach to enhance security in U.S. ports and waterways while concurrently facilitating the smooth flow of commerce.

Our new strategy recognizes that taking adequate precautions in the United States today encompasses more than just protecting the country's national interests against hostile nations. It includes protection against terrorist attacks as well as threats to national sovereignty, natural resources, the environment, and economic prosperity. The collective result of our efforts is aimed at reducing security risks.

Growing, Modernizing, and Realigning the Force

Winds of change are sweeping across the Coast Guard in other ways. Yet the Coast Guard's heightened emphasis on maritime homeland-security is not coming at the expense of our other customary tasks. Supported with the largest funding increases in our history, we have launched a multi-year plan to acquire the necessary resources to implement our strategy for maritime homeland-security while sustaining our other traditional missions near their pre-September 11 levels. We are maintaining a steady focus on our operational commanders' needs to meet the challenges Coast Guard men and women face worldwide.

Due in large measure to the strong support of the American people, the administration, and Congress, the Coast Guard has improved its current readiness and is expanding its ranks so that it can shoulder its growing mission requirements more effectively. Key to our future readiness is obtaining the right capabilities and the right capacity as we grow, modernize, and realign our force.

The Coast Guard's realignment with twenty-one other agencies into the Department of Homeland Security has helped immeasurably in advancing our ability to execute this maritime strategy for homeland security. It united the nation's efforts behind a compelling and urgent mission to protect the American people from another terrorist attack. Guided by Secretary Tom Ridge's watchword of "One Team, One Fight," today's improved unity of effort, greater collaboration, and clear lines of authority are bearing dividends in our quest to protect citizens of this country now and in the future. In recent years the Coast Guard's budget has grown by more than $1.6 billion—a 30 percent increase between 2002 and 2004.

This important infusion has enabled the Coast Guard to make steady progress on our objectives to improve our operational capabilities and cover all missions. Every homeland-security dollar directed to our budget helps us strike a careful balance between security and safety—two sides to the same coin, both important to the prosperity of our nation. As a result of higher funding levels, we are able to sustain a heightened level of operations as well as target high-priority security projects. For the first time in many years, we have restored our maintenance funding. This has enabled us to support electronics and communications systems properly—a huge leap in achieving operational readiness.

A CGC Alex Haley *gun crew stands ready to protect an oil tanker outbound from the Port of Valdez in Prince William Sound, one vital element in the Coast Guard's Maritime Homeland Security Strategy. (U.S. Coast Guard)*

The 378-foot High-Endurance Cutter Dallas *sits cradled on the ship lift for a routine haul-out at the Coast Guard Yard in Baltimore, Maryland. The yard has been in service since 1899. (U.S. Coast Guard)*

Petty Officer Harry Pinti, Seaman Joe Coakley, and Seaman Michael Poles watch vessels entering Umm Qasr, Iraq, from CGC Wrangell. *The Coast Guard deployed four 110-foot patrol boats to the region to stop oil smuggling and to search for terrorists in support of the Navy's 5th Fleet during* Operation Iraqi Freedom. *(John Gaffney, U.S. Coast Guard)*

U.S. Coast Guard Academy

Captain R. J. Copin, USCG (Ret)

The front gate to summer swings wide. As it opens, so does the main gate of the United States Coast Guard Academy at New London, Connecticut, welcoming a new class of cadets. These young men and women step aboard the Academy grounds under an invisible, blue shadow of heroism, competence, and service to nation and humanity.

A Beth and a Mark, along with some 250 other of our country's most promising, well-rounded, and gifted youngsters have arrived at a unique American treasure of higher learning. Many come directly from high school graduation. A few have experienced Coast Guard missions in the enlisted ranks.

These young people represent virtually all lifestyles and ethnicities. Together, they typify the brightest and most physically fit individuals from our nation's youth. Each has met stringent entrance requirements and survived a highly selective screening—based solely on merit—among the most competitive college admission systems applied in this country.

Each cadet receives a tuition-free education with a return, upon graduation, to serve the Coast Guard as an officer for at least five years.

Among Beth's and Mark's class are future leaders trained for roles as engineers, naval architects, marine-safety experts, lawyers, aviators, explorers, earth-science

specialists, law enforcement officers, homeland-security combatants, and perhaps a future commandant of the Coast Guard.

On the first day they are greeted by staff, receive a uniform, and, yes, haircuts, along with instruction in marching. Then they raise their right hands and swear to the oath administered to every entering member of each U.S. military service. Now cadets of the United States Coast Guard Academy, they have taken their first steps to becoming Coast Guard officers.

The shadow in which Beth and Mark will walk, jog, run, march, swim, and sail as cadets casts an inspiring trace of historical devotion to duty and superior achievement. Leaders in the 1920s who envisioned and argued for a four-year school on the west bank of the Thames River in New London saw their dream realized in 1932. Those achievers walked in the blue shadow of seagoing professionals from collective predecessor-organizations to the Coast Guard, who in 1876 began formal officer instruction in the revenue cutters Chase *and* Dobbin. *This is considered the origin of today's Coast Guard Academy.*

Graduates from the past served their country with distinction in every war our nation has fought. Yesterday's graduates now risk their lives daily to rescue people and property from harm's way. Furthermore, they are engaged against many aggressors: enemies who would damage our nation's water transportation system, smuggle illegal commodities, or conduct terrorist attacks.

Life as a cadet is indeed full. A demanding, academic collegiate degree-seeking schedule is sandwiched by military and seamanship exercises, Corps of Cadets' responsibilities, and required participation in an extra-curricula option such as band or singing groups, military drill teams, or other collegiate activities. A cadet experiences a year-round curriculum interrupted only by brief summer and holiday leave periods. "Swabs," first-year cadets or fourth classmen, learn to cope with a regimented

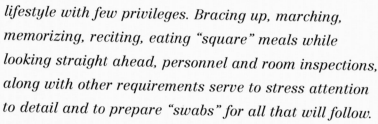

lifestyle with few privileges. Bracing up, marching, memorizing, reciting, eating "square" meals while looking straight ahead, personnel and room inspections, along with other requirements serve to stress attention to detail and to prepare "swabs" for all that will follow.

As they become members of succeeding classes, cadets gain opportunities to assume increasing cadet-corps leadership responsibilities preparing for that day when they become officers. Regimen takes its toll, however. Typically, only two-thirds of Beth and Mark's classmates will graduate.

Change is a regular feature of Academy programs. The academic curriculum evolves to keep pace with technological advancements. Changes in mission demands on Coast Guard forces also result in adjustments at the Academy. For example, cadets receive training in law-enforcement techniques such as handcuffing, searching, and self-defense.

Currently there are more than 900 cadets at the Academy. Societal changes have impacts and have presented opportunities. The Academy, together with the other service academies, admitted women in 1976. The number of female cadets has steadily grown to about 30 percent of the cadet corps. The corps has also gained in minority representation.

Upon graduation, cadets receive bachelor's degrees and become commissioned Coast Guard officers. Swapping first class cadet shoulder boards for an ensign's shoulder boards, they leave the Academy behind with travel orders to their first duty assignments. Likely, it is a floating unit performing Coast Guard missions somewhere on the earth's oceans. These new ensigns will soon stand on a

pier alongside a new home, perhaps a red-hull polar icebreaker or a white-hull medium- or high-endurance cutter, or a black-hull buoy tender. Requesting permission to come aboard and receiving from the quarterdeck a welcoming "Come Aboard, Sir," they will salute the national ensign and the officer of the deck, taking a step they will remember always. They carry with them ethics and a professional capability rooted in their four years as Coast Guard Academy cadets. The gamut of academic, seamanship, and leadership programs and activities is designed to equip the graduate to arrive at an initial assignment ready to perform duties as a junior officer at sea without additional formal training.

As Beth and Mark make their way to their respective shipboard cabins, they are now more aware of the blue shadow of achievement of those who went before. And yet, they are no doubt, and properly so, much too focused on their present to realize that just over their own personal horizons, their individual competence and performance will further broaden that beautiful blue shadow cast upon United States Coast Guard Academy cadets of tomorrow.

Opposite: Coast Guard cutter *Eagle* at the Coast Guard Academy docks in New London just before the summer sailing schedule. The Academy riverside waterfront embraces a variety of vessels to train young officers for maritime service. (David Santos, U.S. Coast Guard)

Top, left: The marching band still presents a classic image of a military organization. Mixing past tradition with future technology leads to a complete education for today's Coast Guard Academy cadets. (U.S. Coast Guard)

Top, right: Academy cadets experience all the emotions and stress of a ship's bridge as they operate SCANTS, Ship Control Navigation Training System. SCANTS is a leading ship and radar simulator used to develop team coordination while providing a collision and seasick-free environment. (Sarah Foster-Snell, U.S. Coast Guard)

High-lining Coast Guard boarding officers to vessels is an operation enabling crews to board vessels quickly for security measures. Boarding officers can rapidly reach the decks of ships where there is an immediate need. This task is as old as the Coast Guard; only today, the helicopter replaces the rowing boat of 1790. (U.S. Coast Guard)

Drill instructor Petty Officer Patrick M. NcNelis is the face first seen close up by the new recruits arriving at Cape May, New Jersey, to begin their eight-week recruit training, or traditional military boot camp. Military training for all recruits includes practical courses for their first jobs in the Coast Guard along with studies in history and naval traditions. Tasks learned include introductions to first aid, fire-fighting, weapons handling, and seamanship. Water-survival techniques are learned along with physical training, marching, and military drills. As future law enforcement officers, recruits learn weapons handling and firing the standard issue 9mm pistol. (Brandon Brewer, U.S. Coast Guard)

Seaman Apprentice Marika L. Hough (left) says goodbye to her former recruit-training shipmate Seaman Apprentice Jesami Statesir. Strong bonds of fellowship develop during shared, demanding experiences such as the training program they just completed, where high school graduates become hard-working Coast Guard members. (Brandon Brewer, U.S. Coast Guard)

We are adding thousands of billets to our enlisted and officer corps. Recruit training at Cape May, New Jersey, is operating at maximum levels to meet our expected growth. During 2003, officer candidate school increased enrollment by 50 percent, and the Coast Guard Academy added 12 percent to the corps of cadets. We also received authorization to increase the ranks of the Coast Guard Reserve. Our reserve component began an incremental growth to 9,000 in 2003, and I expect it will grow to 10,000 during the years ahead. A robust and well-trained force of selected Reservists is an integral part of our plan to provide critical infrastructure protection, coastal and port security, and defense readiness.

Increased capacity will allow us to become as much a "presence" organization as we are a "response" organization. Going back to a central premise underlying our strategy for maritime homeland-security, we simply cannot afford to respond to emergencies. We must be there ready to prevent them.

Closely tied to our efforts to improve capacity, ongoing recapitalization programs will deliver the boats, ships, and aircraft along with systems needed to close the gaps found in today's force. The award of a contract in 2003 for 700 new maritime security boats, for example, allows us to improve our presence and responsiveness on the waterfront. Twelve new 100-person maritime safety and security teams will provide force protection and port security for the nation. More sea marshals are deployed to board ships at sea.

In particular, the long-range *Integrated Deepwater System* will recapitalize the Coast Guard's entire inventory of aging cutters and aircraft, as well as our offshore command-and-control network—all supported with an integrated logistics system.

Our *Rescue 21* project is on track to serve as a modern maritime distress system that provides both a network and an integrated command-and-control system. It improves communication among agencies responding jointly to emergencies. Both *Deepwater* and *Rescue 21* will be interoperable with other directorates in the Department of Homeland Security, as well as the Department of Defense, other federal, state, and local agencies. Realignments at Coast Guard Headquarters in Washington,

Deepwater

Captain Gordon I. Peterson, USN (Ret)

*W*ith its June 2002 Integrated Deepwater System contract signing, the Coast Guard embarked on one of the most exciting chapters in its 214-year history.

Deepwater's *course is plotted and the ultimate destination is clear—designing and building a twenty-first-century Coast Guard equal to the task of defending the United States for its enduring role as the nation's "shield of freedom."*

"We are building a dream into reality," *says Rear Admiral David S. Belz, the Coast Guard's assistant commandant for operations and* Deepwater's *program sponsor remarking on the contract award to the Integrated Coast Guard Systems—a joint venture between the Northrop Grumman and Lockheed Martin corporations. "We are talking about a way of doing business that will set the pace for the future of the Coast Guard."*

Conceived during the 1990s, Deepwater's *recapitalization provides for the Coast Guard's aging and increasingly obsolete inventory of patrol boats, cutters, aircraft, and supporting systems to be progressively modernized or replaced.*

Deepwater *provides the nation with the improved maritime homeland security capabilities it needs to push its borders outward, a critical requirement in the Coast Guard's new* Maritime Strategy for Homeland Security.

In Deepwater's *aviation domain, selected existing Coast Guard aircraft will be upgraded and new airplanes, helicopters, and unmanned aerial vehicles will be acquired, adding a new look for Coast Guard aviation.*

Upgrades to existing surface vessels began in 2003 with the modernization of the 110-foot cutter Matagorda. *It became the first* Island-*class patrol boat converted to a 123-foot vessel.* Deepwater's *new seven-meter Short Range Prosecutor, SRP, will add to the 123-foot patrol boat's capabilities. The SRP will also be deployed on all three new cutter classes: National Security Cutter, Offshore Patrol Cutter and Fast Response Cutter.*

Deepwater *program executive officer Rear Admiral Patrick M. Stillman has nothing but praise for the hard work by the Coast Guard and industry acquisition team and its efforts to equip the Coast Guard in a way that will enable the service to meet the maritime challenges of the twenty-first century. He anticipates that this public-private partnership will continue to reflect a common commitment to impart innovation with the most productive use of technology. "The purpose of such an innovative approach," Stillman said, "is to better serve our customer—the operator in the field." Finally, Stillman notes, "The* Deepwater *team's transformation of operational capabilities, wise risk management, balancing of program cost, schedule, and performance with operational requirements is setting a new standard for the acquisition of a system of extraordinary scope and complexity."*

Above: Future surveillance aircraft planned for acquisition under the *Deepwater System* include unmanned aerial vehicles such as this unique tilt-rotor Bell UAV. The small size with flexibility in operations allows this proposed remotely controlled aircraft to be an excellent ship-based vehicle. (Bell Helicopters)

Below: The upgraded 123-foot cutter *Matagorda* and its new seven-meter Short Range Prosecutor small boat, shown here during preliminary acceptance trials, were delivered to the Coast Guard 5 March 2004. The cutter's upgrade and conversion included the addition of a stern ramp. This new configuration allows the Short Range Prosecutor to be launched quickly and to be driven right up and into the stern of the patrol boat for rapid recovery. Upgrading of vessels in this class, as a part of the *Deepwater* program, also includes the installation of a more capable command-and-control system. The cutter's larger pilot house and 360-degree visibility bridge also are popular with its crew. (Integrated Coast Guard Systems)

Young Chris gives a thumbs up as he sits in the crewman's seat in the "ready" helicopter about to depart on a "rescue mission." Chris is realizing his dream in the Make a Wish Foundation program. (Krystyna Johnson, U.S. Coast Guard)

Petty Officers Matt Gans and Brian Murphy discuss aerating operations aboard a barge on the Kentucky River. The Environmental Protection Agency called the Coast Guard Gulf Strike Team to the scene for a water-pollution cleanup when thousands of gallons of bourbon whiskey spilled into the river. Diversity of responses, going from Ground Zero to anthrax in the capital buildings to oil spills to bourbon in a river, makes working with Coast Guard strike teams a challenging task. (Angel Deimler, U.S. Coast Guard)

Opposite, top left: *The future will mirror the past in one indisputable manner—Coast Guard men and women will make the ultimate sacrifice giving their lives for others in need and to their country in the service of freedom. Venerating those like Medal of Honor recipient Douglas Munro is a reminder of that price some must give. (J. Bigelow, U.S. Coast Guard)*

Opposite, top right: *Petty Officer Joshua Fritzinger aboard a Coast Guard boat on a homeland-security patrol in New York Harbor watches as the British Airways Concorde passes on a barge to the USS* Intrepid Sea, Air and Space Museum. *(Mike Hvozda, U.S. Coast Guard)*

Opposite, center: *Production line for 700 new Defender-class boats ordered as part of the Homeland Security Act. These boats are destined to be on the front line of the war on terror. (Kurt Fredrickson, U. S. Coast Guard)*

354

D.C., help ensure the rapid flow of information, facilitate better decision-making, and improve performance.

This reorganization began with the establishment of a new Assistant Commandant for Intelligence. It includes integration of selected operational functions within the Operations and Maritime Safety Directorates. New posts also were established for an Assistant Commandant for Command, Control, Communications, Computers, and Information Technology, and for an Assistant Commandant for Planning, Resources, and Procurement. This reorganization closely aligns the Coast Guard's resource planning and execution structures, enhancing our ability to integrate information technology and allocate resources more effectively, ensuring we have the capabilities we need to perform all Coast Guard missions.

The Coast Guard Leadership Council at Coast Guard Headquarters—chartered to set organizational direction and review performance—commenced other initiatives to posture tomorrow's Coast Guard properly, notably in the development of long-range strategic plans. Under the "*Evergreen Project*," for example, we will use scenario-based planning to update the Coast Guard's strategic plan. We seek to institutionalize an organic planning process with an innovative agenda that will guide our service through current changes and those yet anticipated. Chairman of the Joint Chiefs of Staff General Richard B. Myers states that transformation goes far beyond technology. In his view, transformation is a process and a mindset associated with managing change entailing intellectual, cultural, and technological dimensions. I couldn't agree more. This is the definition of transformation as we know it in the Coast Guard—and it is our pathway to the future.

Change and Continuity

And what of tomorrow's world? How, amidst transformational change of immense scope and complexity—what the poet Edmund Spenser described four centuries ago as "the ever-whirling wheels of change"—will the Coast Guard position itself to achieve even higher levels of operational excellence in the decades before us? I see two primary and connected ways to achieve this vision.

One is our ability to forge a more robust capability, capacity and strategic partnerships through the fundamental building blocks of people, readiness, and stewardship. I codified this focus in my Commandant's Direction when I assumed my duties as Commandant in 2002, and I reaffirmed it again in 2003. An unswerving commitment to people, readiness, and stewardship will sustain our service, allow us to transform it to meet evolving demands, and preserve our enduring character.

The second is enduring character. These are two important words and suggest another critical attribute for tomorrow's Coast Guard. The Coast Guard will be unavoidably altered during its voyage through the sea of change, but ours will be a transfiguration marked by continuity in individuals as we hold fast our precious core values of honor, respect, and devotion to duty.

Preserving our enduring characteristics, traditions, and values will give the Coast Guard the flexibility, discipline, and capability to respond to evolving national priorities and an ever-changing national-security environment. We will nurture, preserve, and build on a legacy forged over more than 200 years as the nation's maritime guardian.

We begin with people—the bedrock of our service. When I began my Coast Guard career, I reported to my first assignment at sea as an ensign with just enough knowledge to be dangerous! I was fortunate to have a senior chief quartermaster looking out for me. He was always there during the toughest operations—with our cutter coming along tankers at night in heavy seas comes to mind—to offer advice. He did so quietly—whispering in my ear at times—without undermining my authority in any way. I learned much from him and from my other shipmates.

I learned the importance of and necessity for teamwork. We never have much depth on our bench, and shipmates must look out for one another. I called upon my senior chief's experience and expertise. I welcomed his advice and contributions. I learned the value of trusting the team and the importance of having good coaches and mentors—and the criticality of a positive, learning work environment—if people are to develop, mature, and reach their full potential.

Our ability to attract, develop, retain, and deploy quality people is the key to the Coast Guard's future; it is a top priority and perhaps our greatest challenge. People in tomorrow's Coast Guard will operate in a more complex and technologically sophisticated environment—one characterized by modern cutters, response boats, manned and unmanned aircraft, and advanced computer-based systems for command, control, and communications.

Our people must be properly trained, equipped, organized, and motivated. Transforming our service with new technology requires that we also transform our dedicated and professional workforce with the same care and foresight. We must restructure decades-old human resource policies and processes. We must be more agile in adapting to the new marketplace

Above: *Petty Officer Brandon Kealiino-homoka belongs to a forty-member Coast Guard dive team. Among his tasks is searching underwater structures around piers and docks for bombs or other hazards to harbor shipping. (Dave Hardesty, U.S. Coast Guard)*

Chief Petty Officer Trey Loughridhe carries an anchor ashore on a Hatteras, North Carolina, beach to secure their boat. The Coast Guard Atlantic Maintenance and Logistic Command personnel responded the only way they could to this natural disaster. Their immediate task was shuttling federal and state employees by providing them an immediate opportunity to start recovery for a community isolated by transportation and communication breaks caused by Hurricane Isabel. (Dana Warr, U.S. Coast Guard)

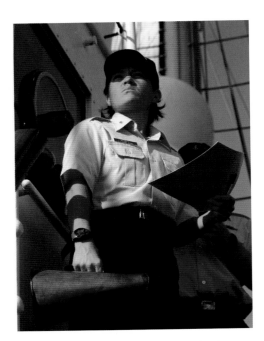

Officer Candidate Sue Kerver, monitoring sailing conditions aboard the barque Eagle, *is prepared to command a sail change.* Eagle, *in the twenty-first century, still offers experience in centuries-old mastery of sea-going expertise to Academy cadets and Coast Guard officer candidates. (Matthew Belson, U.S. Coast Guard)*

for people, provide for both quality of life and workplace, and ensure performance-based policies to lead and manage the workforce.

During the years ahead, we will increase our commitment to people. Our actions will be marked by new emphasis on education, training, and professional growth. We will expand the workforce to meet increasing mission demands. We will identify new approaches to recruit, train, retain, and deploy a diverse, highly capable, and flexible force.

Readiness—a capable, competent, and mission-ready force vigilant in all mission areas—is, simply stated, our *raison d'être*. Superior oper-ational capability is our intent. America expects that we will bring the same level of professionalism and leadership to the war against threats to our nation that we have traditionally brought to all our other missions. We are, and we will.

We must ensure our units employ sound and safe doctrine and tac-tics, supported with integrated logistics systems, adequately staffed with properly trained people, and equipped with modern, well-maintained cutters, boats, aircraft, equipment, and facilities. We are building robust maritime homeland-security strategies, capabilities, and competencies. We are designing and implementing a capability that provides integrated afloat, ashore, and airborne command, control, and communication capabilities as well as improved means for intelligence, surveillance, and reconnaissance.

We will ensure future readiness by leveraging the *Integrated Deepwater System* project, *Rescue 21* and homeland-security initiatives as our recapitalization of the Coast Guard for the twenty-first century.

In addition to the partnerships we are forging within the Depart-ment of Homeland Security, our close relationship with the Navy warrants special emphasis. Our two services always enjoyed close interaction. Today we are working together more effectively than at any time since World War II. This partnership is yielding important dividends in the global war on terrorism. Chief of Naval Operations Admiral Vern Clark and I signed a revision to the "National Fleet" policy agreement that

guides our mutually supportive policies, programs, and operations. This policy guarantees that we will be steaming in close formation with the Navy during our transit through the sea of change. Our National Fleet agreement commits us to shared purpose and common effort focused on tailored integration of our multi-mission platforms, infrastructure, and personnel. Processes are in place to synchronize research and development, planning, fiscal stewardship, procurement, development of doctrine, training, and execution of operations.

The Coast Guard's unique contribution to the national fleet includes its statutory authority in law enforcement. All ships, boats, aircraft, and shore command-and-control nodes of the national fleet will be interoperable for peacetime missions, homeland security, crisis response, and wartime exigencies. Select Coast Guard assets and expertise will shift to the Navy for specific naval-defense operations, and Navy assets and expertise will assist the Coast Guard, when necessary, in our lead role for maritime homeland-security.

Stewardship is the final building block in preparing for the future. This is a reflection on the trust granted to the men and women of the Coast Guard in our role as public servants. We have earned an enviable reputation for excellence in managing our resources as we strive to be the best-led and best-managed organization in government. We must continue to strengthen our commitment to stewardship—embracing innovation, technology together with effective leadership, and management principles to achieve measurable outcomes.

Scientists from the icebreaker Polar Sea *taking ice core-samples in the Arctic icecap. Coast Guard cutters are important mobile laboratories for scientists to conduct research and at-sea studies in remote areas of the world. (Andy Devilbliss, U.S. Coast Guard)*

Admiral Thomas H. Collins became U.S. Coast Guard Commandant in May 2002 and commenced a command that has seen the Coast Guard through its largest transition since becoming a unified service in 1915. Admiral Collins' stated leadership priorities are "readiness, people, and stewardship." He is "personally committed to making effective use of emerging technologies and developing innovative methods to improve Coast Guard mission performance." (U.S. Coast Guard)

357

"Racing Stripe"

Tom Beard

It may have been a suggestion by President John F. Kennedy in the early 1960s that forced the image representing the United States Coast Guard into that of an international icon. A simple colored slash across the side of ships and airplanes became an international insignia making the Coast Guard immediately recognizable everywhere. This paint scheme eventually gained acceptance universally as an insignia for any rescue or law enforcement vessels. Variations appear nearly everywhere displayed on boats, ships, and airplanes adapted for, or involved in, rescue and law enforcement.

The use of the diagonal "racing stripe" started with an effort to make a rather inconspicuous fleet of cutters and aircraft recognizable. From his memoirs, retired Vice Admiral Thomas Sargent recalls, "In 1962, Admiral Edwin Roland was appointed Commandant and brought to the office a breath of fresh air and much innovation." Sargent further notes, "James Read was the Assistant Secretary of the Treasury and had charge of the Coast Guard. He and Eddie [Roland] became good friends, and Jim Read had great regard for the Coast Guard. Between them, they considered that the [Coast Guard] had remained in the background far too long."

Captain Benjamin F. Engel led a board in late 1962 to find and approve a new Coast Guard image. The industrial design firm of Raymond Loewy & William Snaith, Inc., submitted motifs. Captain Gerry Seelman recalls: "At the time of the racing stripe's inception, I represented the Naval Engineering Office, Coast Guard Headquarters, in dealing with Raymond Loewy, Inc., and the contract for designing a Coast Guard logo. Mr. Joseph Lovelace was the Loewy project manager." Others involved in the decision at headquarters were Chief of Staff, Rear Admiral Paul Trimble, and Chief of Civil Engineering, Captain Thomas Sargent. Seelman noted, "At the beginning of the contract to create a logo, Loewy conducted a survey in the New York City area and determined that the Coast Guard had poor recognition

Seaman Sara Rosato (left) and Seaman Jennifer Lanham paint the Coast Guard "racing stripe" on a forty-one-foot utility boat at Station New York. The now-famous racing stripe appearing on all Coast Guard units is imitated worldwide by organizations involved in maritime law enforcement and safety. This symbol set the standard for recognition of units participating in rescue at sea anywhere. (Mike Hvozda, U.S. Coast Guard)

among the public." He further recalls in explaining the color choices, "the color blue was to represent the Coast Guard's seagoing heritage. The orange represented the color identified internationally with search and rescue."

"Two [proposed schemes] survived," according to Sargent, "the scrutiny of Ben [Engel] and his group. One was the slash and a shield of very modernistic design and the other the present seal . . . I was present in the Commandant's office when the Admiral made the decision. In his usual manner, Roland looked at all of us and said, 'Make it go NOW!!'"

The design, approved by the Commandant in 1964, consists of a wide Coast Guard orange color bar forward of a narrow blue bar with the Coast Guard emblem superimposed. The "slashes" or "racing stripes" design, canted at 64 degrees from a horizontal line, was adopted servicewide on 6 April 1967.

Today, this emblem—though widely imitated—adorning boats, ships, and aircraft is unmistakable worldwide, identifying them as belonging to the United States Coast Guard of today and of the future.

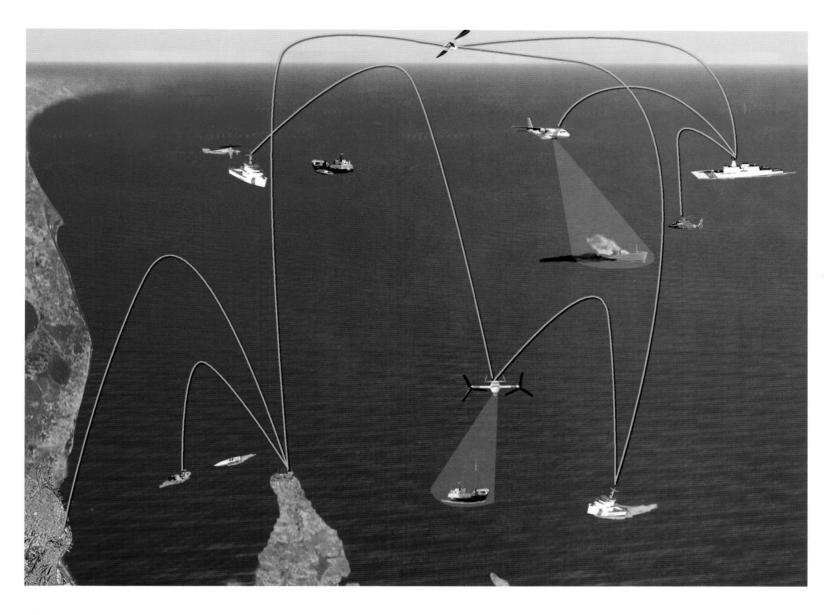

Semper Paratus

Looking to the future, I see a different Coast Guard in many respects. Coast Guard men and women will be at the helm of modern patrol boats and cutters. They will pilot more capable helicopters and airplanes and operate unmanned aerial vehicles. Ours will be a truly network-centric force, with surface, shore, and aviation platforms serving as interconnected nodes in the netted, distributed battle space of tomorrow.

Yet, despite some of the most sweeping changes today in our 214-year history, the constants that have guided our service through other perilous times will endure. We will remain the military, multi-mission, and maritime service that we know today. Mariners in distress around the world will know that when a U.S. Coast Guard cutter or aircraft bears on the horizon, their prospects for survival have brightened. The citizens of America will continue to look to the Coast Guard as its maritime shield of freedom. We will continue to be the leader ensuring safety, security and environmentally sound practices in our ports, coastal areas, and oceans of the world.

And, when the oncoming watch relieves the watch on cutters in home waters and on the high seas, the eyes of Coast Guard sailors will lock during their time-honored exchange: "I offer my relief . . . I stand relieved."

Semper Paratus—Always Ready—today and tomorrow.

Deepwater *graphic shows how Coast Guard units share and dispense data. Satellites connect widespread forces with land-based control centers while remotely controlled unmanned aerial vehicles plus manned aircraft share image data with surface* Deepwater *cutters and control centers through the satellites. (Rich Doyle, U.S. Coast Guard)*

Coast Guard men and women can be depended upon to stand tall and be Semper Paratus. *(U.S. Coast Guard)*

359

Editors and Authors

EDITOR IN CHIEF

LIEUTENANT COMMANDER TOM BEARD, USCG (RETIRED), *New Dimensions*, split a military flying career as a Navy carrier pilot, with a Vietnam tour, and as a Coast Guard rescue pilot participating in numerous rescues, and accumulating 6,000 flight-hours in a dozen operational aircraft, including: attack, surveillance, seaplane, transport, and helicopter. Beard holds a M.A. degree with more than thirty articles, and three books published on American, maritime, and aviation history, receiving an award for maritime writings. He possesses an airline transport pilots rating and Coast Guard masters license. He, with his wife Carolyn, spent sixteen years circumnavigating the globe nearly twice in their sailboats, accumulating over 160,000 miles underway in small boats.

MANAGING EDITOR

MR. JOSÉ HANSON, *Course Changes* and *At Sea*, left high school to join the Marine Corps, but went on to earn a B.S. in journalism at the University of Colorado and a M.A. in Spanish from the University of Texas, where he was also a National Resource Foundation Scholar in Arabic. Hanson worked and studied in Germany and France before moving to Japan to become a technical writer and editor. While in Japan he learned to sail, acquired a small ketch, and through a growing love of the sea, first became interested in the United States Coast Guard. He recently moved to Minnesota, where he works as a writer and Web designer.

GRAPHICS EDITOR

CHIEF WARRANT OFFICER 4 PAUL C. SCOTTI, USCG (RETIRED), *Yered*, *Port Dangers*, and *Point Welcome*, fulfilled a thirty-year military career, serving four in the Air Force and twenty-six in the Coast Guard. Scotti was an X-ray specialist, gunner's mate, journalist, photojournalist, and public affairs officer. Coast Guard assignments included a combat tour in Vietnam as a crewman aboard the 82-foot patrol boats and as liaison officer to the motion picture/television industry in Los Angeles. He is the author of three books; one, *Coast Guard Action in Vietnam*, tells of a little-known but vital contribution to that war.

AUTHORS

COMMANDER THEODORE BULL, USCG (RETIRED), *Secret Wars*, followed a unique career path serving five tours in the Coast Guard Intelligence Program as an intelligence officer in a service with this role yet undefined. He capped his career as speechwriter for the Commandant. Leading to this, Bull's tours included: intelligence watch officer, Miami; Chief of the Intelligence Section, Boston; Coast Guard Liaison Officer, El Paso Intelligence Center; CO, Coast Guard Communication Station Miami; and Deputy Chief of Intelligence, Coast Guard Pacific Area. Bull served a sea tour in USCGC *Hamilton* and was a Coast Guard Academy instructor in humanities. Retired, he serves as special assistant to the director, Transportation Security Administration.

DR. P. J. CAPELOTTI, PH.D., CHIEF PETTY OFFICER, USCGR, *Transitions*, teaches anthropology and American studies at Penn State University Abington College. He is a Chief Petty Officer in the U.S. Coast Guard Reserve and wrote the history of Coast Guard operations on and immediately after September 11, entitled *Rogue Wave*. Dr. Capelotti's awards include the Coast Guard Achievement Medal, Arctic Service Medal, Meritorious Team Commendation with "O," Armed Forces Reserve Medal with "M," and five Coast Guard Reserve Good Conduct Medals.

ADMIRAL THOMAS COLLINS, COMMANDANT USCG, *Semper Paratus: Today and Tomorrow*, a 1968 Coast Guard Academy graduate, became Commandant in 2002. Before attaining this position, Admiral Collins served as the Coast Guard's Vice Commandant, Commander of Pacific Area and of the Eleventh and Fourteenth Coast Guard Districts. As Chief, Office of Acquisition, he managed projects opening the way to the *Integrated Deepwater System*. Earlier, Admiral Collins served aboard the cutter *Vigilant*, as a commanding officer of *Cape Morgan*, Coast Guard Group Commander, and Captain of the Port. He holds the Coast Guard Distinguished Service Medal, the Legion of Merit—three awards, the Meritorious Service Medal—two awards, and the Coast Guard Commendation Medal—three awards.

Captain John D. Dwyer, USCGR, *Harbor Sentinel*, following officer candidate school, was assigned duties in port safety and security, environmental protection, marine inspection, mariner licensing, and investigation. Dwyer left active service in 1985 and joined the Coast Guard Reserve. He was subsequently employed by the Coast Guard as a civilian marine-inspector—the first since World War II. He was activated, following September 11, serving as the Deputy Incident Commander Puget Sound. Following a short release, Dwyer returned to active duty again in 2003 as the Pacific Area Reserve Chief of Staff. Currently he serves as the Chief of the Prevention Department at MSO Puget Sound—again the first civilian employee in this role.

Dr. Ralph Eshelman, Ph.D., *Beacons*, prepared the 1995 Cultural Resource Management Plan for the United States Coast Guard and numerous National Register of Historic Places and National Historic Landmark nominations for lighthouse including the Cape Hatteras Lighthouse. Dr. Eshelman served on the team that wrote the "Historic Lighthouse Preservation Handbook" published by the United States Coast Guard and National Park Service. He currently serves as the historian for the "Star-Spangled Banner National Historic Trail" Study Team of the National Park Service.

Mr. Clayton Evans, *Into the Surf*, serves as a Canadian Coast Guard (CCG) lifeboat coxswain, with a history degree from the University of Victoria and a Master of Laws (Maritime) from the University of Wales, Cardiff, England. He is author of *Rescue at Sea: An International History of Lifesaving, Coastal Rescue Craft and Organizations*. Evans is qualified as coxswain in USCG boats. He served both with the CCG as a rescue coordinator at Joint Rescue Coordination Center, Victoria, British Columbia, Canada and as a SAR instructor in rigid hull-inflatable for USCG crews. For twenty years Evans performed rescues along the rugged Vancouver Island, B.C., coast, where he still stands rescue duty in small boats.

Mr. John J. Galluzzo, *1790–1915: That Others Might Live*, born in Hull, Massachusetts, the home of the "Father of the Coast Guard," Joshua James of the United States Life-Saving Service, served as Education Director of the Hull Lifesaving Museum and as Executive Director of the Scituate, Massachusetts, Historical Society. Mr. Galluzzo authored several books on Massachusetts maritime history, and is editor of *Wreck & Rescue*, the quarterly journal of the United States Life-Saving Service Heritage Association.

Dr. John A. Tilley, Ph.D., *Backup: Auxiliary, Reserve, & SPARs*, is Associate Professor of History at East Carolina University. Dr. Tilley received his Ph.D. in American military history from Ohio State University, and has worked as a maritime museum curator. He is the author of two books, *The British Navy and the American Revolution* and *The United States Coast Guard Auxiliary: A History, 1939–1999*, in addition to numerous research projects conducted under the auspices of the Coast Guard Historian's Office.

Admiral Paul A. Yost, Jr., USCG (Retired), *Roles and Missions*, served as the Commandant of the Coast Guard from 1986–1990. While Commandant, he enhanced the service's military and drug enforcement missions and brought the service to a high state of readiness. During this period, the Coast Guard virtually eliminated the transportation of illegal drugs across the Caribbean. Admiral Yost, a combat veteran of Vietnam, is a graduate of the Coast Guard Academy, the Naval War College, and has master's degrees in both international affairs and mechanical engineering. He is now the President of the James Madison Memorial Fellowship Foundation in Washington, D.C. Admiral Yost's awards include the Distinguished Service Medal, Silver Star, and Legion of Merit with Gold Star and combat "V."

Acknowledgments

The Foundation for Coast Guard History and this book's editors express their grateful appreciation to all individuals supporting our efforts. The generous access to the Coast Guard Historian's office offered by Robert Browning, Ph.D., was invaluable for the source of stories and illustrations, as was the Coast Guard art collection, both at Headquarters and at the Coast Guard Academy, where Cindee Herrick assisted in providing paintings for those photographs that just cannot be taken. The Coast Guard's art program is where the imagination of excellent artists renders in vividness the fleeting mental visions a few carry away from the scenes. The Coast Guard Museum Northwest, Captain Fred Herzberg, Jr., USCG (Ret) (also Executive Director of the Foundation for Coast Guard History) and Captain Gene Davis, USCG (Ret), laid their total resources before the editors with their unparalleled knowledge of Coast Guard history.

The search for graphic evidence in such a diverse organization became the tireless effort of Graphics Editor, CWO4 Paul Scotti, USCG (Ret), a former public affairs officer, excellent photographer, and author. Where words count, Managing Editor, José Hanson, linguist and writer, has no peer.

Several condensed accounts in this book are by individuals, most who receive only the appreciation of a good story well told and a figurative pat on the back. Their yarns depict the unusual experiences where Coast Guardsmen, throughout the history of the diverse organizations, commonly faced exceptional odds sometimes against undetermined challenges. For these stories we are indebted to Mary Louise Clifford and J. Candace Clifford, Captain Ray Copin, USCG (Ret), Captain Gene Davis, USCG (Ret), CWO4 Mark Dobney, USCG (Ret), Commander Eric S. Ensign, USCG, Commander John Fitzgerald, USCG, Captain Jeffery Karonis, USCG, Captain George E. Krietemeyer, USCG, (Ret), Captain Theodore C. Le Feuvre, USCG, John "Bear" Moseley, former Master Chief of the Coast Guard Vincent Patton III, Ed.D., USCG (Ret), Captain Gordon Peterson, USN (Ret), Scott Price, Vice Admiral Thomas Sargent, USCG (Ret), and Vice Admiral Paul A. Welling, USCG (Ret).

My personal thanks go also to all those unnamed whose help is incalculable.

—TOM BEARD, *Editor in Chief*

The Foundation for Coast Guard History project to commemorate a century of flight launched with a 9 June 2003 ceremony at Kitty Hawk near where Orville Wright piloted the Wright Flyer on its historic first flight. The Monument to a Century of Flight created by Icarus International Foundation, shown here being dedicated on 8 November 2003, is composed of fourteen wing-shaped, stainless-steel pylons arranged in a spiral on a brick paved platform. The Foundation for Coast Guard History, with support from The Ancient Order of Pterodactyls (pilots and crewmembers of Coast Guard aircraft, active and retired, plus others supporting Coast Guard aviation) sponsored one pylon bringing recognition to the Coast Guard's flourishing aviation history, which began with its participation even before Wright's first powered flight. (Gary Todoroff)

Index

Page numbers in *italics* indicate illustrations.

(Unless otherwise indicated, all ranks and grades are U.S. Coast Guard)